HANDS-ON CLIENT/SERVER INTERNETWORKING

OTHER McGRAW-HILL CLIENT/SERVER BOOKS

Berson *Client/Server Architecture,* 2d ed., 0-07-005664-1
Berson/Anderson *Sybase and Client/Server Computing, Featuring System 11,* 2d ed., 0-07-006080-0
Dewire *Application Development for Distributed Environments,* 0-07-016733-8
Dewire *Client/Server Computing,* 0-07-016732-X
Dewire *Second-Generation Client/Server Computing,* 0-07-016736-2
Vaughn *Client/Server System Design and Implementation,* 0-07-067375-6
Weadock/Martin *Bulletproofing Client/Server Systems,* 0-07-067622-4
Wise *Client/Server Performance Tuning: Designing for Speed,* 0-07-071173-9

Hands-On Client/Server Internetworking

Bud Bates

McGraw-Hill
New York · San Francisco · Washington, D.C.
Auckland · Bogotá · Caracas · Lisbon · London
Madrid · Mexico City · Milan · Montreal · New Delhi
San Juan · Singapore · Sydney · Tokyo · Toronto

Library of Congress Cataloging-in-Publication Data

Bates, Regis J.
Hands-on client/server internetworking / Bud Bates.
p. cm.—(McGraw-Hill series on computer communications)
Includes index.
ISBN 0-07-005442-8
1. Client/server computing. 2. Internetworking (Telecommunication) I. Title. II. Series.
QA76.9.C55B39 1998
004'.36—dc21

97-37414
CIP

McGraw-Hill

A Division of The ***McGraw-Hill*** *Companies*

1 2 3 4 5 6 7 8 9 0 DOC/DOC 9 0 2 1 0 9 8 7

ISBN 0-07-005442-8

The sponsoring editor for this book was Steven M. Elliot, the editing supervisor was Stephen M. Smith, and the production supervisor was Sherri Souffrance. It was set in Vendome by Tanya Howden of McGraw-Hill's Hightstown, N.J., Professional Book Group composition unit.

Printed and bound by R. R. Donnelley & Sons Company.

This book is printed on recycled, acid-free paper containing a minimum of 50% recycled de-inked fiber.

CONTENTS

ACKNOWLEDGMENTS

Someone once told me that after you've written a couple of books it gets a lot easier. Unfortunately, this is not always the case. This particular book has taken me the longest to prepare of any that I've published. Therefore, it is imperative that I take the opportunity to express my thanks to the unsung heroes who are responsible for its production.

First and foremost I would like to thank the personnel at McGraw-Hill, especially Jay Ranade, Editor in Chief of the Computer Communications Series. Although Jay was continually supportive and understanding of the demands on my time, his pressure on me mounted as delays became protracted. I also want to single out Steven Elliot, Senior Editor at McGraw-Hill, for his patience with and support of me while waiting for the completed manuscript. I am sure there are a number of other McGraw-Hill staffers who were deeply devoted to getting this book produced and published. Unfortunately, the names of those people are not always visible, so I would like to say a "global" thank you to all of them.

At TC International Consulting, two people were responsible for putting together this book. The first was Rhonda Laird. She had to put up with all of the technical mumbo jumbo that I will typically dictate, and translate that into the English language. It could not have been easy to listen to the reels of tape, what with the constant drone of background noises such as airplane jet engines, announcements over loudspeakers, and wind. Beyond all that, Rhonda was relatively new to TCIC. Many thanks go to her.

The second person at TCIC was Gabriele Peschkes. As the graphic artist, the creative one, the person who could most understand my hand-scrawled drawings and turn them into readable, presentable art, she deserves a lot of recognition. It was Gabriele who continually kept after me and reminded me that I had an obligation to finish what I started. Without her constant support and gentle prodding, I may never have been able to find the time to sit down and work on this book. Rhonda and Gabriele are really the creators of *Hands-On Client/Server Internetworking*—I was merely an instrument that relayed content and setup.

Someone else I would like to mention is Dan Stern, a very close friend and assistant, as well as a technical guru, who helped me come up with some of the graphics used in later chapters of this book. It was

Dan's vision and foresight that turned some complex ideas about bridging and routing techniques into usable pictures.

I particularly want to acknowledge the client/server internetworking managers who have frequently spent a great deal of their work time, as well as their personal time, to accomplish what quite often is an unrewarding and thankless task—installing a client/server architecture. Too many of these people have been cast aside by management or displaced in their careers. In the everchanging world of technology, and given the demands and needs of any organization, meeting the expectations of user and management is often difficult at best. The client/server managers have sucessfully put internetworks in place and showed true results, yet their reward has been self-gratification rather than accolades, pats on the back, or thank yous. Indeed, they have faced increasing demands from their organizations that they do more, and do better, and do it faster.

The intent of this book is to view what tasks must be done and what decisions must be made before endeavoring to undertake a client/server internetworking project.

With the movement toward client/server internetworking, vendors have begun selling products and services that have not yet had the bugs worked out of them. This puts client/server managers and other staff members on the spot in the event things don't happen the way they should. It will only be through the maturity of the field that projects will start to achieve the best possible results—namely, that they be done on time, within budget, and as promised.

I must also thank my family for putting up with the fact that I was seldom around. Preparing this book, together with my regular workload and the projects I was involved in, kept me quite busy and resulted in the virtual depletion of the personal time I had to spend with those close to me. They and I know that we share a bond that is special. Although I'm often traveling and constantly under pressure to come up with new material, we still know that, although we are apart, we are together. The support of those around me continues to drive me.

Finally, I want to thank you, the reader, for your sustained interest in the works that I publish. My gratification comes from knowing that the information is being presented in a readable and professional manner. Enjoy, learn, and take heed of what follows.

—Bud Bates

CHAPTER 1

Introduction

This book is about client/server internetworking. When users hear the three words *client, server,* and *internetworking* put together, they often have a misconception about what is being said. This book tries to address the newer, state-of-the-art, common interfaces and communications infrastructures in support of client/server computing platforms. It does not address the computing processes themselves, but rather the way in which we can interconnect computing systems from anywhere in an organization or in the world.

Many internetworking managers have put their jobs on the line. As they looked back at legacy computing platforms such as mainframe or high-end computing systems, they realized that things had to change. Imagine, if you will, an organization that has built its computing platforms throughout its regional, divisional, or branch offices. Over the years data has accumulated on various computing systems, and applications have been written to support those computing platforms. Many of these computing systems and applications are very specific. Now as a new movement is underway to improve on the computing power and the access that an organization requires, the internetworking manager must step forward to justify to management changing the organization's entire computing architecture. Quite simply, the organization is rolling the dice with the hope of seeing substantial improvements in either cost savings, data access, or productivity increases over other systems.

As the research for this book began, several organizations had already taken steps to implement client/server internetworks. This implementation went well beyond just an internetworking concept to include a full computing architecture. The migration from our legacy mainframe environments has brought with it significant risk. These high-end computing systems have been fine-tuned over the years into smoothly operating platforms, albeit perhaps sluggish or delay-sensitive. At least they worked.

Computer manufacturers, networking carriers, and a host of application-specific vendors have all been bidding on a "pie in the sky" challenge. Users are promised pieces that will speed up their everyday processing needs. Management sells its board of directors or senior levels on the idea of saving significant money by moving to lower-cost computing systems. Just moving to a lower-cost computing system doesn't necessarily improve on performance, so management has been led to believe that it would be using faster, smoother, and more reliable computing systems with a step-down in size. Although these ideas are noble in their intent and goals, many of these promises have not been fulfilled. Users have heard about quick graphical interfaces or the ability to link to a data warehouse and retrieve information from any source no matter where it is located.

The ideas sound simple, but they don't even begin to cover the magnitude of the work and the conversion processes necessary to provide harmonious access to an organization's data. Moving, for example, from a systems network architecture (SNA) environment requires the recoding and rekeying of, in many cases, 30 years' worth of data. In trying to draw organizations into client/server architecture, vendors have indicated that the conversion process has been perfected. This is not true, unfortunately, and this empty promise has led to the demise of a significant number of organization staff. Some organizations have undertaken a client/server internetwork and a complete client/server computing architecture and nearly gone broke. Others were large enough to be able to pull back halfway through a process that had taken place over three years.

These items are all covered in the following chapters in an attempt to discuss the differences, the risks, and the possibilities of building a true client/server internetwork. In no way is this book designed to convince an organization to go in that direction; instead, it is designed to look at which pieces can and might work versus which pieces do not work. By viewing these factors from different perspectives, you might see which client/server computing architectures and internetwork concepts may work for your organization. Wherever possible, pros and cons were developed and listed in this book. Several of the chapters throughout this book talk about the possibilities of using different systems, which clearly points to the fact that a single solution will not solve all organizational problems. Before undertaking a client/server internetworking strategy, organizations should look at the skill sets and the strengths and weaknesses of their individual staff members to see just how much talent they have and how far they can go. Stress is the norm. Organizations are dynamic and, as a result, the stress of everyday business operations coupled with the migration and conversion process of full management information systems (MIS) or information technology (IT) departments severely limits their capabilities and impairs the speedy implementation of a client/server internetwork.

As this book begins, the intent is to address two different sides of the business: First comes a look at the different tools that might be available for the computing side of the business; second is a look at the techniques to route or switch information across a wider area, the internetworking side of the business. Protocols, architectures, and devices all play an important role in an internetwork. If one has to choose how to build a client/server network and then internetwork it within the entire organization, it is imperative to understand what pieces constitute the network. The first few chapters of this book cover piece by piece the protocols (Chap. 3) and the components (Chaps. 4, 5, and 12) that must be put together (Chap. 9). It is not the intent of this book to discuss *all* of the protocols and *all* of the possibilities, but rather the more common and more widely implemented ones. Each organization must choose its own devices as it works through this process. However, benchmarking a successful organization's implementation and using that as the starting point for a networking environment may well provide a head start. Looking at the various components provides the opportunity to establish the benchmark from this point forward.

The latter portions of this book, beginning with Chap. 6, look at internetworking. As the carrier community offers newer services and capabilities, we must not forget the old, reliable, staple-type communication systems that have been around forever. Chapters 7 and 8 deal with the availability of options from the various carriers. Chapter 7 discusses the age-old, point-to-point, leased-line circuits still offered by many carriers and then presents the more appropriate bursty data transmission systems that carriers are now delivering to end users. Once again, these processes are shown in this book merely as a mechanism to understand the options that are available. Significant other concerns and issues may well surface on the basis of each individual network. One can imagine the variations, combinations, and permutations that could exist using a multitude of different access links and permanent virtual circuit networking capabilities.

In each case, one must pay a penalty or a price. Where cost is the leading factor, the penalty may be the subsequent result. If a price is paid and enough money is budgeted with the right intent, then the result may well be increased performance across the network. One must clearly look at the amount of information and the delay that is tolerable before engaging in an internetwork.

New techniques to move data fluidly with on-demand capabilities have been developed. Chapter 8 features an overview of frame relay, asynchronous transfer mode (ATM), switched multimegabit data service (SMDS), and fiber-distributed data interface (FDDI) concepts as high-speed, data-moving architectures. Any oversights or understatements can be addressed with the bandwidth on-demand concepts of these internetworking tools. Unfortunately, many carriers and users alike have been steered down a path of using these high-speed bandwidth needs and networks with the promise that they will expand on-demand. An organization in the Midwest thought this description, delivered by its carrier, was accurate. As it turned its network on to internetwork between multiple sites around the United States, it learned a very hard lesson. The vendor promised a network that would allow bursting and expanding of the data capabilities on-demand. The organization therefore sized what it thought was appropriate, expecting that it had a cushion that would allow for minor mistakes. Unfortunately, the carrier's network had already been overstressed with this bandwidth on-demand concept. Consequently, the ability to burst, or send more data than planned, depends on how many other organizations have been promised the same capability.

When working with local and long-distance carriers and computing vendors, many organizations have been surprised to find that the old skill sets of the carrier community have disappeared. What this means is that many organizations have trusted or relied on their carriers to do network design for them to internetwork their client/server computing architecture. Unfortunately, adequately skilled and trained personnel may no longer be with these carriers, and they may have left a significant void. The talent, in many cases, no longer exists. Yet the carrier might not admit this, leaving an organization with the idea that a certain skill and knowledge base exists. In some past instances, as organizations rolled forward to implement client/server internetworks, two possibilities emerged: network collapse or overly designed networks. In the case of collapse, the networks could not sustain the amount of data that needed to be moved. The second alternative nearly bankrupted some organizations.

This book tries to look at those issues. The intent of this critical and hard look is not to dissuade anyone from using the newer techniques, but to help everyone understand that just as strengths exist, risks also exist. A clear understanding of working with the carriers, the protocols necessary to sustain these operations, and the devices necessary to internetwork client/server architectures is a must. From a managerial perspective, this book attempts to look at these pieces, one at a time. Bridging and routing techniques exist to internetwork and interlink various platforms around the globe or across the room. In either case, an internetwork is established. But the significant distance and the necessary routing or bridging protocols could have an impact and consequence on our ability to move data that are not yet understood. The goal then is to bring to light how these things can be achieved, giving the client/server management personnel the tools and understanding of what will or will not work. Bear in mind, however, that no one solution will fit all needs. As a result, all of the techniques have been addressed from circuit-switched, dial-up communications; packet or frame switching; cell relay; and leased lines. Beyond that, the ability to access an internetwork from a regional or remote office is only one piece of how an internetwork must support the organization. This book looks also to the nomad or wanderer who still needs access to the data, albeit smaller pieces of the data, from any place around the world. Therefore, the dial-up telecommuter or remote user is also addressed where possible.

Chapter 10 involves timelines or project stepping-stones that are necessary to develop a client/server internetwork. It is an overview of what an end user might consider in terms of the steps necessary. In no way is it a perfect project plan or timeline; everyone's network implementation will be different. Instead, it highlights some of the initial stages of equipment selection, a test plan, a pilot group, and the resultant checks and balances to ensure that things are working properly. These sections are designed as more of a managerial overview on how to get the client/server network implemented, with as straightforward an approach as possible. Each individual project manager or client/server internetworking manager has to develop his or her own timelines based on the given parameters and the budget expectations of management within an organization.

With any internetwork, the issue of security is always a hot topic. With the emphasis these days on internetworks and the Internet, organizations have grown paranoid and justifiably so. Security has become the hot button in the industry because of the discussion of taking client/server internetworks and intranetworks and exposing them to the outside world via dial-up communications, routers and bridges, integrated services digital network (ISDN) links, and Internet access. More emphasis these days has been placed on the ability to use the firewall communications capabilities to provide the necessary protection against unauthorized access to the data. Subsequently, the use of encryption and authentication on a client/server network has also become somewhat of a hot button. Chapter 11 includes a discussion of securing the network. This security includes such things as dial-in communications, remote access from telecommuters and nomadic users, and access from mobile or wireless communications devices. Several of these issues overlap. We cannot isolate each of the components, issues, or managerial concerns. The network involves all of the components simultaneously, and therefore the overlap is necessary.

Managing a client/server internetwork has always been an issue that is addressed *after* the fact. The intent of Chap. 13 is to at least present the issue in advance. If a client/server internetwork is to be deployed using the necessary tools á la Simple Network Management Protocol (SNMP) as the benchmark or the base from which to look at the variations, one should understand the risks and pitfalls. If, in fact, the decision is to install management after the fact, one is on a fast track for failure. It is through the early stages of planning of a network management system, before the deployment of the network, that one achieves the best results. Once the network management system has been selected, each of the components, such as the routers, bridges, switches, and hubs, on the network can all be purchased to be consistent with the network management system that has been selected. Moreover, the ability to use this network management system as a benchmark for the acquisition of equipment allows cost benefits as well as consistency. Selecting a vendor that does not support the network management system to be installed clearly can cause considerable distress to a client/server internetwork manager. If isolation and individualized network management is a requirement, then the amount of time to solve problems is significantly increased. Therefore, by preplanning a network management system, you can achieve better results if you know what to expect in advance.

This book does not go into the details per se of all the network management structures necessary. Product-specific applications and equipment are avoided as much as possible. However, there are just a few purveyors of network management services, so it was relatively difficult to avoid using product or vendor names. This book does not intend to endorse any vendor products or services; instead it strives for an understanding of what is available from various companies and what might have to be selected. When dealing with this client/server information, one has to understand that it is a relatively new process. Even though client/server internetworks have been touted for the past five to seven years, there have still been only a few that have been finalized and completed.

Other steps throughout this book try to intermingle the managerial, technical, and engineering sides of the network. All too often organizations begin a process of implementing a client/server internetwork without a true understanding of all of the pieces involved. Once again, this book is designed to look at it from various angles. From a user's perspective, the emphasis is on what a user might expect and demand from a networking manager. From the perspective of local and long-distance carriers, the issues of budget, availability, and longevity of protocol capabilities are represented. From a networking manager's perspective, the issues of how stress and conflicts arise are represented. And finally, management's approval and support are always necessary in the development and implementation of a client/server internetwork. Wherever possible, management's approach or opinions are presented to ensure that the network satisfies the demands and needs of the organization technologically, financially, and managerially.

In picking up this book, assuming that everything is very, very precise and specific is misleading. Unfortunately, in a client/server internetworking world, many of the issues are decided "on the fly." Vendors might not understand that every organization does not need the exact same configuration, speed, or facility to support its internetwork. Each organization's data needs and connectivity needs will, in fact, be different. One has to be flexible enough to adjust based on the complexities and the conflicts that might arise once the project is undertaken. Clearly, going into it with your eyes open makes it far easier to see the big picture. The purpose of this book is to create an understanding of a baseline as opposed to a fixed-in-concrete plan. No one solution solves all problems. Keeping this in mind, one *can* adjust with the flow and install accordingly. Recognize however, that the end users are still going to be the deciding factor in determining the mission-critical applications needed so they can accomplish their respective functions. If this flexibility can be maintained to meet those changing demands (and the temper tantrums that might ensue), the project may be far more manageable and more realistic. It is with this intent that the information contained in the rest of this book is presented.

CHAPTER 2

Client/Server Networks

It is interesting that the business community is hyped on the concept of a client/server environment. Whenever the words are muttered, the audience gawks with awe at the person who announced that his or her organization is engaged in a conversion to the client/server architecture for its computing needs. Why should two simple words be treated with such reverence? The client/server words have existed for years. In the old days of computing, IBM and others offered some form of this service. However, this recent trend in the industry has everyone engaged in research or development to make the move. However, one must be careful to analyze true business need, rather than get caught up in the hyperbole of the industry. The move to client/server as we know it can be a very lengthy and costly exercise. This technique of linking computing platforms is not for every organization, at least not right away. Too many organizations have already set out to convert to what the software and hardware vendors have to offer, only to get stuck in the middle. As a result, many have had to abandon the projects and scrap all of the investments and efforts put into the migration. One must be very clear in understanding the rules associated with the need and the conversions necessary before undertaking such a monumental step. This book is designed to clear the air by describing what a client/server architecture is all about.

Once an organization is engaged in installing a client/server environment, the next step is to internetwork the computing platforms, although it is actually a concurrent activity that must be preplanned. One cannot take these activities serially, since the move usually means a directional change in the organization's computing services. To link remote sites to single or multiple servers, the internetworking components must be installed simultaneously. Hence, a lot of preplanning activities and issues dealing with this form of connectivity must be handled concurrently. No single solution exists, however, so this book cannot suggest the entire spectrum of connections, uses, and variations in this arena. One can assume that the move to client/server will

1. Tax the strongest staff organization, regardless of the technical and managerial expertise
2. Take, on average, two to three years to accomplish, if not longer
3. Require every effort to accomplish the goals at hand and stay focused on the goals
4. Cost more than any estimates ever imagined
5. Use more computing and storage (disk space) than current networks
6. Increase the demands on the existing infrastructure and networks

What Is a Client/Server Network?

Herein lies the true dilemma: No one can truly define what a client/server network is. A client/server network is whatever we define it as in our own organizations and with our own expectations! Clearly this concept is very difficult to define, since everyone has a slightly different take on it. It is relatively new in the list of computing definitions, but the concept has been around for years. In reality it is an old concept revisited with a lot of frills attached to it. Ask three different individuals in the information technology business and you'll get four different definitions. This fact obviously makes such a network difficult to install. Since so many variables exist in creating a definition, benchmarking an installation as successful or complete is equally difficult.

The concept of client/server architecture as introduced by the vendor community, both hardware and software, is not totally understood. Various installations already completed were based on some preselected criteria or interpretation of some management objective. Therefore, the solution is really in how we individually wish to define a client/server architecture and network. To further complicate matters, it is a chameleon, changing its identity on a regular basis. No two organizations have the same set of needs. Therefore, each implements this concept differently. How does a new organization go about planning an installation, if no standard exists to steer the way? The answer to this question is to install whatever it takes to create a user-aware network. You can then hope that it will meet or exceed the demands of today's computing needs and that future needs can be incrementally met.

Are There Any Models for Client/Server Networks?

Luckily, the models used to differentiate what a client/server network actually is include the following:

1. All of the components, functions, services, and distributed environments
2. Local area networks (LANs)
3. Campus area networks (CANs)

4. Metropolitan area networks (MANs)
5. Wide area networks (WANs)

Client/server networks as we know them also include the use of distributed services such as

1. Processing power
2. Applications
3. Transaction-oriented services
4. Development and programming

For the novice, the use of client/server is an emergence or evolution from a series of other computing architectures. It encompasses multiple computing platforms from mainframe computers, midrange computers, and even desktop devices. The desktop devices can take the form of terminals, Xterminals, personal computers (PCs) or high-end workstations. The variations are what make this a unique concept. One can mix and match whatever hardware platforms necessary to satisfy the end users' demands and needs, without jeopardizing the infrastructures that are already in place. We can breathe new life into systems that were once thought extinct.

What Issues Surround Client/Server Computing and Internetworking?

First and foremost, the client/server model carries a lot of excess baggage along with the definition. Industry vendors and soothsayers alike continue to bombard us with the key benefits of client/server computing as being all things to all people. Statements abound that this one solution set will bring about a revolution to the computing industry. Some say that we can expect the following improvements from the use of a client/server architecture:

1. *Using a client/server architecture and the internetworking solutions should eliminate all workload backlogs.* The systems and interconnections to various computing platforms suggest that unlimited resources and computing power will be at our fingertips, but this

line of thinking assumes that we have adequate resources to begin with. Many organizations start out with a minimum computing platform. In downsizing from a mainframe computer, organizations use midrange platforms to support new workloads that are to be significantly reduced. Sure, the actual computational power may be spread over smaller machines that are connected together through a WAN or LAN, which offloads the main work from the host computers, but the size and capacity of the LAN device may not be sufficient to perform the work at hand. Additionally, more resources that are diversely spread around the country (WAN) or a campus (CAN) place a larger load on the cable or telephone links that are currently used, which could cause added backlogs if the network is static. Robustness may be required to support all of the additional data that will run across the networks.

2. *Client/server internetworking will significantly reduce the cost of maintenance.* Here again, the assumption is that the mainframe will go away, along with the inherent maintenance costs for the hardware and the licensing agreements associated with the "big iron." However, if we spread these costs across a network of smaller computers, we have to consider the costs associated with licenses on multiple machines, along with ongoing maintenance for a group of smaller machines (PCs and workstations). Can one really factor these all into an equation and come up with an accurate answer? Some organizations feel that paying for maintenance on a PC is unthinkable. Instead they prefer to use a forklift approach in dealing with machine problems. When one breaks, they merely throw it away (i.e., bring in the forklift, take out the old, broken machine, and replace it with the latest and greatest new one). This approach can be more expensive over the long run if we are not careful, although the concept has some merit, whereby it does not pay to fix or upgrade a PC. Indeed it may be far less expensive to replace it with a new model. But one must consider how many times this scenario might occur before getting involved with this theory. One organization benchmarked its expenditures and found it actually incurred greater costs in moving to a client/server architecture.

3. *The client/server architecture has the ability to increase portability of software between and across computing platforms.* This claim may be true, but it is more likely a goal today. Reality says that it is a couple of years away. Further, if the software is portable between and among machines, the burden of maintaining accurate licensing agreements becomes the network manager's. Users are likely to play roulette with software, loading it on any machine that they feel requires it. Launching applications across a network places added loads on the network itself. Moreover, the LANs in use today operate at megabits-per-second speeds, whereas the WAN is typically installed in kilobits-per-second speeds. This cost issue will surface again and again.

4. *Network connectivity will facilitate much quicker rollout of new applications and services.* This belief grows from the network's ability to link computer resources together and get to the development cycle much quicker. However, if the bottlenecks are redistributed across a network, the end result may be as slow or worse. Consequently, the use of a network must be carefully planned before such dramatic expectations can be realized. Throwing resources at this technology is not the end-all solution. The impact of launching multiple sessions or applications on a network is still a design consideration that must be heavily weighed.

5. *The use of a client/server network and the subsequent computing platform will increase the interaction between humans and machines.* Again, this statement may be true, but one cannot ignore the fact that the client/server network may be more complex than previous systems. Thus, the human interaction may diminish as a result of the intimidation factor. Users may fear the use of a complicated network resource and therefore find excuses to avoid it. Nothing can be gained if users are not comfortable with the network. Obviously this fear can be addressed through intensive training spread over time. It may be necessary to start beginners' training, intermediate training, and finally, advanced training. This approach bears the consequences of being very expensive to implement. The PC or workstation that costs a few thousand dollars can well exceed 10 times its original cost when the software (applications) and training issues are finally addressed. These costs must be factored into the original equation before springing forward with the project.

6. *Users will get their programs quicker, because they will be able to use object-oriented architecture to develop their own.* By eliminating the programming staff, organizations think they can save money.

However, the fallacy in this concept is that an organization may well eliminate 100 programmers (or any other number) and let users set their own programming effort through objects. The result is that all 1000 to 5000 (or any other number) employees in an organization become programmers. These users will spend more time developing programs than doing their jobs!

7. *The use of client/server architectures for both computing and networking will increase network performance.* This final comment from vendors deals with network performance issues. This claim is less tangible, since the added bandwidth needed to support the distributed services and the need to cross the network to access these services tend to slow the network down. Rather than improve performance, the network may become a bottleneck. It is a double-edged sword—you cannot predict the impact but you expect the increased benefits. So we are back to square one, a Catch-22 arrangement that leaves the network manager in a quandary. Should you jump headlong into the project and hope for the best? Or should you wait and see? In either decision, users will be demanding more, vendors will be pressuring you to proceed, and management will be looking for financial and productivity justifications that may not be available.

What Is the Goal?

Over the years, organizations have become very dependent on the use of computers. This fact is no surprise. However, a new awakening has occurred. Organizations now look differently at computing power and systems than they did years ago. Instead of being held captive by information systems departments, with all their acronyms and jargon, management can see the true benefit of computing resources. The power of computers has changed our everyday lives. Instead of being excited about the mainframe architectures with their proprietary protocols and locked-in applications, managers see the opportunity to move to smaller systems and less-complicated programs. Graphical user interfaces (GUIs) allow the user to feel less intimidated by the overall connection to a mainframe or midrange system. So the tides have shifted. Further, instead of using computing power for the sake of managing paper, the computer is now seen as a business opportunity Client/

server computing and networking scenarios offer management the opp-ortunity to move beyond the proprietary bounds of the vintage, legacy systems.

The Evolution of Client/Server Networks

The first computers were a rudimentary form of client/server. The diagram in Fig. 2.1 shows a monolithic architecture. Although it is nothing like the picture we have today, this system was effectively used to provide services from the host-based server to the workstation, such as a 327X terminal device (the client). Anything in the form of processing or data manipulation was done at the host from the user workstation. Launching the application was done from the client station to the host machine. Most people involved in the paradigm shift to client/server architectures would not view this arrangement as related in any way to today's client/server setup. However, all services were provided by the server. The distinct difference was the intelligence placed at the desktop device (none). This architecture led to the evolution of the client/server world because the host-based control was something users did not enjoy. The hierarchy is plainly evident—the mainframe housed all of the applications, programs, storage, and access methods. All access to the mainframe was controlled by the front-end processor. Controllers were more of a hub arrangement, linking multiple terminals to the front-end processor over a single high-speed link. One may not want to admit it, but this architecture is very similar to that being touted as the new client/server.

The evolution continued with the introduction of a master host and other subsets driven by the master controller. In Fig. 2.2 we see this next step in the development cycle. Here, distributed application processing under the direct control of the master host system was used. In the figure we see a single main controlling host with two separate hosts served by the main. The subprocesses are dependent on the primary device and therefore somewhat contained in its actions and abilities. This arrangement was often used to limit the access and manipulation to the editing and validation functions. However, one can see that basically three computing devices are involved in the process: the main controlling host, a subprocessor, and a terminal

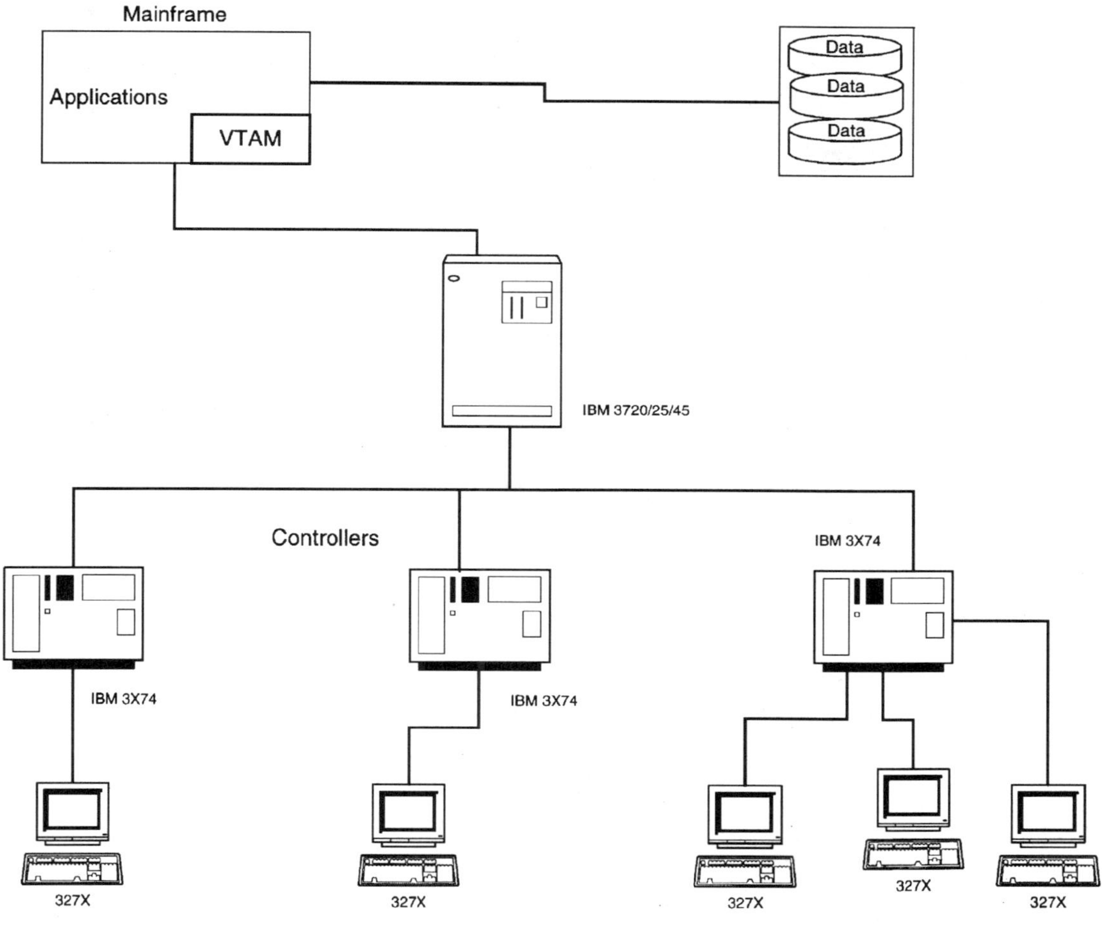

Figure 2.1 The original connectivity arrangement was a rudimentary form of client/server.

device. Granted, the terminal device shown in this figure is a dumb terminal, but the figure could easily reflect the use of a personal computer with a card that emulates 327X terminal functions. We can stretch our imagination far enough to see the basis for this comparison. The client/server computing platform mimics the older mainframe-based architectures.

Next came the peer-to-peer processing concept, as shown in Fig. 2.3. In this part of the evolution, a network of computing devices are connected either in a meshed pattern or a cascading pattern. In either case, all computers in this environment are equal. Each has the ability to

Figure 2.2
The second step in the evolution included a subprocessor host controlled by a main host.

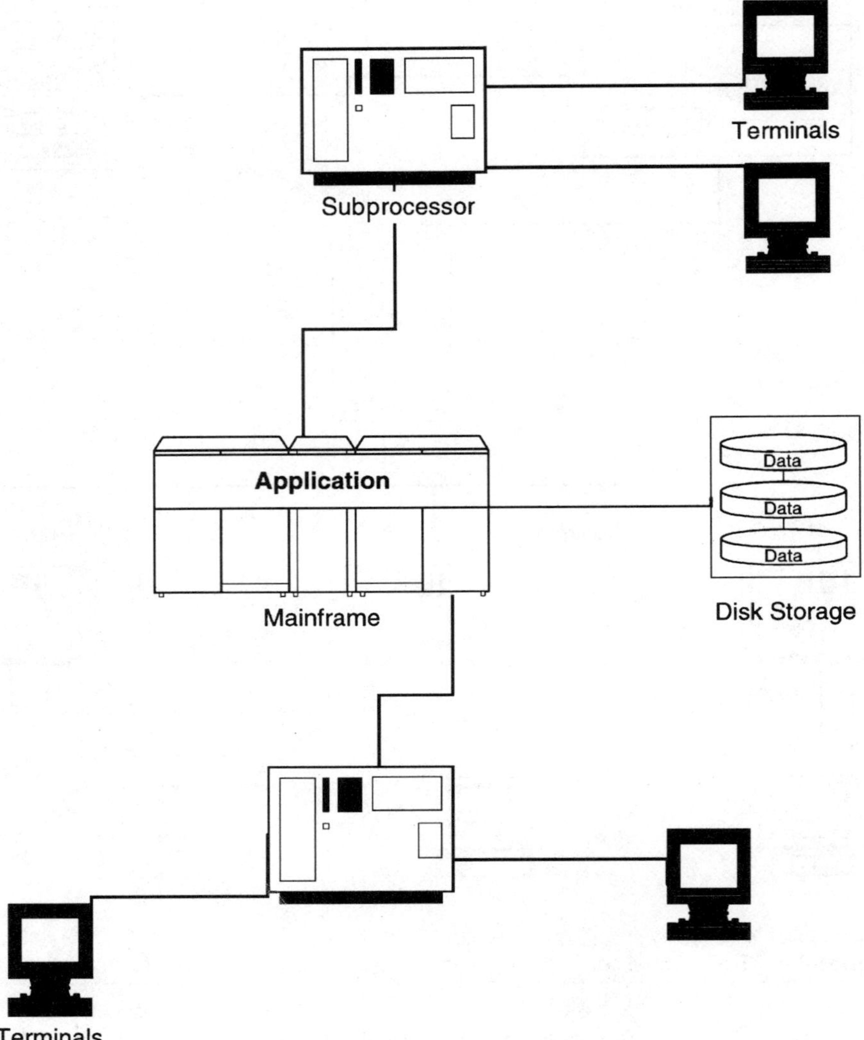

launch applications programs, access data on any other peer, issue requests to each other, and provide services to each of the peers on the network. Processing power is actually provided and performed wherever resources are available, rather than by a specific host system. Although it may not seem like high technology, the fact remains that the evolution of our current way of thinking stems from the 1960s and 1970s. These architectures were changes from the centralized control of the MIS departments, so they were considered radical ideas during their heyday.

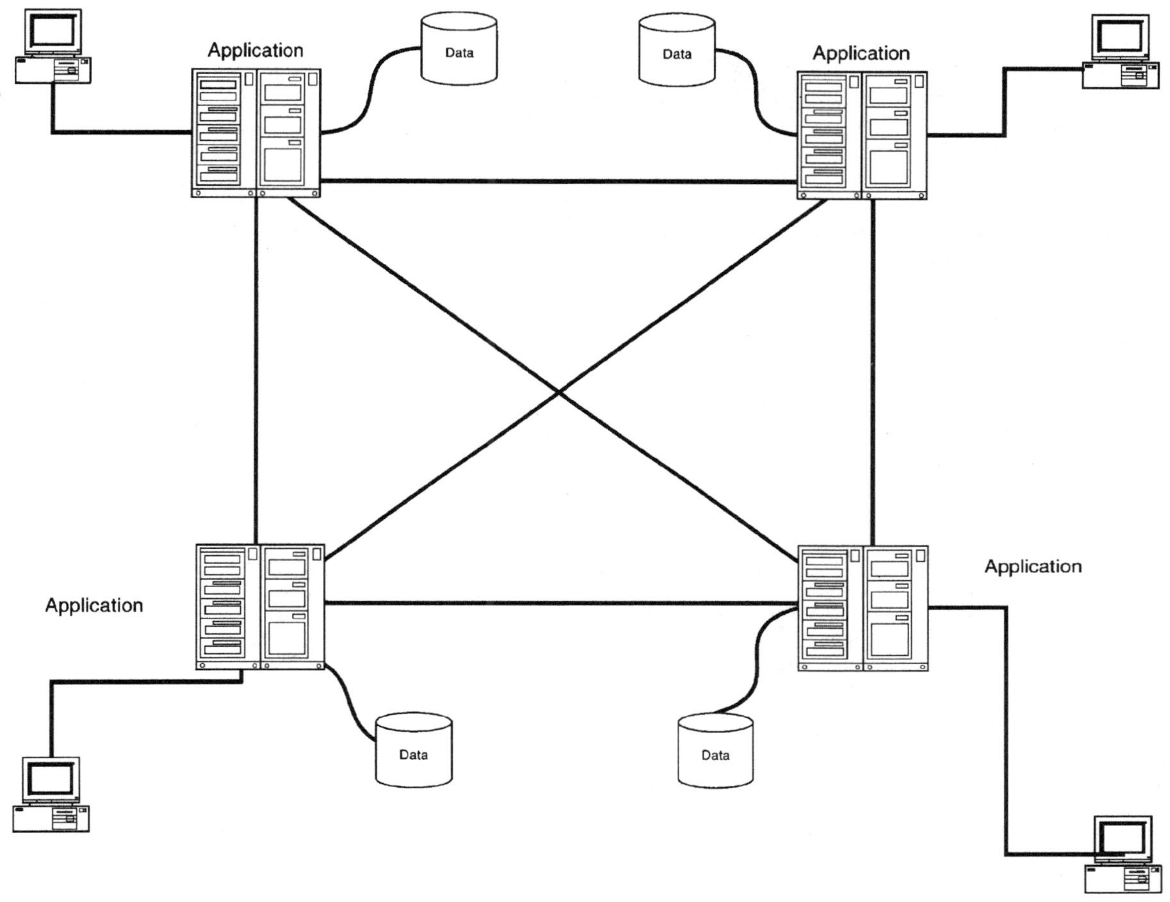

Figure 2.3 Peer-to-peer network processing was a radical step away from centralized control.

Most people believe that actual client/server architecture began with the idea of a local area network (LAN), as shown in Fig. 2.4. A form of distributed and shared processing that emerged in the 1980s, the LAN was a step made by users to escape the control and domination of the MIS departments. End users went out to the marketplace and purchased their own networking solutions. They were typically installed by a systems integrator rather than the internal MIS staff. Thus, the actual precursor to the client/server platform that we discuss now stemmed from the LAN. In this environment the users on a LAN shared devices such as

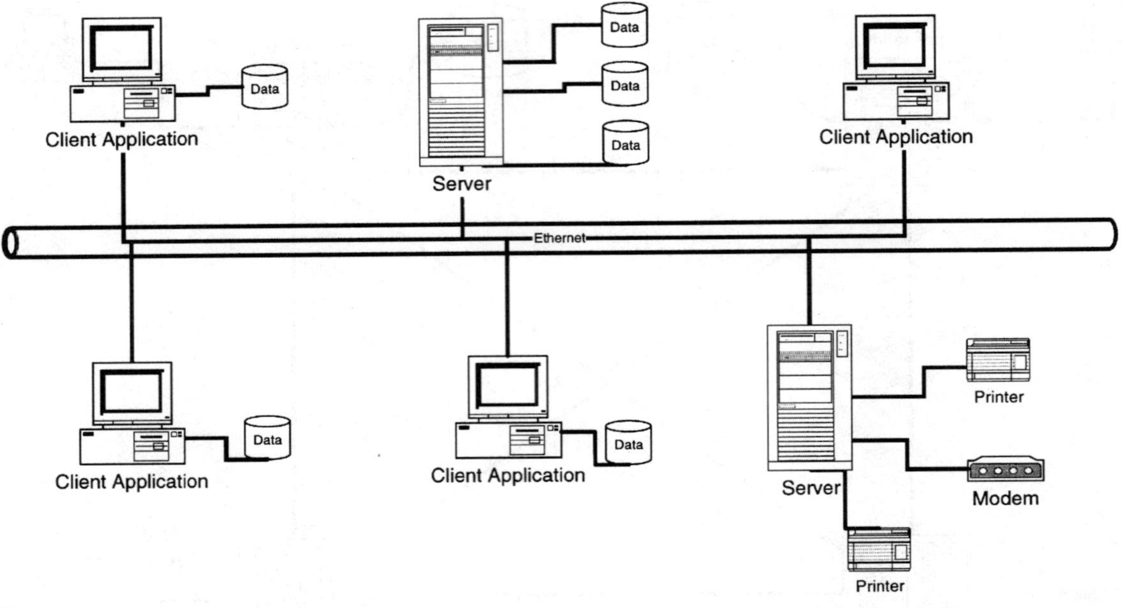

Figure 2.4 The LAN emerged as the client/server model in the early 1980s.

1. High-quality laser printers (given that in 1983 and 1984 dot matrix printers were the norm)
2. Hard disks, which were very expensive during this introductory period
3. Communications services, such as modem pools and other connecting devices
4. Files in a department or workgroup function
5. Programs that resided on the server
6. A single cable connecting all the devices

This concept evolved into the mid-1980s as the rudimentary form of client/server. In this regard the PC-based systems used clients (requestors), which were PCs that requested services and resources from a server. The server performed all of the services for the requesting client.

So, back to the question: What is a client/server architecture? The client/server model revolves around a three-computer architecture. The three computers can include

1. A mainframe host coupled to a midrange application server tied to a PC at the desktop
2. A mainframe host coupled to a PC-based server on a LAN tied to a PC or workstation at the desktop
3. A midrange server coupled to a PC-based server tied to a PC or workstation at the desktop

One can see that the variables are many and that the connections in a client/server architecture take on many forms. The client may be any device. An application server can be PC-based or midrange computer-based. The server can be a PC, a midrange, or a mainframe system. The mix of possibilities can be seen in Fig. 2.5.

One can see that the client/server model resulted in the evolution of various technologies and forms of network services that use various techniques to realize gains in processing and productivity. In all cases, these productivity and processing gains could not be achieved individually. A cooperative processing system exists between partnered devices to share the responsibility to complete a given set of processing tasks. This partnership includes the client (requestor) and the server (one or more cooperative systems that respond to the request). A client/server computing system includes the use of

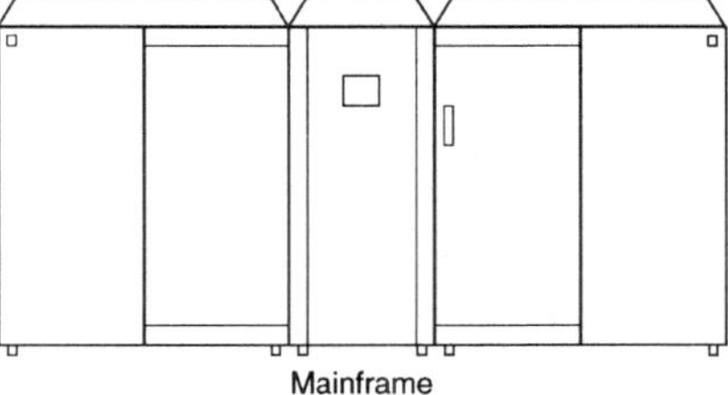

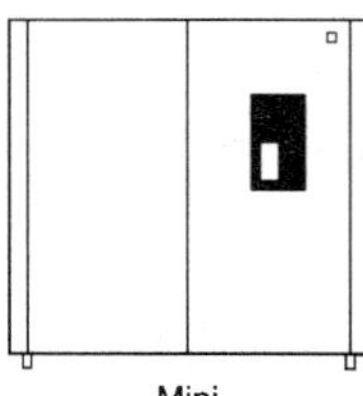

Figure 2.5 The possible variations for a client/server network.

- Applications
- Information (data)
- Processing interrelationships
- Hardware

What, then, is a client/server network?

A client/server network is a collection of computing systems, peripherals, and other devices linked together on a single communication system to serve the end user. In Fig. 2.6 we see myriad devices linked together on a single cable system (the communications system)

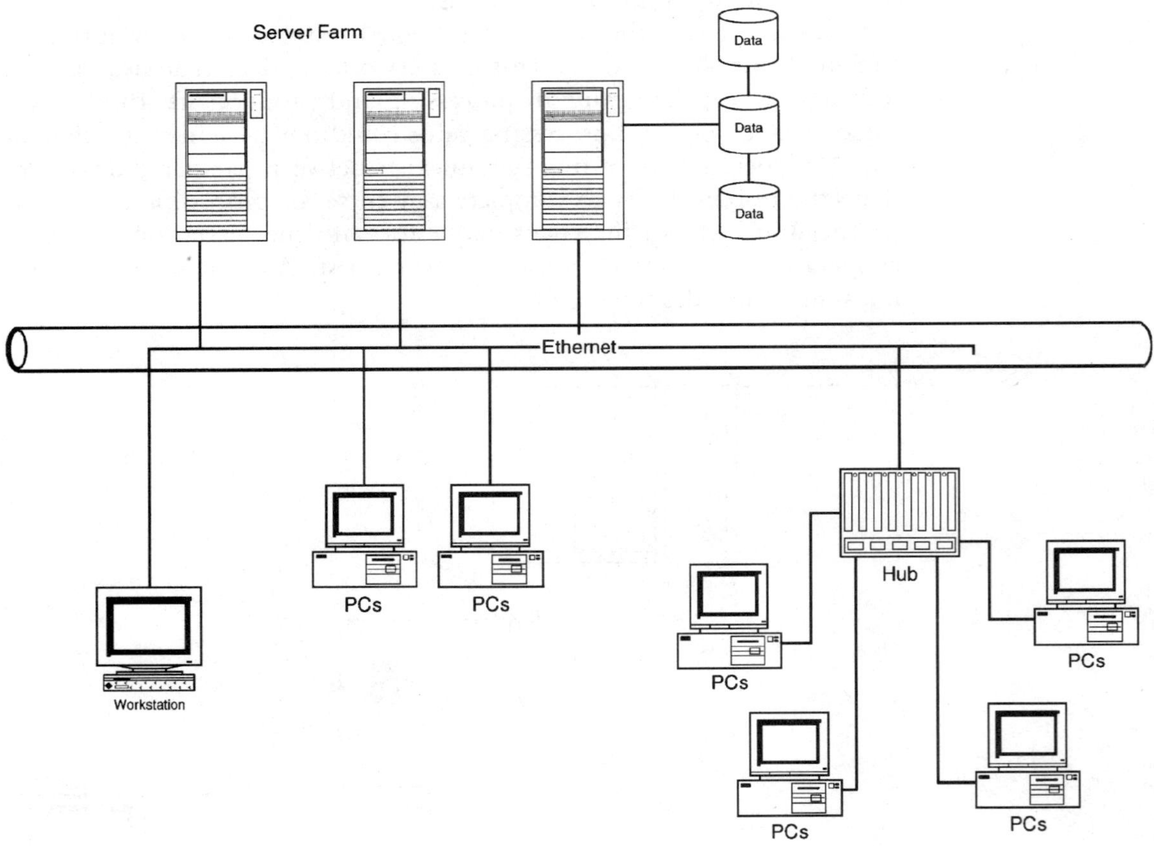

Figure 2.6 The client/server network as it evolves in user environments.

allowing the resource sharing necessary to serve the business need. These computing platforms include such things as

1. *Server farms.* These are groupings of servers that provide specific features or functions to the user population. Server farms can include boot servers, file servers, application servers, print servers, and so on.
2. *High-end workstations.* These are the very high end systems such as CAD workstations, imaging workstations, and the like. Potentially, these workstations will be Sun SparcStations or Silicon Graphics terminals or workstations. They have their own processors, high RAM configuration, and large disk storage capacities.
3. *Personal computers.* These are the 386/486 and Pentium or the newer Power PC families that support the lower-end user. These terminal interfaces are directly attached to the cable with a network interface card, or they can be consolidated in a telephone closet where the hub is used as a concentrator.

We can see that the client/server network is a collection of devices that reside in an organization's infrastructure. It includes the necessary tools and connections to provide the following:

1. Resource-sharing functions that use client/server computing
2. The LAN, which combines the cable system, the workstations and PCs, the servers, and the necessary network operating systems to cohesively bind these all together
3. Specialty devices that serve a single function, such as scanners, plotters, and so forth
4. Flexibility to migrate from one connectivity solution to another with minimal disruptions

Because these components and features are usually tied together across a localized area, we refer to the LAN as a rudimentary form of client/server network. As this evolution continued, the variations of this concept introduced far more complex solutions, as will be seen in this book. Various mix-and-match techniques appeared in the operating environment that required a step into newer architectures. On the client/server network we can use a client/server computing strategy for the masses, which means that the concept of defining a client/server *network* is easier than trying to define a client/server *computing system.*

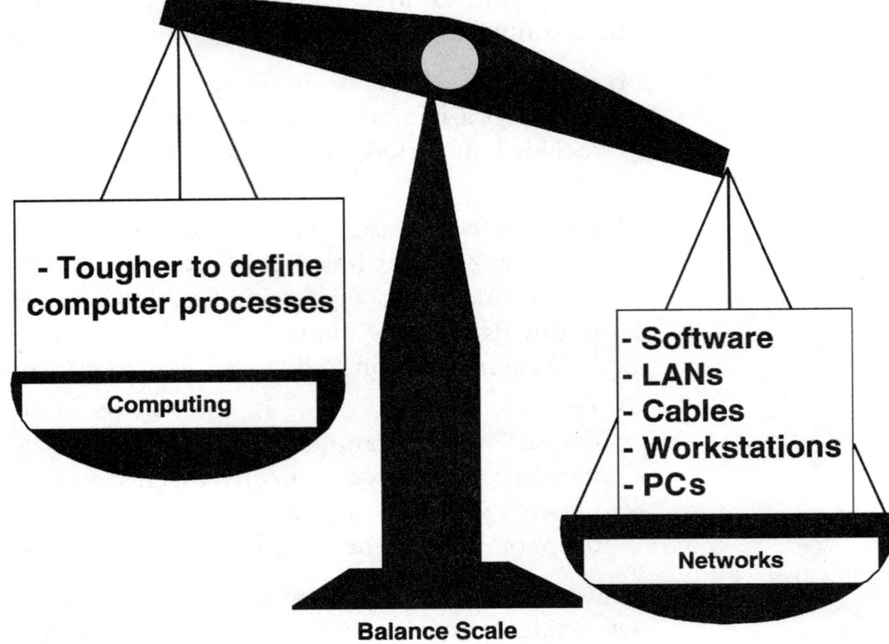

Figure 2.7 The scale of balancing between client/server networks and computing.

As seen in Fig. 2.7, the definition of these environments can be more difficult. A weighting or balance effect makes it easy to visualize new markets and opportunities. Client/server networks include all the physical pieces that we can touch and feel. The networks have readily identifiable components used to link the pieces and services together, in direct contrast to the client/server computing environment, which is a concept that is very difficult to visualize. Where the client/server computing environment entails various definitions, the network is structurally visible. This difference is what leads to the massive confusion in the industry.

Additional Components of a Client/Server Network

When defining the client/server network, we must also include additional items that allow this networking concept to include various enterprise groups. The added components include enough pieces to support the following:

1. A dynamic workgroup
2. An entire department
3. Whole buildings
4. Divisions
5. The entire organization

Differentiating between these groupings is difficult, but doing so creates the many definitions of what a client/server network is all about. Everyone has a slightly different definition, based on individual circumstances. Thus, no one rule really tells the whole story. As can be seen in Fig. 2.8, myriad pieces can be added to the equivalent of the LAN to meld this network into an enterprise solution. The pieces to be added include, but are not limited to, the following:

- Mainframes that act as an organization's central repository of data.
- Database servers that provide database access and manipulation for customer lists, product catalogs, price lists, and so on.
- Specific applications servers that meet very specific needs, such as video servers, time servers, authentication servers, etc.
- Communications servers that consolidate modems into an asynchronous gateway function for inbound and outbound access, or a fax server for sharing across the network rather than supplying each individual, workgroup, or department with its own.
- Multistation access units (MAUs) and hubs that tie the PC-based services together on a more efficient cabling scheme.
- Bridges that work as lower-layer protocol (data link layer) connections between departmental or organizational LANs spread throughout the building, the campus, or the country, depending on the environment.
- Routers that work at a higher-level protocol (network layer) connection between disparate network topologies and wide area networking connections. Routers have also found a new home in the LAN arena.
- Gateways that allow higher-level protocol support (transport, session, and presentation layers) for connections between disparate computing systems, applications, and capabilities wherever they may reside in the organization. These gateways provide for the format

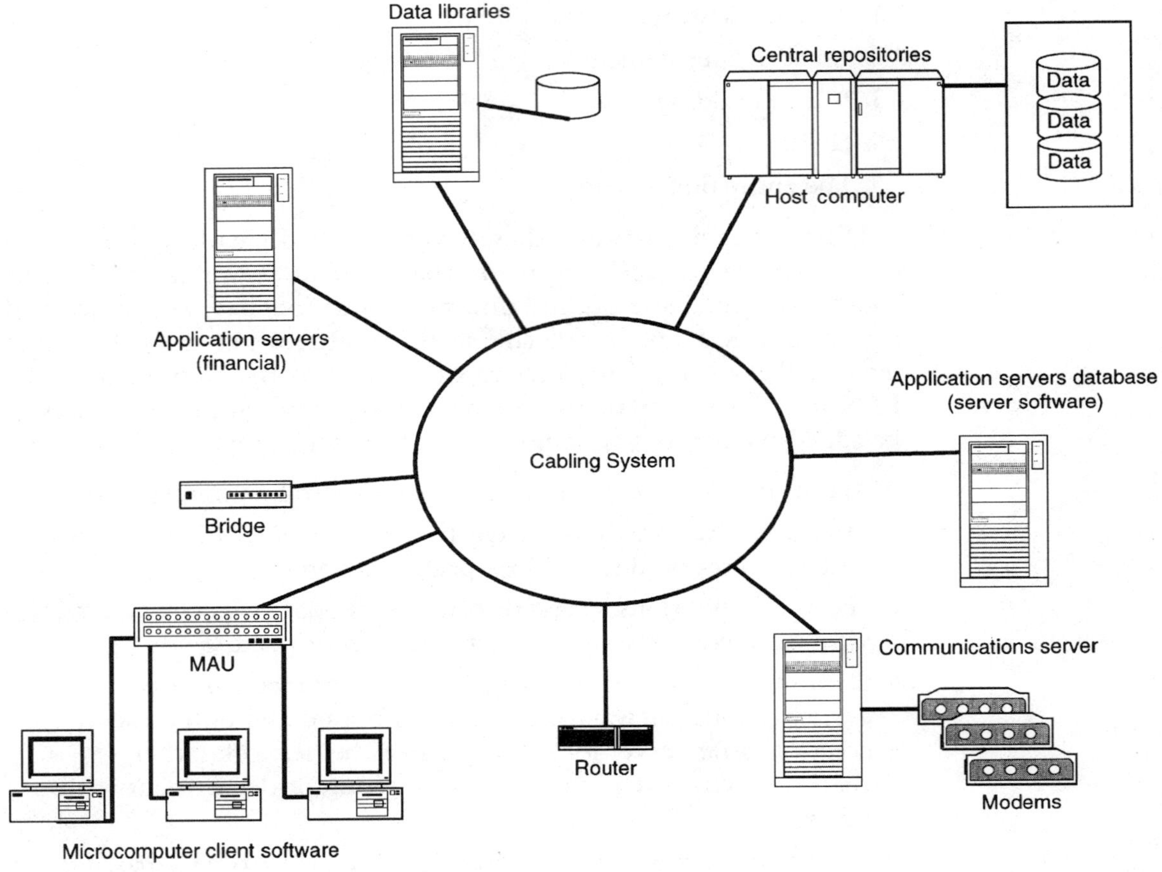

Figure 2.8 Client/server networks include additional components necessary to bind services together on an organization-wide level.

and syntax conversions so that all client/server network-attached devices can communicate and share information transparently.

Why the Hype about Client/Server Networking?

As any industry experiences growth, change, and restructuring, new hype is always introduced. Beginning in the early 1980s, personal computers took the industry by storm. MIS departments in 1980 felt that the

PC was of no consequence to an organization. In their estimate, this semi-intelligent device was no match for the power of their mainframe computers, and the use of a PC in lieu of a 327X terminal made no sense whatever. Why would any user ever want to move away from the simplistic procedures set up on the mainframe to access and manipulate the data? Further, since the PC was detached from the network, it was only a stand-alone device that a user would have to learn anew. No procedures or mass-storage devices were present at the time, so it was just another in a series of nuisance items with which MIS departments had to contend.

However, as users realized that they could connect their PCs together, forming the basis of a mainframe look-alike, they quickly began to demand and acquire the services of multiple PCs in a department or workgroup. This is all history, but it helps to set the stage for this widespread explosion in industry's use of the client/server world. As LANs began to pop up all through an organization, everyone realized that duplication of effort was required when accessing the mainframe for information, then rekeying that same data into a PC-based network device. In response, we had the emergence of the connectivity solutions to the mainframe world through 327X gateways that allowed the user to emulate the 327X terminal sometimes and act as a full-blown computing resource for other needs at other times. This idea was neat, so everyone jumped on the gateway bandwagon. As a result, PC-based networks began to proliferate for front-office functions. What was once a mainframe or midrange computing application was now fast becoming a LAN operation. As this change occurred, various network operating systems (NOSs) began to evolve. Companies like Banyan, Novell, IBM, and Microsoft all began to concentrate their efforts in meeting LAN needs for their customers. The lack of controls established by a centralized MIS department on the LAN was exciting and inviting to the rest of the organization.

Management had a tendency to ignore the migration of the data needs at the individual's desktop. Consequently, they saw the LAN as a departmental computing service but the mainframe as the organization's computing resource. They never saw the migration of mission-critical data to LANs. As a result, the use of the mainframe began to wane. Budgets for computational needs were shifting, so that each department began to build its own staff of LAN administrators and network engineers. MIS staffing came under pressure because the organization was now paying double the cost for the computing and staffing needs. The handwriting was on the wall. Management saw the migration to lower-cost devices such as PCs and PC-based servers hacking away at the need to support very expensive talent and high-end maintenance costs for mainframe systems. The cost of maintaining a mainframe was extraordinary and was escalating rapidly each year. Something had to be done!

The Application Server

As this migration continued, higher-end PCs and midrange computers were finding their way into departments. Users felt that they no longer needed the resources of the mainframe and the control still in place in MIS (now called IT) departments. They went back to the marketplace and found that if a dedicated server (whether PC or midrange) was added to this client/server world that was cropping up, then host mainframes would no longer be required. Naturally, each department felt that its needs could no longer be force-fit into a structured MIS data processing environment. Its needs within the organization were unique. Therefore, departments began buying into the idea of an application server.

An application server provides services to the client, as shown in Fig. 2.9. Here, on a LAN, the application server becomes the worker, providing services to all of the users in a specific department or the entire organization. This server meets very specific needs (e.g., database server, CAD server, etc.) for end users. The client, or requestor, uses the higher computing power of this application server to meet everyday needs, making the client device (whether a PC or high-end device) the traffic cop in the network. Moving the information processing control closer to the end user is what has occurred in this application server world. The client exercises all of the control over what work the server performs. This control deviates from the mainframe environment, where the mainframe dictated what would be done, how, and by whom. The paradigm shift to empowering the user and using the server as the work engine began to close the circle. The server uses all resources necessary to perform a task under the direct control of the user, helping to move away from central-processor control to worker control of data manipulation.

The Workstation

As shown in Fig. 2.10, the client device becomes the workstation controller for the application server. In this regard, the workstation (regardless of the actual device used) becomes a far more intrinsic component in

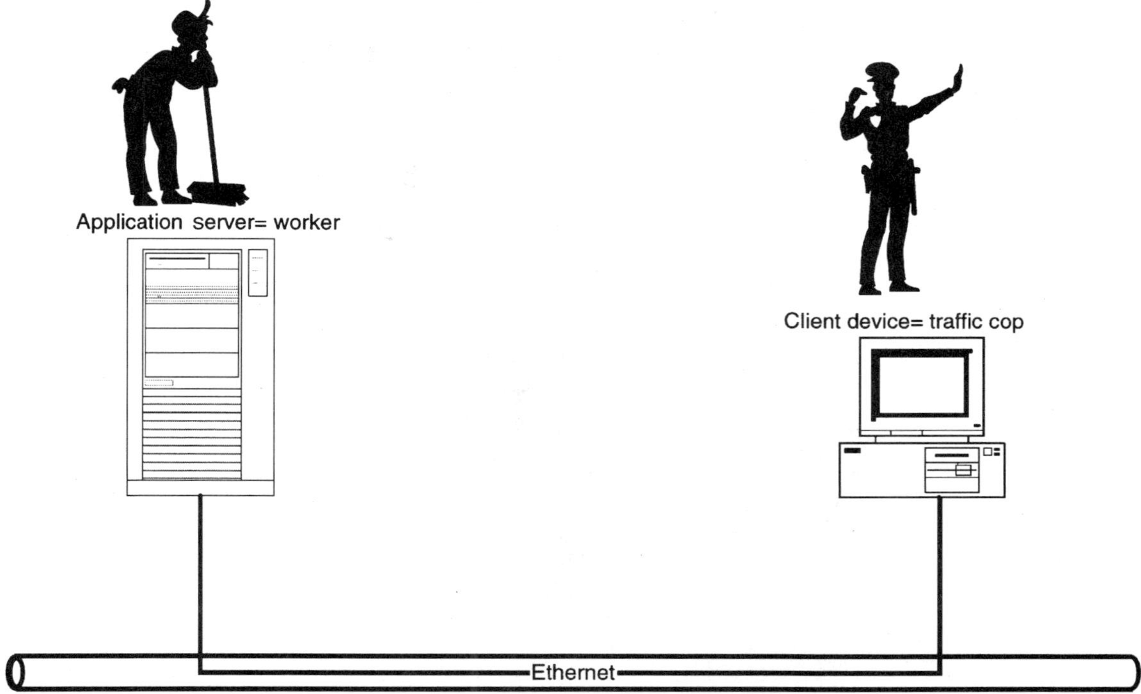

Figure 2.9 The application server becomes the worker and the client becomes the controller in a client/server network.

the client/server network. It is through this device that all of the action is initiated. This desktop device has also gone through several changes. It has become far more powerful in its ability to use processing power with a complete toolbox of capabilities to manipulate and control data. In this figure, the reference has all of the earmarks of a super device. It is typically equipped with the following features and capabilities:

1. *A more powerful processor, working with a 486 processor at 66- to 75- or 100-MHz clock speeds.* Newer devices are now based on the Pentium chip, running at 90- to 200-MHz clock speeds. It is a very powerful device with a lot of computing capacity.
2. *Higher memory capabilities, with 8, 16, 24, and 32 megabytes (Mbytes) of RAM.* What was once the domain for 1 to 4 Mbytes has become far more demanding and requires a minimum of 8 to 16 Mbytes just to operate the operating system and some shells or programs.

Figure 2.10 The workstation has become a powerful computer itself, which is necessary to support the client/server architecture.

3. *Very large storage capabilities on hard disks in the workstation.* In the old days, a 30- to 40-Mbyte hard disk was sufficient. Now these devices are typically configured with a minimum of 100 Mbytes, but the norm is becoming a 1- to 3-Gbyte disk subsystem.
4. *Powerful graphics on the PC screen, supporting SVGA and better standards with color.* It wasn't that long ago when color was the exception rather than the norm.
5. *The ability to run high-end client software such X-Windows, Windows 3.x, Windows 95, Windows NT Workstation, or some form of UNIX.* In the Macintosh world, we are looking at System 7.
6. *Multitasking capabilities for newer systems and software using full tasking operations.* In the Windows 3.x series, task swapping is the environment, as opposed to multitasking.
7. *Strong GUI interfaces to facilitate the ease of use.*
8. *Better memory management for all memory resources, as well as support for greater than 8 Mbytes of memory.* Many typical applications and operating systems have changed to recognize memory availability greater than 8 Mbytes.

9. *Full 32-bit support in newer devices to take advantage of the new applications and operating systems that are rolling out.*

Shifting the Problems on the Network

One of the reasons that workstation power is required is to shift the data manipulation closer to the desktop. In a client/server network, this shift may or may not be employed. Thus, the real risk is the possible bottlenecks that can occur on the network. The issue is where to place the processing power. The industry gurus all state that the power is needed at the server, since it is now the worker. However, if all the power is moved to the application server, then the potential bottlenecks will mimic the age-old problems experienced with the mainframe computers. In Fig. 2.11, we see where these bottlenecks may appear.

This figure shows that the following areas may become risks for the future:

1. *Access through the network to the application server through the network interface card (NIC) could become one of the bottlenecks.* If all requests must be processed through a single NIC, then this device must be able to support the priority and the size of the files, coupled with the sheer volume of requests that will follow.

2. *Assuming we can get through the NIC, the next area of possible problems is the computer processor.* If the processor is not fast enough, then the cycles will all be expended, causing queues or "server not responding" messages across the network to the client workstations.

3. *A third area of risk is the amount of memory available.* The application server will have to use substantial amounts of memory to support simultaneous sessions from a multitude of users. Memory at 256 Mbytes on up to the Gbyte range may be required. Unfortunately, this amount of memory is expensive (although rapidly dropping in price) and requires a high-end memory manager to support this service. If not enough memory is available, the applications could crash, or the page swapping may take a significant amount of effort to serve the users, causing noticeable delays.

Figure 2.11 Potential bottlenecks are created by using all processing power at the server.

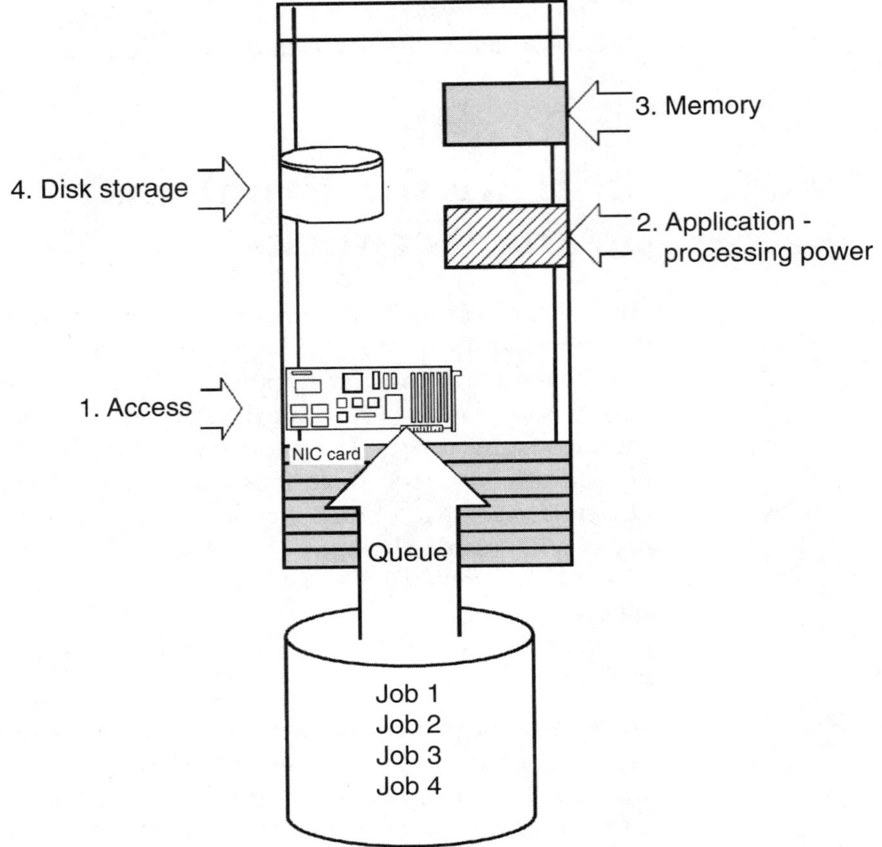

4. *Disk storage cannot be ignored.* Where we once had servers with 1 Gbyte of storage, the newer application servers and the ensuing programs, mixed with user storage needs, lead us to 20- to 50-Gbyte storage needs. When using GUI-based information, complex documents with graphics, and object orientation, the storage demands will increase. The use of a client/server architecture may well cause the storage demands to double or triple over those to which we are typically accustomed.

5. *Queues to the servers and storage systems could get bogged down considerably.* This possibility is at least as problematic as the other potential bottlenecks, but users will perceive more delays and will not be happy.

The move is to put more power at the desktop in a client/server network. The server still facilitates the application process, but the workstation performs the operation. If this is the actual case, then a new set of opportunities arises. The opportunity to move this power to the desk is one that may shift the risks of congestion to a new location. In the network, more data will be required across the network to move megafiles to the workstation for manipulation. In Fig. 2.12, the client sends out the request to *get* a file, whereas in the past the server would *use* a file. Now as the get request is sent across the network, the server needs only to move the entire file across the network and deliver it to the workstation. A typical application may be a database inquiry that requires that the entire database be downloaded to the workstation. The problem for the late 1990s and beyond, then, becomes the bottleneck on the cabling systems and NIC cards to support these massive files moving across the local networking scheme. In Fig. 2.13, as the server responds to the *get* request, it sends the entire file across the network, causing a delay for any other user looking for a similar-sized file. One can see that this problem can become exponential. Where does this all lead? The answer still resides on each network, because the use and capacities are all variables in every network.

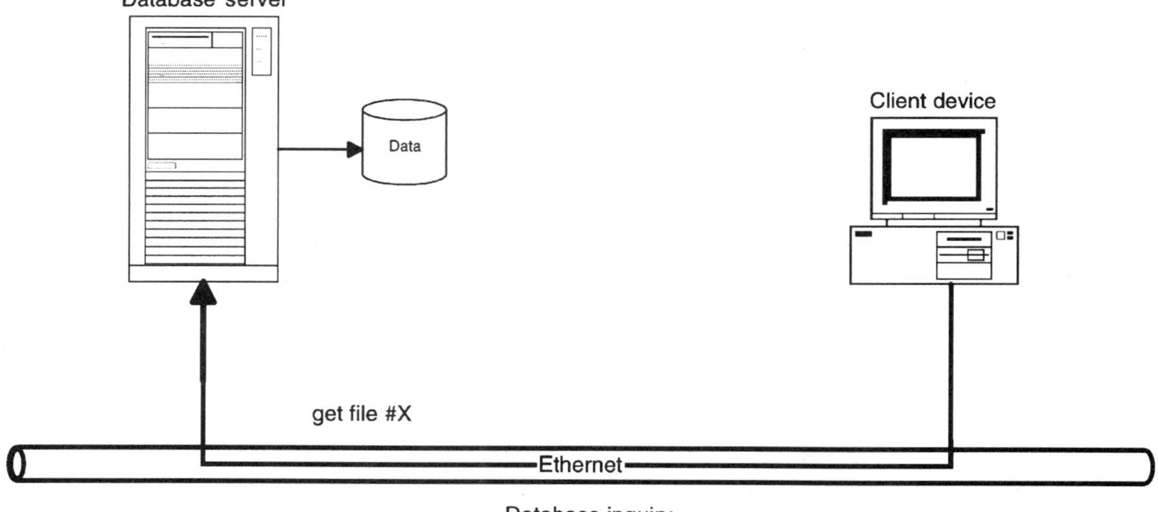

Figure 2.12 As the *get* request is now issued by the client, the server no longer has much responsibility.

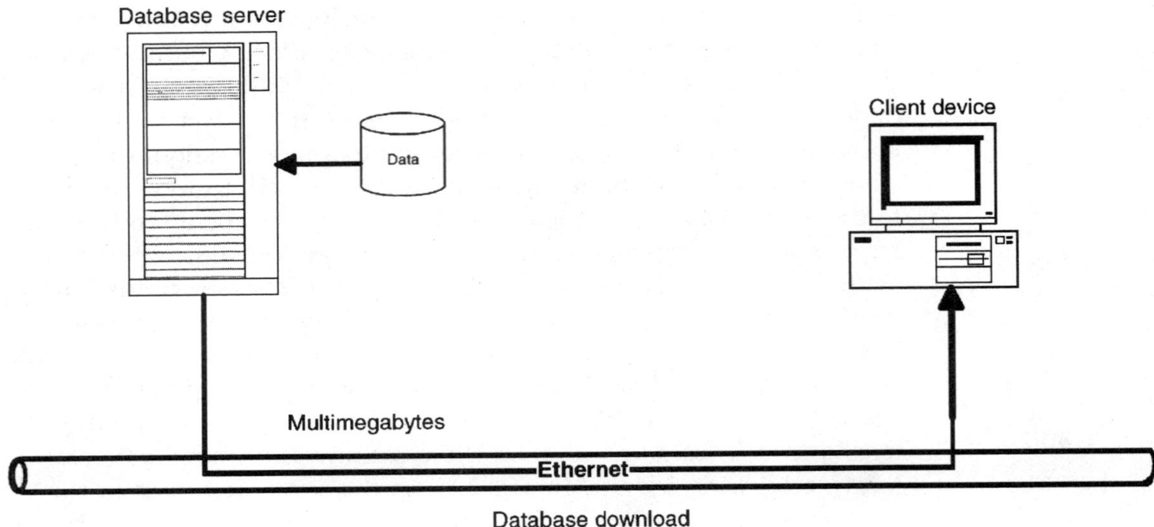

Figure 2.13 The response from the server to the client means that huge files will be moved across the network, which becomes the challenge of the 1990s.

Additionally, a new problem is working in this same arena. The applications are themselves getting larger. What was once a 10-Mbyte file in mainframe days has now become a 50-Mbyte file in this new architecture. It is an understatement to suggest that applications programmers working for the various software houses are developing less finely tuned (sloppy) code. It is really a money issue. In Fig. 2.14 we see that the size of these applications and the ensuing data are getting exponentially larger. The argument here is that the code is constantly changing and therefore does not need to be fine-tuned, because it will likely be changed soon. Further, programmers don't have to tune the code because the hardware (disks) is much less expensive. Thus the hard disk subsystem must be considerably larger at the desk and at the server level. One can see that this issue is getting out of hand, but because the hardware is less expensive, no one has the patience to go back and revisit the problem. We therefore need larger disks and faster throughput to move these applications and files across the networks of the future. This scenario is already painting us into a corner in our efforts to support the needs for both present and future applications.

More pieces must be included into the overall equation, but these are addressed in later chapters in this book. However, the myths and

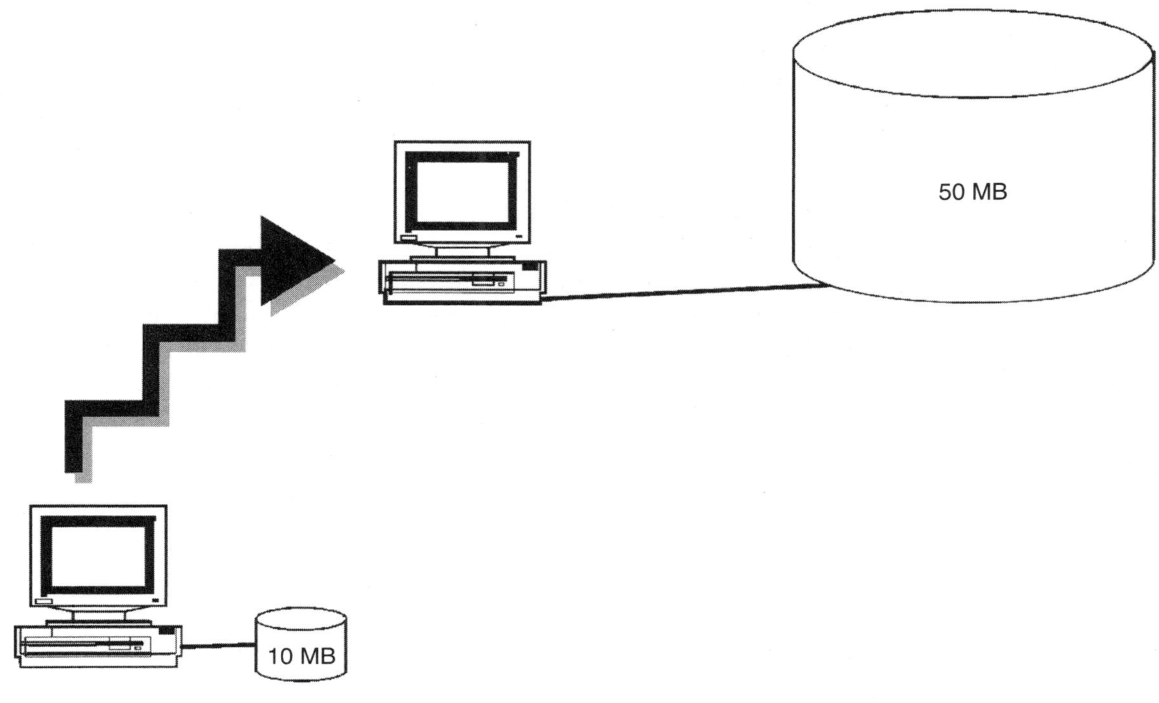

Figure 2.14 The applications are four to five times larger than they were in the days of mainframes, requiring larger disks and faster throughput across the network to support them.

fantasies that are looming in the industry are all leading the way for users and vendors alike to get into a bind that will be very expensive to reverse.

Management is looking for the logical replacement for the mainframe, a move away from the controlled days of the MIS departments. User department managers are looking for the freedom to manipulate their information as easily as their needs dictate. Workers are looking for simplified ways of accessing and manipulating their data, without the heavy command-line interfaces. They prefer the use of GUIs where possible. Vendors are looking to get new blood into the business to sustain the rapid growth and pricing benefits of the 1980s. Therefore, they needed to come up with the next generation of computing platforms.

Network suppliers also are getting into the picture. Where they once were able to sell an organization kilobits-per-second data transport across the country to link computers, today they are in the megabits-per-second stage. Users are buying into this concept to prevent bottlenecks. How, then, does one look at this market and concept with an air of caution? Organizations are jumping headlong into projects without a clue about what is real and what is fictional. Movement into client/server networks means that major upgrades and investments will be the norm. Furthermore, the timing to implement these projects has been grossly understated in the industry. We are running at a brick wall with all stops removed. What follows depends on the relative success and failure rates of those who attempt to implement client/server networks. However, many organizations are entering this project phase without being fully equipped to manage such a conversion or without the necessary staffing and funding. Will this be the pace that leads our way?

CHAPTER 3

Evolving Standards for the Client/Server Network

When looking at a client/server network, one has a potpourri of various protocols to choose from. This situation may sound like a panacea, but at the same time it can lead to a lot of confusion. Which protocols are best for your particular network? Should one standard be selected, or should the network be dependent on the various user-based services? If one chooses a single standard, things can be much simpler. However, if one standard is selected, the possibility of incompatibilities exists. This being the case, one would have to choose to ignore added protocol stacks or attempt to support them as best possible. The users, on the other hand, generally lack compassion about the needs of the network manager, since the applications that fit their needs dictate the protocols that must be supported. One cannot ignore the fact that several client/server networks are supporting multiple protocols as a matter of necessity. Therefore we have to assume that the network will have multiple protocols provided by multiple vendors. Whether products or services, these protocols have to be met straight on. The network manager can provide some level of support, but will attempt, over time, to mitigate these into a manageable number. A statement of just how many protocols will be supported and to what degree is necessary.

First, before getting into an argumentative position with the users, one should do some homework. One can spend some time researching the available standards to support the client/server network and choose the strategic directions for the future. This research will look at a variety of inputs from the standards bodies responsible for the industry and from the vendors providing the services and applications. In Table 3.1, we look at some of the variety of protocols that are currently on the dockets for the standards committees. Some of these include operating systems; others adhere to standard architectures. However, they are all protocols based on the need to connect various computing platforms. This table attempts to provide some semblance of just what popular sets of protocols are available and which ones may be safe bets. This information is all contingent on the actual network supported and the various applications being introduced.

Many client/server networks were started and finally abandoned due to the cost and difficulties encountered by network managers who attempted to support every protocol imaginable. One recent discussion with a very large *Fortune* 100 company led to the revelation that their users use more than 40 various protocols to meet day-to-day needs. What they will ultimately do is only a guess. The network managers felt that they had no choice but to try to develop a strategy to support everything.

TABLE 3.1

Summary of Standards and De Facto Standards Emerging in Support of Client/Server Networks

Standard/de facto	Works on	Benefits
OSI	All LANs, WANs, and MANs	Works within all platforms if adopted and implemented fully by vendors
DCE/DME	All client/server platforms	Designed to be transparent based on using the best of multiple vendors' products in the client/server network environment
TCP/IP	All platforms, LANs and WANs especially	Robust and works just about everywhere; however, there are several different versions and implementations of this protocol, meaning that not all do the same things; vendor-specific
UNIX	Server arena, but is limited for the client; thus far, too powerful for a client device	Robust and based on the use of TCP/IP in its implementation. Other versions exist for various UNIX platforms such as AIX, HP UX, and several others.
SNA/SDLC	Mainframe server; can work in a client/server world	Very proprietary with few interfaces to other vendor products; will support multiple protocol stacks such as TCP/IP
APPN/APPC	Peer-to-peer networking architecture for the WAN	IBM's counter to the WAN services and TCP/IP; based on IBM's mainframe and midrange server line
DecNet	Works in the enterprise so is geared for the client/server architecture	Some proprietary features and services; requires DEC interfaces and products; runs in multiprotocol network with TCP/IP and Novell
Novell	LAN; client/server network; the de facto standard for the LAN; recently began supporting full routing protocols as a WAN capability	Supports both the IPX/SPX and TCP/IP protocols. This support is intrinsic for 65% of LANs being converted into client/server networks. A full stack of other supporting protocols are resident. Now with UNIX support, it is becoming a standard.
NT	Client/server architectures; LANs and WANs	Full support of TCP/IP protocols for the NT version of Microsoft's new operating system
Others	Emerging for LANs and WANs	Other standards and de facto standards are emerging based on implementations.

Although this effort may have been noble, it was bound for disaster. How can one set of network staff members attempt to learn everything there is to know to ultimately support such a wide variety of protocols?

One can see from this table that the choices for some of the standards and de facto standards are varied. All of these can work together in the same network if some gateway functions are used. Doing so adds complexity to the network and could confuse the user. This multiple-protocol approach must be as transparent as possible and use GUIs to ease the implementation.

A First Look at These Standards

Before we can discuss these standards and the ensuing variations (de facto), it is wise to understand that use of the variations is inevitable. When we research the standards, we have to understand that they are based on some form of an architecture. With the client/server architecture, remember the use of a three-computer system that shares resources among and between computing platforms. All products and services offered by the vendors are based on some form of architecture. Whether proprietary or standards-based, these products are the direct result of some form of standard.

Regardless of the consequences, many vendors derive a product in advance of standards being completed or, in some cases, a variation of the standards. An architecture designed by vendors and standards committees is an attempt to develop logic in the implementation of a service. This architecture describes the interoperability of the products that will evolve based on the architecture. In the event a vendor applies all of the rules and definitions of the architecture, then all vendor products should be interoperable. Here is where the purpose of the architecture and the standards comes into the most play. Unfortunately, though, when the standards are set, they describe the protocols and the interoperations between two systems using the same implementation. However, the standards usually fall short of mandating the way the implementation and interpretation of the architectural design will be conducted, which means a vendor can produce a product that abides by the general guidelines of the standard but performs some proprietary tricks internally that differentiate its product from others. Let the buyer beware!

Although the architecture lays things all out, the actual production of a final service or product is what makes everything come together. A product abiding by the standards will be a vendor-specific implementation. This means that many vendors will tell their customers that they are compliant with a specific standard, for example, but their products may not be able to interoperate with a different vendor's standards-based product. Once again, the one in the middle of this dispute and situation is the network manager who thought that the standards protected the investments being made. Products will be short- or long-term solutions to your networking needs but will be like chameleons over time. They can change, be modified, or be completely scrapped midstream of an installation in favor of the latest and greatest new product. This issue must be addressed up front by the network manager before embarking on a long-term solution for the organization, especially if the product is de facto in nature.

The Longer-Term Solution

The longer-term solution is to attempt to select a standards-based architecture that supports a 5- to 10-year solution for the network being considered. Since the client/server architecture means so many different things to so many different people, it can only be a best guess to decide on the overall architecture to adopt. Thus, one must be wary of the implications of the definition and implementations of the particular architecture selected. It is very easy to lose sight of the ultimate goal if one is not careful. The charter and goals of the organization are all-important. The installation of an enterprise-wide client/server network and computing architecture should serve these goals—nothing less than that will do.

If the installation takes several months to several years, then reminders are necessary to keep everything in focus. Too many organizations have lost their vision after beginning the journey to client/server due to the constant changes and misdirected efforts by the vendor and user communities. No one can keep on course if the target is constantly moving, so very specific needs and goals must be stated up front. If these goals cannot be defined, a forklift mentality may slip into the overall equation. The approach may quickly become one of "If this solution doesn't work, I'll just throw it out and add a new one." This approach can be dangerous to the network that is going to support the entire organization's informational needs. The wrong decisions could cripple an organization or its profitability. Therefore, when dealing with the client/server network, one should clearly remember that

- Openness is a goal.
- Interoperability is a must.
- The client/server network started at the LAN.
- Inevitable migrations are now spanning the MAN and WAN architectures.
- Distributed computing and processing on the network will happen.
- The selection must be based on standards.
- Many systems are already in place, and adherence to these standards must involve some flexibility.
- The selection process may be limited!

In later chapters, this discussion is driven home for both the client and the server components as they deal with the operating systems, protocols, and interoperabilities across a LAN or WAN. To implement this networking structure, we must pay very careful attention to these guidelines and be aware of the complexities involved.

Figure 3.1 shows a pyramid approach used to conclude the installation of the standards needs for the organization. What this pyramid is attempting to show is the relationship to the selection and installation processes. These pieces can be seen in their own regard as follows, working from the bottom of the pyramid to the top, where the actual concept of the client/server network will be completed:

1. Interoperability between and among systems facilitates the ease of internetworking. What this attempts to define is the overall concept of the internetworking side of the business. If, in fact, the capabilities of these services cannot be internetworked, it will be extremely difficult to get to the goal of the client/server network. However, some other tools may be used to replace the connection through a gateway or a private leased line. The only risk here is that although connectivity may be achieved, interoperability may not be realized.

2. Interoperability therefore must be based on an open standard to allow the various connection arrangements and the multiple protocols to coexist on a single platform. It is openness that is a goal at

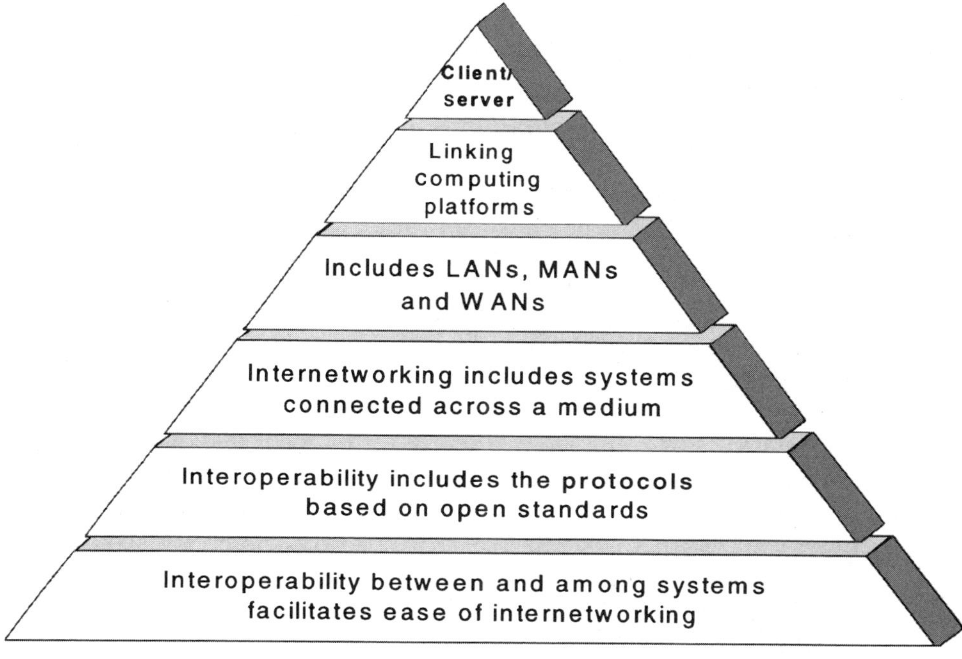

Figure 3.1 The pyramid that leads to the client/server network.

this level. Other aspects are considered in higher layers of the pyramid.

3. Internetworking includes the interconnection of various systems across a communication medium, requiring the use of communications protocols in a standards-based environment. Once again, the actual networking strategy used depends on the way the network is designed. No one solution exists at this level, so each network manager must look at the connection as a link across a private, public, or virtual networking scheme.

4. The network spans the various platforms used in our environment. A client/server network includes the connection at the LAN and may stop there. In other cases, it may span the LAN and continue across to a MAN. Still others include the LAN, MAN, and finally breach the WAN. The possibilities and the combinations are endless.

5. Linking these systems requires the ability to span different computer platforms, such as the PC and the mainframe, across a boundary through a communications subprocess. Finally, the communications and computer platforms become a homogenous, linked system based on the open set of standards.

6. What sits on top of the pyramid is the final client/server network. It is the composition of all standards and protocols—both computing and communications—linked across myriad topologies to create the final connection of transparent networking.

This scheme may seem too simplistic, but inevitably the use of such a model can make the difference between an interoperable and interconnected system and a patchwork of connections and computers that do not transparently interoperate. One cannot assume that a single vendor's products and services will match all of these requirements, but some derived benefit can come from understanding what it will take to make these systems work with each other. As one looks closer at the model, the need to find protocols, operating systems, and communications systems becomes imperative. In Fig. 3.2, the relationship between the words *interoperable* and *interconnected* is shown. This figure merely reinforces the point made in the model, but it drives home the point that many vendors and network managers overlook.

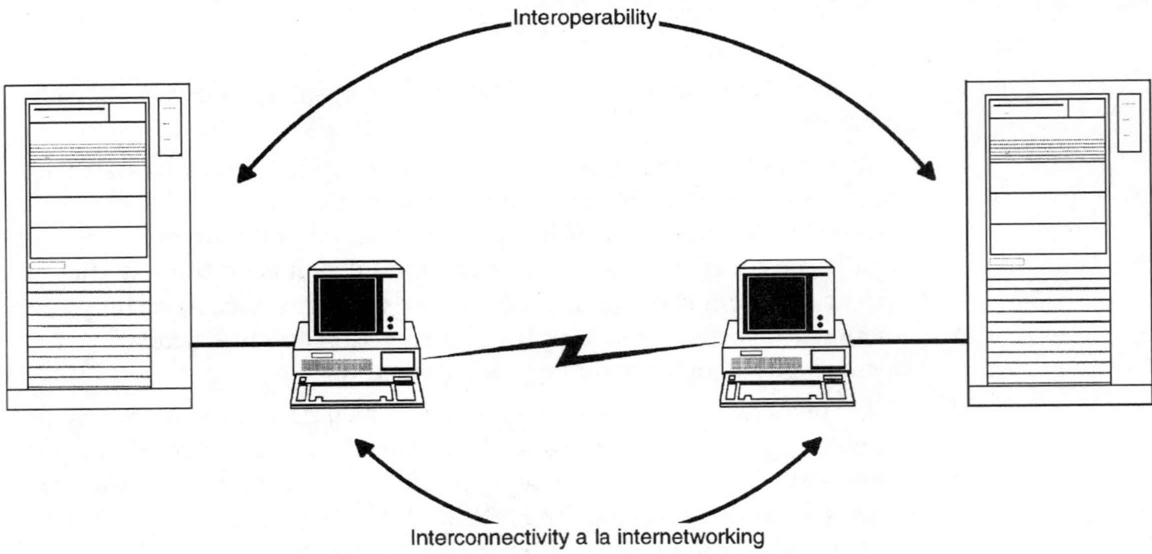

Figure 3.2 The final relationship between interconnected and interoperable networking.

The Benefits of Standards

The use of standards in this new internetworking arena yields significant benefits to end users and networking managers alike. The benefits can be assessed as follows:

1. Standards do not lock the network manager into a single vendor product.
2. By keeping to a standard, proprietary solutions are kept at a minimum.
3. Support for systems (computers, communications, and networks) and software is available even if the selected vendor does not succeed.
4. Systems are far less complex in their installation if openness is maintained.
5. Maintenance and support issues can be handled with relative ease if more than one vendor can support the system and software installed.
6. Faster rollout of products and enhancements to the installed base can be achieved, because a single product or protocol requires less complex hooks to other systems.
7. The end result is a more productive environment.
8. Users appreciate the standard look and feel of the delivered products.
9. All users and management can assimilate the information more quickly, making the installation run more smoothly.
10. Overall, the cost of such an installation should be less expensive. This benefit may not be immediately evident since a heavier front-end cost may be required. However, over the life cycle of the project, one can anticipate less expensive, open solutions.

One cannot overstate the actual benefits of a standards-based installation in client/server networking systems. This is such a variable and new opportunity in the industry, confusion and chaos reign. To eliminate this risk and be more financially prudent with an organization's money, the whole situation must be boiled down into a financial and factual model. Too often this piece is overlooked in favor of the slick new set of products that have all the bells and whistles no one else can deliver.

Selecting the Standards

The steps necessary to get toward the end of the project must start up front, not at the end of the project. Figure 3.3 reflects the basic selection process for the standards available and the possible outcomes. The chart is linear rather than multiphase by design. This way we can gain an appreciation for the steps and the process for each of the steps.

The steps may be self-evident to some, but some explanation is necessary to ensure that the reader understands that this selection process is far more complex than dealing with a simple point-and-click selection. As each of the steps is covered in checklist form in Fig. 3.3, one can derive that this is a suggested checklist of the major steps involved. Far more complex decisions are required to get to that point, but a summary like this one is a useful tool.

Selecting the Standards

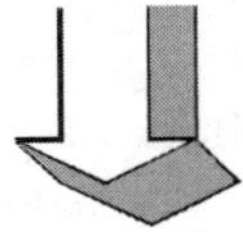

1. Establish a standards committee
2. Identify goals for the organization
3. Select the best mix of protocols and applications
4. Develop a networking strategy
5. Determine the best way to move beyond the LAN
6. Decide on the connectivity choices
7. Remember the nomadic user
8. Establish a set of security rules
9. Ease of use and implementation is imperative
10. Evaluate the carriers' offerings for internetworking
11. Consider new and emerging transport systems
12. Order the network
13. Put the pieces together
14. Test and accept

Figure 3.3 The steps in selecting and implementing the standards for client/server networks.

1. *Establish a standards committee.* A committee is necessary to gain some form of business perspective on the process. If only a technical solution is used, the possibility of missing the needs of the organization is always present. It is very easy to get caught up in the process and look for the latest and greatest technical or computational solution. However, doing so could lead to meeting only a portion of the business needs. The standards committee should act as a steering committee and help in the process of keeping everything focused. By using a standards committee, one can also be assured that a limited set of protocols are endorsed and recommended to senior management. Using key members of management staff, technical, and business groups also aids in the ease of transition for user departments. After all, it is those users who are setting the rules. The standards committee members gain an appreciation for the problems that the network manager encounters, which also helps smooth out the objections from other users who feel that they know best.

2. *Identify the goals of the organization.* As the standards committee becomes involved with the selection process for standard hardware, software, and protocol support, it also assists in keeping the strategy straight. Meeting the needs of the business is what this network is all about. However, one must consider that the entire process of moving to a client/server network can take three or more years. What about changes in the organization's direction over time? This is where a set of goals must be clearly charted out for the committee and the network manager to adhere to. For example, if the goal is to move to client/server to produce better widgets, and as this process is being developed, the organization plans to get out of the widget business, then it is a waste of time and money to continue down this path. Does the mechanism exist to keep the team involved in the organization's strategies? If not, something must be done to change that fact.

3. *Select the best mix of services and protocols for the organization.* Clearly this can be "voodoo science." How do you select the best mix when everything is constantly changing? Here is where initial research starts to pay off. If the best choice is the only one available, it becomes a moot point. However, in a multivendor, multiprotocol environment, finding the best mix becomes very complex. The committee should look to the network manager to provide

the guidelines. A presentation on the status of the standards and the openness of the architectures may be in order. There are no right and wrong answers here, only varying degrees of correctness. The best available information is all that one can base a decision on, as long as the best available information is known. Many people who have begun the journey into a client/server network have just jumped at the standard protocols that they currently have installed. It becomes a force-fit situation in which every application and hardware platform is forced to operate in an particular environment, regardless of the costs and productivity consequences. Trying to get away from a set of canned packages that remain inflexible to the users' needs is what the LAN and client/server concepts are all about.

4. *Develop a networking strategy.* Client/server networks cover the gambit of local and wide area networking, as well as everything in between. The strategy is first a local decision about bringing the client/server network up to standard operating procedures. From there, the topologies and specifications must be developed. For example, does the network require the use of a specific topology? If so, what should be done about it? A strategy that allows protocol and topology independence is best. This is easier said than done, but it is better in the overall scheme of connectivity. The integration of various topological services is easier to accommodate than trying to limit all applications and protocols to a specific network design.

5. *Determine how to move beyond the LAN.* To set a course of action, consider rolling out the network to a specific region or section of the country as a starting point. As new nodes are added to the network, the strategy grows to encompass the newer locations into the architecture. However, there will be many chances to reevaluate the network strategy as things progress; implementation must therefore remain somewhat fluid and flexible. The suppliers and the carriers alike will introduce several new opportunities to network the systems together. Look at what is happening in the carrier arena—many new players are emerging in competition with the local and long distance suppliers of bandwidth. Be careful with this multistage technique; too many organizations have attempted to bring their very large locations up first, causing a disjointed system with regional locations spread throughout the world on one platform, with districts and sales or production offices supported by the regions operating on a different network. Another risk is to attempt to cover distances that are too great for the initial programs. One organization wanted to do just that, so it selected to use the corporate location in the Midwest networked together with its largest location in the Far East. The problem became difficult since the time zone differences caused some conflict. Additionally, as problems arose, there was no simple way for the networking staff to get to the site and resolve issues quickly. Using two sides of the world for an initial rollout complicates the situation exponentially.

6. *Decide on the connectivity choices.* What are the best arrangements for the connectivity? Will the services be localized only? Will the network be based on leased lines or dial-up services? These and many other decisions are involved in selecting the best mix of services. The operative word here is *mix,* since no one solution may fit all needs. Some of the services and connection arrangements may not be available in parts of the country or the world, which limits choices if a single solution is selected. Thus, a mix of compatible networking services is needed. Price also plays an important factor in this decision process; no one can afford to break the bank while implementing a network.

7. *Remember the nomadic user.* Tools have to be put in place to support the "road warriors" of an organization. Keep in mind that the client/server network is there to support the *entire* organization. Although it may require a longer-term rollout, traveling employees must have access to the organization's business information to successfully accomplish their mission. This factor also creates new possibilities of complexity based on speed, connections used, and security issues. Each new device or employee added to the network can create a separate situation. Plan for this part of the network capability, because the network will not suffice if it does not serve the needs of the user population.

8. *Establish a set of security rules.* Linking remote sites and traveling employees onto the network through some form of casual or on-demand connection opens the door to security issues. Therefore, a set of security procedures must be established in advance of the network rollout. The rules should not be so complicated that users cannot gain valid access. Moreover, the rules should be straightforward and applied to all. Security should be transparent in some regards, allowing the user unimpeded access to the information needed to accomplish the job. However, security should also be very visible to prevent unauthorized access to the network by anyone other than valid users. A challenge/response system may be the best solution to meet this need, but it varies by organization.

9. *Ease of use and installation is imperative.* One must remember that the client/server network and the computing platforms must be easy to use. If not, they will not be used, and all the time and effort will be for naught. The systems must be somewhat transparent for end users to access their data, manipulate it, and save it. Remember to keep them as simple as possible, preferably with a look and feel similar to those users are already accustomed to. Additionally, the installation of the network should be as simple as possible so as not to complicate its overall operation. One cannot maintain the most difficult and complex network with a limited staff. Consider how things will work on a day-to-day basis before the selection process. Where possible, have the vendors and carriers show you a working network that they have installed that is similar to what you need.

10. *Evaluate the carriers' network offerings.* Client/server and wide area networking are almost becoming synonymous in this industry. Although they are different, many have applied the same general rule to both networking concepts. The carriers have moved beyond localized service and are migrating to wider areas, to include the MAN and the WAN. Several different carrier offerings exist that can serve an organization's needs. New players are emerging with service offerings every day. As telecommunications reform in the United States and privatization in the rest of the world catch on, new offerings will become commonplace. Do not lock yourself into a fixed networking strategy with a carrier. Allow for changes as the industry changes.

11. *Consider new and emerging transport systems.* Regardless of networking strategies (the local transport to the desk, the metropolitan area services, and the wide area), new things are happening every day. The transport systems that hindered us in the past will become the legacy systems of the future. One can see the emergence of the higher-speed connection and the dedicated bandwidth to the desk in support of the client/server network. But the wider areas also have some attractive offerings developing that will bring suitable connectivity to bear. Where once the LANs operated at shared capacities in the low-end (4-, 10-, and 16-Mbits) speeds, they now dedicate capacity to each desktop (10, 16, 25, and 100 Mbits). The WAN that traditionally was used in the kilobits-per-second speeds will now offer megabits-per-second speeds on demand. All opportunities to get to a virtual networking strategy may be in the best interest of the user and the organization. Consider what is emerging in terms of protocols to support these speeds and connections for the future.

12. *Order the network.* One cannot say enough about the lead times associated with the connections around the entire organization. Whether local or international in nature, the wide area client/server network will take some lead times that can become extraordinary. No one wants to admit that the service may take longer to install than anticipated, but the fact is, it does. One may also consider that the ordering process for the network is not strictly a circuit order; many other pieces exist. Local loops, local connection devices (like CSU/DSU units), and access to buildings across wires or fibers may not be available. In wide area networking, local sales representatives have a tendency to overstate what wide area installations teams can do, which may not be consistent with the overall wide area schedules. Be aware.

13. *Put the pieces together.* Once the order is placed for the network, several components, such as routers, bridges, and gateways, may be required. One should time this portion of the networking hardware to arrive close to the time the circuits are due. Keeping these on site for months is inappropriate for many reasons: Warranties expire before the equipment ever gets installed, equipment can get damaged or lost, and vendors take a lackadaisical attitude in getting them installed on time. This is not a criticism of the vendors, just a statement of fact.

14. *Test and accept.* The pieces are in place. Circuits are installed, hardware is attached, protocols are selected, and the connectivity is finally there. Now is the time to start testing and acceptance of the overall network. One cannot get beyond the pilot program if the network does not function properly. All the promises and crisp data transfers now have to happen. If it does not happen according to plan, allow enough time to resolve problems before the acceptance of the network. Make sure all the mechanisms for supporting and troubleshooting the network are in place. If not, go no further until the vendor (carrier) solves the open loop. If you continue to accept even though no solutions are evident, it is much harder to get the solutions after the fact. One must be appropriately cautious at this juncture of the project. Make sure everything works as defined, with no exclusions or excuses. Test every single aspect; leave no stone unturned. Remember this network is what will support the entire organization's critical business data transport. Without the connection performing transparently, it is useless.

Standard Protocols for the Client/Server Network

Several protocol stacks are designed to fit nicely into client/server networks. Some of these are summarized here, but the list is not all-inclusive. It would take a book unto itself to discuss all the network protocols and services available. The intent here is to gain an appreciation of the various services that are off-the-shelf brands of protocols. Following is some limited discussion regarding their use and ability to support the internetworking schemes approached by many companies and organizations. Each of these sets of protocols is based on a protocol stack. The stack is referenced against the model of models: the Open Systems Interconnect Model as defined by the International Standards Organization (ISO), which completed work on this model in 1988. Several years of effort went into the development of the model as a communications technique to allow for transparency between and among disparate systems. Unfortunately, too much time was used to develop this model and the world could not wait. Consequently, other models that have become firmly entrenched in our networks will be tough to displace. The investment in the installation of the various transport systems and the associated protocol stack does not easily lend itself to displacement. Thus, the multiprotocol network is a regular occurrence. The protocol stacks that we compare here are

1. Transmission Control Protocol with Internet Protocol (TCP/IP)
2. Open Systems Interconnect (OSI)
3. Open Systems Foundation (OSF) and the Distributed Computing Environment (DCE)
4. Systems Network Architecture (SNA)

Although these protocol stacks vary in availability and use, many have become the de facto standards in the industry. As long as a critical mass of systems has been installed using these proprietary protocols, they become the standards on which vendors' implementations are based.

Transmission Control Protocol with Internet Protocol (TCP/IP)

TCP/IP has made significant inroads as the protocol stack of choice for WANs and, more recently, LANs. No one can claim in this day and age that they have never heard of TCP/IP or that they have not piloted it into their networks. It is a very robust stack of protocols that has taken the networking industry by storm. Initially, this protocol stack, shown in Fig. 3.4, was designed around the original ARPANET for the U.S. government. It was designed to be a robust set of network protocols allowing for the open interchange of information and ease of connectivity. Initially the data networks in the late 1960s were not designed to share and exchange information between each other. It was also a parameter that network managers did not want others to tap into their computing resources or their data. It was mostly a security concern, but it also led to the proprietorship of the network. Many networks were incompatible, which led to the support of the theory of closed architectures. A set of common protocols were developed to allow for resource sharing and openness between different networks by computer manufacturers. The TCP/IP stack emerged as this interface.

The stack is actually a four-layer stack designed around a comparison of the OSI model that we reference against. The first layer shown in this architecture (Fig. 3.4) is the subnetworking layer. It is not a part of the TCP/IP stack but is used to show the interaction between the various LAN and WAN subnetworks that are used in an organization. These subnetworks include the use of LAN architectures such as the Ethernet and token ring network topologies and protocols. A subnetwork uses a

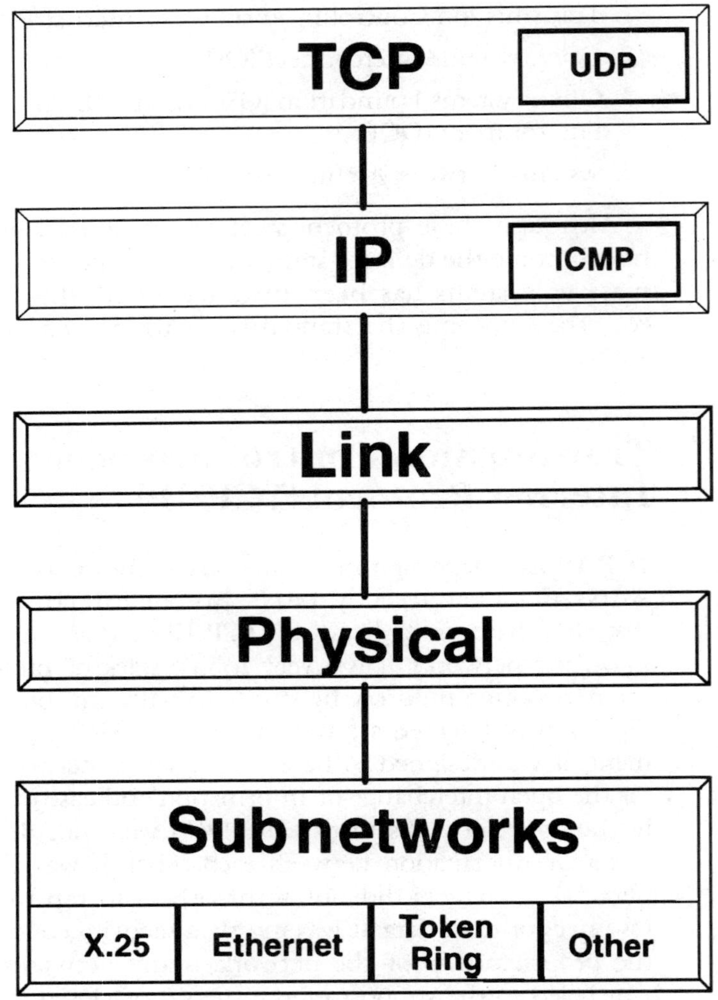

Figure 3.4 The TCP/IP protocol stack.

router (or, to some, a gateway) to interconnect the various networks. The subnetworks, although separate, perform as a full network in a logical sense.

What is actually the first layer incorporates the *physical* layer of connections. This layer defines the electrical and mechanical interfaces to the physical medium. TCP/IP runs on any medium, as long as the user knows how to configure the physical network. Working up into the stack, the next layer is the *data link* layer that describes the framing and formatting of the data for the physical link.

It is above this data link layer that the *Internet Protocol* is introduced at layer 3. The IP layer is where the data is segmented into more manageable pieces and sent across the network as IP segments. Actually, the segments are sent across the network in a willy-nilly arrangement, meaning that IP makes no guarantee that the data will get to its end destination. This is where some logical control is needed. Therefore, sitting on top of IP is the *Transmission Control Protocol* (TCP), which is responsible for the guaranteed delivery of the data in a reliable manner. What TCP does is reassemble the data into its original state and take up the slack for IP's indifference to the data. We shall see more on TCP/IP in Chap. 6 as we discuss the variations and addressing schemes used. What is important here is the following:

1. Although not a standard per se, TCP/IP is a set of rules and protocols that specify the open communications between and among various computing platforms.
2. Open connections are an integral part of TCP/IP.
3. TCP/IP is widely implemented throughout the world and is therefore a de facto standard.
4. Its stack supports client/server internetworking exceptionally well.
5. It is not without its limitations, however. Overhead is a major concern in the internetworking arena, and TCP/IP has a lot of it.
6. Overhead shows its impact in costs and time for the delivery of the data between systems.
7. The robustness of TCP/IP tends to make up for the overhead limitations.

In Fig. 3.5, the TCP/IP stack is shown differently, with the hooks at layer 4 (TCP) to various other protocols and interfaces available. The various links to applications are through the TCP architecture directly to an application that has a socket (or address) that interrelates with TCP, or through some other user interface such as an applications programs interface (API). Note that this figure shows the various applications that are integral to the operation of TCP/IP, such as

- The Simple Mail Transfer Protocol (SMTP), allowing internetworks to pass electronic mail among the devices and users.
- The File Transfer Protocol (FTP), for a simple and easy-to-use binary file transfer system, allowing the interchange of information between computing systems.

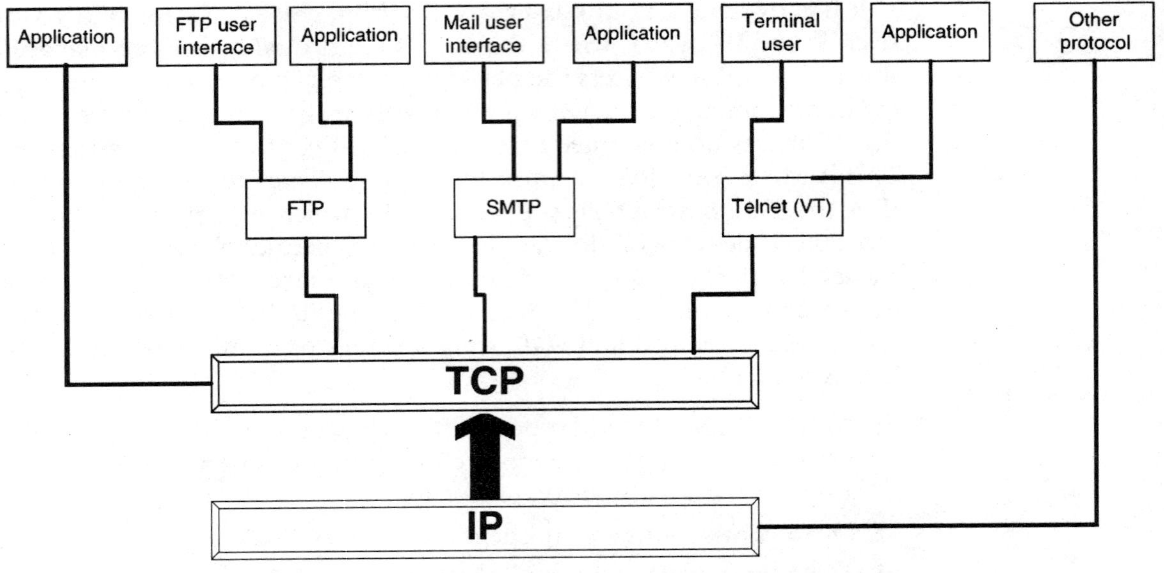

Figure 3.5 Direct access to services or user interfaces to these services are allowed for in TCP/IP.

- Terminal emulation through the Virtual Terminal Emulation Protocol (VTEP), allowing the mapping of keyboards and the syntax conversions between terminals from different manufacturers.
- Other applications that are directly linked or that have an interface written for the interconnection via TCP/IP.

TCP/IP deals with most of the issues associated with internetworking. It is actually called the middleware in a client/server network. It is the glue that melds the various systems and protocols together. TCP/IP is supported through multiple network integration schemes at various hardware levels, such as

- Token ring LANs
- Ethernet LANs
- X.25 packet-switching networks
- Frame relay networks
- SNA/SDLC (synchronous data link control) networks
- DecNet networks

Further, it is supported by the various network operating systems manufacturers in their implementations of the operating systems software to network computing systems together. The major players that support the TCP/IP stack are

- Novell, with a dual stack running on its clients and servers
- IBM, in the OS/2 operating system
- Banyan Networks, which bases its core protocol stack on TCP/IP
- Microsoft, with its Windows 3.x, Windows 95, Windows for Workgroups, and NT architectures
- UNIX

This list shows the full support at multiple vendor and hardware levels, which is why TCP/IP is so popular on LANs andWANs. It is a very robust set of protocols and is widely accepted throughout the world, meaning there will be limited risk in adhering to the stack in a client/server network.

The Open Systems Interconnect (OSI) Protocol Stack

Actually the OSI model is one that was designed as a direct result of the inherent problems experienced back in the late 1960s and early 1970s. In this period, many organizations made a decision to deploy computing architectures across the organization. Many were centralized computing systems, and internetworking was just beginning, which is when the problems arose. As users who had selected a particular vendor architecture (such as IBM, Burroughs, Honeywell, or DEC), they experienced the realization that they were using proprietary protocols and that the fix to this problem was extremely expensive. Users were unhappy with a single-vendor solution, since they had different specific applications that were developed on special hardware platforms. This setup was all well and good until the need to share information, hardware, or communications surfaced. Then the true revelation came to the front. No easy solution existed to connect the various systems and terminal devices delivered by the big players of the day.

The call went out to the ISO for help in solving this dilemma. ISO assigned a working committee to review and recommend the solutions to this problem. What the committee came up with was a seven-layer model called Open Systems Interconnect. The seven layers were nothing new; many other seven-layer architectures already existed. This model, however, states that systems should be universally open if they all adhere to the same standards and protocols, if they deal with and between each other on a layer-by-layer basis, and if the vendors adopt this open interface ubiquitously. Unfortunately, this issue took quite a long time to resolve, as it did to develop the protocol stack to model against. The world, however, was not sitting still waiting for the model, so many proprietary systems were installed. They will be around for awhile before we achieve the necessary depreciation write-off on equipment and software. While this is ongoing, the problem keeps rearing its ugly head. Costs skyrocket when we lock into a single-vendor solution. However, the costs of attempting to internetwork disparate systems are exceptionally high. Figure 3.6 shows the OSI reference model. The seven layers are identified on the left-hand side of the figure, while a description of the service provided at that layer is shown on the right side of the figure. This model, if implemented, would revolutionize the entire industry since all systems would be manufactured and delivered to a particular specification. It is now used as a base model for all industry implementations even though the model has not been fully adopted by the manufacturers. It also

1. Handles data sharing and data processing transparently
2. Is extremely complicated to understand
3. Is very expensive to fully implement
4. Provides a definitive structure through the seven layers for client/server networking
5. Deals with communications as its sole basis for interconnection; everything is built on communications
6. Has transparent communications
7. Overlays other models nicely, such as OSF, TCP/IP, SNA, etc.
8. Eliminates the proprietary solutions if implemented
9. Is more widely installed in Europe than the United States
10. Offers users, but not vendors, incentive (openness will curtail future revenue streams)
11. Complements the client/server internetwork through a mix of services and communications protocols

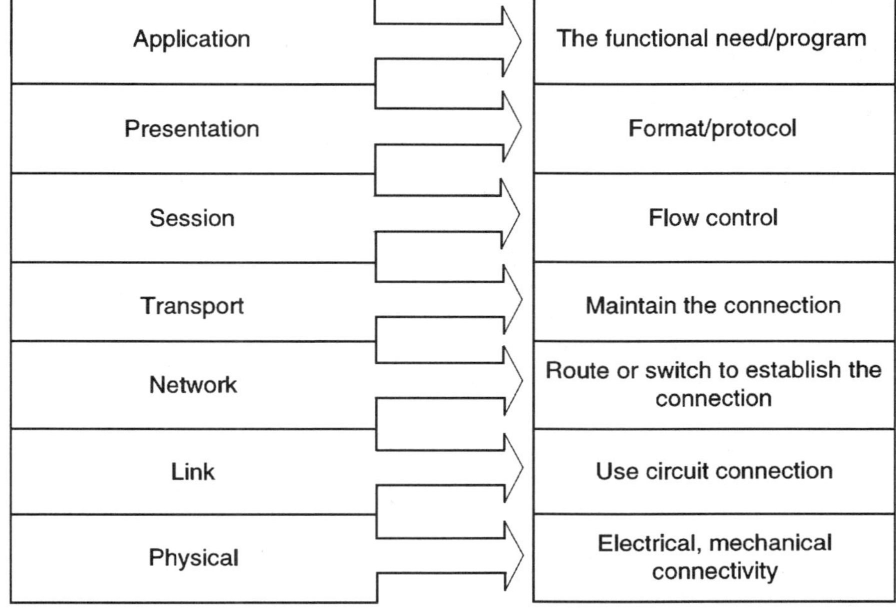

Figure 3.6 The OSI reference model uses a seven-layer protocol stack.

12. For internetworking, uses the bottom three layers of the model for communications across the various WANs, such as X.25, frame relay, leased line, and others, as shown in Fig. 3.7

Although OSI is a complicated and expensive model, there is no doubt that eventually all vendors will be forced to migrate to support it. Users are getting tired of proprietary solutions and the ensuing complications in trying to provide transparent connections around the proprietary network protocols, and they are demanding more support for the OSI model. The jury is still out on when it might happen, but the best guess is 1999 or 2000 before we see total acceptance and implementation.

The Open Systems Foundation (OSF)

Several vendors got together and decided that the industry needed a new set of open protocols that treats all devices on a client/server network as transparent connections. They were frustrated with the lack of support for the OSI model and the constant costs associated with making their products open, while others declined to do so. Consequently, a consortium of vendors formed the Open Systems Foundation

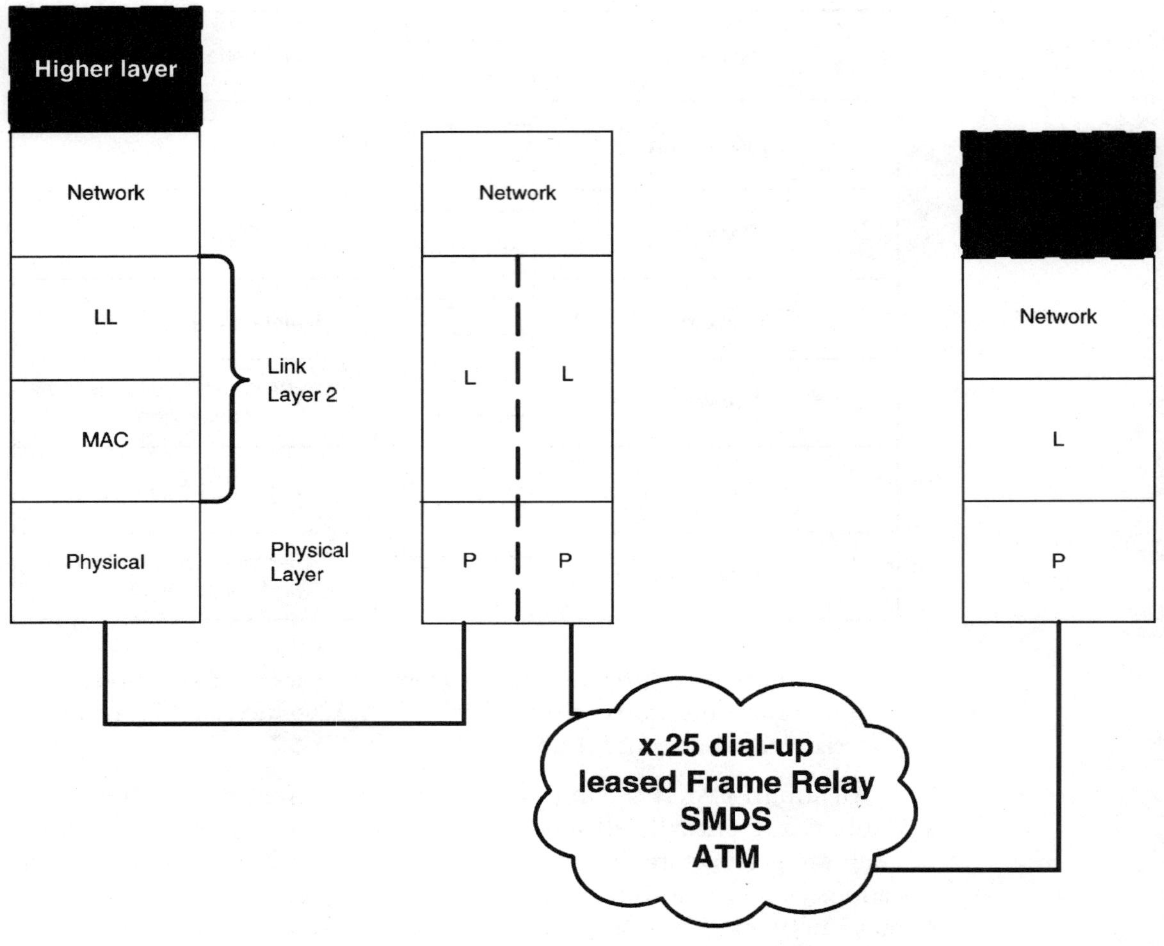

Figure 3.7 OSI uses the bottom three layers to internetwork across the WAN.

to develop a Distributed Computing Environment (DCE) stack of protocols to support the true client/server architecture. In this development of the DCE, the standards are developing quickly. With all the vendors having a vested interest in its success, there should be no doubt that it will succeed. It is based on the OSI model with limited differences, but the goals of the OSF in producing DCE are

1. Openness
2. Distributed computing as the basis of the entire stack

3. Remote procedure calls (RPCs) as one of the foundations for the distributed computing architecture, since they have extensive support from the industry
4. Separating the middleware from the actual network, allowing for the transparency of applications

DCE also includes several features for distributed file systems, directory services, time and synchronization services, and threads that tie the processors all together in a networking environment. European acceptance of the DCE is moving faster than it is in the United States. Many European communities have adopted the DCE as their next generation for distributed applications.

Using the best services and definitions from myriad vendors, the model for the DCE is shown in Fig. 3.8. This model is a bit more complicated than the simple seven-layer architecture of the OSI, but it yields the same end result when fully developed and accepted. The

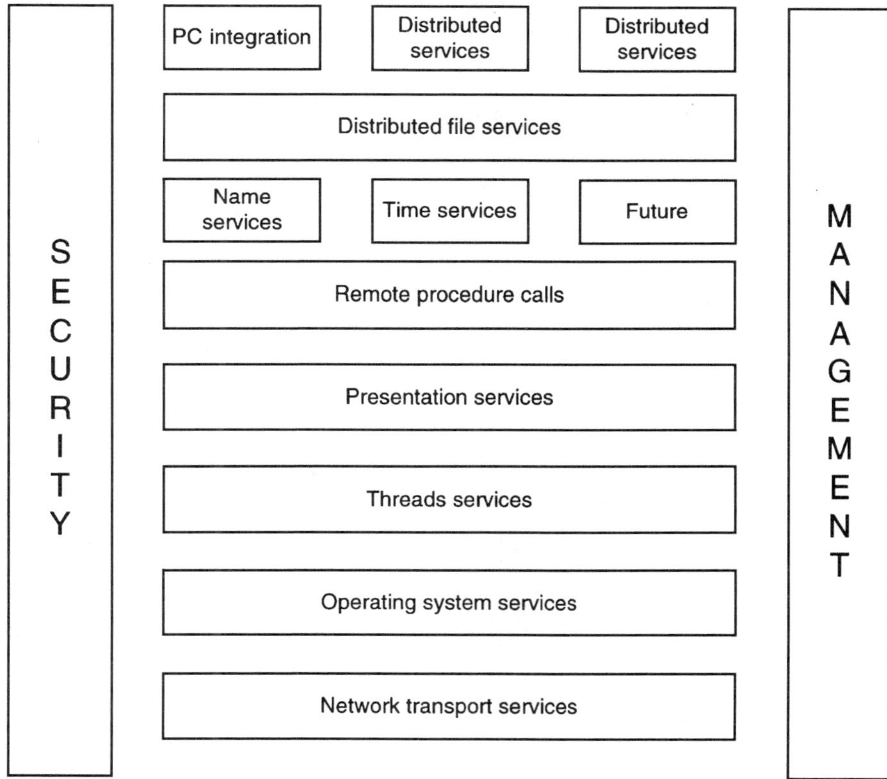

Figure 3.8 The DCE architecture is built around an open client/server environment.

DCE has also built around it a series of other features that incorporate the security of data at all layers and the distributed management environment (DME) using a network management tool at each layer integrated in the model. This is a switch, since in the past the network management of systems was usually the last thing developed by the providers. Note that this model is the basis for the client/server internetworking architecture, but it is still not completely ratified. It appears complex, but many of the services are already in place.

Some of the more popular pieces include the use of

1. Distributed file services (DFS)
    - Allows a user on one system, connected to a network, to access and modify data stored on another system
    - Defines the user as the client
    - Defines the system with the data as the file server
    - Handles problems with multiple users accessing the data by caching the data and issuing a *token* (permission slip to use the information)
    - Accounts for tokens issued to the users at the server
    - Allows a client to modify the data by requesting a write token
    - Keeps track of users with tokens and issues a notice to the other clients that the data is now changed
    - Designed to maintain security, availability, and reliability of the data through replication services
    - Supports local and wide area networks
    - Provides distributed management of the data
2. Directory services
    - Keeps a list of names and where they reside on the network
    - Interconnects with the X.500 standard for directory services (electronic yellow pages)
    - Is portable between systems
    - Integrates with the DFS to allow for location services of the files and file servers

3. Time services

   - Provides a synchronization mechanism for all network nodes to control the network as one, regardless of time zone differences and variations in the clocks in the nodes
   - Uses the best of DEC's Distributed Time Synchronization Services (DTSS)

4. Remote procedure calls (RPCs)

   - Allows the code of a called procedure (process) on one network to spawn a process on another node transparently
   - Comes from HP/Apollo Network Computing Systems
   - Designed around the transparency across the internetwork
   - Uses and supports threads

5. Threads

   - Uses the best of DEC's concert multithread architecture
   - Links all participating processors on a network
   - Is used to implement parallel processing
   - Issues a subprocess call (called a thread)
   - Has special synchronization tools to control the access to a common resource by multiple users on a network
   - Is fully supported by the IEEE Portable Open Systems Interexchange (POSIX) standard

Shown in Fig. 3.9 is a procedure call, which issues a named procedure call and a stub as the locator and controller of the call. Figure 3.10 shows the thread that links the processors together on a network.

Bringing these features all together, the DCE is loaded as a protocol stack at the client and the server level, as shown in Fig. 3.11. Note that this architecture uses the basis of the executive in the client and the data-sharing services in the server, a slight turn from the LAN architecture of the past. The two systems share the distributed application so that they can spawn appropriate processes (subprocesses) across the network.

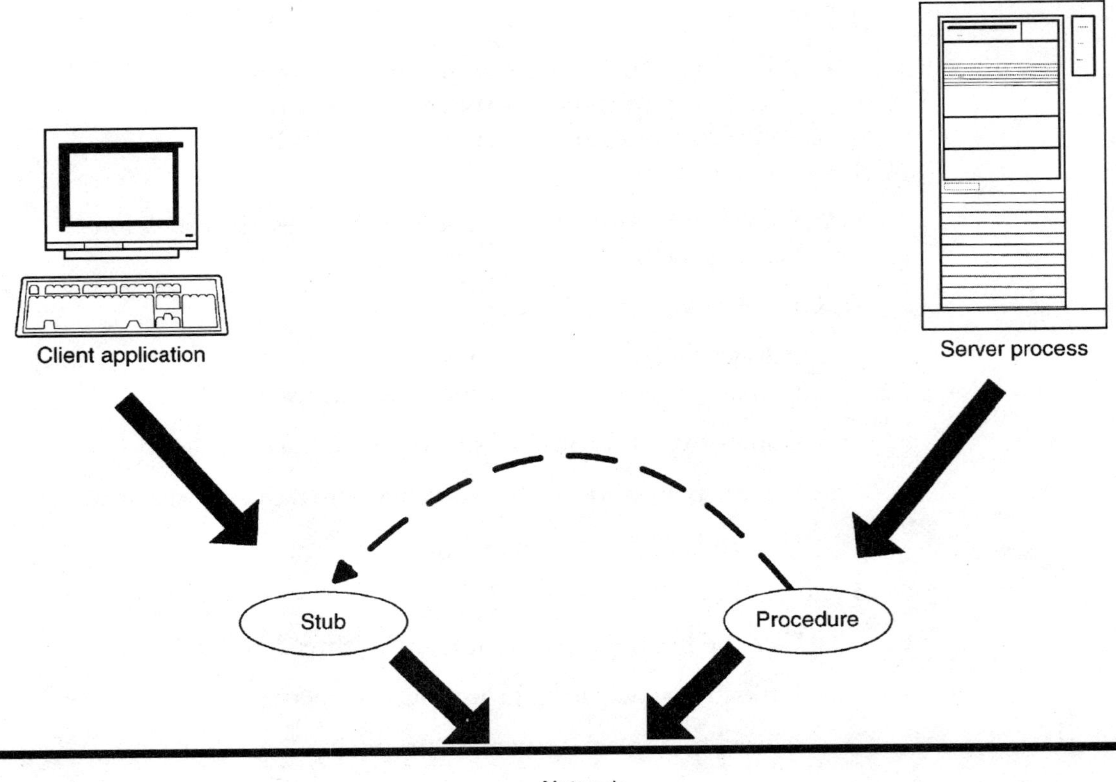

Figure 3.9 The remote procedure call issues a stub to a known procedure and executes the code at the server owning the process.

Systems Network Architecture (SNA)

IBM developed its Systems Network Architecture back in the early 1970s, just about the time everyone was screaming to the standards committees for help in dealing with all the proprietary protocols and services. It was unfortunate that the end user had to suffer through a single-vendor solution back then. However, in the 1970s, we were far less sophisticated and perhaps needed the single-vendor architectures to keep everything harmonious. When SNA was introduced in 1974, the conversion was both expensive and complicated. The users who had older IBM architectures relished the idea of a structure in the internetworking arena. For 20 years (and counting), IBM continued to support

Figure 3.10 Threads are used to link all processors together on a network. This can operate in a parallel processing connection.

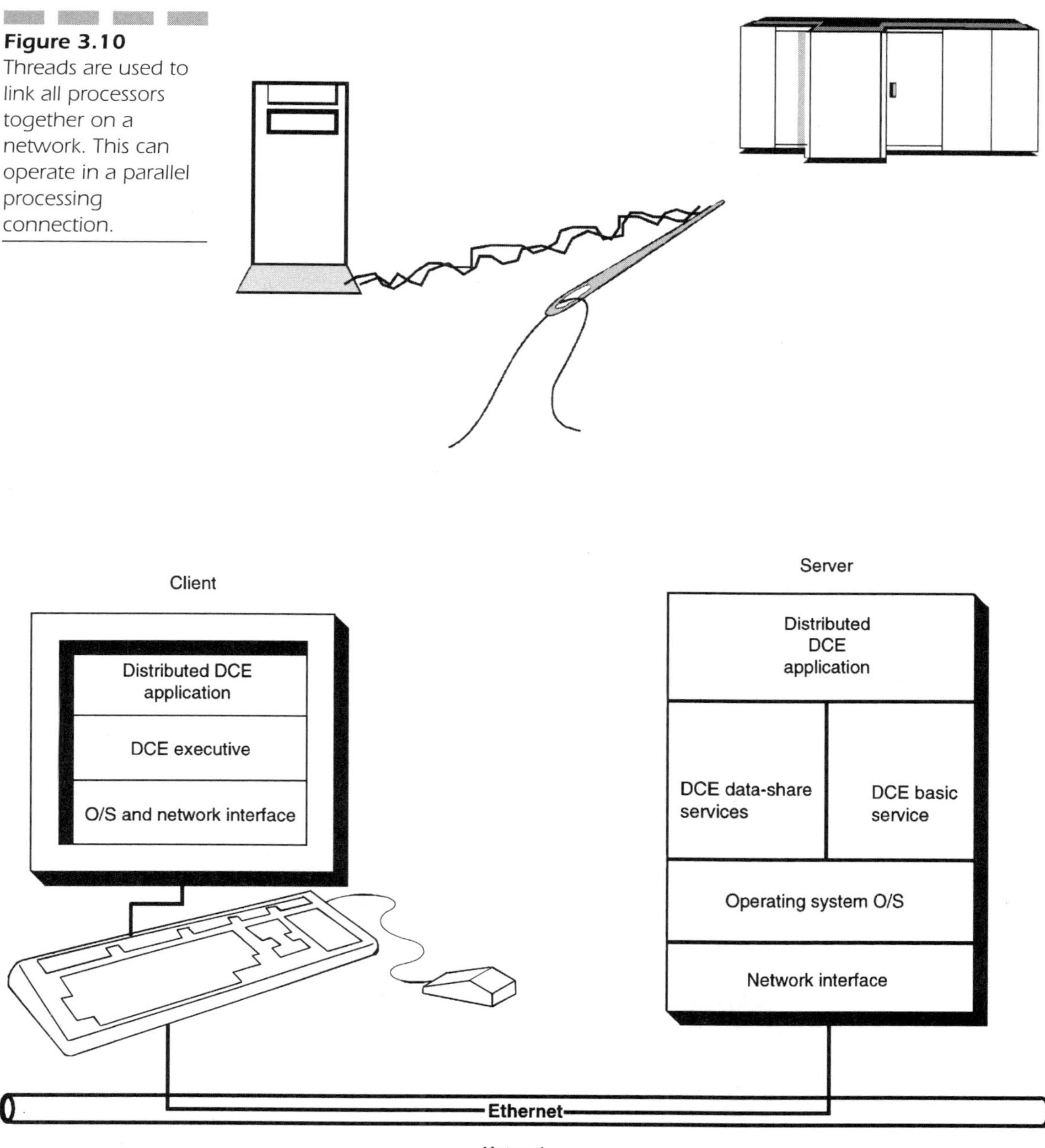

Figure 3.11 The DCE stack as it appears in the client and server devices.

this architecture for the mainframe environment. In keeping with a sole-vendor solution, IBM has met the requirement to support the networking process and lived by its customers. Say what we will about the organization, it clearly met its customers' needs head-on. It may have been expensive, but it worked.

The SNA is a seven-layer architecture that deals with the interconnectivity of clients and servers (in IBM's words, the mainframe and the terminal). However, IBM was influential in the development of the OSI model with significant contribution of resources and labor to get this model developed, even though IBM had no incentive to move away from the installed base of SNA users. In IBM's view, it had the single largest networking architecture installed, and there was no need to move away from it. See Fig. 3.12 for the architecture of SNA and Fig. 3.13 (p. 68) for the protocol stack. SNA brings to the table a lot of capabilities:

- Host based in a server architecture
- Thousands of networks installed worldwide
- Rules defined for intercommunications through ACF and VTAM
- Truly a resource-sharing environment
- Dependable and reliable data transfer
- Easy (albeit expensive) to grow
- Full history of problem resolution and determination tools over 20 years
- Excellent security enhancements

In Fig. 3.14 on p. 69, a typical client/server internetwork using an IBM SNA mix-and-match of services is shown. One thing about IBM—it has the ability to get things linked together. In this architecture, please note the three-computer architecture as stated in the beginning of this book. The server just happens to be an IBM mainframe (or two), the application server can be an AS400 or a RISC 6000 computer, and the client can be a terminal or a PC-based system. Linking these together across the network is as simple or as complicated as one needs to make it. We see that these systems can be used in various locations through interconnection devices such as bridges, routers, and gateways—a complete mix of goods and services across an internetwork that all come together in a single picture.

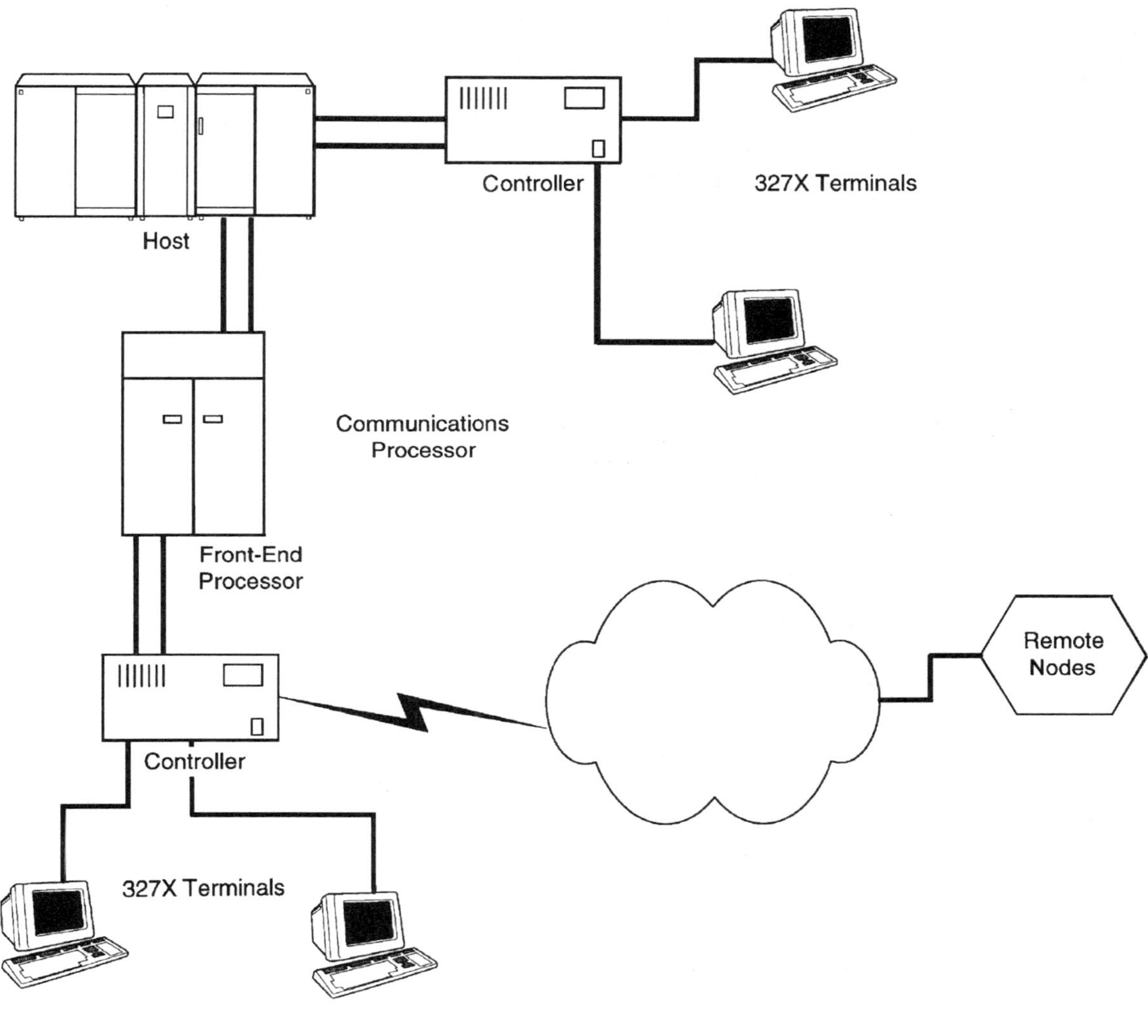

Figure 3.12 IBM's SNA architecture.

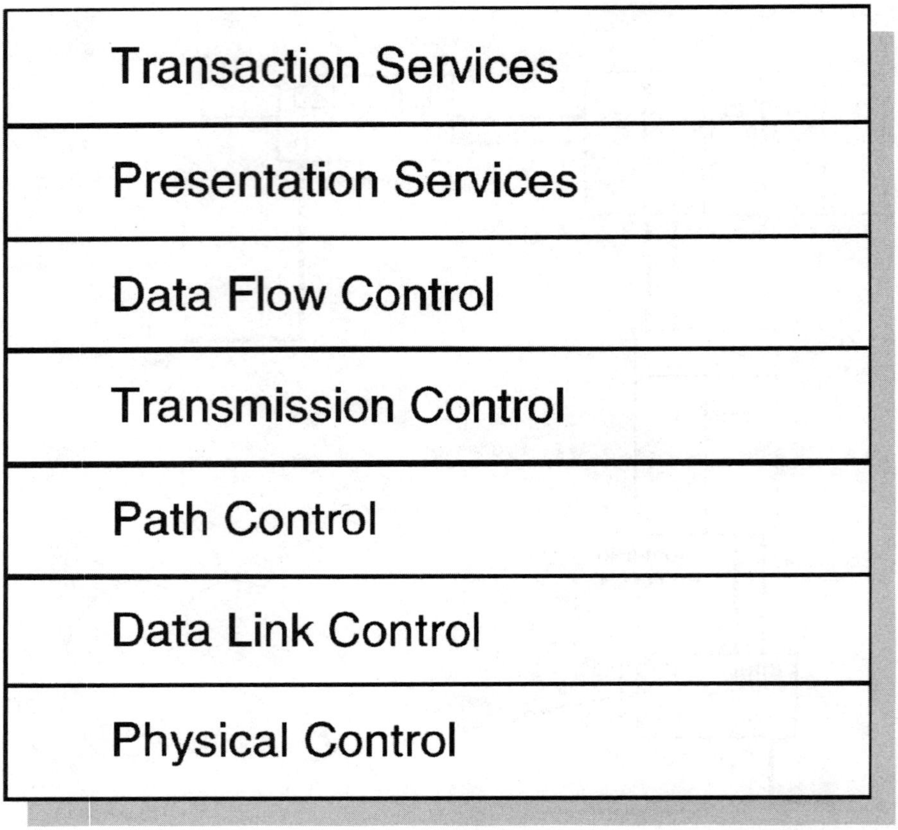

Figure 3.13
The SNA protocol stack.

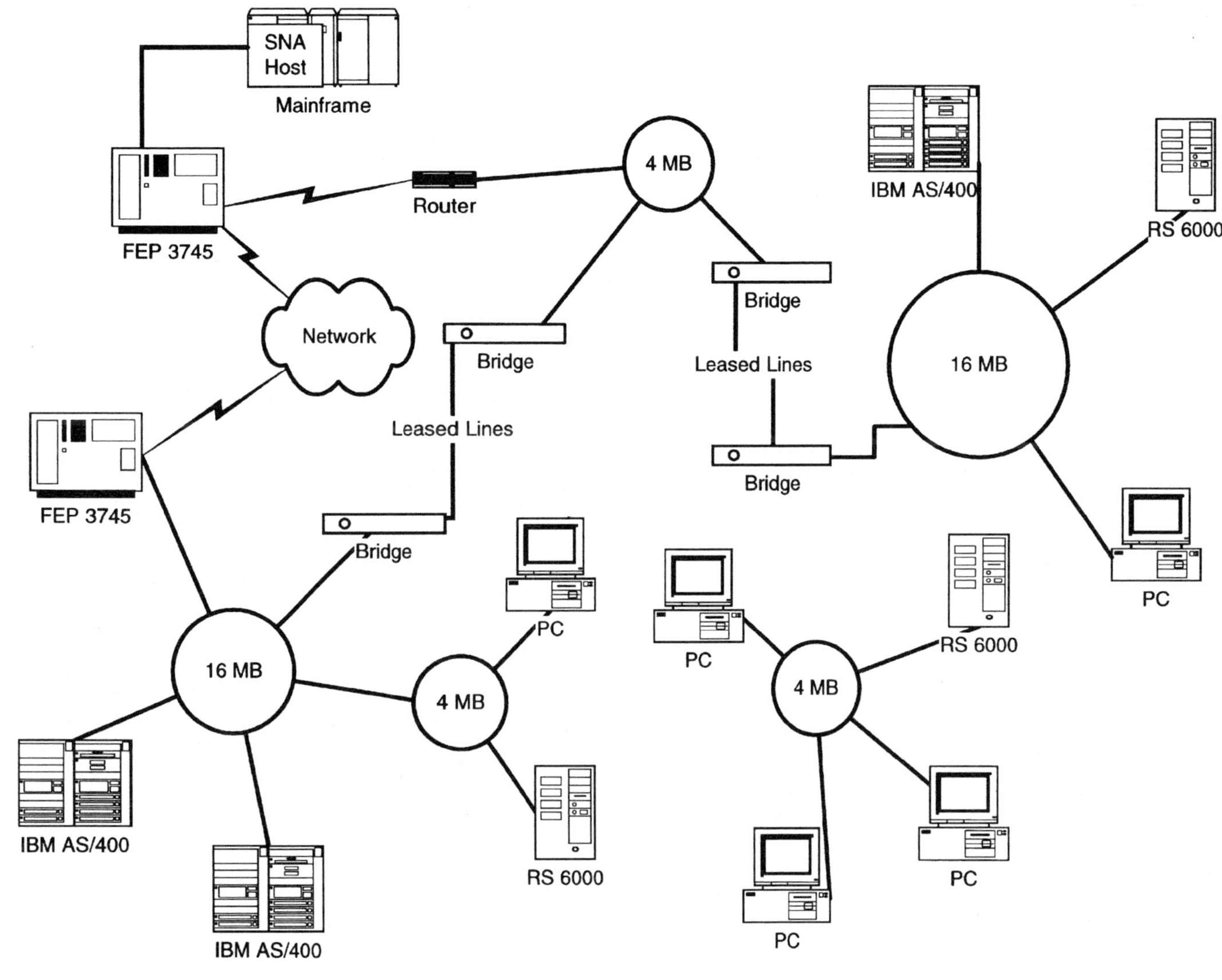

Figure 3.14 *A client/server network using an IBM solution of mainframe, midrange, and PC-based systems.*

CHAPTER 4

The Server

One of the essential ingredients of the client/server network is the server. It is one of the key components of the network. It does no good to have a client/server architecture if the server does not exist. Furthermore, the LAN or WAN has no need for the network if it is comprises a group of stand-alone devices such as PCs and workstations. Thus, the need to define the components of the server is integral to this discussion. The server, for all intents and purposes, can be a central server providing a combination of services to the clients. Another way to look at it is to consider the server as its name and function implies. For example, as shown in Fig. 4.1, servers provide the following services on the network:

- Mainframe servers provide access to a centralized database or corporate data that spans many years. In some cases, this server has

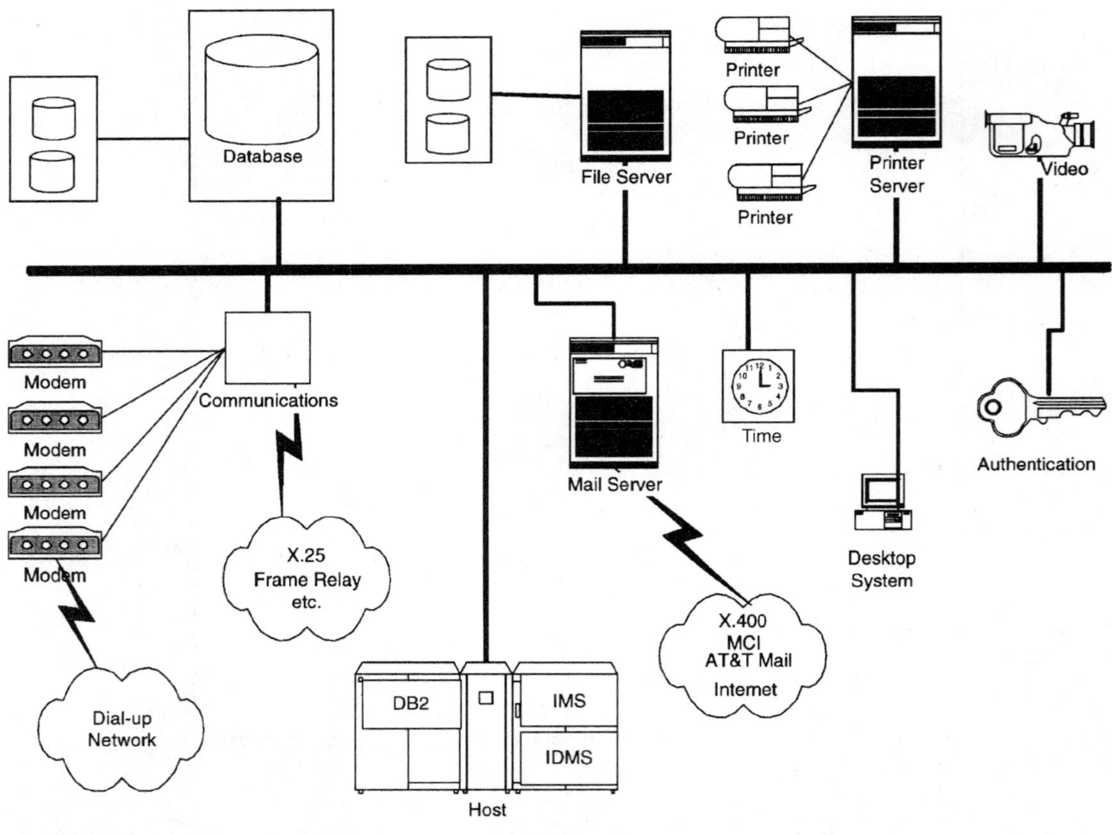

Figure 4.1 The many types of servers and functions that can exist on a network.

been renamed the central database server or the central repository in the client/server architecture.

- Database servers store the organization's database and allow access to the information for queries from a multitude of simultaneous users. It is this server that must be made wary of the constant changes to the data by multiple users so that overwrites and dreaded record lock do not occur on the network.
- Application servers store and launch the programs that are used by the clients. This server can be a mainframe, a midrange computer system, or a PC-based server. The flexibility and differences discussed here are reinforcement to the discussion in Chapter 2 about client/server meaning different things to everyone. A host of different concepts can be met and served by this one service alone.
- A file server can also be any of the aforementioned computing platforms. This device provides file storage and retrieval for the clients on the network. In the file server is the structure for the directory services in use on the network.
- Mail servers provide access and retrieval of e-mail for the clients. This device acts as the post office for the client and provides the store-and-forward functionality of the mail system. The mail server may also house a gateway to other public mail services, such as MCI Mail, AT&T Mail, Internet mail, and X.400 services. The possibilities vary quite a bit depending on the organization and the network.
- The print server, as its name implies, provides the capability to access printers on the network. Print queues are built on this server. All print files are spooled to this server for temporary storage (possibly in memory or on a disk) and then sent out to the actual printer for completion of the job. In some cases, the printer server formats the data for the appropriate queue; in other cases, it does not. For example, if a user sends a file that is HPGL-5-compatible and spools it to a Postscript printer, a different page description language is required. The server may intervene with the print job and reformat it into a Postscript file before sending it off to the actual printer.
- Disk servers are different in that they may be strictly large disk farms for use by the client. They may be just raw storage or they may have duplicate functions for disk and file storage.

- CAD and video servers are typically specialty servers that serve their own niches. CAD servers are becoming more commonplace. However, as more emphasis is placed on client/server networking to support multimedia applications, the video server is becoming more prevalent on larger networks.
- Boot servers are servers that allow the client to boot up on the network. These servers provide the services for compatibility on the network and offload this responsibility and boot files from the individual client. The boot server is the first thing that the client sees when booting up. It does not allow access to the network until a successful login has been achieved. A substitute name for this server may be the login server.
- Time servers are devices that synchronize the clocks on the network so that the entire network looks like one homogenous clocked system, preventing problems from different host clocks and time zones.
- Authentication servers are security devices that reside on the network. Upon successful authentication and naming of the client, access to the network is allowed. The authenticator may also be used as a security device for remote access use.
- Communications servers are computers that provide access to the communications portion of the network, like modem pools, gateway services, Internet access, frame relay and X.25 services, and other miscellaneous communications services.

One can see from this mix and match of servers on a single network that the possibilities are endless. How complex or simple we make a client/server network depends on the organization's needs. Looking at these servers as computers that serve a function, we can then categorize them as mainframe, midrange, or PC-based servers. In this light they can spill over in the definition of the services they provide, but the size and cost are what separates them from others.

Mainframe Servers

Someone once said that the mainframe is dead. Pity we didn't mourn and have a funeral procession for the big iron. As shown in Fig. 4.2, the mainframe has not been killed off. While we recognize that big main-

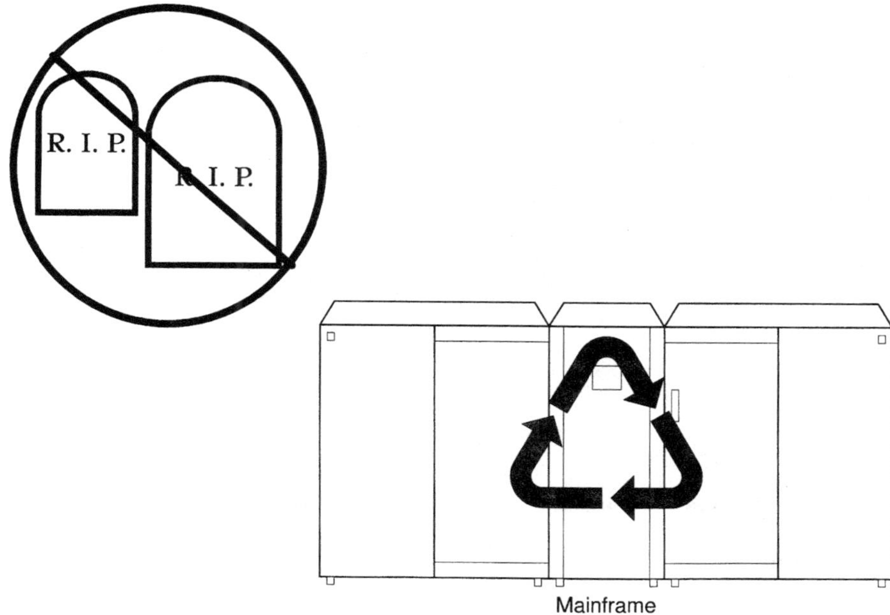

Figure 4.2
Host computers still have a major role in the client/server role–the mainframe is not dead!

frames are no longer being produced, a lot of life still resides in the ones that have been in place for years. Typically an IBM (but not only), the mainframe has the infrastructure of the master and subserver from the SNA days. True, many companies have abandoned their mainframes for greener pastures on a midrange or super server. However, one cannot lose sight of the overall cost of running and licensing the software for these devices. Still, replacing a mainframe takes years of conversion and migration onto a high-end server. It is safe to say that the mainframe is a server of the central repository type or a database server for the entire organization, as shown in Fig. 4.3. For these very reasons, one cannot dismiss the use of the mainframe on a client/server network:

1. 30+ years of evolution in a distributed processing environment has not gone for naught.
2. Users see it as a big engine for server functions until the contracts on their maintenance and lease arrangements expire.
3. Lots of money has been invested in the mainframe for software development and customizing programs, which is not easily discarded.
4. Security on this machine has been fine-tuned over the past three decades; therefore, it may be more secure than the lower-end servers.

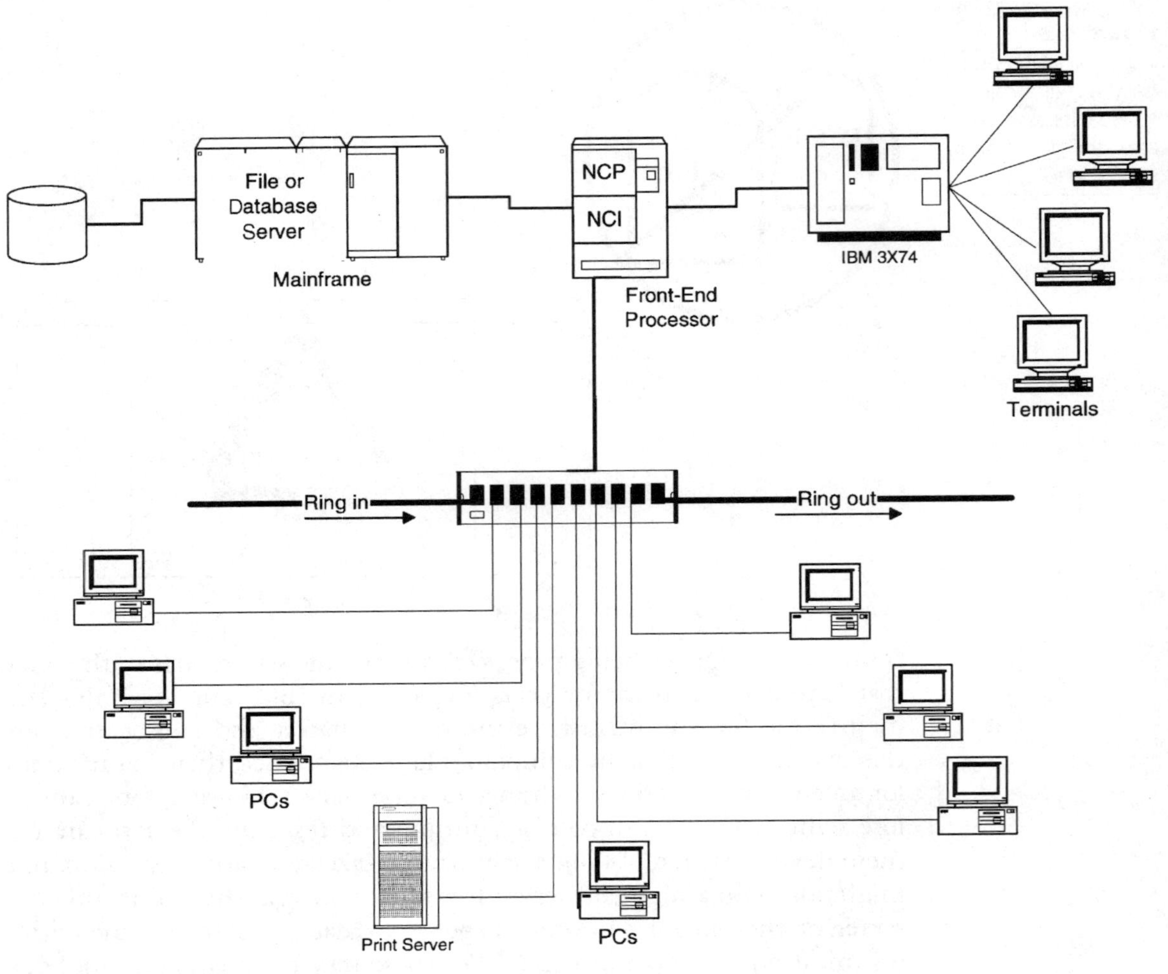

Figure 4.3 The mainframe as a server or central repository.

5. In the three-computer architecture known as the client/server architecture, the mainframe can be the database server for the organization.
6. This device has lost some of its popularity over the past decade, but it continues to linger on and gain new respect as the high-end server through redeployment of its applications and interfaces.
7. It supports a full range of interconnectivity devices and arrangements.

8. A sufficient number of programmers to convert all the code and the data sets that reside on mainframes does not exist. If they did, the cost would be prohibitive.
9. It has an extremely solid operating system and very reliable operational characteristics, even if it is proprietary.
10. Mainframe performance for an entire organization's database inquiries may be a useful thing to have around.
11. Ad hoc reports and queries are fully supported and well worked out.
12. It certainly has a lot of processing power that many of the smaller servers have not yet achieved.
13. It has a high-capacity bus architecture with very strong input/output (I/O) capabilities.
14. A more recent innovation is the support for UNIX on the mainframe, making it more robust in the client/server network.

Using the three-computer approach in defining the client/server network, one can see in Fig. 4.4 the tiered approach that shows where the mainframe may reside in the overall scheme of things. The use of this

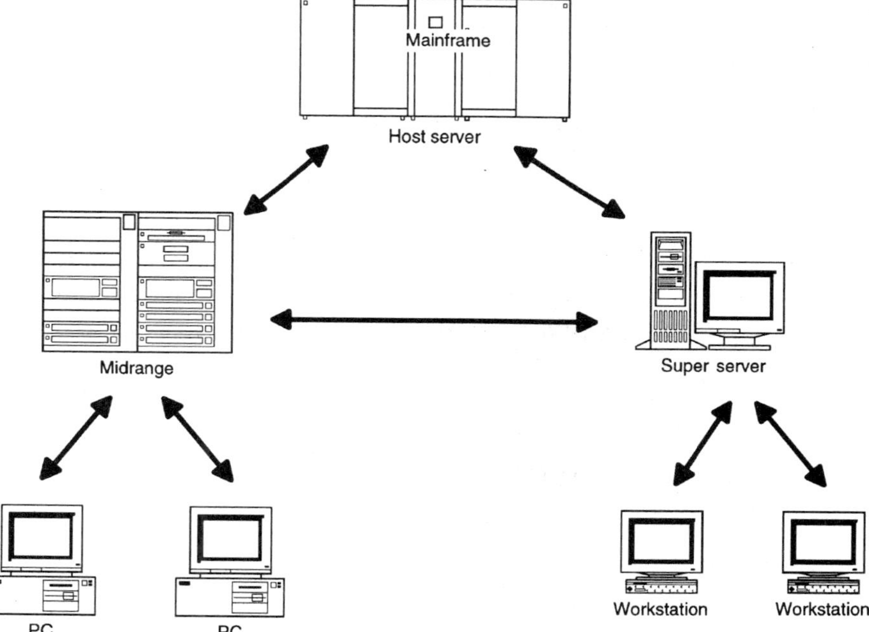

Figure 4.4 The mainframe in the three-computer architecture known as a client/server network.

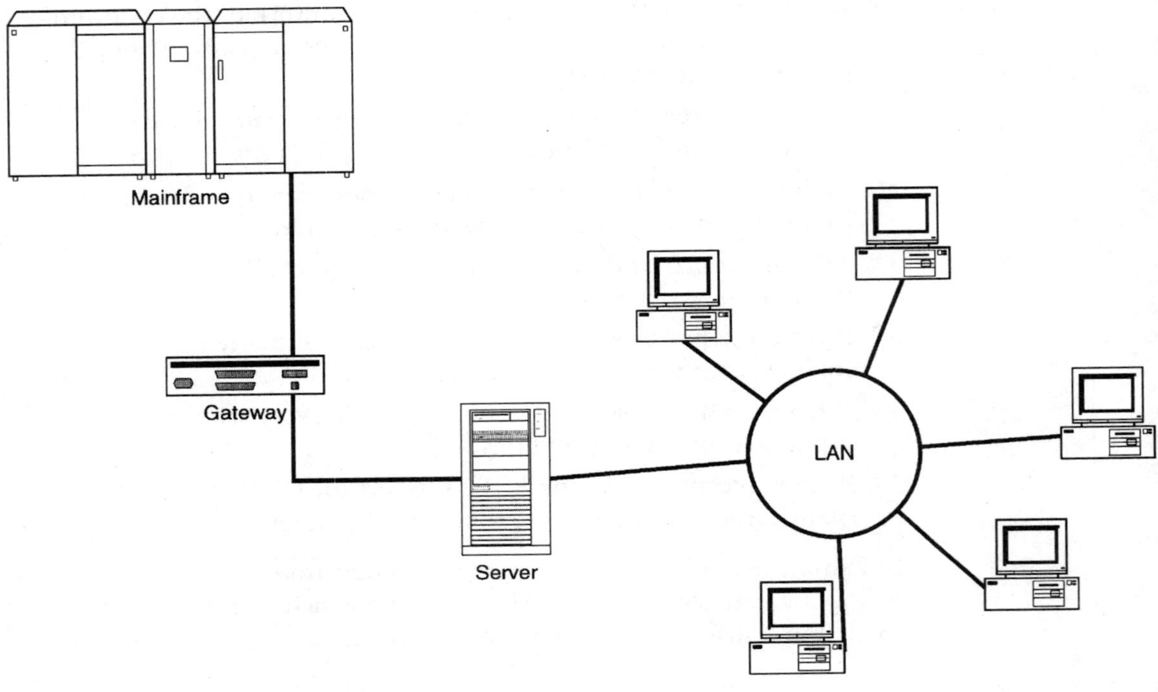

Figure 4.5 Multiple computing platforms using a LAN connect to the mainframe via the gateway and application server.

mainframe as a centralized repository can breathe new life into the architecture and provide high-end support for the organization. In Fig. 4.5, we see a similar position from a LAN through a LAN server and gateway function to access the mainframe data. Again, this structure supports the multiple computer architecture in our definition of client/server. Call it what you will, but we can expect to see these boxes around for some time to come.

Case in Point: The U.S. Government's Move to Client/Server Networks

The U.S. government hired a group of very talented and brilliant minds to study how it might abandon the mainframe architecture in favor of a midrange client/server networking environment. Government officials felt that to keep pace with the corporate world, the government should move to the latest and greatest technologies. The head of this operation looked over the situation and realized that although it would not be a popular decision, the only conclusion that could be supported was to continue to hold onto the network of mainframes. First, the amount of data that needed conversion in the best of times would require approximately 2000 programmers to write the code to convert the various amounts of information amassed over 30 years. Second, the conversion process itself with 2000 programmers would take some 200 years of effort each. Some problems do not get better by throwing people at them. If more resources were deployed, the conversion would not happen any sooner.

Armed with this information, the director of this project had to approach senior management and recommend that they stay put on their mainframe architecture. Realizing that this would not be received easily, the director had a secondary plan that all new installations, such as moves, adds, and changes to various government agencies, would migrate to client/server on a midrange computing system. Any new applications would be built on a UNIX machine with TCP/IP support, and interfaces or hooks to the mainframe data would be handled through a GUI-based point-and-shoot connection. This idea was well received as being brilliant and forward-thinking. The author agrees and feels that is why the government hired these people. It has saved us millions, if not billions, in expenses that would have reaped us nothing had the original plan to abandon the mainframes been implemented.

Midrange Servers

The midrange server market has really heated up in the last three years, simply due to the use of the client/server architecture in many midsized to large organizations. These servers have an edge right now on the market for a few reasons, not the least of which is the acceptance of the price. However, price alone is not what has made possible this leap of faith into the client/server networking world. It would be better to suggest that the real move has been caused by the chameleon-like performance picture of these servers, whereby they can be as powerful as a mainframe or simply faster than a small, PC-based server.

These devices are rapidly gaining acceptance by the user community because they are more open than a mainframe by design. The midrange computer manufacturers saw the niche for a specialty machine that allowed computational power to be placed closer to the user. The midrange platforms have very robust protocols and support myriad applications that never existed before. Instead of being a back-office computing system, they are now performing front-office functionality. A subtle difference is that these computers are a lot less expensive than a mainframe, and they fit nicely into the tiered approach of client/server. However, in the tiered approach of the three-computer architecture, the midrange can reside as the high-end corporate server, as shown in Fig. 4.6, or in between as the application server that issues the remote procedure calls to the mainframe or another midrange processor, as shown

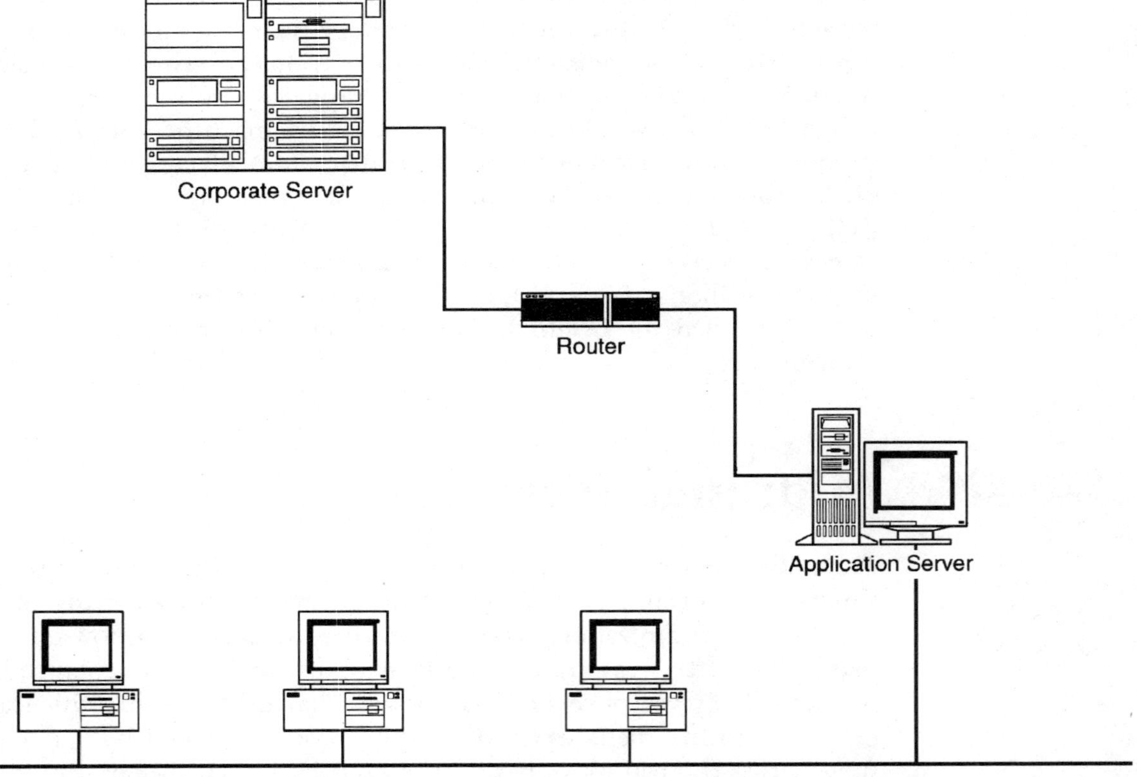

Figure 4.6 The midrange computer can satisfy the role of the corporate server or the application server.

earlier in Fig. 4.4. The midrange server can be the engine that supports the organization. It is a dual role of this particular device that lends more credence to its role in the client/server architecture. Specifically, the computers are geared to work in a UNIX operating system (or some deviation thereof) with robust interfaces to the applications and networks that support the end users' computing needs.

In Fig. 4.7, we see the typical spread of main players in the midrange computing platforms serving the client/server networks of today. Although this information is subject to change at any time, the gist is that the players are emerging stronger in this new market. Where they used to serve the niche market, they are now significant contributors to the industry. These midrange servers are used in a multitude of different ways in the client/server networking arena, but one finds that they are the more prevalent players in the U.S. marketplace. Similar performance ratios can also be found in the international market, but the players' positions may shift by several percentage points. Note that no one player dominates this market by virtue of size or volume of sales in the client/server market for systems ranging between $100,000 to $2,000,000, as one would expect these systems to cost.

Super Servers

Differentiating between the midrange suppliers and the role of the super server is difficult and a value judgment. These devices can be the application servers or the main servers (such as the database servers) in a smaller organization, a branch office, or a large regional office of a major corporation. They take on many forms and have a multitude of suppliers that are stepping up to the forefront of the industry. To summarize their capabilities, the super servers are the high end of the PC networks for LANs and WANs. In Fig. 4.8, we see the super server as a vehicle for the computing needs of the organization. Super servers typically

- Are UNIX-based systems
- Cover the midrange plus more services
- Are alternatives to the mainframe
- Are similar in capacities to the host (mainframe) computers
- Support symmetrical multiprocessing
- Are fairly open in their architecture

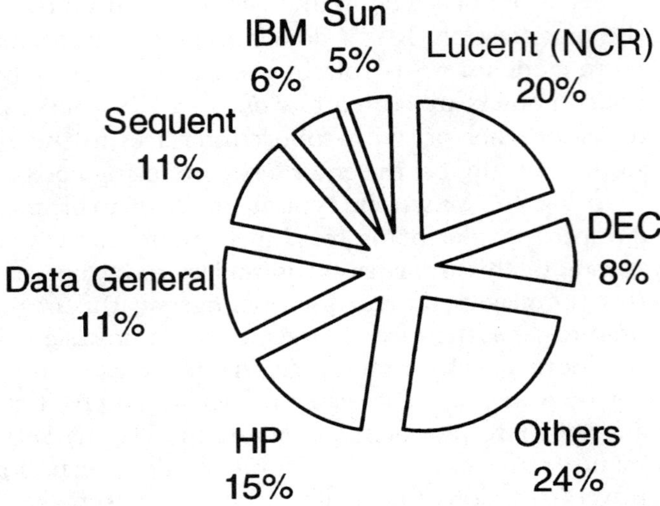

Figure 4.7
The percentages and providers for midrange servers.

- Support the client at the DOS or Windows platform (also the Macintosh)
- Provide server support for full UNIX services
- Have large memory configurations
- Use graphical user interfaces (GUIs)
- Have very fast CPUs
- Have high-performance bus architectures
- Are optimized for use in the client/server networks
- Support multiple software programs that are used in the client/server network
- Are great database engines
- Are becoming a specialty market supplier

Some of the key players in this market include the following vendors:

1. Sun Microsystems (Sparc)
2. Lucent (formerly NCR)
3. Hewlett-Packard (Prism)
4. Sequent Computers
5. Pyramid
6. MIPS (a division of NEC)

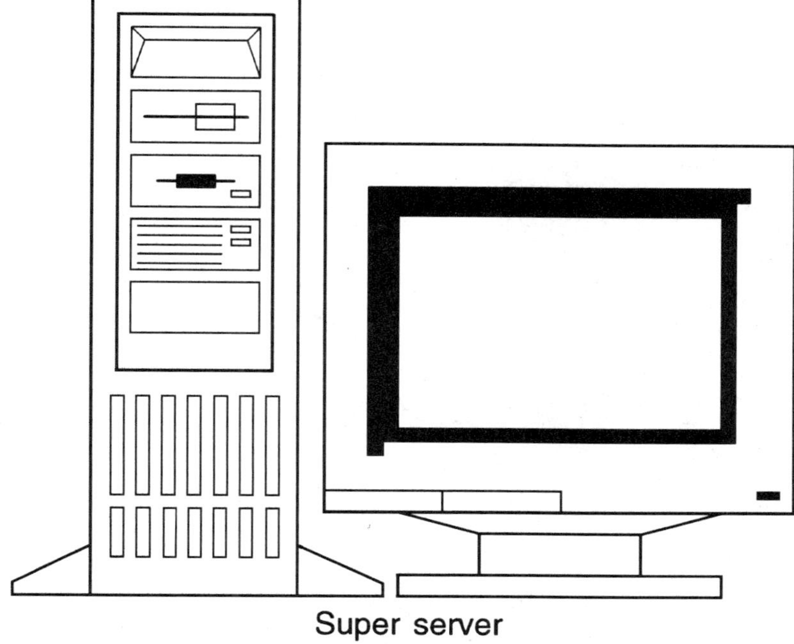

Figure 4.8 The super server is emerging as the specialty niche market for client/server networks.

7. IBM RISC 6000
8. DEC Alpha
9. Compaq
10. Motorola 88000
11. Intel i860/960

These super servers are rapidly becoming the de facto standard for client/server networks and architectures due to their robustness and the power of their systems. Certain pricing advantages make them attractive in the overall scheme of the network.

In Fig. 4.9, we see a representation of an HP 9000 super server acting as the database engine for an organization running on a high-speed LAN connection using fiber distributed data interface (FDDI). Note that this is a single database server for the entire organization, located at the corporate headquarters for a $500 million manufacturing company. On the front end of the database server are a group of application servers (HP 735 workstations) that act in the three-computer architecture. Clients use the access to the client/server network

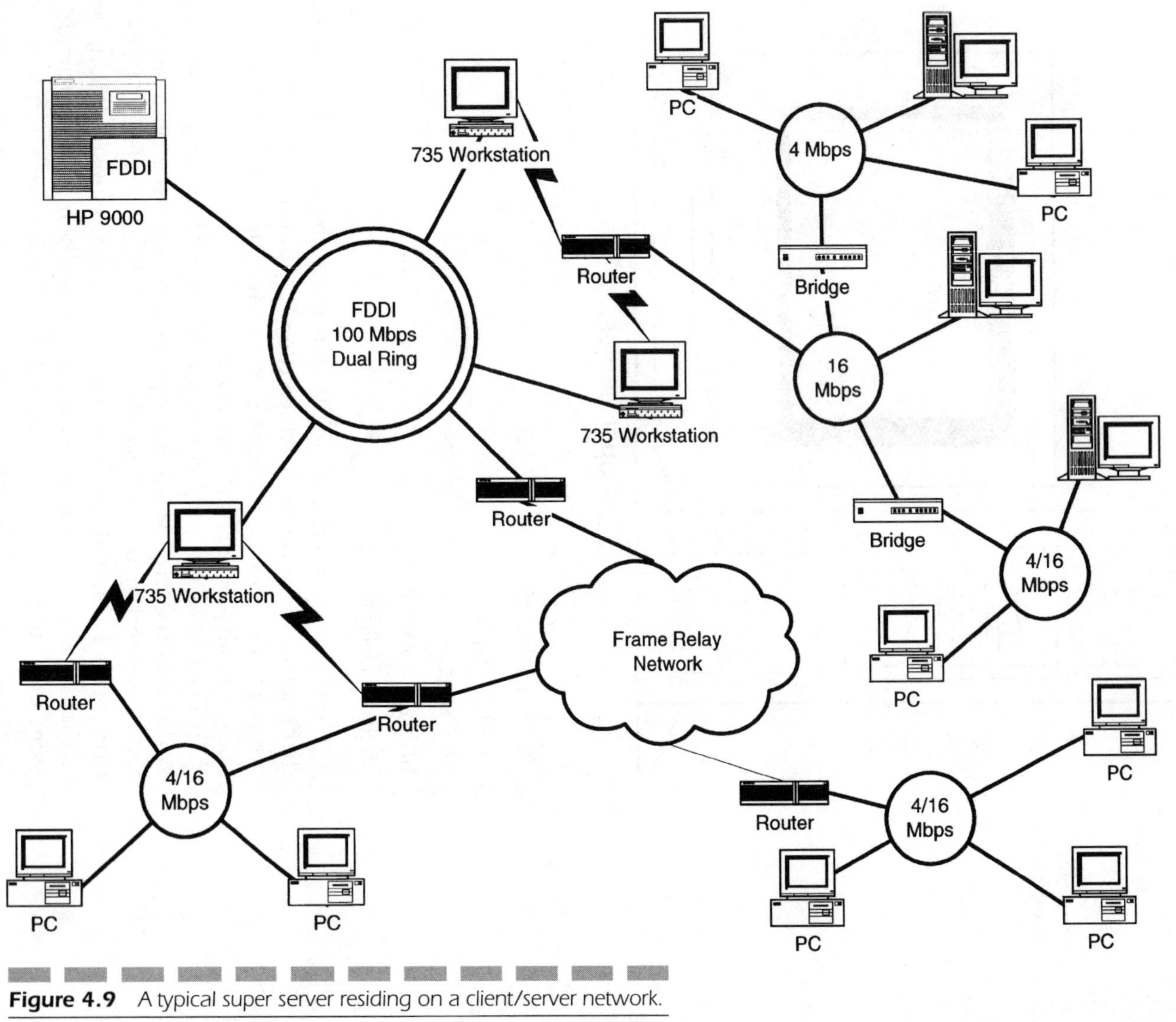

Figure 4.9 A typical super server residing on a client/server network.

through a series of internetworking services on a token ring with a Windows interface. It remains transparent to the user as the local server places a remote procedure call across the network and accesses the corporate database engine regardless of where in the world the user resides. This is a true client/server internetworking scheme. When the network user begins the connection to the server, the system automatically looks for the closest and least busy application server through a routing system to gain access to the host (super server). This network is in production but took nearly three years to build and convert to the state that it is in today. Interestingly, the network was chosen for its robustness as a suitable replacement for several IBM mainframe and midrange systems spread throughout the world. Duplication of effort was to be totally eliminated with this architecture. Unfortunately, it is taking much longer to break the umbilical cord to the IBM mainframes due to application support of the database services, not the server. However, when completed, this network internetworking scenario will produce savings in excess of $1 million per year.

These super servers will be necessary for the future of the client/server networks because the processing power required to support all of the applications that we hear about daily will have a significant impact on the network. For example, as we hear about the graphics-based services and applications development of the future migrating to the desktop, we will need a higher-end network to support this added burden on the network (Fig. 4.10). In this scenario, we hear that the applications and tools necessary to manage such a network will be readily available. However, one can only wonder if such added pressures will be sustained on this networking architecture. The use and integration of data, video, imaging, and, later on, voice to the desktop will add to the complexity of this network and the need to manage and power such applications. These multimedia applications can, however, be broken down from the larger systems problems and distributed across a client/server network. The super server will help to break massive problems down into more manageable, independent problems that can be shared across the network resources, as shown in Fig. 4.11. This breakdown will require strict performance tools and diagnostics to manage the workload across the network no matter where the resources exist. They should be available on the true client/server network. The client/server network was actually designed to facilitate this distribution of problems across networking resources.

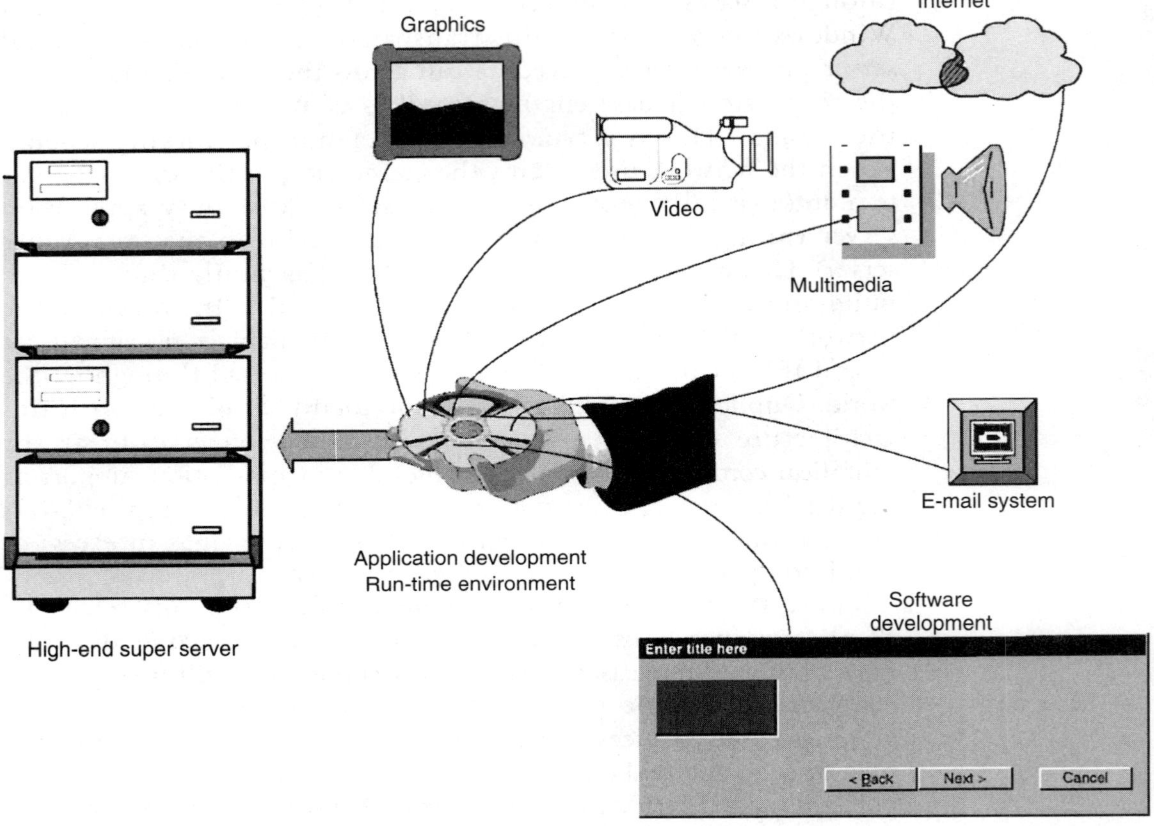

Figure 4.10 *High-end super servers are needed to sustain the graphical interfaces and applications development of the future.*

Network Operating Systems for Servers

Before progressing into the art of internetworking, these servers will require a high-end operating system to support the applications and the future distributed multiprocessing services. The network operating systems (NOSs) are very crucial. In selecting the appropriate one to use on the network, one must be careful that the NOS is capable of the demands and the parallel processing capabilities needed to sustain an

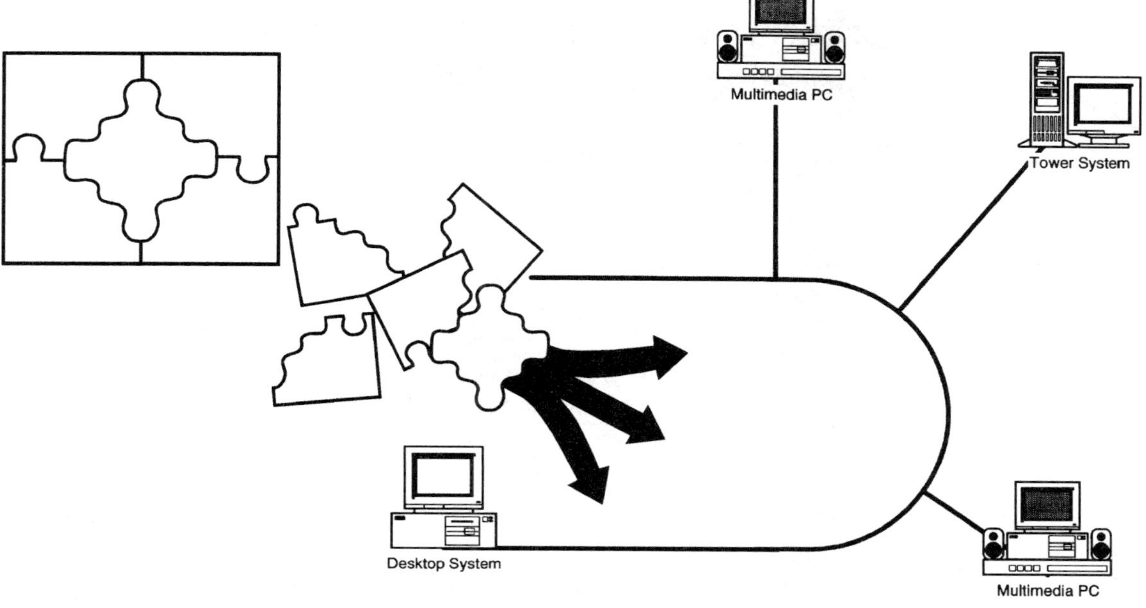

Figure 4.11 The client/server network can help by reducing larger computing problems into smaller ones and distributing them across the network.

organization's current and future needs. Some of the decisions in the selection process require caution due to the following factors:

1. Many applications in use on client/server networks are operating systems-specific, thereby limiting the choices to the few for which the application is written. Otherwise, multiple operating systems and protocol stacks may be required.
2. Proprietary systems that are developed for the LAN and WAN arena are in abundance. So, too, are the proprietary applications that have been custom-designed for the organization in meeting a niche application or departmental need. Here again the limitations of the systems and applications that are hardware- or software-specific create a risk in the design and selection of the client/server network.

Before selecting the NOS, one should consider several criteria. A checklist is shown in Fig. 4.12. The list is not all-inclusive, but it does contain

Criteria for selecting the Network Operating System (NOS):

Must support multitasking services
Must support multiuser environment
Full support of a minimum 32 - bit operating system
Hardware-independent
Variety of applications support
Operating system in the architecture
Ports between various platforms

Figure 4.12 The selection process for the network operating system (NOS) is critical.

some of the minimum requirements for the NOS to be considered in your network.

The operating system should have, at a minimum, the following capabilities for the server:

1. Multitasking support that can sustain and handle symmetrical multiprocessing operations inherent in the operating system.

2. Multiple user support for the needs of the organization. Many servers use network operating systems that are built to handle this. Be aware that some are limited in the number of users supported. In this case, the larger the number of users supported, the better the operational needs will be met.

3. Minimum of 32-bit operations at the operating system. Newer operating systems are now becoming 32-bit-compatible, but many still reside on a 16-bit platform. Clearly, full support for 32-bit operation may be a hindrance due to some of the applications' inability to support the 32-bit operation, but the industry is rapidly catching up to this new standard. Newer operating hardware platforms are migrating to 64-bit processing power, meaning that the 32-bit operating systems will have to catch up to the hardware systems. This is a short-term problem that will be solved in the near future. Currently, work is being done on 64-bit UNIX operating systems. It is only natural to recognize that the rest of the operating

systems will follow suit shortly after the introduction of the first versions.

4. The operating system should be hardware-independent so that it will not limit the future porting between servers and other associated hardware. This issue can become critical since so many of these systems have a tendency to be hardware-specific.

5. The operating system should be based on an open architecture from a standards perspective so that new applications and services can be added. One must be very careful in selecting the operating system so that a proprietary solution does not creep in unexpect edly. One note here is that some solutions are purchased with the knowledge that they are proprietary. If the operating system is selected for whatever reason and is proprietary, that is not all bad. So long as the standard is known and the decision is made with open eyes, then so be it.

6. The operating system should be fully supported in the industry and by multiple vendors. Too many client/server architectures have been installed without full support of the industry and vendor communities. This problem leads to solutions being created in a workaround or in excessive delays in producing newer versions of the software. Some organizations have even been placed in situations where the supplier of the operating system abandoned the software because they went out of business. What resulted was client organizations being stuck with an operating system that was not supported and, therefore, they needed to change in midstream. One particular case occurred in which the customers literally funded a company for months to get new revisions to an operating system, only to have the vendor go under anyway. How could this be explained to management?

7. The operating system should be easily ported from communications subsystems such as LANs, MANs, WANs, and remote access arrangements.

8. Lastly, one should be careful to get an operating system that will port from platform to platform transparently. Working at the server level, the hardware platforms may incorporate the PC, workstation, midrange, super server, and mainframe. Doing this at the server level prevents the operating system from mandating the solutions that are available for the overall network implementation. This is serious input that requires a full understanding of how the operating system may also port down to the client level, where a host of different hardware solutions may exist from the 386-, 486-, Pentium-, PowerPC-, and even some Macintosh-based client devices. Hardware compatibility lists should be provided by the vendor and tested to be sure. One can just imagine the impact of selecting an operating system that does not support multiple vendor platforms, memory configurations, or peripheral products that need to be incorporated. In the interest of being fair, some of the incompatibilities are often unknown because the mix of hardware systems has never been reviewed or completed as they appear in your environment. What if the operating system did not recognize the various server devices that are combined on a network? Should you get into a workaround in this matter and hope that the systems suppliers will resolve the conflict? This could mean an extensive delay in meeting the needs of the organization. One case in point was a mix of server platforms and the associated printers and tape backup systems attached to the server. Unfortunately, the tape subsystems were not recognized and supported by the operating software, and the necessary print drivers were not provided. This meant that printer emulation was used, creating a slower print queue, and a separate backup systems software was required to see the tape subsystem, at a substantial cost. Even then, the systems required special instructions every time the server was rebooted. The time and effort are things that cost the most.

This list above is only the beginning of the story, but it accentuates the difference between standards and proprietary solutions. The overall goal of this discussion and checklist is to arm the network manager with the necessary insight so that unexpected events do not slip into the equation. You may be surprised that when a dialogue is opened, the vendors will offer more detailed information than what is in the printed glossy pages they use for advertising. Read the lists and be amazed at what may or may not work in your network. Do you want to change the pieces or force-fit the connection? What if some specialty hardware is attached to your network that your users cannot do without? If you buy a proprietary solution and try to make this come together, then the odds are against you for the long-term success of the network.

List of Operating Systems for the Server

At the server level, there are many options for the network operating systems. Some have been around for some time; others are newer. Some are deviations from other operating systems for whatever reason, such as legal trademark restrictions. Examples of the trademark restrictions include the use of the word UNIX. Several flavors of this one operating system exist with various spins on the name just because of the legal situation. Therefore, one should understand the differences, which are more complicated than this book can cover, and the restrictions or proprietary spins on the same product. Thus, the generic list of operating systems for the server include the following:

1. UNIX
2. IBM AIX[1]
3. HP UX[2]
4. Novell
5. Banyan Vines
6. Microsoft NT
7. IBM LAN Server
8. IBM OS/2
9. DECNet (Pathworks) and Ultrix[3]
10. Sun
11. Solaris
12. Other specialty products

The network operating systems are quite varied in terms of their approach to meeting the needs of the organization. However, a quick look at a couple of these can give the reader a sense of the overall power

1. IBM's version of UNIX due to the restriction on the use of the UNIX name; a little proprietary in nature.

2. HP's version of UNIX, again from the legal restrictions on the use of the name; more open and compatible with UNIX than most.

3. Still another version of UNIX from Digital Equipment Corp.

of these systems. This way the process, rather than the product, will be compared. The intent is not to endorse a specific product or service but to see the overall comparisons and capabilities of these operating systems.

UNIX

Since its creation back in the 1969 era, UNIX has met with very strong success because of its ability to port between and among many hardware platforms. In the beginning, it was exceptionally widespread in colleges and universities around the world in the midrange and mainframe applications. It is the most popular operating system for midrange, super servers, and now PC-based servers. Its popularity is due to the robustness and the overall acceptance of the protocols and operations from the computer industry. Further, the wide use of reduced instruction set computing (RISC) platforms make UNIX an easy migration path.

There are several flavors of UNIX on the market (as many as hundreds), each with its own spin on the product. Because of the legal and trademark provisions, every manufacturer of a UNIX product has added some proprietary piece or a twist from the norm. In its command-line interface, UNIX is very powerful but complicated for the novice user. Most individuals steer clear of this platform from the desktop because of its complexity. However, in the server world, it is a very strong platform on which to base an operating system. Because it is used heavily at the server level, we find it most common there. However, it is not a server requirement. Many organizations around the world, regardless of their vertical position in the market, are well versed in UNIX. UNIX is favored in the U.S. government, well accepted in the European and Japanese markets, and gaining new influence in the developing countries. Other characteristics of the UNIX platform include the following:

- Support for a large number of users
- Symmetrical multiprocessing (SMP) power
- Support and endorsement by the OSF
- Support also in an OSI and X/Open standard
- Full kernel support for internetworking
- Heavy communications subsystems support:
    - TCP/IP support
    - SNA interfaces

- OSI
- X.25
- NFS/NCS

- Spanning many hardware platforms
- More openness than other operating systems (but proprietary versions do exist)
- Excellent price/performance ratios
- Heavy penetration into the high-end workstation and LAN-based server markets
- Support of graphical interfaces including Motif and X/Windows for ease of use

One can see that the use of a UNIX-based platform is fairly popular; therefore, each computer manufacturer has developed its own version of this system. It is very portable, allowing the manufacturers to cross their various hardware platforms easily. Figure 4.13 is a chart showing the popularity of the UNIX platform in the industry. The chart reflects the number of UNIX systems sold over the past few years. This steady

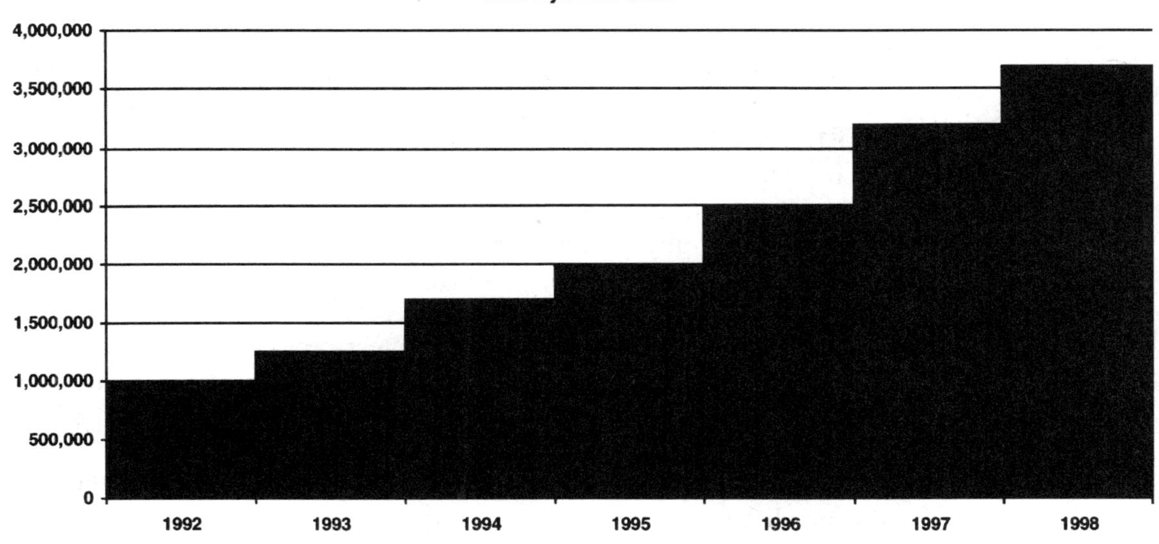

Figure 4.13 Estimated number of UNIX systems sold (and to be sold).

growth drives home the realization that more users are moving toward the power of this operating system. (Note that the number of systems sold includes the variations of the different systems suppliers.)

IBM AIX

AIX stands for Advanced Information Executive. It is a spin on the UNIX operating system. Due to the legalities in using the name, IBM came up with AIX as its proprietary UNIX operating system, which spans all of IBM's systems to include the following:

1. 386/486 Pentium-based systems
2. PS/2 family
3. RT product line
4. 370 computers
5. RISC product line

As shown in Fig. 4.14, AIX is the basis for IBM's Advanced Information Executive. It uses interactive programs to support multiple users, similar to the UNIX world. Because it is designed to span IBM's entire hardware product line, the AIX is hardware-independent. The Open Systems Foundation has selected the AIX as the sole operating system for its DCE. IBM uses the AIX as a port to its Systems Application Architecture (SAA), the surrogate to SNA. In this configuration, the AIX as the core has total interfacing capacities to industry standards based on OSI and OSF proceedings. Further, it has all the necessary drivers and interfaces for a connectivity solution that works well in the client/server network. It is designed around a distributed rather than a centralized computing architecture, although it can work either way. Several end-user interfaces have been provided for, so the system network manager can support the GUIs necessary based on the X/Open standards. Several application program interfaces have been provisioned for common programs that are used in a networking environment. AIX also has all the bridging services to SAA and other architectures, allowing for transparency across the network.

Looking a little closer, the AIX interfaces to the IEEE 1003.1 (POSIX) standard. It uses several UNIX components, such as the kernel, which allocates basic computing resources. It has a UNIX shell and runs UNIX-based programs. The kernel supports 10,000 processes (newer ver-

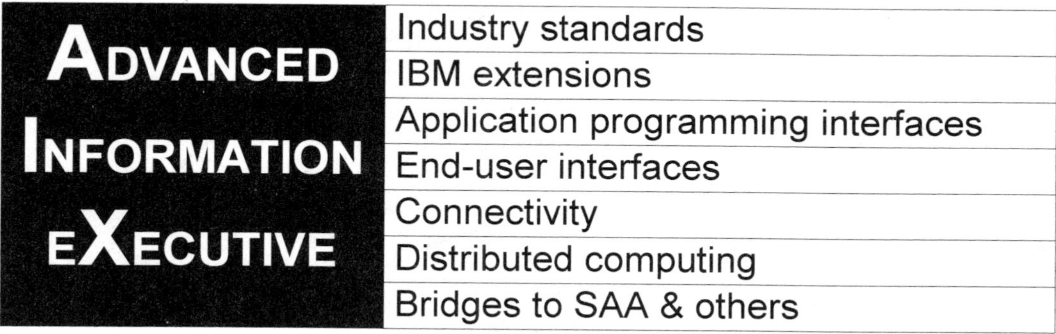

Figure 4.14 The interfaces supported in IBM's AIX.

sions will support 100,000 processes) and has all the hardware support for virtual memory management and virtual resource management in the RS/6000 product line. In Fig. 4.15, we see a reference to these as they are structured around the AIX operating system. The heart of the operating system is the basic kernel in this figure. As the circles work outward, the shell and user interfaces are supported. On the outer edges of this figure are the interfaces to the applications.

DECNet

Another very popular operating system in the client/server network is Digital Equipment Corporation's DECNet. It is a well-developed set of standard protocols and support for various interfaces on a DEC network. A suite of communications facilities is provided between various DEC systems. It was designed to provide a cohesive and seamless communications infrastructure between dissimilar processors and architectures. In reality, the DECNet was developed around a peer-to-peer networking strategy, but it has since been modified to support the client/server network. Ultimately, the DECNet has no one controller node on a network, although these functions can be set up on a network. It was modeled around the original concept of a LAN where the control over the network is shared among all cooperating processors. In general, any DECNet node on a network can communicate with any other node as long as they both abide by the rules established in the architecture. This makes managing a network a little more complex. DECNet was built around

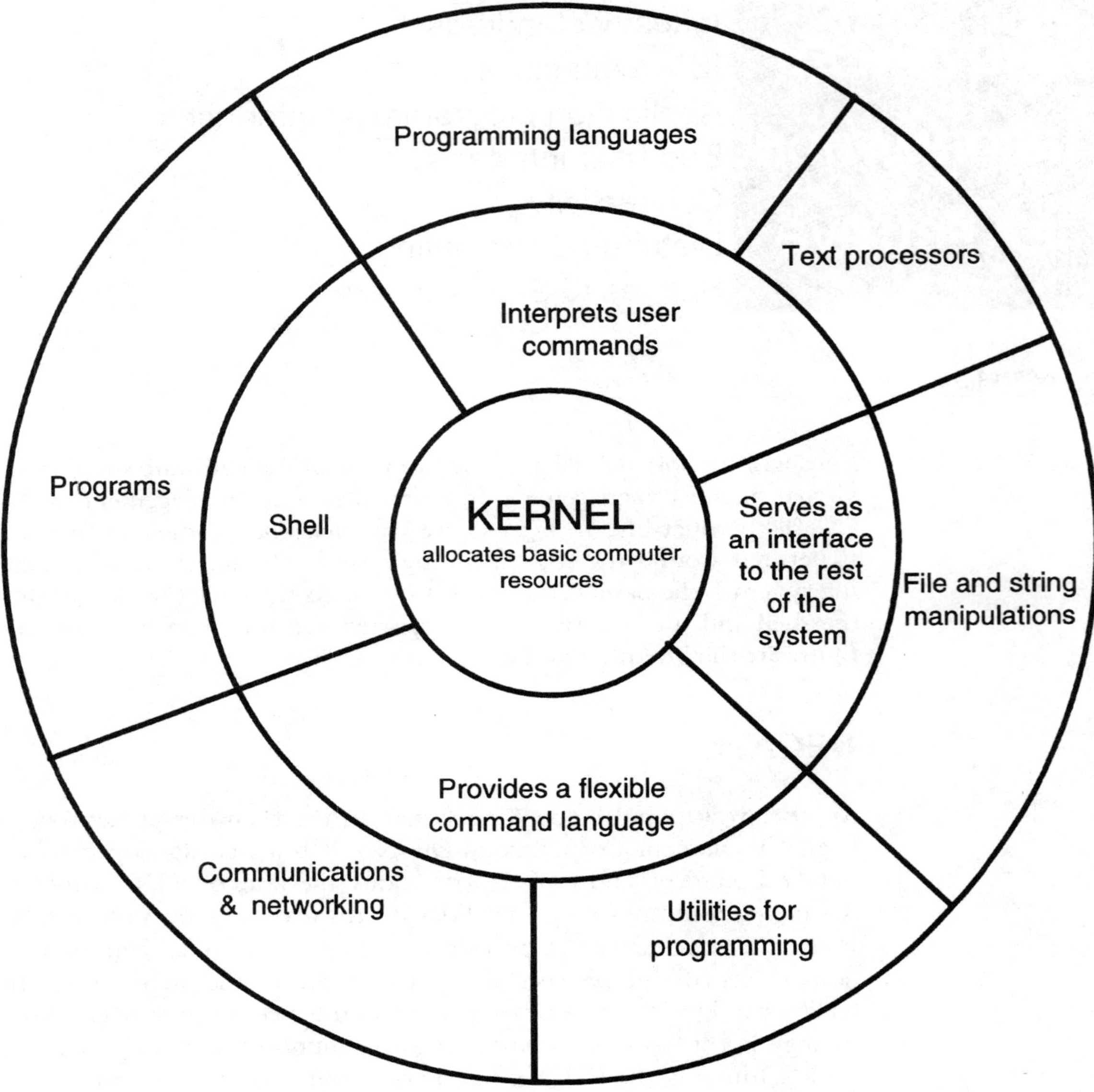

Figure 4.15 IBM's AIX uses the kernel as the heart of the operating system. Each concentric circle provides hardware or software interfaces.

several iterations or releases that added features and complimentary products with each new release, called phases. Each phase specifies:

- The operating system support within the release and supported by phase
- Communications hardware supported by the new phase
- New features and functions introduced in the phase

DECNet came in five phases:

1. Phase I was introduced in 1976 as a basic file transfer and task-to-task communications process. Communications was only supported for a few nodes via asynchronous communications. Routing on this network was not available.

2. Phase II provided some enhancements to better support the OSI model as it was being developed. DEC was an integral part in the development of the OSI model, because it had a vested interest in making sure the new model would not obsolete their existing infrastructure. It comes as no surprise—any vendor that had an operating system on the market played an integral part in developing the OSI. In this phase, manual routing was introduced, as well as additional operating systems support for the Virtual Machine System (VMS) operating system.

3. Phase III brought full routing capability, full file transfer support, and task-to-task facility enhancements. In this phase, remote (virtual) terminals allowed a user to log into a remote system as though it was the local host. Transparent programming facilities (for the VAX family) for opening remote communications, very similar to opening files, were added.

4. In Phase IV, introduced in 1984, DEC attempted to meet the OSI compliance more efficiently. In this phase, support was extended across Ethernet[4] LANs, MS-DOS, and Ultrix systems. Further support of non-DEC computers and non-DEC operating systems was added.

5. Phase V, announced in 1987, brought about more support for the OSI model, which was nearing completion. DEC announced that it would support a dual stack of protocol suites (DEC and OSI stacks) running either stand-alone or side by side. This came to a

4. A LAN standard for CSMA/CD networks introduced by DEC, Intel, and Xerox.

full seven-layer architectural support for the OSI model. Added features included distributed naming services, distributed file and queue services, file transfer access and management protocol (FTAM), virtual terminal protocol (VTP), and domain network support. Many of these features and support issues were the basis of the OSF selection of the queue and file services, as well as the naming services.

Although DECNet was widely implemented as a networking architecture, DEC also introduced its version of UNIX, called Ultrix. It supports the full stack of features and portability for a UNIX environment but has some proprietary spins on it. Further, as DEC moved toward Phase V of DECNet, the response from the user community was less than enthusiastic. It is very expensive to implement a fully compliant OSI system, so when DEC introduced Phase V, little user response was evident. In comparing the DECNet and OSI models (Fig. 4.16), we see

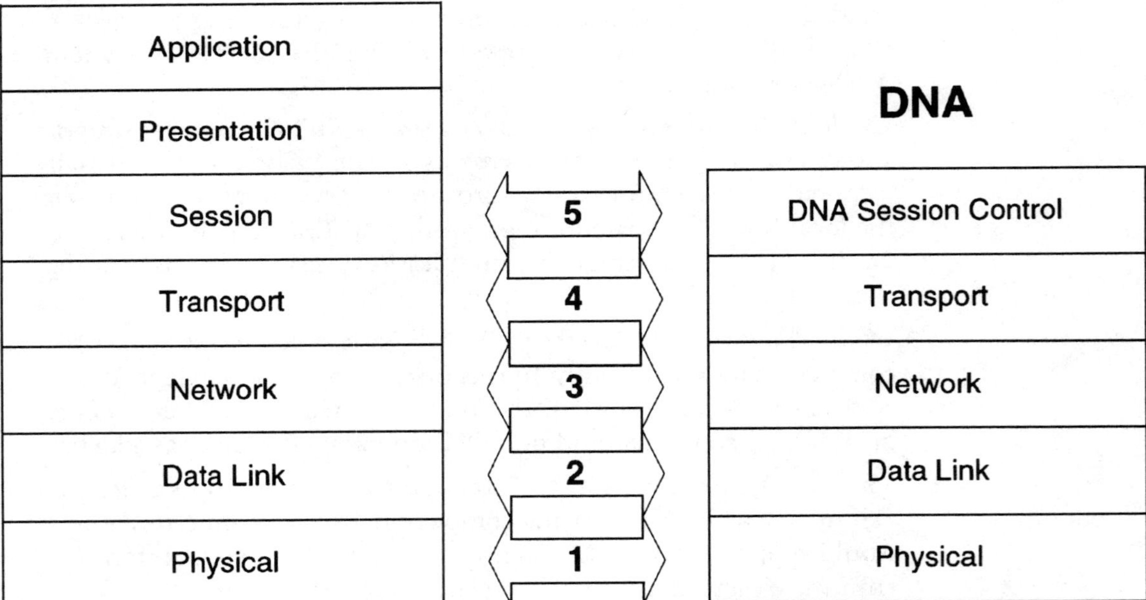

Figure 4.16 Comparing DECNet and OSI protocol stacks.

the original DecNet as a five-layer stack, whereas the OSI model is the full seven-layer stack.

Novell NetWare

No other network operating system has taken the industry by storm like Novell's NetWare. This operating system came into existence in the early to mid-1980s as a counter to the NOSs developed by 3Com, Banyan, Corvus, and others. Many of these operating systems were built as a basis of an add-on. Some of the initial suppliers were hardware manufacturers that made cards and, oh, by the way, made the software that used the NICs. Others were software suppliers who built on the basis of an enterprise networking strategy, but the code was very bulky and the controls implemented on the LAN mimicked the data-processing department's heavy-handed control. These others were destined to shake out because of the misdirection in their market niche.

Novell came along with a simple-to-use and less bulky operating system that dealt with the individual departmental LAN. This caused the entire industry to stand up and take notice. Later, as the product matured, Novell got into the enterprise networking strategy, but this was after amassing a full 65 percent of the NOS installations around the United States and abroad. This pervasiveness set the stage for many of the enhancements and competitive products that followed suit. As a network operating system for the LAN and specifically for the server environment, Novell's NetWare has definitely taken a very large chunk of the market. In the client/server architecture, Novell is continually upgrading the power of the operating system to offer more robustness. NetWare is an operating system that has traditionally been considered a LAN product but has since gained new acceptance in the WAN and client/server networking arenas. In general, it meets the best of all worlds for the applications that we have already addressed. Specifically, NetWare offers

- Robust LAN support for all networks, including
  - Ethernet
  - Token ring
  - Star LANs

  - IBM PC networks
  - NetBios emulation
- Full support for file and print sharing
- E-mail services
- Remote access
- Inter-LAN communications
- Gateway services to SNA/SDLC networks

Rather than attempting to extol the benefits and pervasiveness of NetWare, one merely needs to understand that the market share still resides at the installations out there in the industry. However, shifts are beginning to take place in this market niche. More and more pressure is being placed on Novell to hold onto market penetration. Some of the robustness, however, is evidenced in the support from myriad vendor products in this industry. For example, Novell is fully supported on the following platforms:

- UNIX
- DOS/Windows
- OS/2
- Data General
- DEC
- IBM (MVS, VM, OS-400)
- HP
- ICL
- Interactive
- MIPS
- Pyramid
- Unisys
- Apple

No single other vendor product or operating system has matched the robustness of this NOS to date. The versions of the operating system allow for some forward and backward compatibility (but obviously not 100 percent). The cost of the NOS and the user licensing is far less than mainframe operating systems, and the interfaces to the end user are

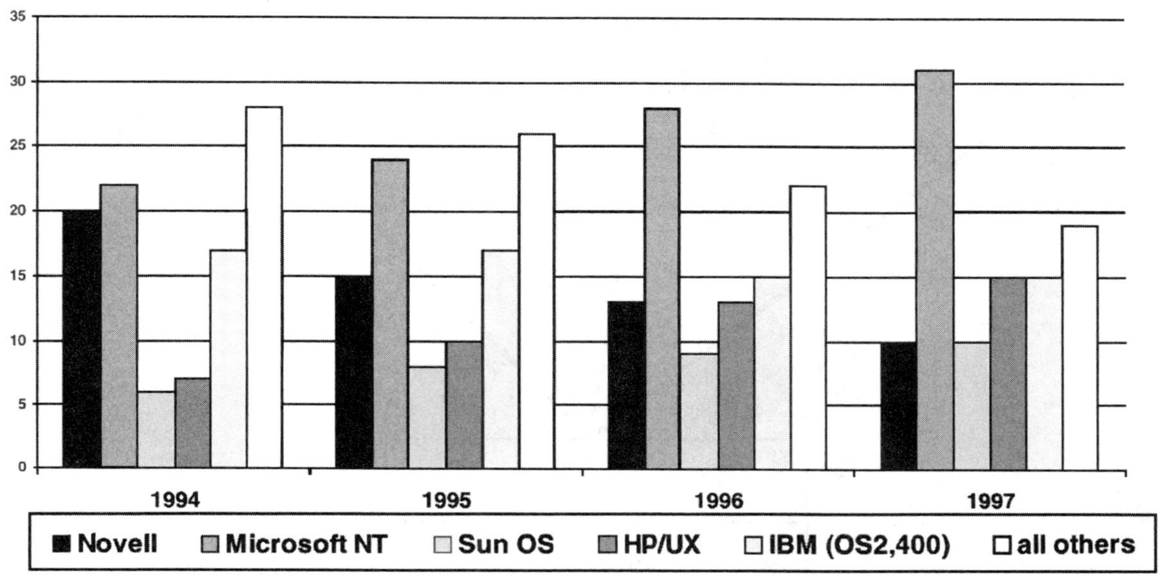

Figure 4.17 The shifts in the operating-systems marketplace over the past 4 years.

straightforward. Therefore, NetWare is the de facto LAN client/server architecture to follow. This is not to say that it is the only operating system that will port between and among the various hardware platforms, but it is the most widely used to date. The chart shown in Fig. 4.17 indicates the shift is to support the Novell world but also to move into other operating systems as well. This chart reflects some of the dominance of NetWare but also the changes in the client/server world.

Microsoft NT

Microsoft has been pushing hard against Novell's operating system with its new technology (NT) operating system. Windows-based server software was always a limitation, since it was 8- and 16-bit operating code. The NT Server and NT Workstation operating systems are 32-bit operating systems like Windows 95. They support the older services of a Windows 3.x platform and, of course, the older-yet DOS platform. What NT also provides is what Novell started early on, that is, multitasking, multiuser operations. Windows was always called a multitasking system, but in reality it was a

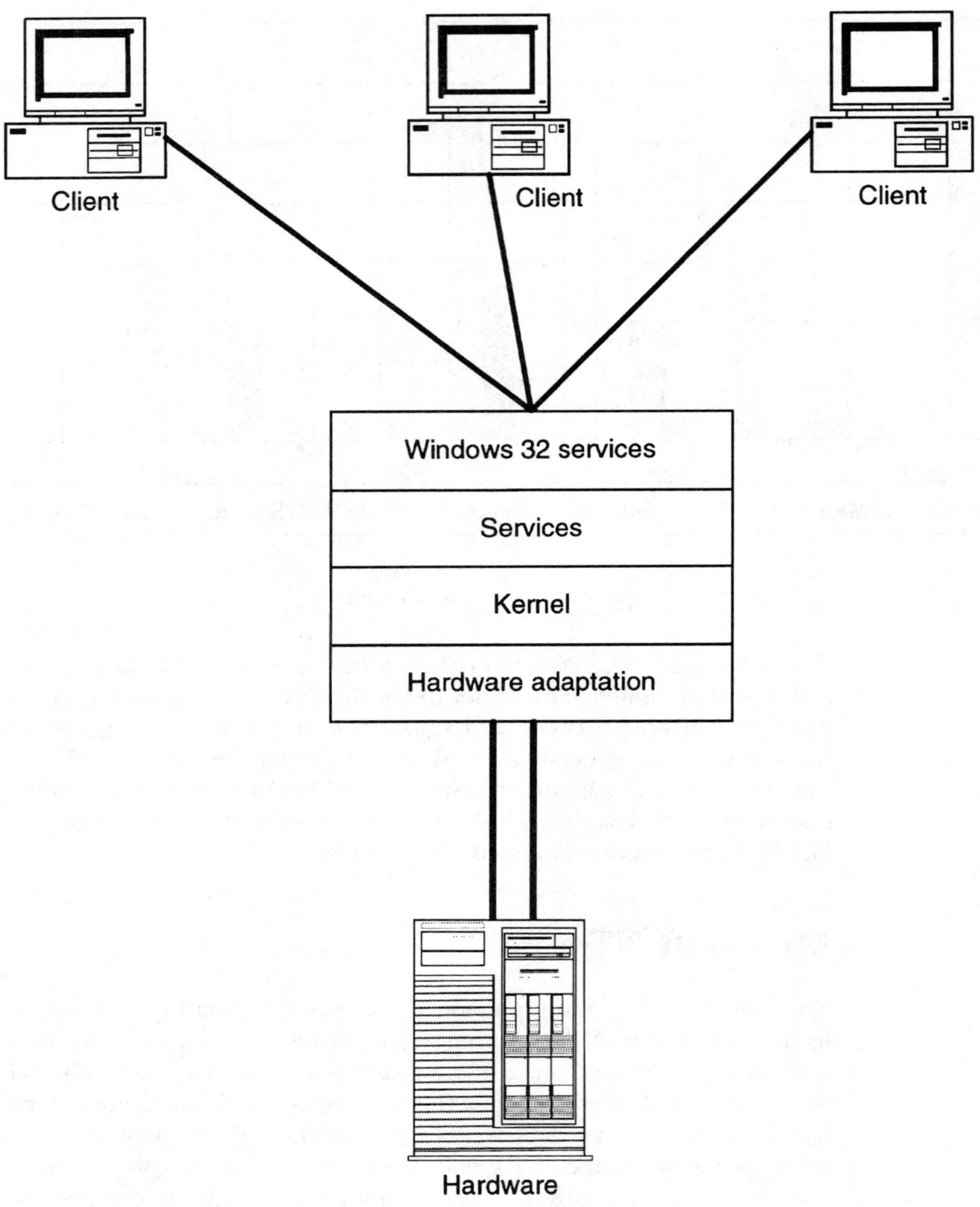

Figure 4.18 The NT architecture is Microsoft's answer to Novell's NetWare.

task-swapping system that sat on top of DOS. As an operating system for a server environment, it left significant voids. Therefore, NT was introduced.

NT Server 4.0 has increased in its robustness and support for myriad systems. It is an emerging operating system, so the jury is still out on its acceptance. However, one should watch the U.S. government, where plans are to migrate to NT at the server level for all standard installations. This decision is not final, but reliable interviews have shown that this is the direction. The same holds true for many *Fortune* 100 and 500 companies, where the NT server will be used at the high end, and Windows 3.x, Windows 95, and NT Workstation will be used at the user end.

Since NT is a full 32-bit operating system, it supports multiple users easily. Multitasking and swapping are inherent in the OS. However, LAN Manager (an older version of OS) add-on modules are used to create the multitasking services. The NT is client-independent, hardware-independent, and POSIX-compliant for portability across platforms. The use of the NT server will be a high-end performance capability. Primarily, the NT server is used in LANs and networks as a database server, but this is an implementation rather than a limitation of the system. Figure 4.18 is a representation of the architecture of the NT operating system. It is a reflection of the interfacing between the client and server on an NT platform. This system is gaining a lot of acceptance, including from IBM in its implementation of the PowerPC-based networks that are coming along. Several issues are being considered by IBM, one of which includes using NT at the server and OS/2 at the client. More will have to be provided on this later in the evolution of the client/server networks.

CHAPTER 5

The Client

The previous chapter discussed the considerations for selecting the server and the operating system to use. After reading Chap. 4, it was probably obvious that the preferred operating system for most organizations is the UNIX environment. It is the preferred operating system for vendors of midrange and super server hardware, as well as an acceptable arrangement for the mainframe server environment. This situation is not unexpected, but our intent is not to force the overall operating system onto an unsuspecting reader. Therefore, we now look at the operating system environment and the hardware associated with the client.

The client, as already expressed in this book, is the traffic cop for the client/server architecture. Thus, it would be normal to expect some emphasis on the use of the hardware and software that run at the client level. One should understand that the client has undergone metamorphoses. Initially, the client, in a mainframe world, used the characteristics shown in Table 5.1. This table is a summary of the evolution of this all-important component on the network.

When the migration to a LAN-based system began in the early 1980s, the move was away from the 327X terminals to a PC-based client. This shift required some adaptation of the end-user perspective and the ability to move more of the services away from the mainframe and closer to the desktop. Although it was not as quick as one might perceive from other readings, the replacement of dumb terminal devices did take the industry by storm. In general, the movement toward empowering the end users to control their own data in a form and format that these

TABLE 5.1

Summary of Evolution of Client

Characteristic	Client capabilities
Evolved from	The older terminal
Screen-based	Originally text- (character-)based and interfaced to host
Robust	No robust interfaces
Options for the client	Limited options and operational interfaces
Where the work is performed	Relied exclusively on host to do the work
Applications located	At host
Communications capabilities	None; required at host
Interaction with other devices	Limited, through the host
Memory capacities	None
Type processor	None

TABLE 5.2

The Introduction of the PC as the Client

New characteristics	Client capabilities
Terminal-based	No; evolved as a result of the introduction of the PC
Processor	Low-end, using 80X186 Intel processor; limited processing
Memory	Limited
Screen	Still text-based, similar to 327X devices
Host-based	At first, but moved away from dependency on host quickly
Resources shared	Yes
Services shared	Disks, programs, and print capabilities

users wanted caught on with record-breaking speed. Data-processing departments were reluctant to view the original client (PC) as a viable alternative due to some of the initial PC-based characteristics shown in Table 5.2.

Access to the Host

Figure 5.1 shows the access method used from the PC-based client to the original host-based server. As the migration continued with the installation of the PC at the desktop, the client still needed access to the organization's data. This access was achieved through the use of a gateway. The gateway handled the differences in

1. Access methods
2. Protocols
3. Language and formatting
4. Common shared communications channel
5. Other keyboard mapping and templates

The client made the move away from the hierarchical network and internetwork by moving the resources onto the common medium now known as the LAN. The requirement for interconnectivity and access to the host (mainframe) became evident as users had to manipulate and enter data into the host-based system. PC-based servers also needed to be interconnected to the host. Thus, the applications were moving

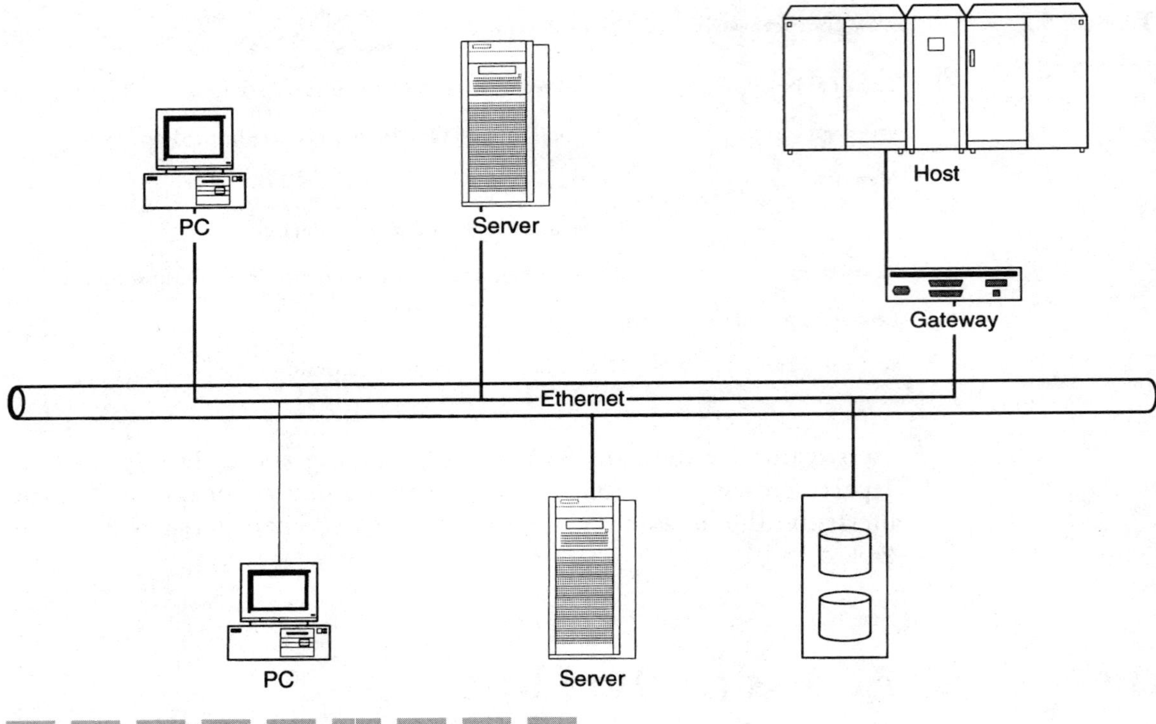

Figure 5.1 *Client access to a host running on a LAN.*

away from the host and closer to the desktop. However, the power to handle this access was not readily available. Simple PCs and other terminal devices did not have the necessary power to command the respect of data-processing departments, but, the server was powerful enough to maintain this control. Thus, operating systems were developed around the server being the controller of the access and data storage. PC-based hard disk farms emerged as file and disk servers, requiring the desktop device to remain dependent on a host replacement. The server was nothing more than a substitution for the mainframe with a higher-end PC that controls the data. This situation did not satisfy the end user, who was looking to gain more control over the data and the ability to manipulate the data in an ad hoc fashion. Therefore, client evolution continued to move the desired control closer to the desktop, which necessitated the continued development of hardware platforms.

The Next Phase

As the evolution continued, Intel influenced the movement from the mainframe and dumb terminal with the continued development of higher-end processors and less expensive end-user devices. It was this power and pricing strategy that caused the proliferation and the movement to the client/server network en masse, as shown in Table 5.3.

Figure 5.2 shows a representation of the new desktop-based client hardware. Note that the disks are larger to support the amount of data to be stored on the local drive. Further, this figure also shows a representation of the windowing terminal interface and the GUI interfaces using a mouse for point-and-click services.

The Client Architecture

A four-layered architecture for the client emerged that covers the characteristics just discussed. This architecture is shown in Fig. 5.3, beginning at the bottom layer with the operating system that drives the client and the network operating system that provides the resource sharing and common network interface. The application sits on top of the operating and network operating systems. From there, the presentation layer provides the actual presentation to the PC-based system and interacts very heavily with the actual application software. Lastly, to make this all

TABLE 5.3

The New Client Strategy Compares the Differences in the Development of the Desktop Device

The new client	Client capabilities
Desktop improvements	More powerful
Type of devices	Workstations and PCs based on Intel 486, Pentium, PowerPC, and X-Terminal/Windows
Memory	Requires 8 to 16 Mbytes of RAM, with 32 to 64 Mbytes becoming common
Access methods	Far more robust interfaces to networks
Hard disk	Capacities that exceed 300 to 500+ Mbytes with 1.0+ Gbytes being commonplace
Screen	Color, SVGA
Client interface	GUI-based and NOS-driven

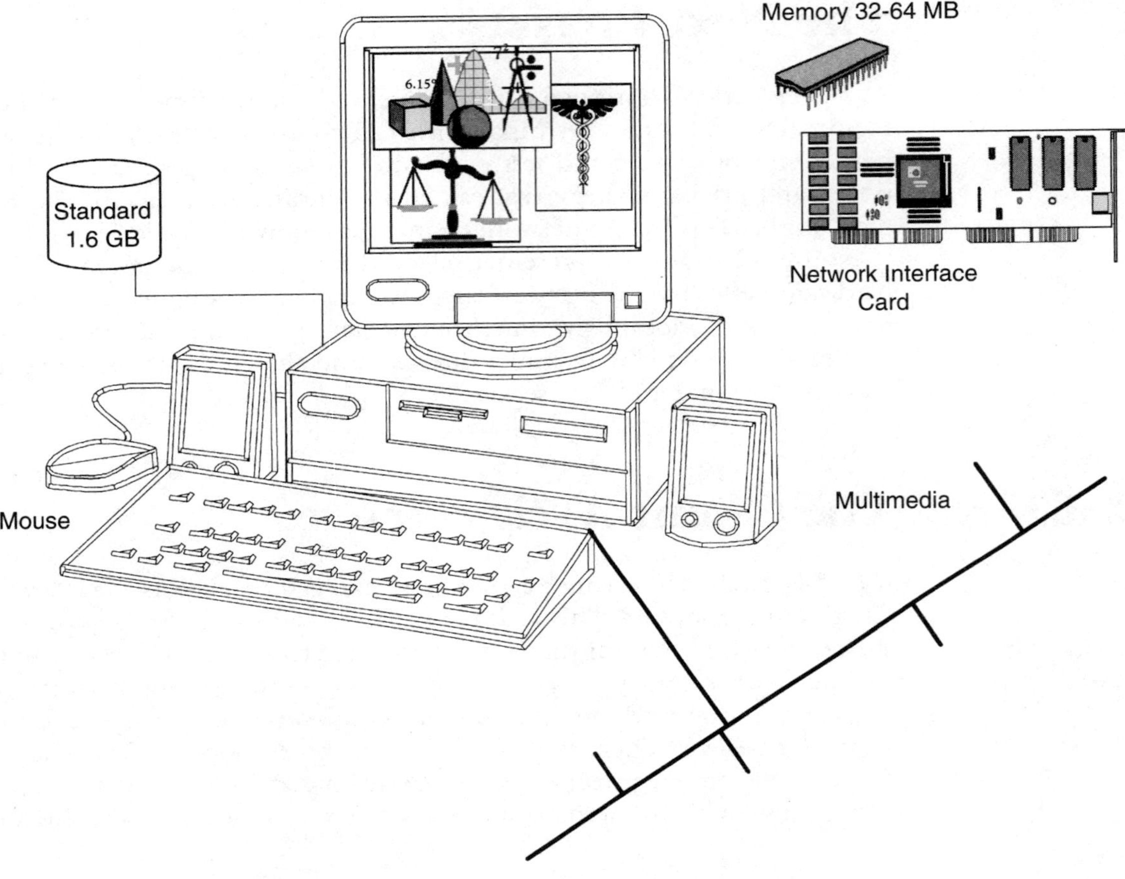

Figure 5.2 The new client is far more powerful.

work simply at the user level, the client architecture incorporates a GUI based on a standard interface such as Windows, X-Terminal, or Motif architecture.

This architecture is a mapping of the functionality of the actual workstation, PC, or other device. One has to realize that the client can take on the form of many devices, from a dumb terminal to a fully powered and configured workstation. Therefore, the architecture accounts for the differences in the equipment. As we look at this architecture, the client becomes an integral part of the internetworking infrastructure. Without the ability to access the data in a reasonable fashion that allows

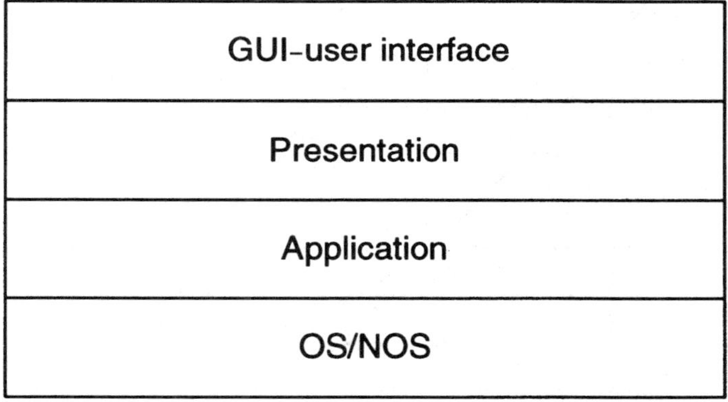

Figure 5.3 The client architecture.

the transparent manipulation and creation of the data, the services will be impaired. Because the client acts as a traffic cop in the movement and storage of the data, the functions do require a capability beyond the original hierarchical and distributed networks. Now the processing power may be a component of the client as opposed to the mainframe or midrange computing system. Hence, the expenses we sink into the hardware and software are going to increase dramatically. The only salvation is that while the need to beef up the client is driven by the application, the overall cost of the hardware is constantly dropping. In Fig. 5.4, the cost versus power of PC-based systems is reflected over time.

Defining the Client Software

As can be seen in Fig. 5.5, defining the client software entails several different operating systems and hardware platforms. We cannot assume that the actual client is a standard PC or other workstation. As a result, we see that various platforms can be integrated onto the client/server internetwork. The options shown in this figure are as follows:

1. *486 PC-based system.* This system operates on a 486, 33- or 66-MHz hardware system using DOS as the primary operating system and Windows 3.x on top of the DOS environment. The older versions of these operating systems do not lend themselves to the newer, more powerful operating systems, but one must recognize that hundreds of thousands of these systems still exist in the industry. Further, they will stay in existence for some time to come.

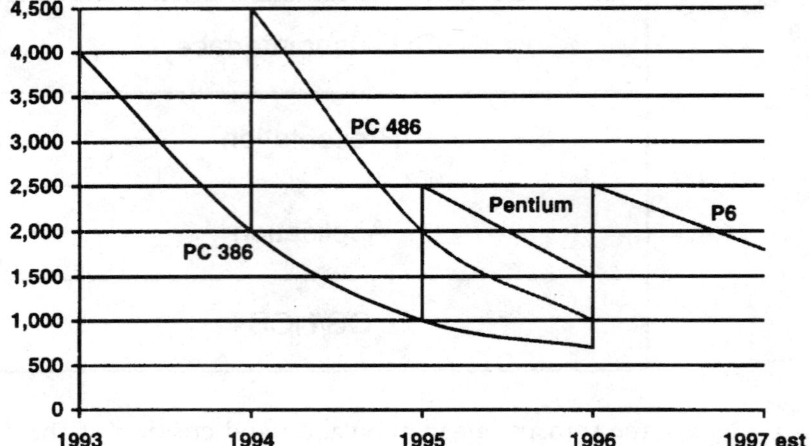

Figure 5.4 The trend in hardware costs over time.

2. *Pentium-based systems.* This system is the later version of the Intel-based computing hardware using a higher-end chipset at 60 to 200 MHz. The primary operating systems are a selection of Windows 3.x, Windows 95, NT, or a UNIX operating system. The use of any of these operating systems in the client makes for a very powerful system on the desktop.
3. *DEC Alpha.* This system is the high-end client of the future. Although the Alpha chipset is currently used in a server-based environment, the time is rapidly approaching when it will become a desktop powerhouse. Running at 133 to 500 MHz, this hardware platform meets the demands of the multitasking and operating systems environment. At this level, UNIX, DECNet, and Ultrix[1] can all be accommodated as high-end operating systems.
4. *Macintosh.* The Mac is still alive and well at the client level. More applications will run on this hardware platform operating at 30 to 200 MHz in a somewhat transparent fashion. The Mac runs System 7 or 8 client software at the operating systems level. One cannot discount the Mac unit's contribution to the client model. Many of the Windows-based systems are direct descendants of the Mac operating systems.
5. *IBM RISC 6000.* The RISC 6000 product is a hardware platform operating at 60 to 200 MHz to support the server and now the

1. Ultrix is DEC's version of UNIX.

client. Once again, the power of a single RISC chip is more than is required at the desktop level, but it's just a matter of time until it moves in as the operating system. Running an IBM OS/2 or an AIX operating system allows for a robust device. Although some of these are more expensive than others that are available, the price declines of the past indicate the potential of this platform as a client.

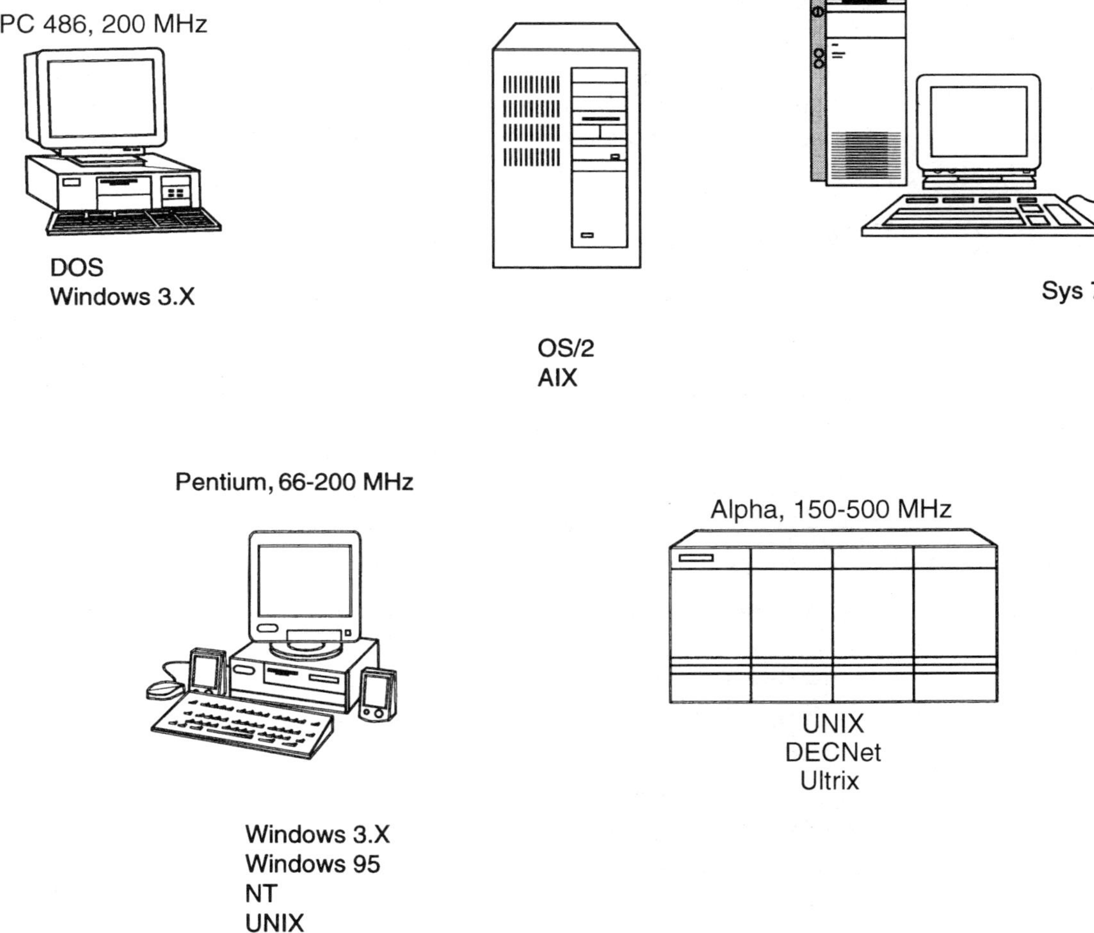

Figure 5.5 The powerful multitasking client operating systems that must be internetworked.

Graphical User Interfaces

The GUIs used at the client level require a friendly interface. It only takes a short visit with today's users working on these new client/server architectures to see that the workplace has changed dramatically. Users are faced with new challenges every workday. In the era of client/server architectures, the user is empowered to make business decisions at a lower management level than ever before. With the power of the processors coming at a very rapid rate and the operating systems changing dramatically, the end users are being asked to perform more on their own. As we started this discussion in earlier chapters, the suggestion of the client/server networks providing the users with a programming interface is a matter of course. Using an object-oriented service, the GUI standard emerged to facilitate the interaction between the client and the server.

Windows

The GUI standards emerged as a means to simplify the connection and interaction of the applications.

- Many changes in the client provided differences between the older, terminal-based systems that depended on a character-based screen as opposed to the graphics-based interface that uses pixels instead of characters.
- Instead of using a command-line interface, the GUI presents an icon-driven interface to ease user manipulation of the data.
- Applications use an event-driven sequence rather than a data entry sequence, allowing the data manipulation and gathering to be controlled more efficiently.
- With the GUI, a user selects the best or easiest buttons, scrolls, and screens.
- Customization of tool bars and screens gives the end user a more comfortable interface with the client.
- The GUI further uses the presentation to base the output and results of data manipulation in a friendlier format.
- Lastly, the GUI must be able to port across the various hardware platforms listed previously. It is through this portability that the open standards are achieved and the user can move between and

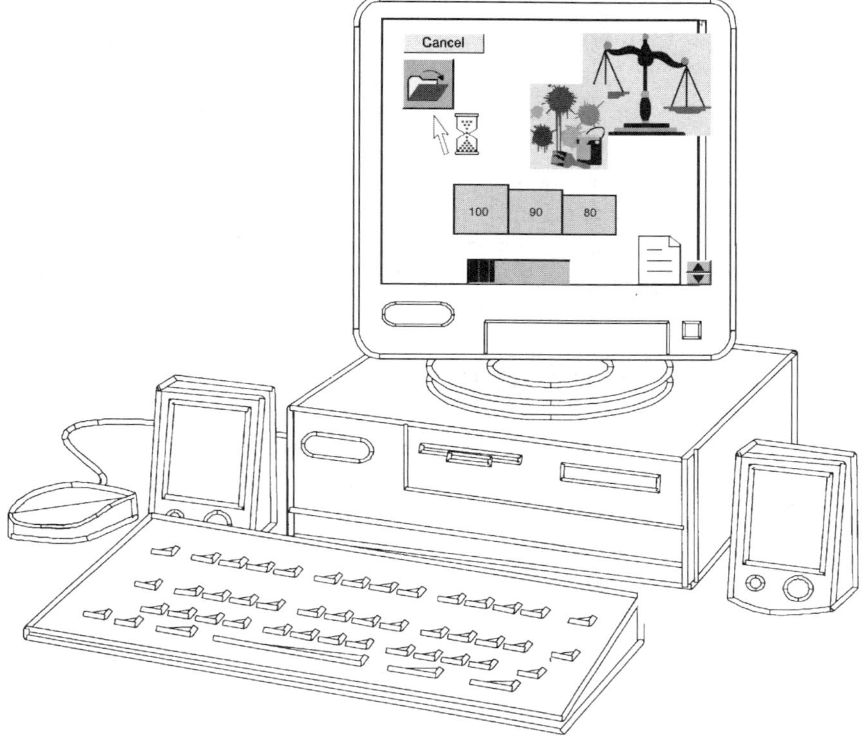

Figure 5.6
The GUI allows the client to set the environment.

among various interfaces on differing hardware. Yet the presentation at the screen is the same regardless of the hardware platform.

Figure 5.6 shows the use of a Windows-based GUI. It presents the interface using the various object-linking environments (OLEs), dynamic link libraries (DLLs), and dynamic data embedding (DDE) capabilities through a windowing interface. The client using the GUI selects various tasking operations in multiple overlapping resizable windows to view and link the actual data. Mouse-driven interfaces to the GUI facilitate the use of icons instead of a command-line interface, making the overall job easier. The GUI standards adhere to all of the standards from the Institute of Electrical and Electronics Engineers (IEEE), American National Standards Institute (ANSI), and National Institute of Science and Technology (NIST) as interoperable. They provide flexibility for various displays, drivers, applications, and I/O devices. However, the use of this GUI-based interface also adds overhead to the data storage and the transport across a network. Graphics, and particularly bitmapped graphics, are data-intense as they travel across the cabling system. Thus, the GUI adds a level of sophistication in planning for the implementation of the client/server internetwork.

Along with these interfaces, development tools in the form of toolkits are available on many interfaces, thereby allowing additional customization at the client level. International character sets are added benefits of the GUI where a global or universal numbering system is applied, characters are used, and specific symbols are required. Again, these sets allow flexibility at the client but place the burden on the network. Hardware and software interfaces and NOS transparency are a must for a GUI to be effective.

X Windows

A standard emerged that allows for network transparency in communications between the client architecture levels at the application and the presentation. In the X Windows environment, the roles of the client and the server have shifted. The presentation can reside at the server rather than the client. Figure 5.7 shows X Windows. Here we have a high-performance graphics interface as a GUI with the ability to resize multiple overlapping windows. Note that the physical client now runs the server application software and the physical server runs the client interface. The client interfaces between applications are loaded on the physical server. The traffic-cop functions and roles are reversed in this architecture. Thus the client becomes the server, and the server becomes the client in an X Windows environment. X Windows can run on most of the hardware platforms discussed earlier, but it is best served on high-end workstations such as Sun Microsystems SparcStations and Silicon Graphics workstations. It also supports the RISC, Alpha, and Pentium hardware platforms. Through this high-end graphics and presentation package, the client can access the various multitasking operands on the client/server network.

Motif

Still another interface standard is emerging to facilitate the object-oriented, icon-driven client/server network. The use of Motif as a standard rides on top of the X Windows interface. It uses a different window manager. Motif is a compendium of various manufacturers' products. It uses

- The best of DEC Windows

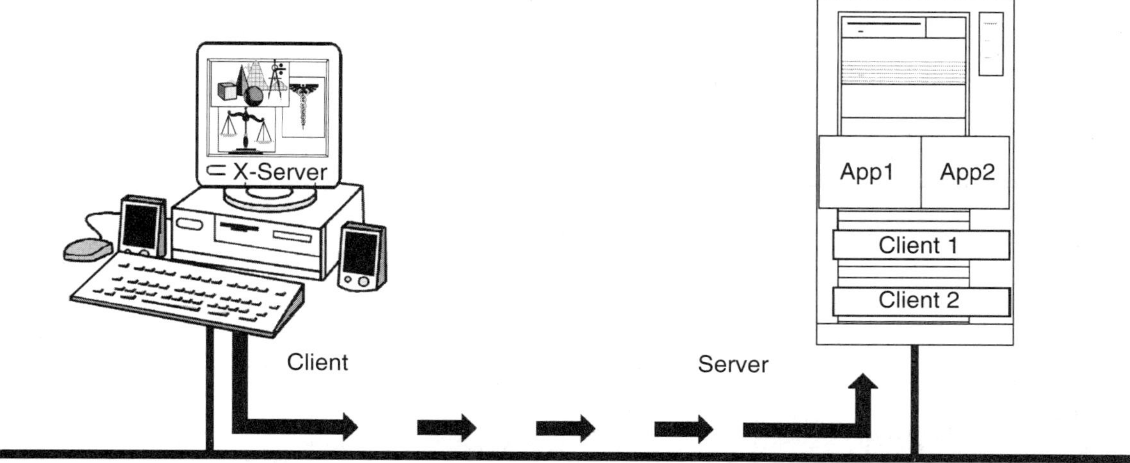

Figure 5.7 The X Windows GUI interface presents a role reversal on the architecture.

- HP Toolkit and Window Manager
- Microsoft Presentation Manager

Motif carries a lot of UNIX vendor support in its capabilities. It offers portability through the X/Open (XPG3) standards and is heavily supported by users. Motif is the preferred GUI of the U.S. government. Thus we can expect to see much more support and development in this arena.

Figure 5.8 shows the compatibility index and architecture of the various GUIs available. Here we see the various GUIs offered by different vendors and how they stack up against each other. Note that in this architecture, Motif runs on top of X Windows. The application program interfaces sit between the GUI and the application to interface the two together.

The Operating Systems

DOS

The most common and still prolific operating system for the client is Microsoft's DOS. DOS is quite common at the hardware level on PC-based networks. As we all know, DOS is not a network operating system, but rather a hardware platform operating system. DOS is not a

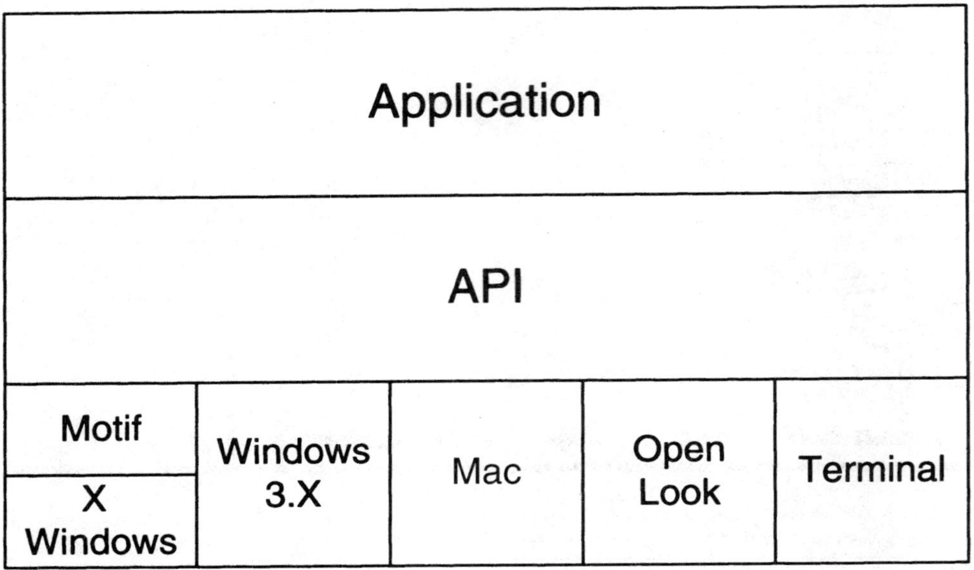

Figure 5.8 Compatibility and architecture of various GUIs.

multitasking or an integrated operating system, but a single-user, single-tasking system. Even with the installation of a user interface such as Windows 3.x, the system is not multitasking, but task-swapping. Despite this drawback and the fact that the industry continues to pretend that DOS is on borrowed time, one can imagine how long this migration away from DOS will take. With millions of installed copies of the operating system in place, the movement will be long and arduous. Figure 5.9 is an attempt to look at the simplistic architecture of a DOS-based PC network. This graphic represents the simplest form of networking services such as a Windows for Workgroups (3.11) to support resource sharing. The use of WFW is a peer-to-peer environment rather than a client/server. However, as stated in the beginning of this book, client/server networks mean different things to different people, depending on the installation.

Windows NT

Running Windows New Technology (NT) either at the workstation or the server level may become far more prevalent in the client/server networks. NT was Microsoft's answer to Novell's NetWare. Because there was no true NOS in the Microsoft lineup, NT was developed. The principal characteristics of NT are

- 32-bit operating system
- True multitasking capability
- Hardware-independent
- POSIX-compatible
- Good file transfer capabilities in the operating system
- Built with networking in mind
- Supports OS/2
- Microsoft's direction away from the DOS world

At the client level, NT Workstation 3.51 and 4.0 provide some powerful capabilities. However, the minimum RAM configuration is 16 Mbytes,

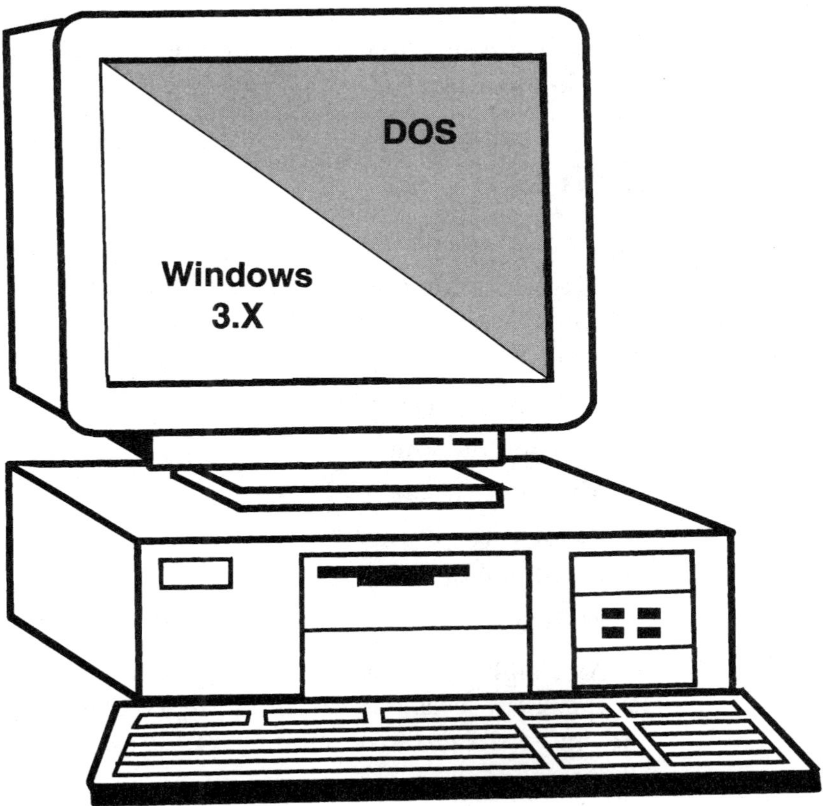

Figure 5.9 The simple DOS/Windows architecture is the most common in existence in the industry.

despite what the manual states. If the ability to be robust and fully interactive with multiple sessions on the client is a requirement, there will be no substitute for the 16- to 32-Mbyte RAM requirement. Further, running all 32-bit applications will be necessary to get away from the older DOS and Windows worlds. If all applications are not 32-bit-supported, then the NT file system and benefits are lost. One will then have to run DOS and Windows beside NT regardless of the version of NT used, which slows things down considerably and adds to the storage requirement. Evolution and customer support will drive this as the preferred Microsoft solution in the future. Whereas Microsoft has developed Windows 95 as a step to get away from the DOS/Windows 3.x systems, it does not fully provide the user needs. Windows 95 still requires a substantial amount of interaction with DOS and old Windows. Several steps are needed to move completely away from the legacy systems. Further, many organizations are establishing policies to wait out the NT evolution rather than take the leap of faith to Windows 95. Most government agencies are heading in the direction of NT as opposed to Novell, Windows 95, or OS/2.

UNIX

Still another client operating system that will emerge as a possible winner is the UNIX operating system. It is also one powerful operating system that will support the new interfaces and GUIs for the client. Some of the client characteristics are

- 32-bit operating system
- True multitasking system
- Multiuser system
- Requires lots or memory
- Requires faster CPUs than today's
- Runs and fully supports X Windows

Although UNIX is still too powerful today for an individual user at the client level, one can only foresee that in the future, UNIX may be one of the most common operating systems at the client and server levels.

NetWare

Enough was said about NetWare in the server discussion, but we cannot ignore that it is still a widely implemented and installed operating system at the client level. Novell's NetWare offers the client many advantages:

- 32-bit operating system
- Multiuser system
- Multitasking operations
- Windows 3.x/95 support
- UNIX support
- Widely installed and supported between organizations
- OS/2 support
- Migration strategies from Novell in support of client/server networks

Novell is still the dominant force in the client networking interface; however, industry experts agree that the NetWare operating system may be running out of steam to support future client demands.

The Client Shell

In Fig. 5.10 on p. 122, the emphasis is on the use of the client shell to access the services of the server on a network. Regardless of the location of the client, data access and manipulation is the goal. Therefore, the tools and interfaces must be positioned so that transparency is the final result.

To finalize our thoughts on the client interfaces to the client/server network, Table 5.4 on pp. 122 and 123 is a checklist to select the appropriate operating system and interfaces to the client/server software engines on the market. It offers selection criteria or evaluation criteria for the client.

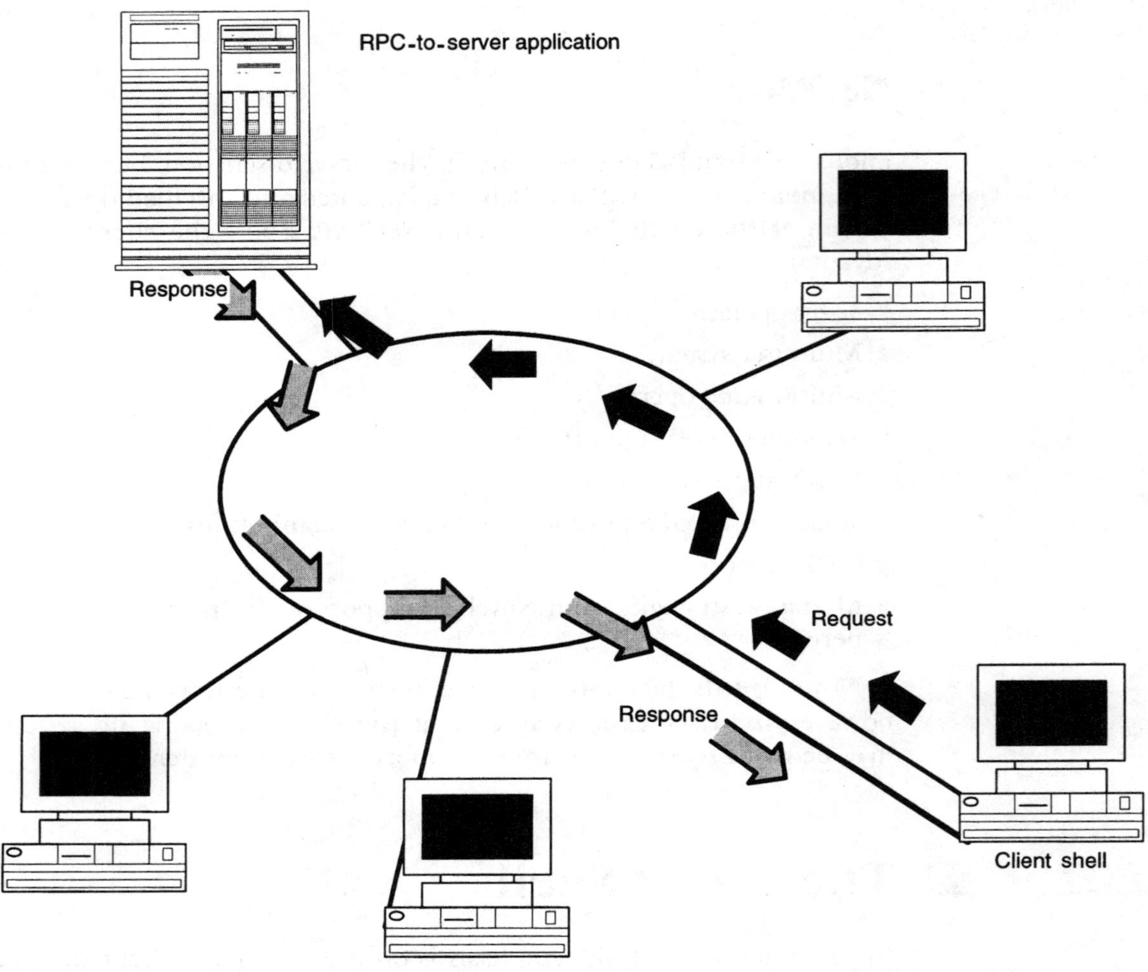

Figure 5.10 The client shell is the interface to the services provided by the server. Shells from various applications are provided through the communications medium.

TABLE 5.4 Summary of Criteria for Selecting a Client Interface

Issue	Yes	No
1. Is the client interface transparent and friendly?		
2. Are standards-based graphical user interfaces employed?		
3. Can the users devise and modify their own screens?		
4. Are the GUIs based on Windows, X Windows, OS/2, or UNIX?		

TABLE 5.4 (Continued)

Issue	Yes	No
5. Is the use of the client both icon-driven and command-line driven?		
6. Is the client interface fully hardware-independent?		
7. Does the client interface allow a Windows-based access to host systems and data?		
8. Are the windows fully resizable and scalable?		
9. Is the number of windows that can be open simultaneously greater than 5?		
10. Does the interface support a WYSIWYG (what you see is what you get) report generator?		
11. Do the interface and operating system fully support ease of use on an internetworking environment?		
12. Are the interface and operating system independent of topology?		
13. Is networking a part of the interface or an add-on module?		
14. Is security available as a standard feature?		
15. Do the interface and operating system meld the host and the LAN together transparently?		
16. Are multiple protocols supported simultaneously?		
17. Does the supplier have a migration plan that supports this interface for a period of 5+ years?		
18. Can users jump or hot-key between applications easily?		
19. Can the current suites of applications be supported transparently?		
20. Are the system and the interface fully portable between the host and the networking strategy?		
21. Can multiple database engines be supported simultaneously on the operating system through a standard interface?		
22. Will the interface work on Alpha, RISC, Intel, and other platforms?		
23. Is vendor support readily available?		
24. Does the vendor have a proven track record of past performance and successful installations?		
25. Has the vendor completed other installation on time and on budget?		
26. Is an operating client/server internetwork demonstrable, other than in a showroom environment?		
27. Do all applications running on the network operate seamlessly on the new operating system and interface?		
28. Is a conversion utility available for all applications running on other systems that need to be ported to this one?		
29. Are timed backups available on the system?		
30. Are screens able to be refreshed on an auto-timed basis?		

CHAPTER 6

Client/Server Internetworking Architectures

As we have seen in previous chapters, the use of client/server architectures offers the ability to link multiple computing systems together transparently across a wide area network. But is it really transparent? One can imagine that the overall architectures will allow for multiple protocols to run on a single infrastructure, but the ability to interface a combination of services may cause confusion to the end user. If the overall structure is not carefully planned, the users of the network services may become frustrated. Worse yet, users can get apathetic if they have to go through convoluted gyrations to manipulate their data. Consequently, one must be very careful in planning the installation, and always keep the end users' needs in mind.

Several architectures are emerging that will help to simplify the process, but the simple fact is that not all architectures are transparent and interoperable. So caution is still the operative word when choosing the services and the protocol stacks to use. Thus, when selecting the right operating systems and protocols, one has to use some standard architecture. Several architectures for multiprotocol (and single-protocol, for that matter) environments exist. We do not always have to scrap the environment that is in place. Moreover, we can make several operations function together, as long as a plan is in place. Some of these multiprotocol environments include the following protocol stacks:

- SNA/SDLC using the IBM client/server model
- TCP/IP on any platform, supporting a multivendor situation
- Open Systems Foundation using the Distributed Computing Environment (DCE) and a Distributed Management Environment (DME)
- The Open Systems Interface model as the networking model
- Other proprietary solutions

IBM's SNA

IBM's SNA is the predominant architecture, but several others are offered on a vendor-specific solution. Nowhere is it written that these are the only sets of solutions on the market. Personal experience from past clients and contacts points to these as the most prevalent installations in the industry.

One example of SNA architecture is a major bank in South Africa that spent more than two years putting in an IBM solution for its client/server internetwork. In this particular case, the bank was looking for a new solution to an old problem. Several branch offices and subsidiary locations were entertaining bids from various suppliers to replace their existing dependence on mainframes. In an effort to thwart the insurgence of new architectures, the bank's information technology department sought out new solutions. The result was to keep the IBM mainframes in place and use them as a repository for all bank transactions.

Since much of what a bank does is based on transaction processing, the mainframe applications were preserved. However, what did change was the networking solution. Using the IBM mainframe as the server in this situation, the bank installed a group of LANs, eliminating the reliance on coax-attached 3278/3279 devices and placing more intelligence on the desktop. Using IBM's OS/2 operating systems for the LANs was a given in this situation. Then, to link more than 100 branch offices back to the mainframe server, the bank used IBM's Nuways routers from each of the offices back to the central processing facility.

This solution was total IBM, although it was a close call. The bank did evaluate other solutions in this change. Initially, the need for routers was close because of the preponderance of Cisco routers in the South African marketplace. Secondly, the bank considered using a database engine from SAP AG in Germany. From an internetworking perspective, this combination may have made sense. Many organizations have already made the switch to this form of architecture. In this particular case, however, the bank IT group recognized that SNA still offered solutions without the need to change all of the operating software and applications. To convert the code and to rebuild the entire applications base would have been far too expensive. The IT group was convinced that this was its best solution and stayed with SNA/SDLC for its transaction-processing environment. Training was limited because users were already somewhat familiar with the screens and forms. The main need imposed on the bank included LAN access training and the ability to integrate front-office functionality to the user on a GUI-driven system.

SNA is still a connection-oriented protocol using the definition of an end point. The LAN node was addressed in this architecture as the LU 6.2 end point. The network isolated the user from the physical network

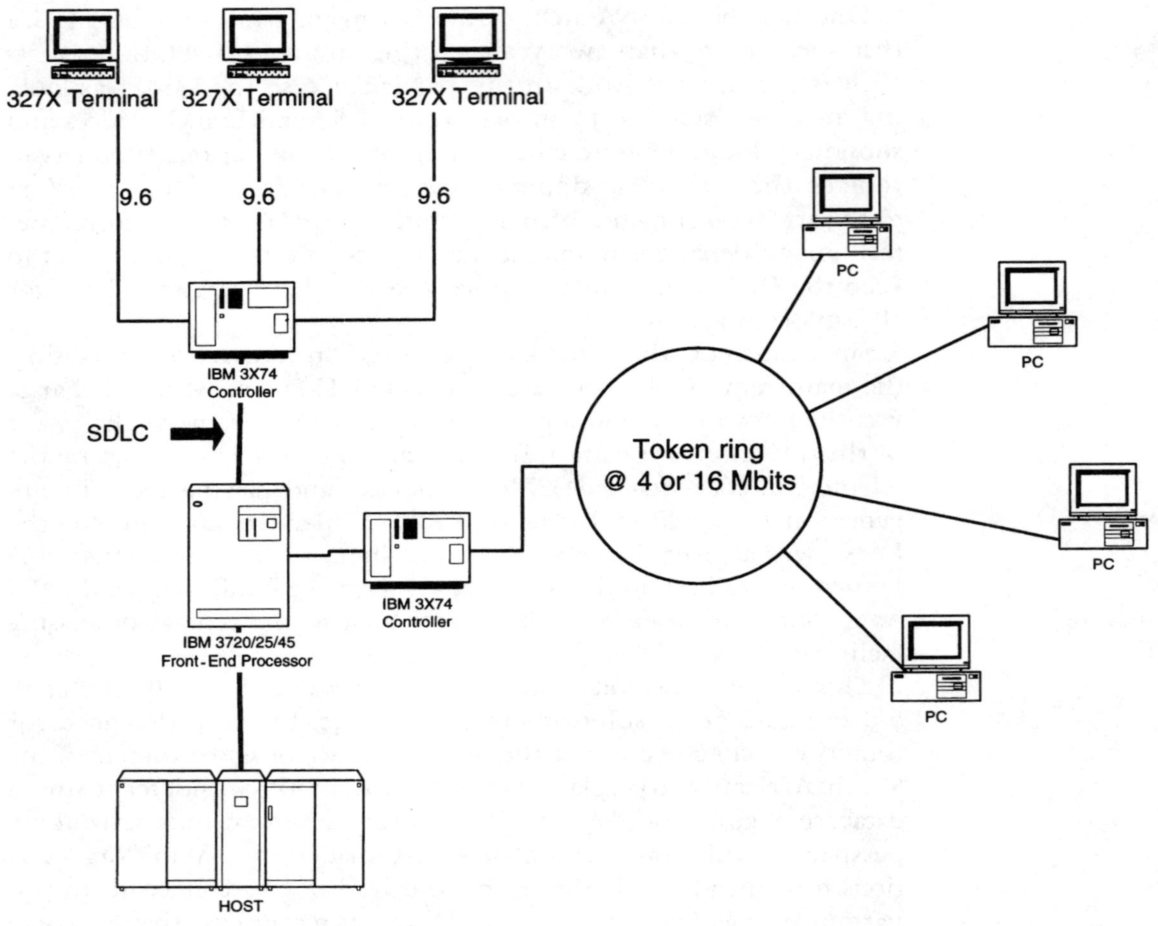

Figure 6.1 Mixing and matching 327X terminals and LANs in the SNA architecture.

devices as an SNA node would normally do. Figure 6.1 shows the network as finally designed. Several dumb terminal 3278/3279 devices remained intact, allowing some of the end users to stay on the network unchanged. Where no changes were necessary, none were made.

Distributed processing is IBM's goal using SNA/SDLC. Many organizations are in a mode to change from their mainframe. However, the mainframe still offers some solutions in a client/server network. It is not easily displaced, because too much time and money have been invested in developing the original solutions. Consequently, IBM evolved the SNA architecture to meet the changing needs of organizations. Where the SNA systems do not meet the overall goals of the organization, IBM came up with the next step. Introducing the Systems Application Architecture (SAA) through Advanced Peer to Peer Networking (APPN) and an Advanced Program to Program Communications (APPC) solution, the organization may still be able to preserve 80 to 90 percent of the original networking investment.

With SNA and APPN/APPC, the ability to internetwork is possible as an interim solution. Although the peer-to-peer implication in APPN varies from the client/server concept, the actual master-slave computing infrastructure is the primary implementation. The mainframe can therefore be preserved as a central repository, and the internetwork can facilitate the connectivity through the three-computer architecture. The LAN node (PC) running an OS/2 network operating system is connected through the LAN to a LAN-based server. This server can issue remote procedure calls (RPCs) to the mainframe, offloading the work function to the application server. The mainframe acts as the data repository or data warehouse.

Using the IBM approach, many organizations can install client/server architectures without the need to redeploy an entirely new set of operating systems and hardware platforms. This does not imply that the use of IBM's SNA in the server world disallows the use of other platforms. To the contrary, a Novell NetWare or Windows NT architecture at the client layer allows access to the SNA server through a solid gateway platform. Now the two architectures can act as a hybrid to serve the needs of the organization. In Fig. 6.2, the Novell NetWare solution is shown with the client running NetWare while the server is running SNA/SDLC. Although it is using a simple e-mail application, the same rules apply for access to transaction processing. In Fig. 6.3, the SNA protocol stack is used as a comparison for access from the NetWare architectural stack. This comparison uses the various levels of protocol support for the various applications.

SNA and NT

Another method of preserving the SNA architecture is to use a combination of Microsoft Windows NT and the host-based SNA. The use of Windows NT is a coming approach that offers a lot of flexibility and robust connectivity. Originally, the NT networking strategy was considered a

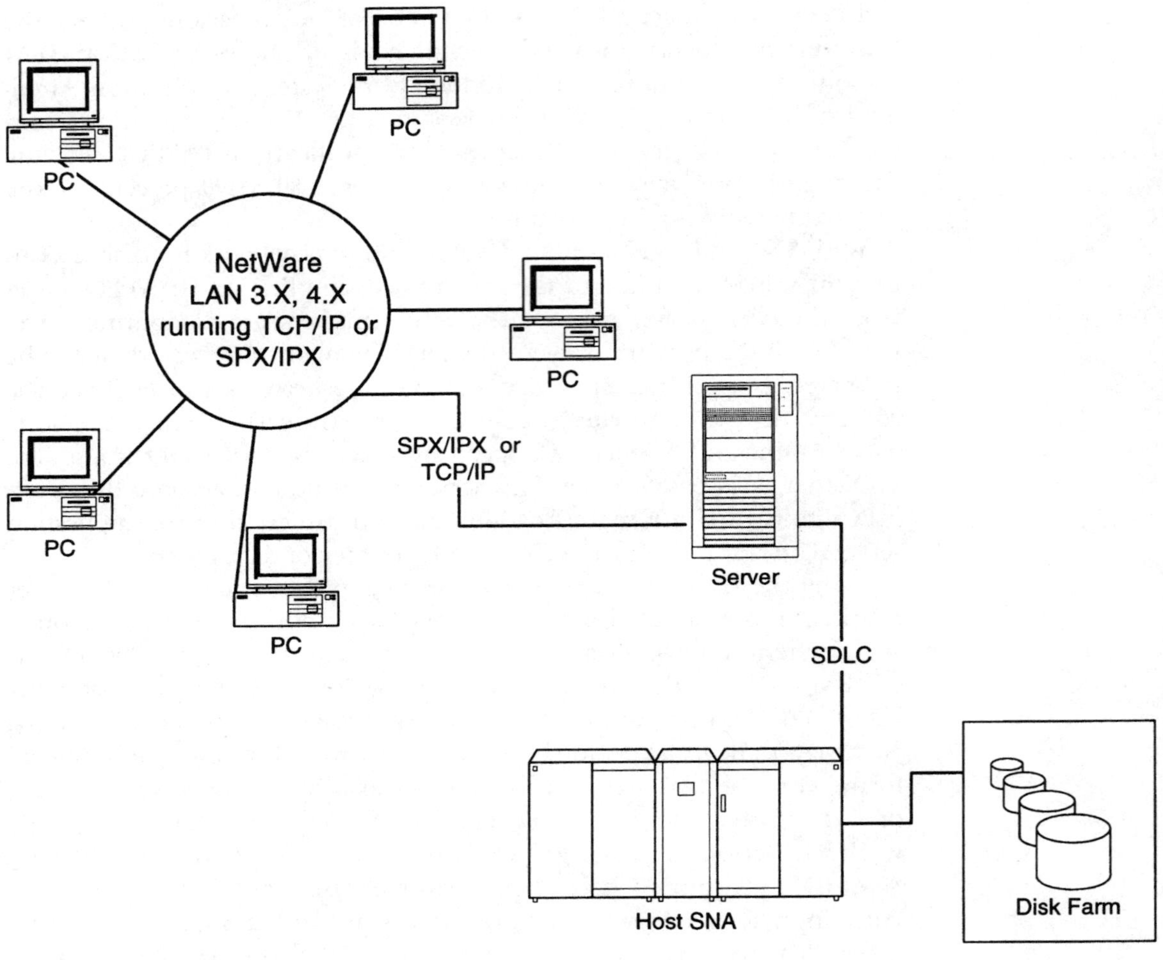

Figure 6.2 Clients running on Novell's NetWare but accessing the SNA server.

minor influence in the overall client/server architecture marketplace. Users felt that it was too little, too late. Microsoft improved the NT architecture dramatically, introducing the SNA server and offering the ability to use the full complement of the 32-bit architecture and operating system to incorporate these two architectures together.

IBM obviously had a different approach with the use of its OS/2 architecture for LAN and WAN connectivity for the client/server

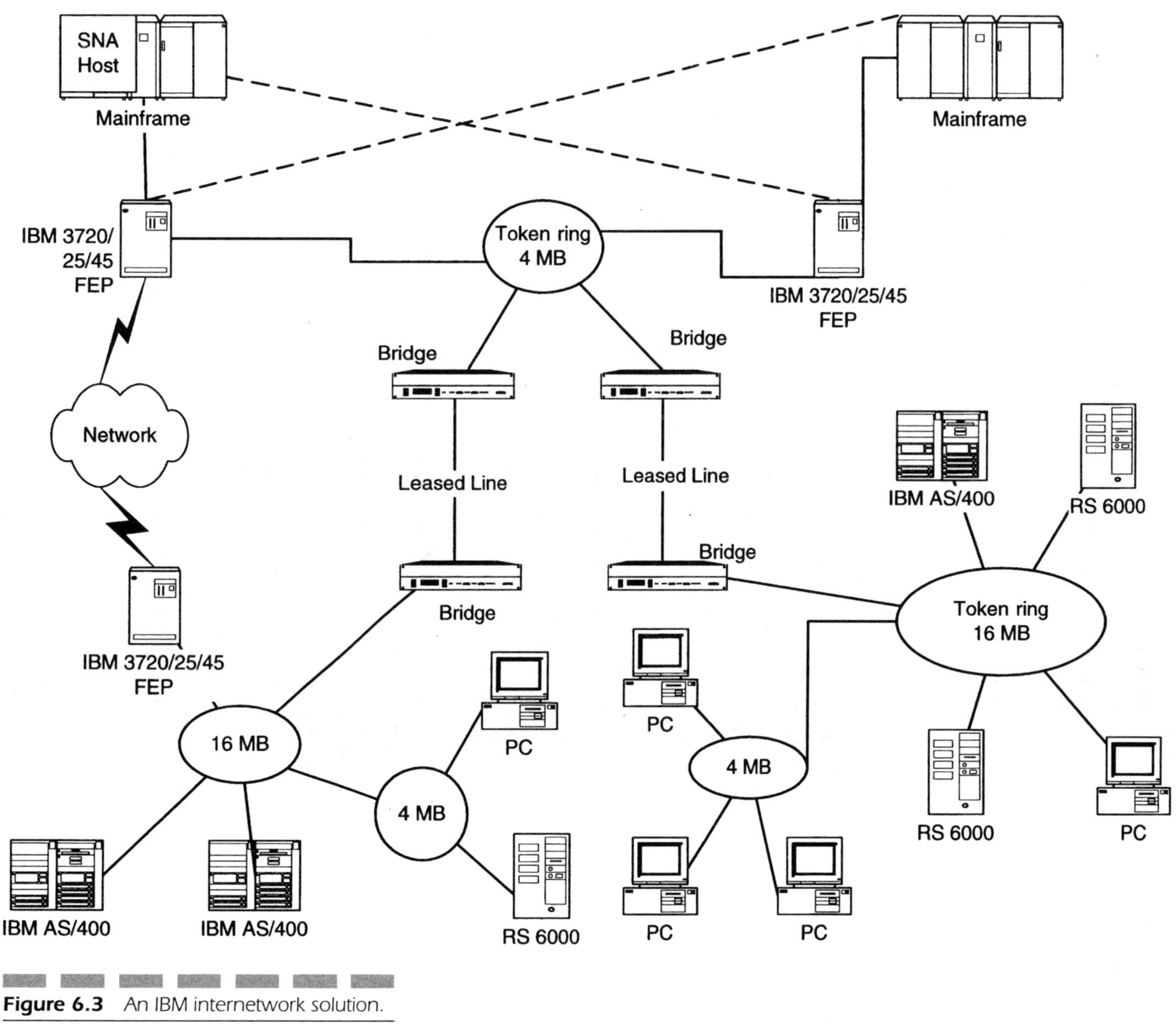

Figure 6.3 An IBM internetwork solution.

networks it was marketing. The introduction of the PowerPC, which is destined to infiltrate the LAN networking strategies of a massive customer base, was originally related to the OS/2 platform. However, recent announcements from IBM present a different picture. The operating system that will likely emerge as the basis for the high-end PowerPC interconnected in a client/server network will be NT. Therefore, the use of Microsoft's architecture in conjunction with the SNA architectures in place complements the overall networking installations at many organizations.

The SNA server makes use of an enterprise-wide connection that is both easy to configure and economical to use. The SNA server provides the consistency of today's desktop Windows-based interfaces with the strength of the LAN architectures to access the host-based SNA systems. Using the advances of the client/server architecture to distribute corporate processing and communications capabilities, the desktop device uses standard LAN-based protocols (even NetWare and TCP/IP) to access the servers running SNA protocols somewhat transparently. The SNA communications infrastructure uses the SNA protocols to provide all of the sharing of links to the hosts, reducing the need for extra storage and processing power on the desktop devices and simplifying the need for multiple protocols on the PC. Fortunately, the ability to provide management across bridged or router-based networks is also included using NT's remote access services (RAS).

The SNA server has other distinct advantages in that it does not add any burdens on the devices in the client domain, nor does it limit the type and number of LAN-based protocols you can support. It does allow for the ease of integration of multivendor and multiprotocol support that is common in enterprise networks. Scalable bandwidth utilization is possible on this architecture, thereby reducing the need to add resources to the existing network infrastructure. Figure 6.4 shows a central host-based system with the combination of the NT and SNA architectures in place. This figure shows the benefits of using the two architectures to combine the best of both worlds in the client/server network.

Following the centralized networking need is the ability to link remote sites together with a host-based solution. Figure 6.5 shows the remote branch office environment. This architecture takes advantage of the remote clients using the LAN-based protocols and the WAN-based SNA/SDLC protocols. While individual servers are remotely located and distributed around the organization, the NT SNA server is

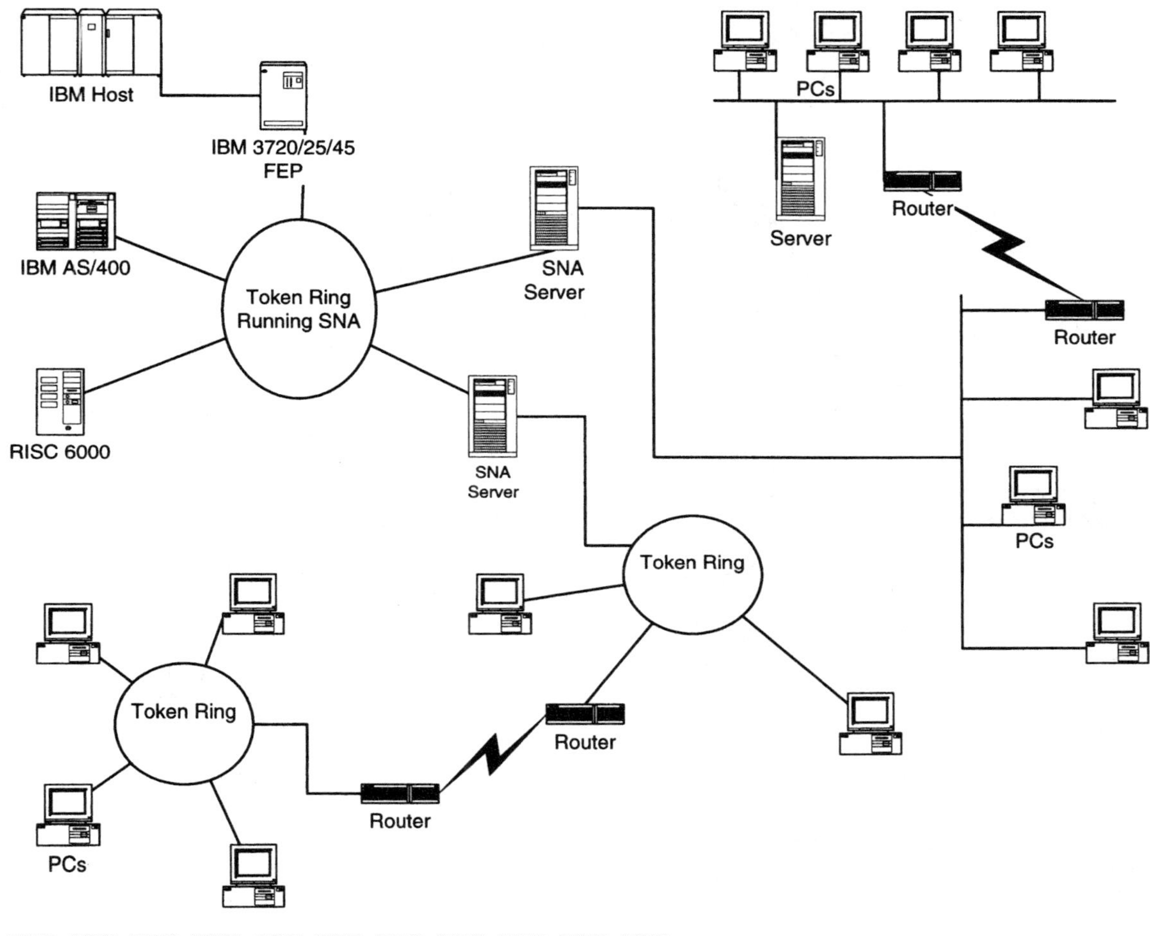

Figure 6.4 The SNA server in a centralized host environment.

used as a multifunctional device. It provides the necessary applications and protocol support for the branch office and, at the same time, the WAN connectivity server function to the remote host running SNA.

Table 6.1 shows the analysis of features and functions of the NT SNA server. This list is not all-inclusive, but it does address the most common interfaces and protocols in use today. The table shows the benefits of comparing an architecture and the supporting subsets that can be integrated to form the true internetwork.

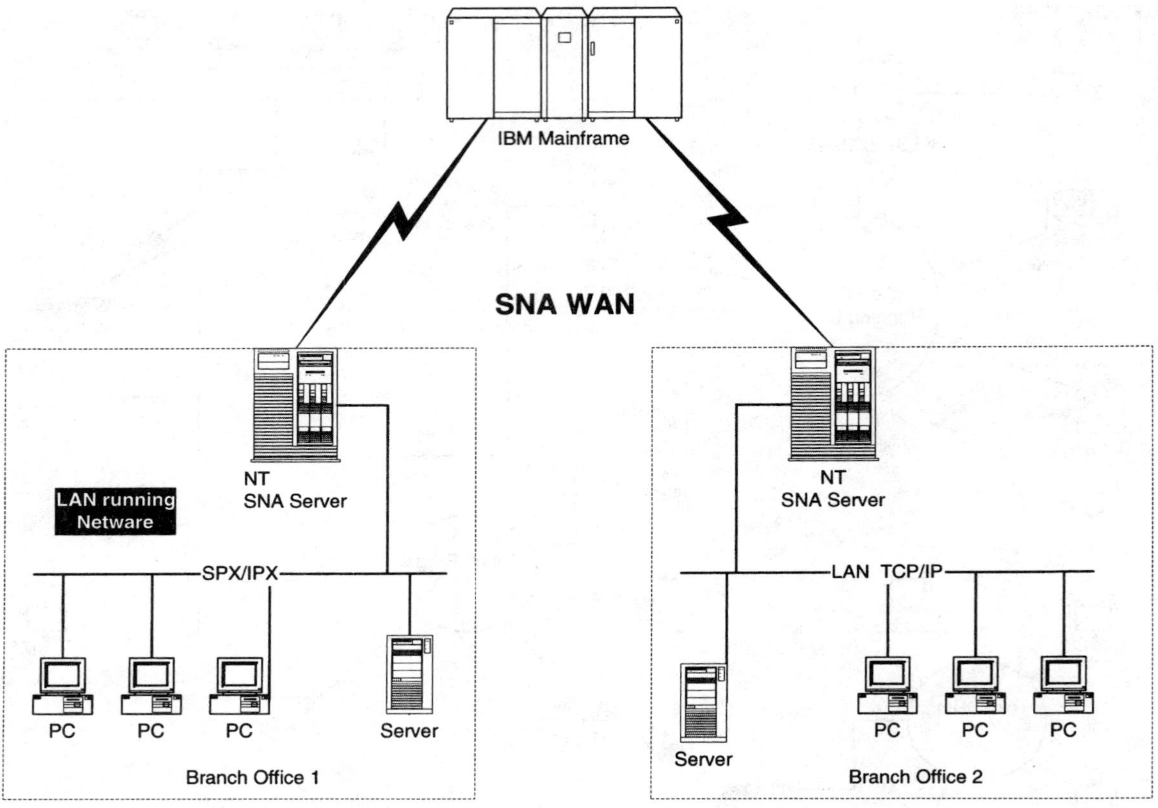

Figure 6.5 Using an SNA server for a remote office.

From this table we see that a combination of protocols and physical devices can be linked. In Fig. 6.6, this major network internetworking solution is shown with myriad connectivity schemes included—the heart of what the entire client/server internetworking strategy is all about.

SNA and Novell's NetWare

One can integrate several different approaches in a client/server architecture. Using one of the industry's largest market-share holders, Novell, the client/server network can come together nicely. In this case, one can inte-

TABLE 6.1

A Summary of the NT SNA Server Features

Item	Description
SNA protocol support	Physical unit 2.0; APPN LEN node; TN 3270; logical units 0, 1, 2, 3, and 6.2
Data link protocol support	802.2 LLC; Token Ring (802.5); Ethernet (802.3); SDLC (leased line or switched service); X.25; Twinax; channel attach
Client/server protocols	TCP/IP; IPX/SPX; Vines; AppleTalk; others
SNA distributed APIs	APPC using LU 6.2; LUA using LU 0, 1, 2, and 3; others
Server capacities	2000 clients/server; 10,000 LU sessions/server; 50 SNA servers on NT per domain
RAS support	SNA over RAS using dial-up, X.25, or ISDN; RAS over SNA using LU 6.2
Emulation protocols supported	5250; 3270; TN3270
Security	C2-level security integrated in NT

grate the connectivity through various service and feature offerings from Novell, as shown in Fig. 6.7. The SNA Branch Office solution allows the remote LAN user to gain access to the IBM mainframe running SNA. The Branch Office suite of Novell-based products allows both mainframe and AS/400 access applications while sharing the file, print, messaging, and hub services. A single branch office server is all that is needed with the SNA service installed. One benefit of using this setup as a connectivity solution is the reduced need for IBM data-processing personnel at each of the remote sites. The administration and management functions can be provided at the corporate central location and be transparent to the remote office.

NetWare SNA Branch Office also provides the key functionality to internetwork the remote offices. Some of these features are shown in Table 6.2.

One can see why this option provides a simple and efficient service. NetWare 3.x and above are the most popular and widely used network software installations in the world. In the LAN arena, Novell has approximately 65 percent of the overall operating systems installed. One cannot ignore the powerful marriage of these two products.

NetWare for SAA provides the connection and the resource-sharing mechanism for the network and host environment. Where an organization has an existing hierarchical network installed, it does not make sense to attempt to scrap this architecture and start anew. Therefore, NetWare for SAA allows the clean connection of the branch office to the

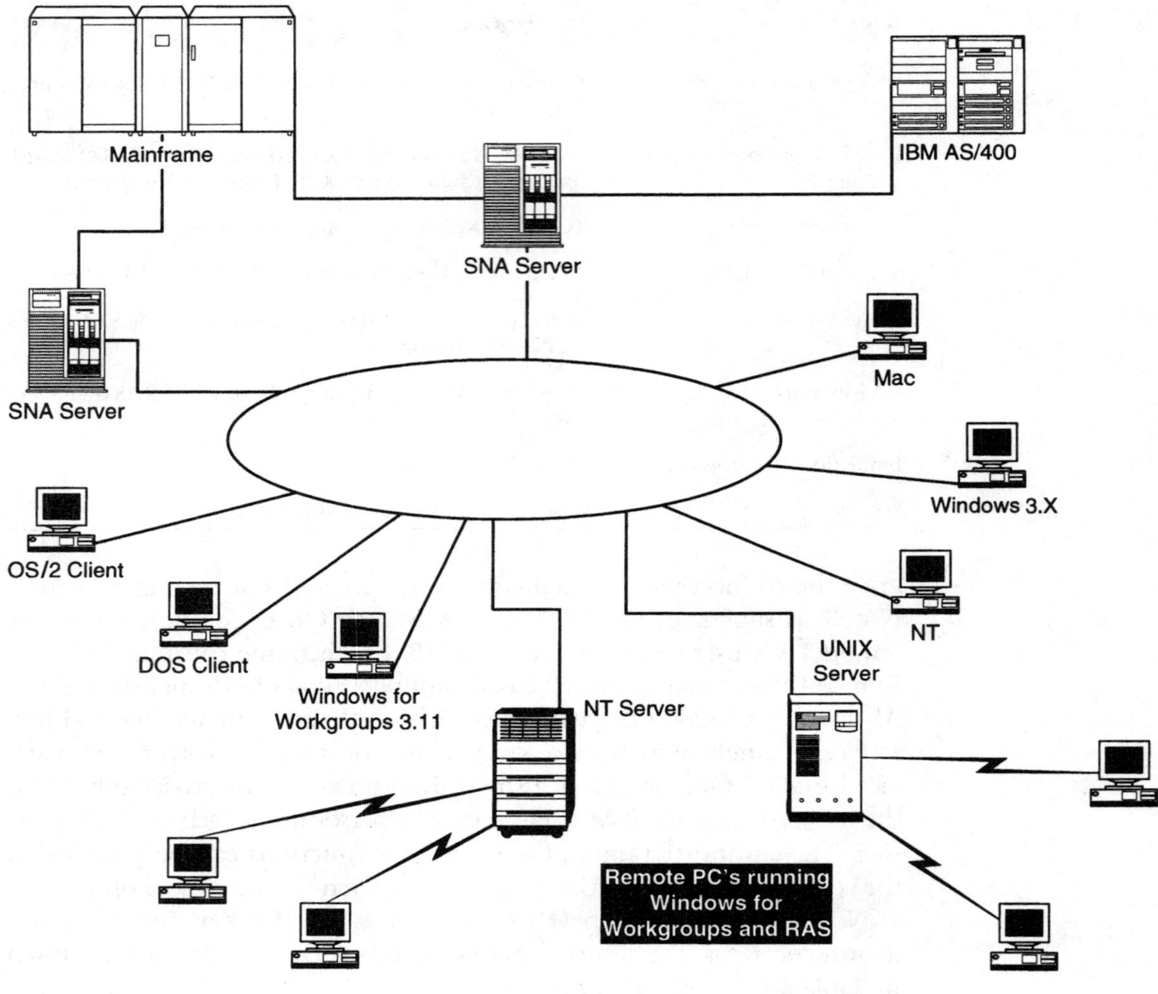

Figure 6.6 The true client/server internetwork supports myriad operating clients.

SNA mainframes and AS/400s among the locations. If an existing leased- or switched-line network is already in place supporting an SNA link network, then the NetWare for SNA links application allows communications over the existing SNA links. This setup provides such features as e-mail and network management over an SDLC link, as shown in Fig. 6.8. The global MHS gateways allow electronic messaging among multiple sites for a wide array of services, such as automation for mail, forms, fax services, and workflow products. NetWare hub services let you build an

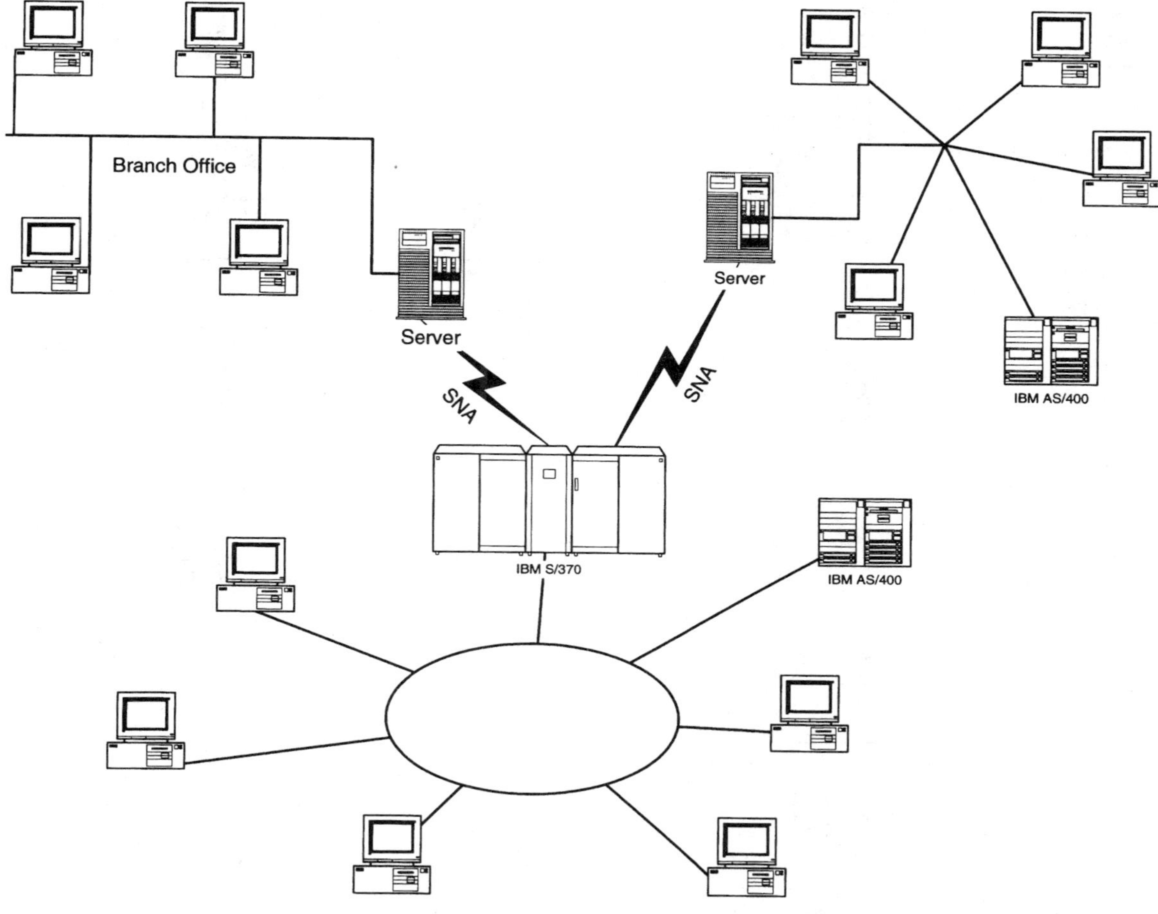

Figure 6.7 Using NetWare at the branch office to link mainframe and AS400s in an SNA environment.

TABLE 6.2

Integration Services from NetWare SNA Branch Office

1. NetWare 3.12 or later for up to 25 users
2. NetWare for SAA supporting 16 sessions
3. NetWare SNA links
4. NetWare global message handling services supporting 50 users
5. NetWare hub services
6. NetWare management agent services

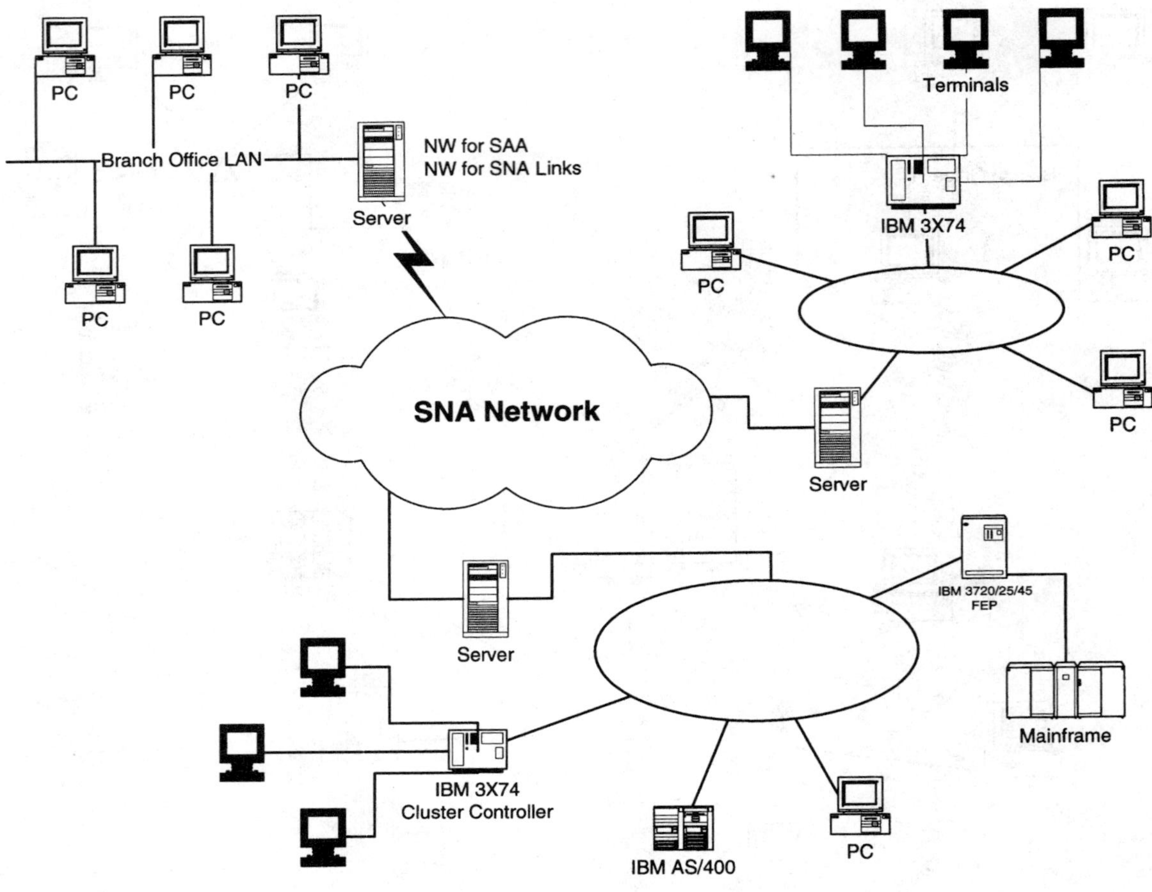

Figure 6.8 NetWare for SAA supports geographically dispersed NetWare LANs.

intelligent hub function in the file server, eliminating the need for separate hubs and their associated proprietary management schemes.

Another service from Novell is the NetWare host printing capability. The end user needs access to the server-based IBM printer without constraining the capability of the workstation's memory and CPU to run other applications. This access allows for better use of the network and the ability to centrally manage and control the print services. In this setup, an NetWare Loadable Module[1] (NLM) offers IBM

1. A NetWare Loadable Module is a NetWare-based module offered by Novell or third parties.

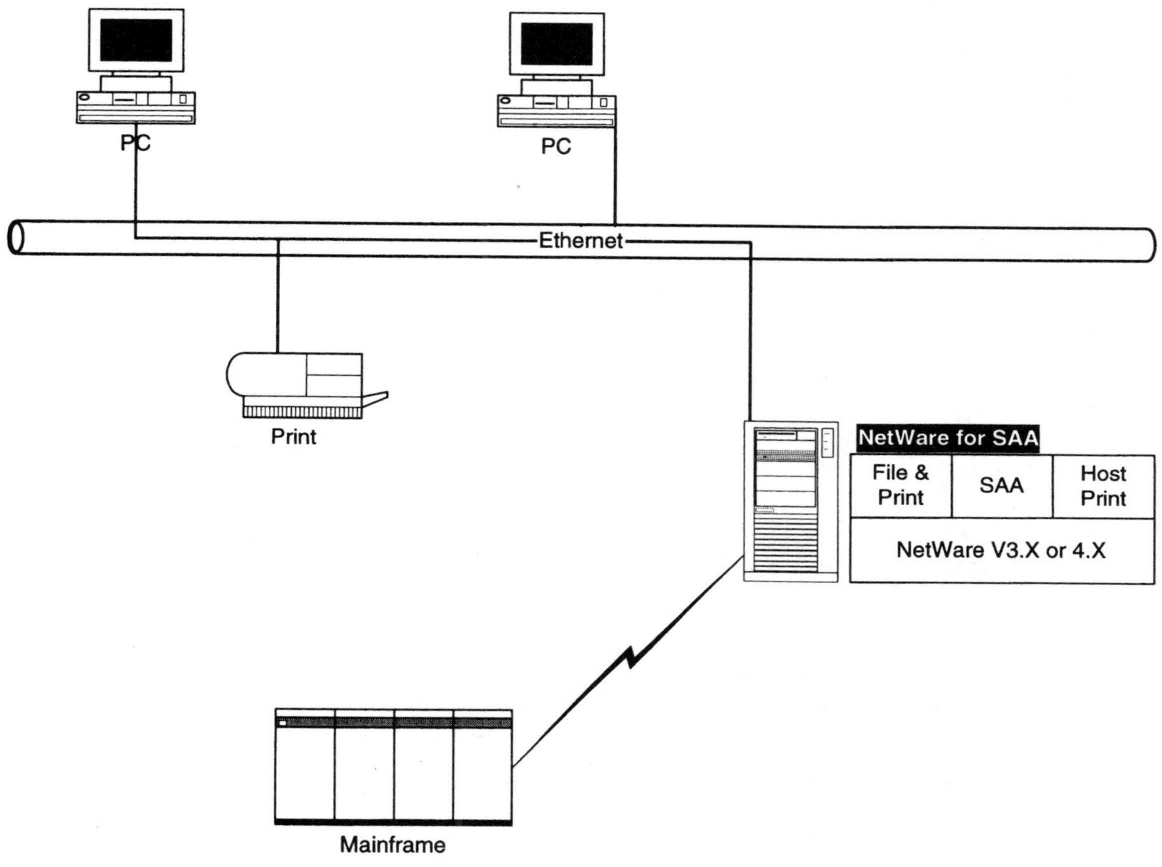

Figure 6.9 The host print function provides IBM print emulation.

3270 LU1 and LU3 printer emulation that coexists with the NetWare for SAA server. Interfaces to the normal print queues on the LAN are provided transparently. In Fig. 6.9. we show the server environment with NetWare for SAA on a LAN. From there, the addition of the host print service is added at the workstation level. Note that this platform has the various hooks to the file and print capabilities, as well as the host print service. Figure 6.10 shows the NetWare server with and without the host print function. The flow between the devices is shown as a more complex operation (Fig. 6.10*a*). Eliminating this complexity is performed with the use of the host print NLM, as shown in

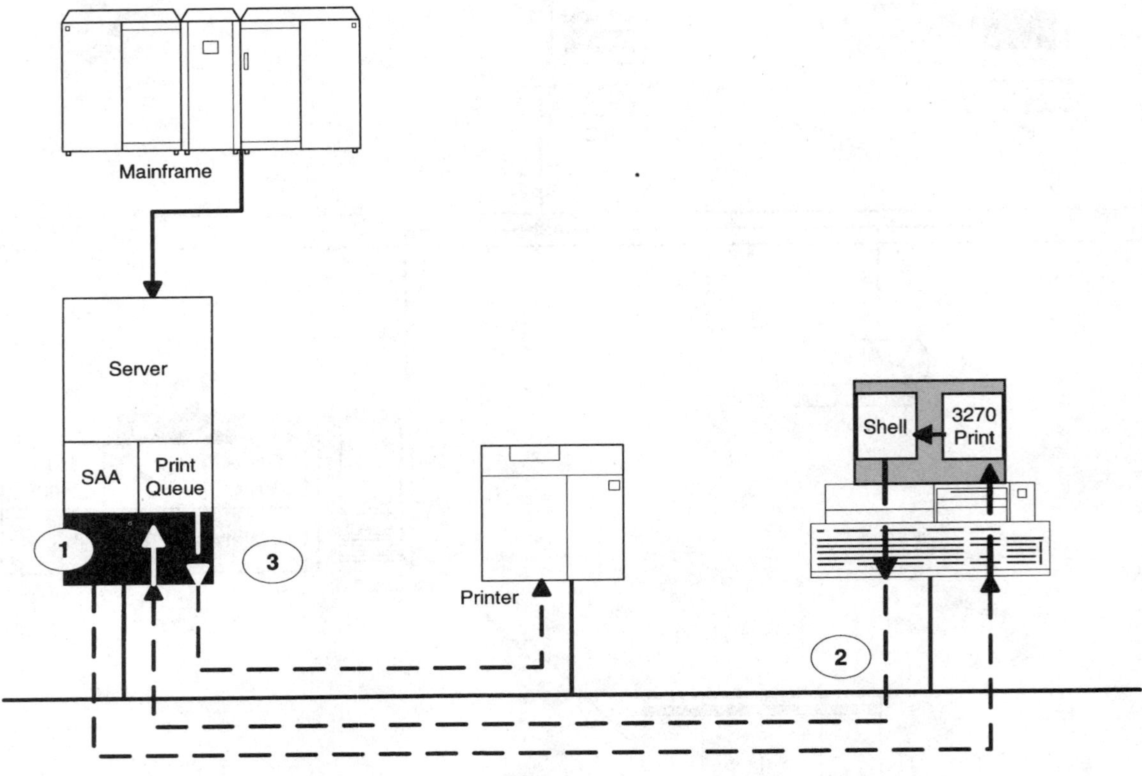

Figure 6.10*a* Without host print, the process is more complex and uses the PC CPU and memory to print.

Fig. 6.10*b*. Note the simplicity in this configuration, which uses the print queues to perform the host print function by offloading the extra overhead from the individual workstation. This configuration frees up the end user's CPU from the work and spares the memory usage.

The SNA internetworking schemes within a client/server once provided a significant challenge to the manager of the overall network. Data-processing departments struggled with the question of whether to replace the older mainframe and the SNA architecture with the new client/server PC and midrange computing platforms. However, if this decision went away from the mainframe, how then would the conversion be handled easily? The solutions are less difficult with the two architectures complementing each other in this networking topology serving both the LAN and the WAN services for the organization. Additionally, newer applications can be migrated off the host onto the

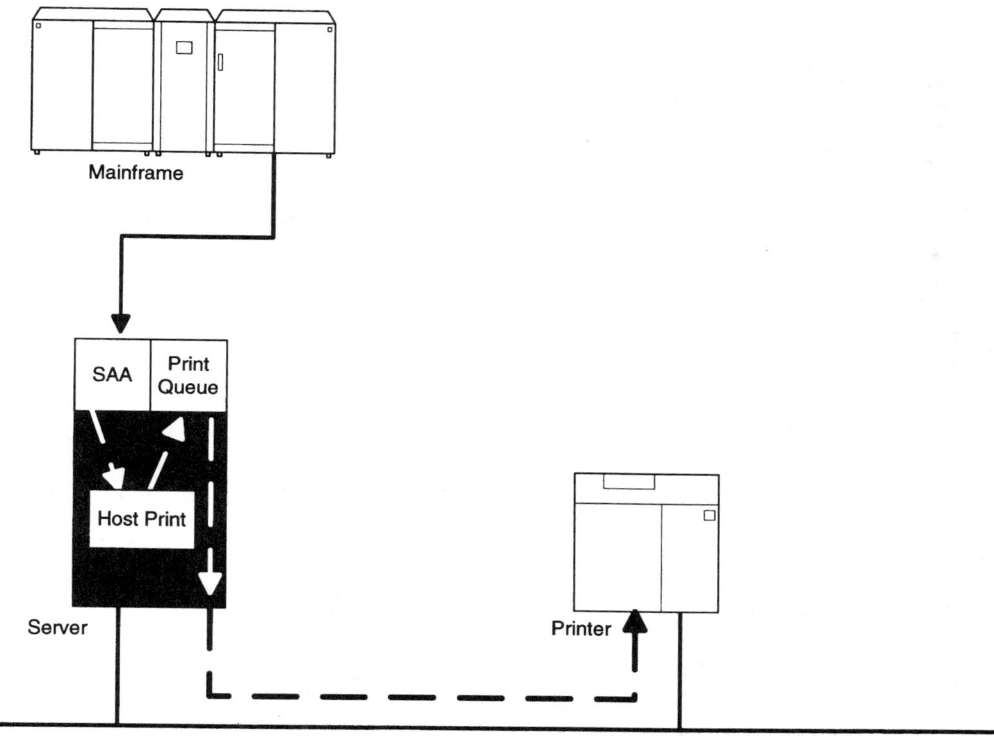

Figure 6.10b With the host print function, the PC is removed from the cycle, simplifying the process.

lower-end servers as time passes without the need to abandon all of the older applications and code written and tuned over the past 30 years. Lest this sound like a IBM/SNA-only solution, understand that this is one of many architectures that emerged as a winner. Others exist and are discussed in subsequent sections.

TCP/IP Architectures

It is important to note that TCP/IP is a de facto standard and not a de jure standard developed by the international and industry standards bodies. TCP/IP is a set of routed protocols and, as such, the use of its robustness is extremely popular in a client/server internetwork. We can understand and

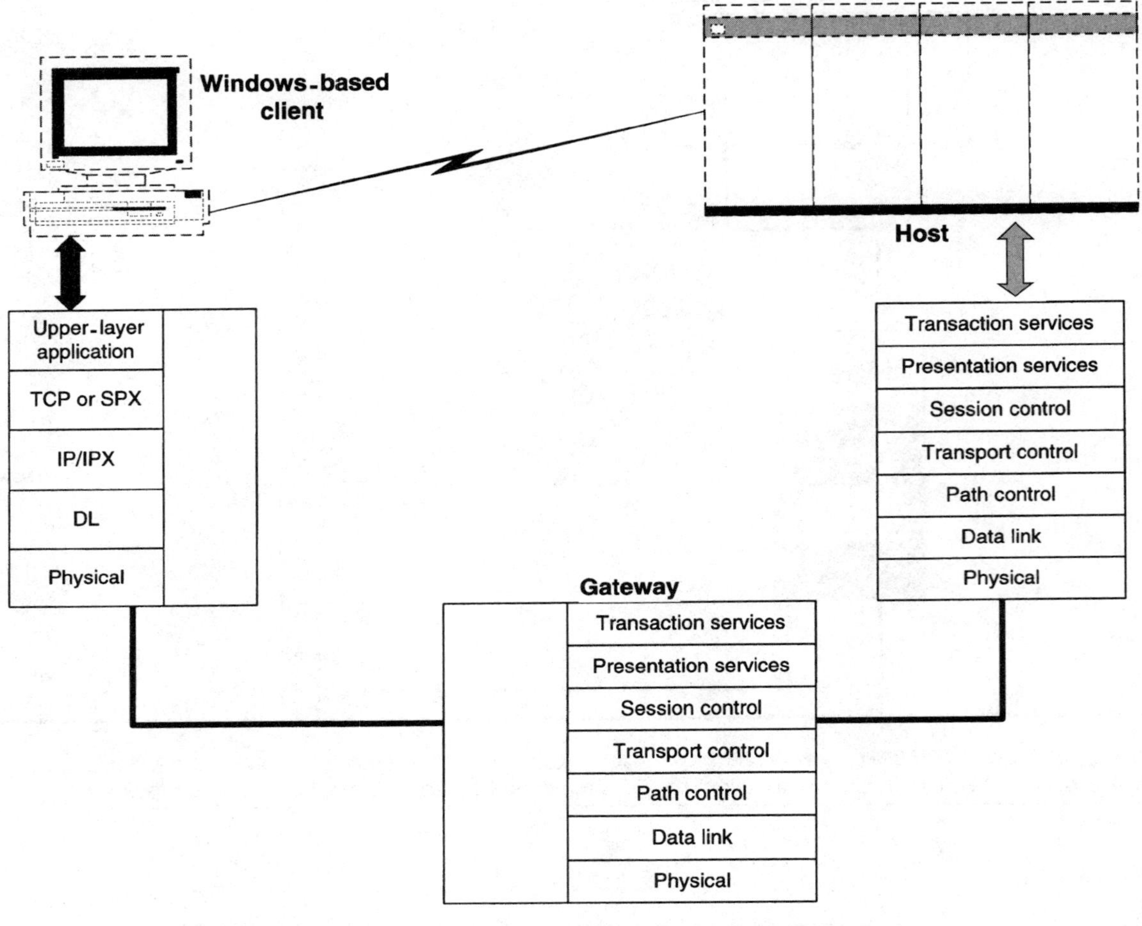

Figure 6.11 Matching the protocol stacks (Novell and TCP/IP) in an SNA architecture.

appreciate the importance of this architecture of protocols when we see in how many different environments TCP/IP is used. From the LAN area, we see TCP/IP emerging as an accepted set of protocols in use with Microsoft's Windows, Windows 95, and NT. Further, in Novell NetWare environments, many organizations have installed a dual stack of IPX/SPX and TCP/IP, as shown in Fig. 6.11. This installation allows a network the flexibility of using Novell's protocols when applicable and TCP/IP when required for interconnectivity between other platforms, such as HP, DecNet, SNA, and NT. The use of TCP/IP is rapidly surpassing other sets.

As possibly the widest set of protocols in use today, this architecture allows for total transparency in the client/server internetworking architecture. It provides support for many of the data link protocols, as shown in Fig. 6.12, and just about all LAN services and other subnetworks can adapt readily to TCP/IP implementations. It is not without its limitations, but its strengths far outweigh its shortcomings. When considering what architecture to use, remember that this one set of protocols can mitigate some of the other complexities of the proprietary architectures available in the marketplace. Many users and opponents of this architecture continually bring up the overhead associated with TCP/IP, but once again, the overhead, although hefty, can be overcome through other techniques. It allows you to support myriad operating systems and architectures on a single platform.

Above and beyond the actual protocol stack, TCP/IP includes very robust methods of data transfer dealing with just about all internetworking issues. Through the use of a middleware function in the client/server world, it provides support from all operating systems manufacturers and interfaces to most of the wide area networking schemes in place or planned today. Using techniques to map TCP/IP addressing schemes to a frame relay, ATM, or SMDS wide area network, the TCP/IP service becomes transparent. Further, at the subnet level, Ethernet, token ring, and token passing bus architecture are all fully supported. Every hardware manufacturer of computing systems, routers, bridges, and other associated peripheral devices offers support for the TCP/IP architecture. Whole TCP/IP networks have emerged from major players in the industry (such as IBM) as a transport system and an architecture to support a wide array of connections around the world.

In Fig. 6.12, we see a network of many complex pieces that support the client/server network across a LAN, CAN, MAN, and WAN. How many other architectures fit into the same amount of service areas as simply as this one stack? The answer is very few, and they can be counted on one hand. Since it is widely implemented on UNIX platforms, integrated on NetWare and SNA, integral to NT, fully supported by the midrange computer manufacturers, and standard on the super servers, one can take comfort in considering TCP/IP as the architecture of choice. For all intents and purposes, this one set of protocols forms the basis of the internetworking model. It has a common means of reaching any node on a network through the use of the IP addressing scheme. TCP/IP deals well with the public-domain specifications through the use of its IP and UDP protocols. TCP/IP also uses sockets (the combination of IP address and port associated with a LAN address) to provide the necessary connectivity.

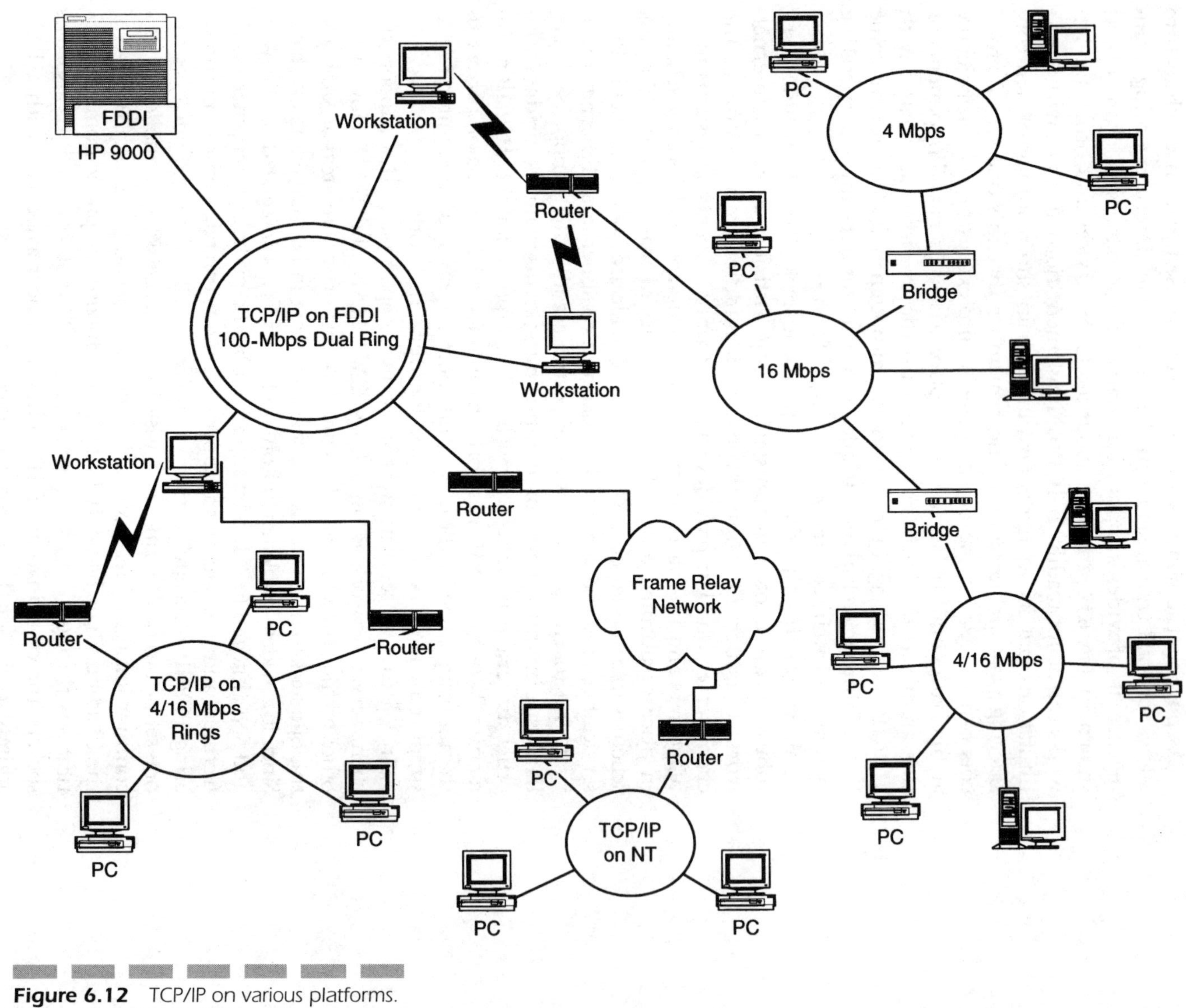

Figure 6.12 TCP/IP on various platforms.

IP

IP is a connectionless-oriented service that handles each packet (segment) as a stand-alone, independent data-transfer element. It routes its packets between dissimilar networks and remains transparent while doing so. IP makes its best effort to deliver each packet, but it does not guarantee delivery. Reliable and guaranteed delivery is not a function of IP but of higher-level protocols, such as TCP. IP is also not concerned with the integrity of the data it transports across the network; that again belongs to a higher level of protocols in the overall stack. This fact gives IP its robustness, allowing it to carry the data independently and quickly. If something goes wrong, IP ignores the problem. If something happens to totally corrupt the data and the header, then IP merely discards the packet and goes on to the next one. Many data-processing and network managers find this somewhat disconcerting, feeling that the protocols should pay more attention to the sequencing and reliable delivery of the data. However, in real life, when this problem happens in other protocols, the delay in dealing with the data can be excessive. Rather than bog down the entire network, it is far simpler to let a higher level of intelligence be responsible for the data integrity.

Looking at the IP layer in the networking scenario, we see the overall connection in Fig. 6.13. IP is the networking layer in the internetwork and handles the equivalent lower three layers of the OSI model. Using the addressing scheme (class of network), the IP mechanism supports a significant number of interconnections. Enough has been said in the industry about how addressing works. Table 6.3 summarizes the actual numbers of addresses available. These are the public-domain networks' addresses; one cannot predict how many organizations have established and installed their own private networks using a proprietary or private network addressing scheme with IP.

TCP

TCP is the actual traffic cop that puts everything back together in an orderly fashion. TCP is a connection-oriented protocol and has to know that the two connection points exist. The two points are not the individual end points, but the two network points or sockets used in the application layer of the connection. This part of the protocol stack and architecture is responsible for guaranteed data delivery that is properly

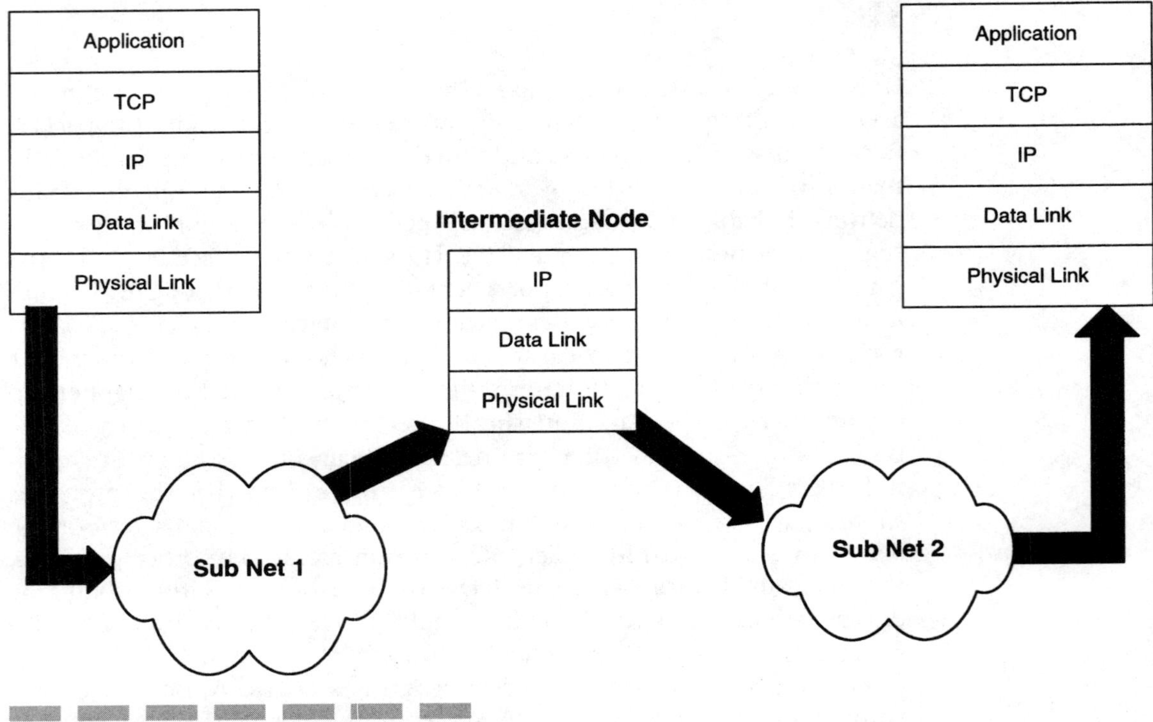

Figure 6.13 The IP function in a network.

sequenced with true integrity. Therefore, TCP must ensure concurrency and sequencing of the data back into the original form, as well as error checking and recovery. If a segment arrives corrupted, IP delivers it to TCP. TCP, on the other hand, requests a retransmission from the originating end device. Once the data is checked and properly sequenced, TCP then provides the connection to the end application. Supporting many different higher-level layers of the OSI model, TCP provides the interfaces to

- Network file systems (NFS)
- Remote printing
- Remote program execution
- Name services and domain name services (DNS)
- Networking windowing and X services
- E-mail (SMTP)

TABLE 6.3 The Yield of Networks and Nodes Using IP Addressing Scheme

Class	Network header	Network number	Host number	Yields	
				Networks	Hosts
A	0	7 bits	24 bits	128	16,777,216
B	10	14 bits	16 bits	16,384	65,536
C	110	21 bits	8 bits	2,097,152	256
D	1110	Multicast			

- Telnet services for terminal emulation (virtual terminal)
- File transfer protocols (FTP)

TCP is a very robust interface and architecture in supporting the overall networking needs of a client/server world. In Fig. 6.14, we summarize the connection to the SNA architecture by connecting TCP/IP systems to a host through a cluster controller (3172/3174) to a TCP/IP stack running on the host. This connection can be achieved in many ways, as shown in this single figure. It can be made using gateways or separate protocol stacks to access the host print queues; it can access applications through the sockets and the front-end processor through a LAN running TCP/IP. One can see the true robustness of a single architecture, but when it is combined with others that serve application- or program-specific needs, we can only look at it as the glue that holds everything together.

OSF

As stated earlier in this book, the Open Systems Foundation is currently working on the Distributed Computing Environment (DCE) and the Distributed Management Environment (DME) to solve the ills of past interconnections and interoperabilities. This architecture will be a contender in the client/server networking arena in the future. Although it is not a simple product or family of products that one can easily purchase and install, significant strides have been made to improve its user adaptability. The OSF created the foundation of openness to allow the end user to access computing power regardless of where it is. Further, the goal of OSF is to empower the end user with the computing resources necessary to

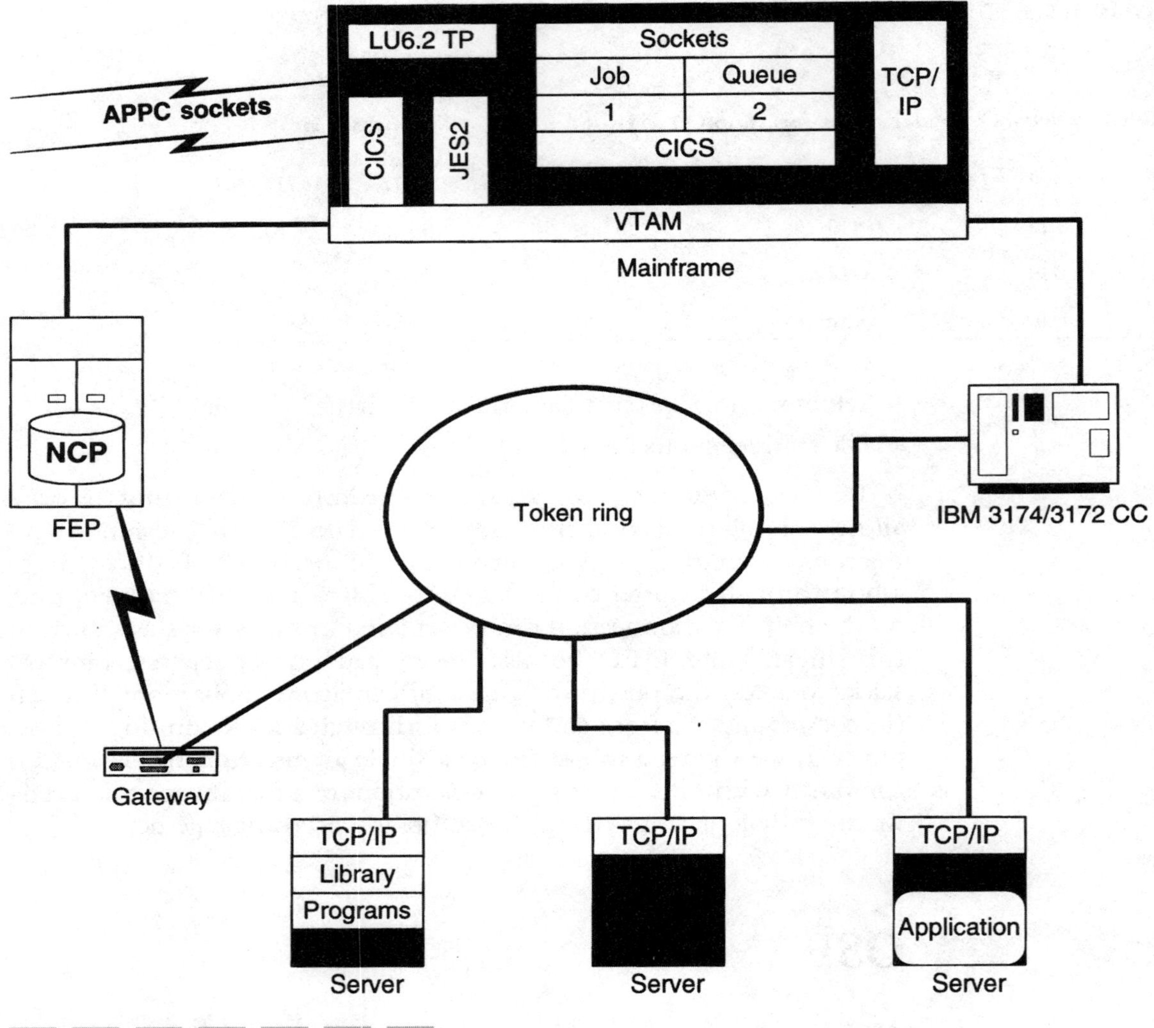

Figure 6.14 Linking hosts with TCP/IP.

accomplish the mission at hand. This empowerment means that the user can access any resource through a mix of various vendor products and services. The OSF's DCE and DME are designed to take the best techniques from a mix of vendors that sponsored the development effort. The vendors included in the DCE development are Digital Equipment Corporation, Fujitsu, Hewlett Packard, Sun Microsystems, and several others.

Nothing comes without a price, but we do know that in the long run, DCE and DME will have significant benefits in the client/server world.

TABLE 6.4

Summary of Manufacturers and Platforms for DCE Architecture

Manufacturer	Operating systems	Platform
IBM	AIX	Full coverage
	OS/2	Basic client
	Windows	No server support, basic DCE client
	OS/400	Basic client, no server
Sun Microsystems	SunOS	Full support
DEC	Dec-Ultrix	Full support
HP	HP-UX	Full support
Microsoft	Windows (3.x, 95, and NT)	Client only with restriction on preemptive tasking

Linking a three-tiered network architecture instead of the normal two-tiered network is one of the strengths of the OSF development. However, like any other set of operating systems and protocols, many variations in the implementation have occurred. Consequently, running a straight TCP/IP platform for UNIX or running a Windows 3.x-based system loses some of the functionality of the DCE. Threads and other cell-based operands are not as clean when variations are implemented. NetWare IPX can be a bottleneck and a detriment to running DCE. One must be very selective in choosing the appropriate sets of operating systems and protocols. In terms of topology, DCE is transparent. It works on the platforms and operating systems shown in Table 6.4.

CHAPTER 7

Carrier Offerings to Connect Client/Server Networks

Getting beyond the overall strategies for the client/server architectures and the hardware platforms needed to support the client and the server was a tedious process. As many organizations began their migration to this architecture for internetworking, they quickly discovered that after selecting the equipment and software, a new roadblock was introduced. This new roadblock is the cost and availability of transmission systems to support the speed and the data volume that is part of the internetwork. How can one get to the decision process of where to locate the data, what transport systems and protocols to use, and what price to pay, if, in fact, the transport systems will not support the rudimentary network? We get a rude awakening when we realize that in the late 1990s we still have to struggle to get the necessary bandwidth to the locations that need to be linked.

As the time drew near to implement a distributed computing architecture in support of a client/server internetwork, the last consideration was the communications infrastructure to support this network design. Even when vendors quoted connectivity, the hidden agenda was that it did not exist. Therefore, vendors had to mask the way the connections would take place. Let us learn from the misconceptions, misinterpretations, and general frustrations of the organizations that went before us. There is no such thing as a ubiquitous network for all locations at the same speed, access, and cost. The following guideline should help you to prepare for the inevitable shock you will get.

Rule: If all your locations are in downtown metropolitan areas in major National Football League (NFL) cities, you have a good shot at getting the speed and access that you need. If, however, you have locations that are remote, in the suburbs of the NFL cities, or in smaller, less populated areas, then the risk is that you will have to compromise your needs with your budgets.

Once accepted, this fact of life has less impact on the overall project plan than you may believe. As long as the situation is addressed up front, the plan can be modified to accommodate lack of services and carrier peculiarities. One can imagine that the network design will take longer to implement if this area is skimmed in the beginning stages and surfaces as a problem in the later stages of a network implementation. Why should this be so?

The Carriers

The carriers are quickly deploying several techniques throughout their networks to support the ever-changing needs and demands of

TABLE 7.1 Summary of Differing Offerings from Carriers

Technology	Local exchange carriers	Interexchange carriers
Leased lines	Yes	Yes
Dial-up analog service with modems	Yes	Yes
Packet data switching (X.25)	Limited	Yes
Switched multimegabit data services (SMDS)	Yes	Limited/no
Integrated Services Digital Networks (ISDN)	Yes, but proprietary in some LEC areas, distance-limited in others	Yes, but proprietary
Switched digital services	Yes	Yes
Frame relay	Yes	Yes
Transparent local network services (TLNS) dedicated	Yes	No
Asynchronous transfer mode (ATM)	Limited	Yes, but evolving
Fiber distributed data interface (FDDI)	Some	No
Wireless offerings	Some	Some
Customized offerings	Some	Some

the computing architectures. This, of course, is a problem for them as they do not know exactly which technology we need or want. In Table 7.1, we see a summary of the various alternatives available to an organization. This table is the foundation of the entire chapter as we discuss the options and the risks associated with each.

So where does this leave the end user who needs a clear connection across the network to link the distributed computing platforms? One can say that the end user is out of luck or must integrate various offerings into a homogenous network and hope that they all work together. The intent of this discussion is not to cast stones at the carriers—they are trying to get their offerings up to speed. However, the changing demands of our computing architectures and our organizations' data needs have the carriers in a catch-up mode. The standards committees take a significant amount of time to arrive at a standard technology and topology, placing the burden on de facto developers to fill in the gaps. The carriers get caught in this web all the time.

Defining the Role of the Carriers

What is the actual role of the carrier in supporting the client/server internetwork? One can say that their role is

> To provide the goods and services necessary to meet the changing needs of the customer's data and voice networking strategies. Further, the carriers are expected to provide a highly reliable, integrity-based, cost-efficient, and totally available network service.

Not a bad start at what we are looking for from these providers, but this role must be analyzed from the beginning. The differences among the various operators of the network are many.

Local Exchange Carriers

Local exchange carriers, for example, are constantly trying to deliver their services as allowed but limited by the local regulatory bodies. Recent changes in the telecommunications industry will revise all of the offerings and remove many of the constraints that were passed down over the years. In the United States, the Telecommunications Act of 1996 allows for competition in the local provisioning of services by the telephone companies (or LECs) and a myriad of new competitive entrants, called competitive LECs (CLECs). These suppliers are responsible for the communications connectivity in the local areas. The LECs, consisting of the Regional Bell Operating Companies and the more than 1460 independent companies (PTTs) in other countries around the world, try to provide as much service as possible, but they must make some decisions. Whenever an LEC wants to offer a new service in support of customers' needs, it must conduct a business case. This case determines just what the demand will be for a specific product. Following this business case, the next decision is what the price will be. In the regulated world of the LEC, this means that it must determine what the tariff will be and how to best offer the service. With many of the newer technologies, the LECs have been offering the service as a special pricing model not contained in the embedded base. The LEC is not lumping the cost of build-out for the service in its installed base for average costing, as required by the local regulators. Even in the rest of the world, many local suppliers (PTTs) are being deregulated to offer competitive services to an installed base of customers.

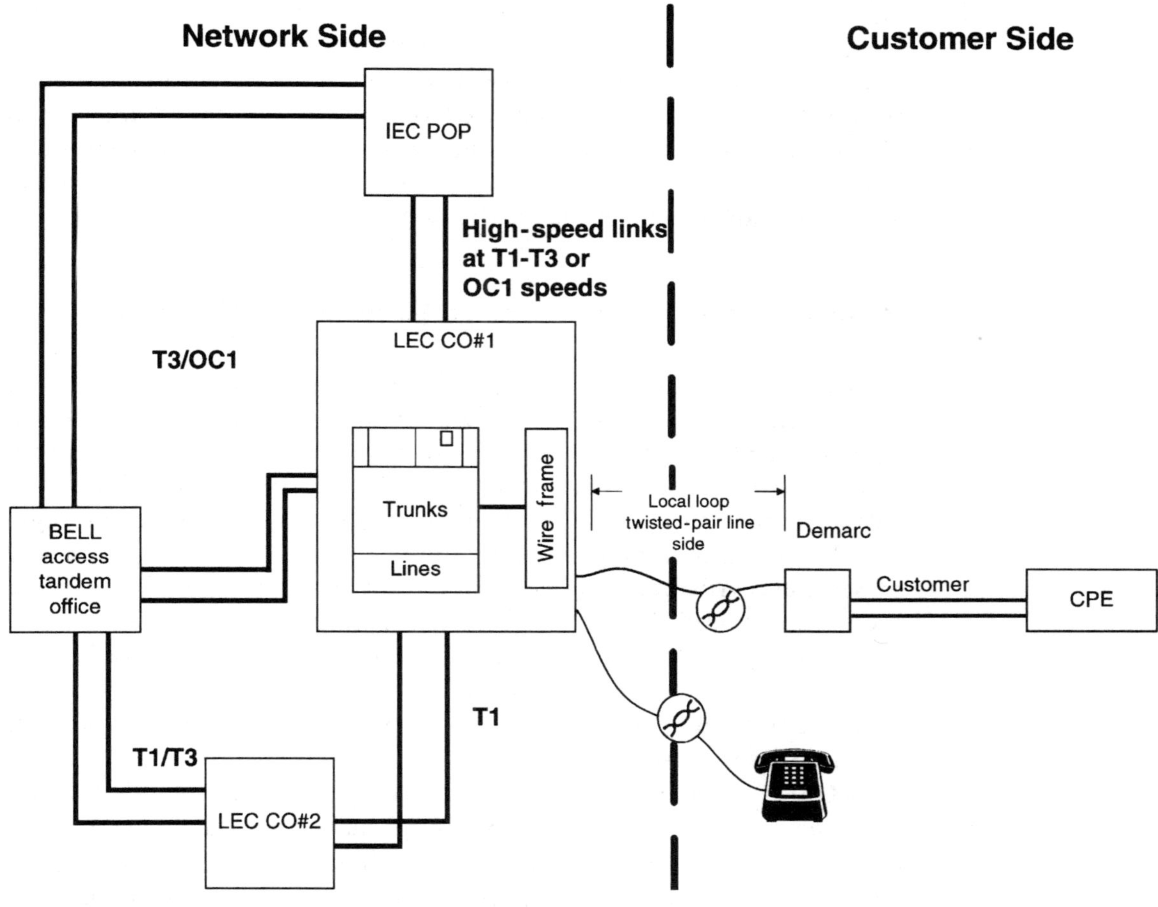

Figure 7.1 The normal building block at the LEC office to customer and to network.

Figure 7.1 shows the typical layout of the local loop services as the basic building block for an offering from an LEC. This figure describes the need for the local access to the customer's location to connect to anything. One should not interpret this figure as the only way to provide the connection. Competition is creeping into the localized connection to provide various business customers with services that may not be available from the LEC. This again is where the LEC is trying to use a shotgun approach. Instead of locking onto a single technology and providing that as its basis for all connections, it offers various services and pricing arrangements to counter the threat of competition. These services are covered later in this chapter as we proceed to discuss the options available to link the networks together. In many cases, the offerings may only satisfy a limited need, or they are not always available in all locations. The user creating a network design must understand just what is and what is not available. Along with this knowledge of availability goes an understanding of the pricing arrangement.

The Competitive Access Providers (CAPs)

In many parts of the United States and other parts of the world, newer players are emerging. These providers are called competitive access providers, or CAPs. What was once a mere hardwire provider that linked together two or more organization buildings or that provided access to interexchange carriers (IECs) has now emerged as a provider of high-speed access and cost-efficient methods of connectivity using a variety of services. CAPs were originally fiber providers that offered leased-line access to customer locations on a high-speed backbone, typically fiber. Now these providers are offering various other access methods. Fiber is still the primary service for the CAPs, but microwave radio and coaxial cable are becoming alternative methods of connection. The use of these technologies is shown in Fig. 7.2.

A CAP can bring one of many alternatives to the table for the end user. Newer players are entering the CAP marketplace, such as cable TV (CATV) companies, electric companies, wireless companies, and others, and all are vying for a part of this business. One can look at the availability of service from the LEC, and, if there is a limitation, look at the CAPs as alternatives to connecting the sites and networks for distribution around the local community. Still others offer wide area connectivity, bypassing the LECs' and even the IECs' backbone networks. Such is the case with an organization called Metropolitan Fiber Systems Data Networks, which completely builds out around the LEC and IEC. MFS Data Networks is located in many parts of the United States and is now international in scope. However, as with any alternative, the service is available in only a limited number of locations. The network manager (client/server internetwork manager) must therefore consider using multiple providers in a single networking platform, adding to the management complexity.

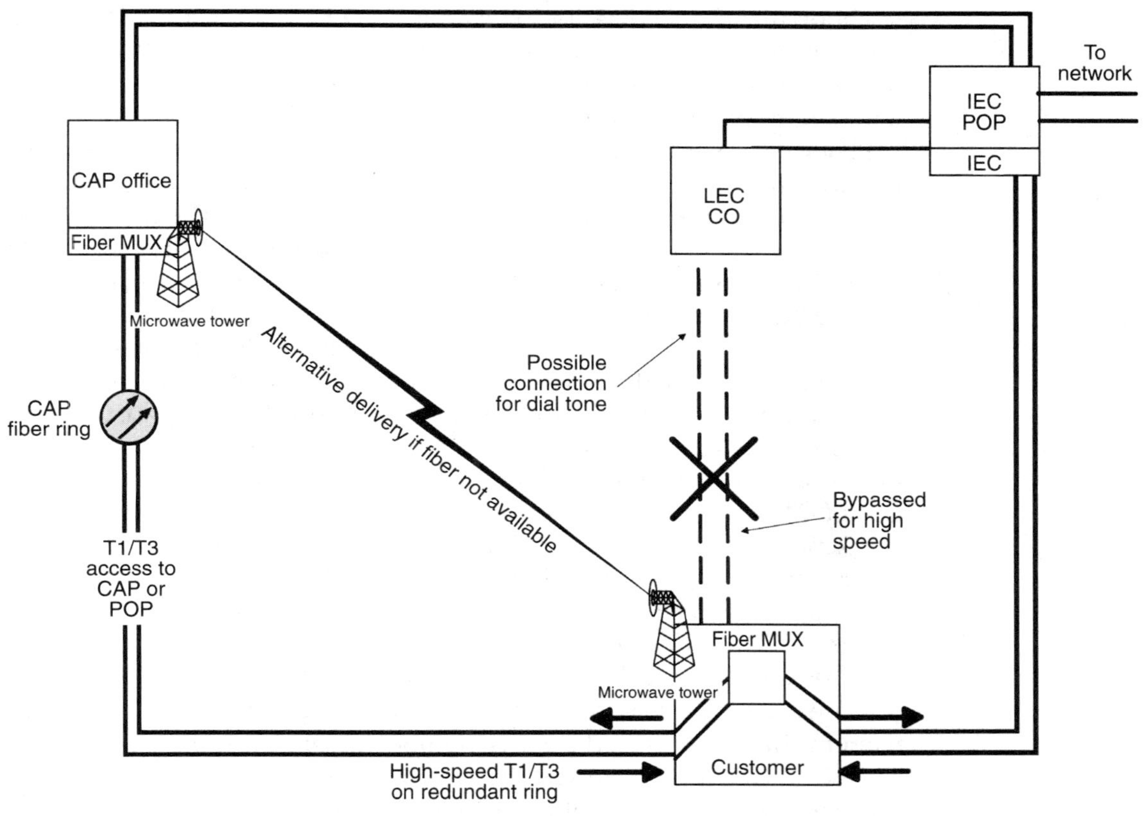

Figure 7.2 The competitive access provider (CAP) delivers high-speed access, bypassing the LEC, via fiber, coax, or microwave.

Interexchange Carriers (IECs)

One of the other providers that can allow access to the interexchange network across local boundaries is an interexchange carrier (IEC). IECs are the major providers of long-distance services; they offer various services and connections to other suppliers. The IECs emerged from the LEC backbone over the years as providers of voice dial-up and leased-line services. As the evolution and competition for long-distance connectivity continued, IECs got heavily involved in data networking. Now as the conversion from analog lines has been practically completed, their digital backbones are used for the higher-end services.

Unfortunately, the base of experience for LECs, CAPs, and IECs—and their bread and butter—came from voice networking expertise. This limitation poses some unique complications as the providers get into newer offerings and the migration to distributed computing continues. Whenever a system is connected, the experience of the carrier is one of the crucial factors in determining the success or failure of the installation. Too often organizations experience problems with the transport of data across the network of leased, dial-up, or packetized networks, only to find out that the IEC misinterpreted the installation instructions. Some cases have surfaced that clearly point out the limited data coverage from these suppliers. One cannot begin to understand the risks associated with the providers of service until experiencing a problem, and then suffering through days (or weeks) of guesswork. In one instance, an IEC had a network installed for months before a problem arose. This carrier was contractually bound to provide reliable service at an availability rate of 99.99 percent. All was fine until one occurrence on a leased line (T1) kept the circuit down for five days, bringing the internetwork to its knees and costing the organization immense losses in terms of productivity and sales. The carrier's only response was that it had never before run into that particular situation.

What can the user do if the providers are confused? This is one of the dilemmas facing the network manager today. Jargon and colonialism still reign in this industry, and carriers are not regulated as tightly as the local suppliers. In Fig. 7.3, we see the connection to a wide area network through the IEC. This graphic shows a combination of all three providers discussed so far. An LEC connection is used for access in the localized network, a CAP is used to access the WAN, and the IEC connects the WAN across the country (although it could be around the world).

New Players

New players are emerging all the time in this industry. Cable television companies offered high-speed access to the local customer via their coaxial networks, or through their newer fiber backbones. As the cable companies learned, the market for new suppliers is ripe: the cable companies must either team up with another player (an RBOC, for example) and offer competitively priced services on cable modems at hundreds of times the speed of dial-up communications from the LECs, or provide leased-line access to the IEC backbone networks. Enough of these are evident in

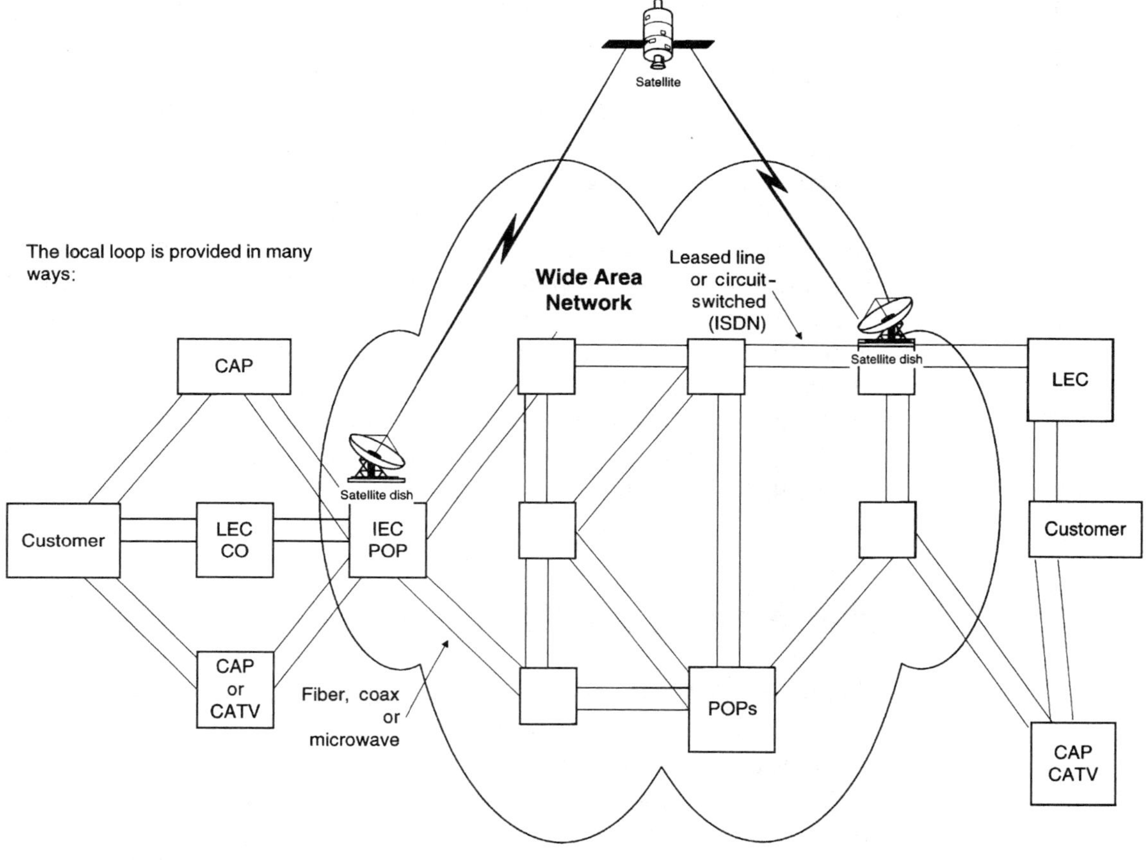

Figure 7.3 The IEC provides the long-haul circuitry via various delivery mechanisms.

the United States and the United Kingdom to show that this is a reality. As telecommunications reform gained attention in the U.S. Congress, the new players began preparing to provide Integrated Services Digital Network (ISDN) switched services and Asynchronous Transfer Mode (ATM) services in their backbone networks because they have been building this architecture for some time now.

Another new player that will be seen in the United States especially is the electric utility. In 1996 deregulation took effect for the competitive service offerings of electric companies; this part of the regulated monopoly is gone. Now many competitors can offer the same customer access to electricity. The local electric provider must allow access to their customers, instead of the new competitor's suffering the disadvantage of having to build a duplicate infrastructure. This new regulatory environment was anticipated years ago by electric company executives, so a strategic plan was followed by many companies. A major part of the plan involved installing fiber optics in the ground wire along electric rights of way, the purpose of which was serving the electric company's needs for process control and internal voice and data communications. Now a new plan is being undertaken. Excess capacity exists in these ground wire optics networks, so providers are dropping fiber links down from their pole lines and hooking up to the electric access points of buildings. Electric companies will use their immense amount of capacity to serve a customer's high-speed data, video, multimedia, and voice needs, and even as an alternative supplier of client/server internetworking access. These companies have also been buying ATM switches and routers, telephone interfaces, and ISDN-compatible equipment.

The Service Offerings

As shown in Table 7.1 earlier, each of the providers has a potpourri of service offerings. Many are the old reliable ones that have existed for decades, such as leased lines (analog or digital) and switched services. Newer switched digital services also emerged amid a rash of confusion in the industry. Other forms of services emerged using packetization of the data needs of the organization. These forms include packet switching (X.25), frame switching (frame relay), and cell switching (cell relay, i.e., ATM and SMDS). Regardless of the name, the issues concern

- Availability
- Connectivity options
- Interoperability in the network you are building
- Cost efficiency

Normally, the carriers offer services to meet the demands of the network, rather than the needs of the organization. This means that past installations limited the throughput (bandwidth) and the connectivity based on where the carrier provided access. Too often we have been limited to less throughput for many reasons, such as

- It was not available at the speed we needed.
- It took too long to get it.
- The carrier service was not in the correct location.
- There was no financial enticement for the carrier to provide the service.
- The cost was prohibitive to the customer.

Now the older offerings are becoming more attractive, with modification. However, newer offerings, such as high-speed cell and frame services, are overtaking the industry to meet the bandwidth needs of the organization. Let's look at these in more detail.

Leased Lines

For years, the old, reliable analog or digital leased line was one of the preferred methods of transport. This method is still used extensively in the industry, if for no other reason than because it is there. One can order a leased line (a dedicated point-to-point circuit) between any two points anywhere in the world. For the most part, lead times are simple. A 10-day-installation cycle is not uncommon. As long as the local loop facilities are available, the carriers can accommodate this schedule. Prices are based on mileage sensitivities—the greater the distance, the higher the total cost on a monthly basis. One should also be aware that although the total cost is more expensive, the price per mile drops, making this service somewhat attractive.

As hard as it may seem to imagine, many carriers still offer the use of an analog leased line, due to the local exchange carriers' limitations to provide service to some areas around the country. The LEC will provide the connection to the customers premises and terminate the circuit. Upon handoff to the IEC, the analog link will undoubtedly be converted to a digital link and be multiplexed onto a higher-speed digital trunk. In Fig. 7.4, we see the local loop being provided as an analog circuit, and then multiplexed onto a digital link. As the circuit is carried to the far end, it is then reverse-multiplexed and sent out to the end user as an analog signal. Modems are used to provide the interface to the link. The maximum speed that organizations usually install is 9.6 kilobits per second (kbits/sec), but variations do exist where a 19.2-kbits/sec circuit may be used. These leased lines are expensive by

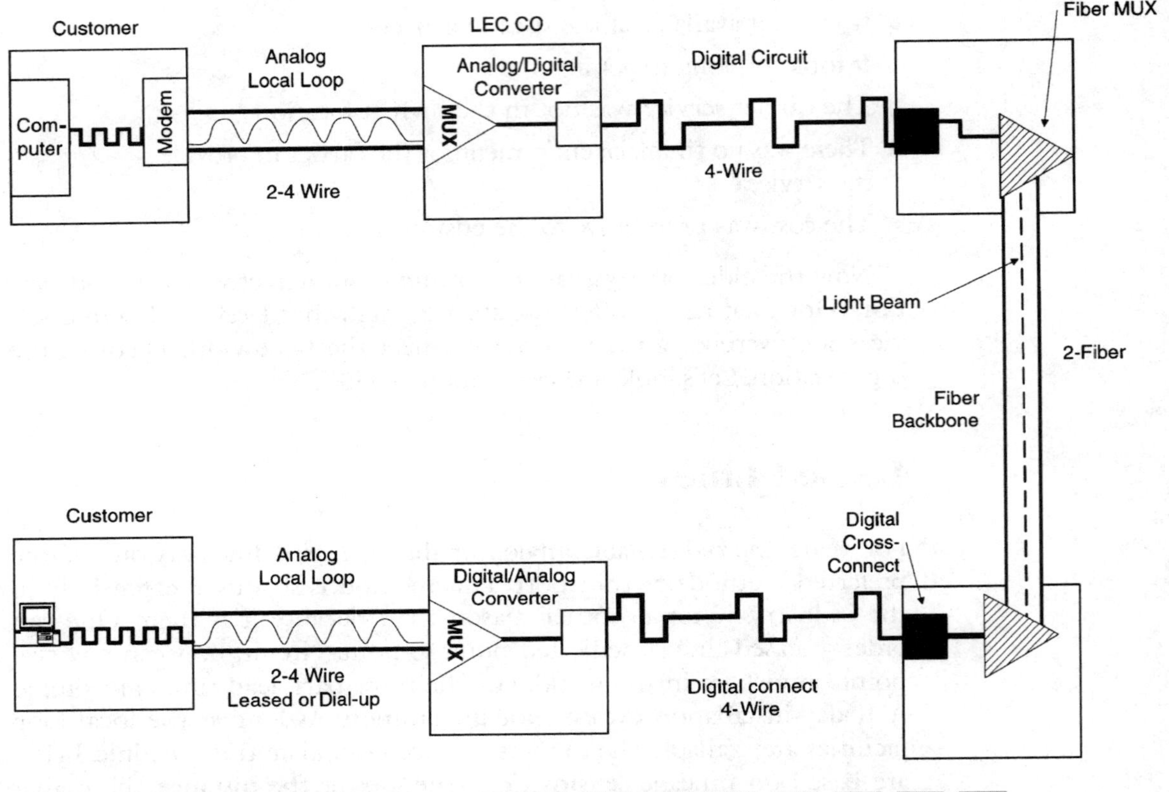

Figure 7.4 The digital signal is processed several times from digital to analog and back again.

today's standards, but they may be all that is available. Linking a branch office to a corporate office for the client/server network is impaired at this level of service because the amount of data may well be too great for the link speed.

Another variation is the use of a multipoint, multidrop leased line. Using a single circuit to connect multiple locations on a network offers a pricing advantage. The risk is the throughput disadvantage. If one looks at this alternative, the volume of data throughput must be carefully weighed. I recently ran into a situation where approximately 35 sites needed connections to a host-based SNA architecture located on the East Coast. The carriers quoted a network that was made up of seven multipoint circuits. The connections were all to the single corporate headquarters' host-based system, and the bulk of the data was inquiry and status checks for a transaction-based network. In Table 7.2 we model

TABLE 7.2 Summarizing the Costs for Analog Leased Lines to 35 Sites from a Corporate Headquarters Using SNA

Circuit	Number of sites connected	Terminals	Local loop	IXC mileage	Total cost	Average cost per site
1	6	37	$900	$1700	$2600	$433
2	6	25	$450	$1200	$1650	$275
3	3	20	$850	$800	$1650	$550
4	4	20	$750	$1300	$2050	$513
5	5	33	$600	$1200	$1800	$360
6	5	24	$1150	$3500	$4650	$930
7	6	33	$1275	$3350	$4625	$771
Total	35	192	$5975	$13,050	$19,025	$544

the traffic to look at the possible throughput of this link, based on the necessary data throughput. This table uses certain assumptions and is actually run through a spreadsheet. Not all of the possibilities are considered here, but enough are shown to give you an idea of the impact. For pricing considerations, we used generic costs, rather than nailing something in concrete and have you, the reader, think that circuits will cost this amount. The average cost per site to connect an analog leased line from the Midwest to the East Coast on a monthly basis is shown as $544 per month. This price is for a shared leased line at 9.6 kbits/sec. Although the price doesn't look bad, we should continue with the overall analysis. What is the need? In Table 7.3 we show the volume assumptions for this connection, which are moderate at best. No one can ever really predict the actual data, so assumptions have to be made.

TABLE 7.3

Assumptions for Modeling the Data on the Network

Number of transactions per hour per user	30
Number of screens per transaction	6
Number of bytes per screen	1900
Number of active devices	192
Total data needs	65,664,000 bytes/hour

TABLE 7.4 Assumptions Applied to the Model Showing the Shortfall as Data Is Applied across the Network

Circuit	Number of terminals	Number of screens	Number of bytes	Number of transactions*	Bytes	Bytes available	Difference
1	37	6	1900	1110	12,654,000	4,320,000	(8,334,000)
2	25	6	1900	750	8,550,000	4,320,000	(4,230,000)
3	20	6	1900	600	6,840,000	4,320,000	(2,520,000)
4	20	6	1900	600	6,840,000	4,320,000	(2,520,000)
5	33	6	1900	990	11,286,000	4,320,000	(6,966,000)
6	24	6	1900	720	8,208,000	4,320,000	(3,888,000)
7	33	6	1900	990	11,286,000	4,320,000	(6,966,000)
							(35,424,000)

* Assumes 30 transactions per hour per terminal.

Finally, using this assumption set for the data modeling, we see the overall response time for the network using only the circuit throughput desired. We do not consider the overall impact of the actual end devices and processing of the data, merely the data throughput as it works for the overall design as shown. The results are shown in Table 7.4, where the assumptions are laid out across the overall network to arrive at the needs for throughput.

From this table one can see clearly the risk of installing what the vendor offered. Although this problem can be solved quickly by adding additional circuits, the risk is that the data is not predictable. In this model we used a factor of 30 transactions per user per hour. What if the volume goes up? The data is already a fixed number of screens and a fixed-size transaction (1900 bytes per screen), so the variables are in the number of transactions and the size of the link (bandwidth) to carry the data. In Table 7.5, we add some sensitivities of varying types of data transactions per user into play to see the overall impact. Again, this table is strictly a model that we assume will work for the organization in linking the mainframe-based server and the terminal client.

These tables are reflective of how one must be involved in the data-modeling effort for the client/server internetworking capacity. This model was developed by the carrier with limited information. The carrier made

TABLE 7.5 Sensitivity Analysis of Varying Transactions*

Transactions @ 30 users	Bytes available	Bytes required	Difference
20	4,320,000	6,840,000	(2,520,000)
25	4,320,000	8,550,000	(4,230,000)
30	4,320,000	10,260,000	(5,940,000)
35	4,320,000	11,970,000	(7,650,000)
40	4,320,000	13,680,000	(9,360,000)
45	4,320,000	15,390,000	(11,070,000)
50	4,320,000	17,100,000	(12,780,000)
55	4,320,000	18,810,000	(14,490,000)
60	4,320,000	20,520,000	(16,200,000)
Transactions @ 20 users			
20	4,320,000	4,560,000	(240,000)
25	4,320,000	5,700,000	(1,380,000)
30	4,320,000	6,840,000	(2,520,000)
35	4,320,000	7,980,000	(3,660,000)
40	4,320,000	9,120,000	(4,800,000)
45	4,320,000	10,260,000	(5,940,000)
50	4,320,000	11,400,000	(7,080,000)
55	4,320,000	12,540,000	(8,220,000)
60	4,320,000	13,680,000	(9,360,000)
Transactions @ 25 users			
20	4,320,000	5,700,000	(1,380,000)
25	4,320,000	7,125,000	(2,805,000)
30	4,320,000	8,550,000	(4,230,000)
35	4,320,000	9,975,000	(5,655,000)
40	4,320,000	11,400,000	(7,080,000)
45	4,320,000	12,825,000	(8,505,000)
50	4,320,000	14,250,000	(9,930,000)
55	4,320,000	15,675,000	(11,355,000)
60	4,320,000	17,100,000	(12,780,000)

* Using the same criteria from earlier assumptions.

assumptions and looked for the least-cost alternative, based on what the customer told the carrier. However, at any number of transactions modeled, we see that the results could have been devastating to the network manager. The systems would not have been able to move enough data between the sites in a reasonable amount of time. Response times in this instance would have been at a snail's pace. The entire organization would have been unhappy. But what alternatives exist? As stated earlier, the data can be handled on more circuits or faster ones. In either case, however, cost factors will go up considerably.

Digital Leased Lines

Analog leased lines can be replaced by a digital leased lines provided by an IEC; however, getting to the IEC's point of presence (POP) may still be the problem. Many of the remote areas around the country still do not offer digital services to customer locations. Therefore, a leased line is only as good as the end provider (called the last mile). If digital is available, then the use of a digital leased line operating at 56 kbits/sec or 64 kbits/sec is an alternative. Using digital at these speeds will obviously improve the peformance of the scenario we used earlier. Using the 56 kbits/sec trans-

TABLE 7.6 Comparing the Use of a Digital Circuit for the Same Data, with the Network Using 56 kbits/sec Digital

Circuit	Number of terminals	Number of screens	Number of bytes	Number of transactions*	Bytes	Bytes available	Difference
1	37	6	1900	1110	12,654,000	25,200,000	12,546,000
2	25	6	1900	750	8,550,000	25,200,000	16,650,000
3	20	6	1900	600	6,840,000	25,200,000	18,360,000
4	20	6	1900	600	6,840,000	25,200,000	18,360,000
5	33	6	1900	990	11,286,000	25,200,000	13,914,000
6	24	6	1900	720	8,208,000	25,200,000	16,992,000
7	33	6	1900	990	11,286,000	25,200,000	13,914,000
							110,736,000

* Assumes 30 transactions per hour per terminal.

mission, we see in Table 7.6 that the speed should be sufficient to support this same network. This time, the speed and capacity are shown in the same vein as the original traffic used in the earlier tables.

One can see that the difference is now in a positive capacity, meaning that excess capacity is available for added transactions or other data streams. The difference in capacity allows for a better response time and less user frustration. The assumption in both cases is that the data is transferred without any data-compression techniques. Some benefit can be achieved by using a compression technique that derives a four-to-one ratio of compression. However, the price of compression is overhead and time in preparing the data for the link. By using straight data transfers without compression, we can compare the anticipated results. Later, if the need exists, then the compression can be included. Local loops can be accessed by the LEC. However, if the LEC does not offer this service, alternate suppliers (CAPs) can and should be considered. An alternate access supplier and the IEC providing the long-haul portion of the network can provide the same link.

When this digital link is used in a multipoint circuit, the IEC actually multiplexes the circuits onto a higher-speed link, such as a T1. This multiplexing is transparent to the end user, but it allows the connection to take place smoothly. The link is not a true multipoint, passing through one site to another. Reality slips in where the links are individual local loops and multiplexed at the POP to appear as a single circuit. What then of the cost for this service? Table 7.7 compares the price difference for the circuits only. One should remember that the cost of equipment could also change. Further, the scenario for the analog and digital circuits used in these tables is based on terminal traffic (327X) as opposed to a GUI that would add significantly to the amount of data needed. This may further bear out the comparison of the analog-to-digital link, where the digital excess allows for the more dense data that is graphically represented. The terminal interface assumes that only a character-based data transfer is taking place.

Note the difference for the cost of the digital circuits has increased by $10,000 per month, or a 50 percent cost penalty. This is not always the case, but the options must be closely analyzed based on this difference. The budgeted amount for linkage may well be shot in the first month if the actual costs increase by this amount. Also, remember that this scenario is a leased multipoint circuit (seven of them) instead of individual point-to-point circuits. The costs must be considered under the different options to financially justify the client/server internetwork. Imagine if

TABLE 7.7 Cost Assumptions using Digital Circuits to 35 Sites from a Corporate Headquarters Using SNA

Circuit	Number of sites connected	Terminals	Local loop	IXC mileage	Total cost	Average cost per site
1	6	37	$1800	$2200	$4000	$667
2	6	25	$1800	$2400	$4200	$700
3	3	20	$1250	$1550	$2800	$933
4	4	20	$1200	$1700	$2900	$725
5	5	33	$1500	$1800	$3300	$660
6	5	24	$1610	$4400	$6010	$1202
7	6	33	$1975	$4250	$6225	$1038
Total	35	192	$11,135	$18,300	$29,435	$841

you had 200+ sites to link. The costs could easily exceed $200,000 monthly. Although this cost must be considered in direct relationship to the data needs of the organization, the costs still have a lot of bearing on acceptability from a management perspective. One can never assume that prices will be discounted for quantity, but the opportunity exists to reduce the monthly rates by as much as 25 percent for quantity and long-term contracts (three to five years). Unfortunately, the risks to this option are the uncertainty of a carrier's ability to sustain the need for and reliability of the network. If things are not going smoothly, then escaping the contract must always be an option kept in the forefront.

All of this service assumes that the end user is performing the data-processing function at the host system. We cannot forget that the other alternative is to download the actual application to the end user (client) device. If this is the choice, then the data analysis that we are comparing and contrasting is all moot. The real amount of data that needs to be moved is based on where we select the applications to run.

Packet-switching Techniques

Beyond the fixed-price connection of a leased line, either analog or digital, other options exist. Each of the carriers that we discussed can provide an alternative to the data needs of the client/server architecture and network. Using a packet-switching technique, the IECs especially are prepared and well-versed in the ability to transport information across their networks. Packetizing the data is not new by any stretch of the imagination. This technique emerged back in the 1970s, and it has been a reliable and guaranteed form of data transfer for all that time. The analog network was unreliable, causing a significant degree of overhead and degradation over time. As the links degraded, data suffered. To solve this problem, packet switching offered the ability to guarantee the data delivery in proper sequence. Packet switching means that the data is truncated (or packetized) into smaller segments, and then assigned a sequence number. As the data packets are transmitted across the network, they are checked for integrity to ensure that corruption has not occurred. Then, if any corruption occurs, a retransmission is requested by the switching system that experiences the receipt of bad data. While this is all happening, the data is buffered, and the additional packets that follow the corrupted one are kept in a buffer until the error is corrected. This buffering guarantees the orderly and reliable delivery of the data to the far end, where it is then reassembled into the actual data request.

All this action has a price. The price is the potential for delay and excessive buffering. However, if one is looking for an international connection of the data needs for a client/server, packet switching is an alternative. Figure 7.5 shows the connection among the carriers to provide packet-switching capability. This illustration shows the connection as a leased line from an LEC or a CAP and the packet network as part of the IEC backbone. Other variables work in the packet switching systems. A packet-switching drawback, as mentioned, is the delay of sensitive information. When dealing with client/server networking needs, this may be a small portion of the demands to provide connectivity. In the public packet networks, the carriers installed a limitation of 64 kbits/s for transfer rates. This limitation is not one of the technology, but of implemented networks by the suppliers. Private packet networks exist that run at speeds of up to T1 (1.544 Mbits/s) and E1 (2.048 Mbits/s), but they are expensive to build for the average-sized organization looking to provide connectivity to hundreds of sites. In developing countries around the world, however, it may be the only available reliable service offering from the PTT and international carrier combination. Using a packet network for client/server may cause

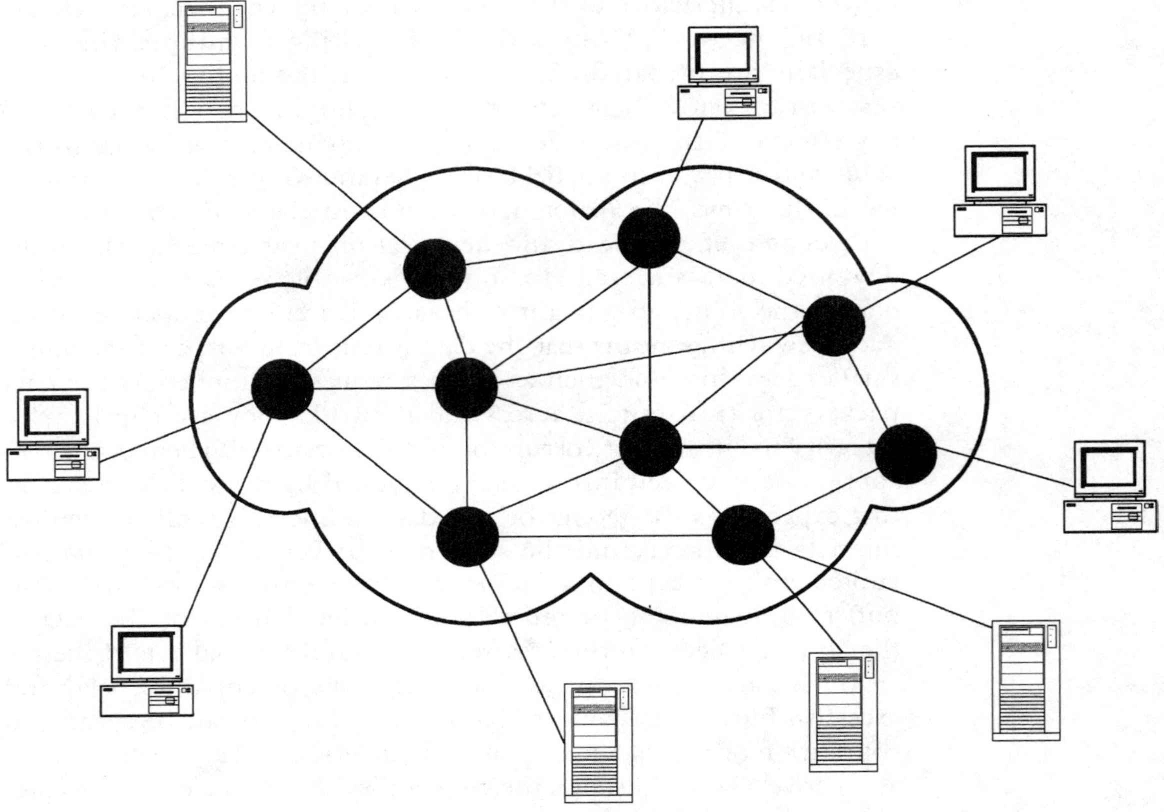

Figure 7.5 Packet switching.

significant delays to the data transfer or increased response times that are perceived to be intolerable. One can only model what the expected response times will be, then hope for the actual traffic patterns to fall within the scope of the design. Unfortunately, this packet technology may be one of the only choices available to you. In many parts of the world choices are limited to the following:

1. Leased lines that can be inordinately expensive.
2. Dial-up data transfers that can be both expensive and unreliable.
3. Packet switching that offers lower costs and reasonable speeds for the dial-up network, coupled with guaranteed delivery and integrity. Yet this solution may take a long time to install.

New technologies are emerging both in the United States and abroad. One must keep a close watch on what is available and from whom at all times. Surprisingly, in this day and age of fast networking technologies, the LECs are all still deploying packet-switching systems in the backbone networks (X.25), because not all users need or can afford the higher speed that attracts attention in the trade magazines. Thus, LEC networks are being expanded with packet-switching alternatives. Even in the ISDNs of the present and future, packet switching is and will be a viable offering. Does it meet the demands of the client/server internetwork though? The answer is a function of the network being built by the end user, speed requirements, and the volumes of data that must be moved. Only the actual network user can say for sure.

CHAPTER 8

New Carrier Offerings to Internetwork a Client/Server Architecture

Chapter 7 discussed the older analog leased-line and multipoint circuits to connect a client/server architecture. It also provided an overview of the digital leased-line services available from a combination of carriers. These carriers include IECs, LECs, CAPs, and PTTs. What now follows is a look at some of the emerging technologies that will be available for data needs across a global community. Many of the international and domestic U.S.-based carriers are deploying several new techniques, including frame relay, ISDN, SMDS, and ATM. These newer technologies were designed around a digital infrastructure. The carrier community recognized the impairments, limitations, and lack of speed and connectivity, as well as the overall cost to communicate among computing systems. Therefore, they introduced these newer technologies at various times in the evolution to digital transmission systems. Many of these newer technologies are available in differing places. In the LEC environment, ISDN and SMDS are two of the primary offerings. Although other options are available, these are the primary initial services. Now many of the LECs also offer frame relay services with the ultimate goal to move to ATM in the future.

The IECs, on the other hand, have already rolled out several ISDN offerings, frame relay services, and limited ATM application support. The IECs have a propensity to roll out services in the major metropolitan areas. The benefit of the IECs is that they merely have to connect on an interstate and inter-LATA basis, because they typically do not have to go to the end loop or, as we refer to it, the last mile. Therefore, IECs only need to connect among their own office communications capabilities; then they have the customer use the local exchange carrier network to connect to the wide area network.

In the CAP environment, the services cover the ability to provide leased-line services, access to a frame relay carrier, access to an SMDS network, or access to an ATM environment. Originally, the CAPs did not offer any form of switched services but merely provided the access links. Now, with the change in regulatory environment, CAPs are beginning to roll out products and services that mirror the capabilities of both the LEC and the IEC. Today, depending on where you are in the United States or in the international sector, CAPs can provide varying degrees of connectivity throughout their own backbone network or act as wide area and local area suppliers. CAPs, however, have the advantage in that they can pick and choose the buildings or organizations they wish to serve. In most cases, CAPs select large, multitenant, high-rise office buildings or large campus environments. By doing so, they can serve a very select population while providing services to these limited customers. CAPs also have the ability to be very creative in their provisioning capabilities. Today many of the CAPs offer switched multimegabit data services (SMDS), transparent local area network connectivity, fiber distributed data interface (FDDI), or limited ATM capabilities. Through the use of these different services, the CAPs can provide very creative, as well as cost-effective, solutions. Their pricing mechanisms are very attractive and competitive. It is not uncommon to find a CAP pricing a high-speed communications channel capability at anywhere from 30 to 40 percent less than what an LEC charges.

Newer opportunities exist from a CAP perspective to offer access to frame relay services. Therefore, these providers now offer a complete line of products and services that meet the client/server internetwork demands of a large consumer. This statement does not mean that a smaller organization cannot reap the same benefits. When a CAP locates its equipment in the basement of a high-rise office building, the smaller users being served in that same building can reap access capabilities from this first connection to the larger company. Figure 8.1 shows a connection from a CAP's location to a high-rise building. Note the competitive equipment is located in the basement of the building, but the connectivity is run throughout the entire high-rise backbone. Any tenant in this building can gain access at a lower cost. In Fig. 8.2, the capability of providing access also exists when two or three high-rise buildings adjacent to the first connection are also connected. This figure shows where the fiber multiplexing equipment located in Building A is extended (tail circuits) to the adjacent buildings, offering high-speed connectivity to more than one user simultaneously.

Cable TV Companies

The idea of cable TV companies gaining access into the telecommunications arena already has been discussed in detail. But one should remember that the cable capacities bring an enormous amount of bandwidth services to the forefront. Figure 8.3 shows a cable TV infrastructure being delivered to each of the residential and business users in a major city block. Note, however, that the cable companies have now provided high-speed fiber communications capabilities in their backbones. Looking at this fiber backbone, one can just imagine the capacities that the

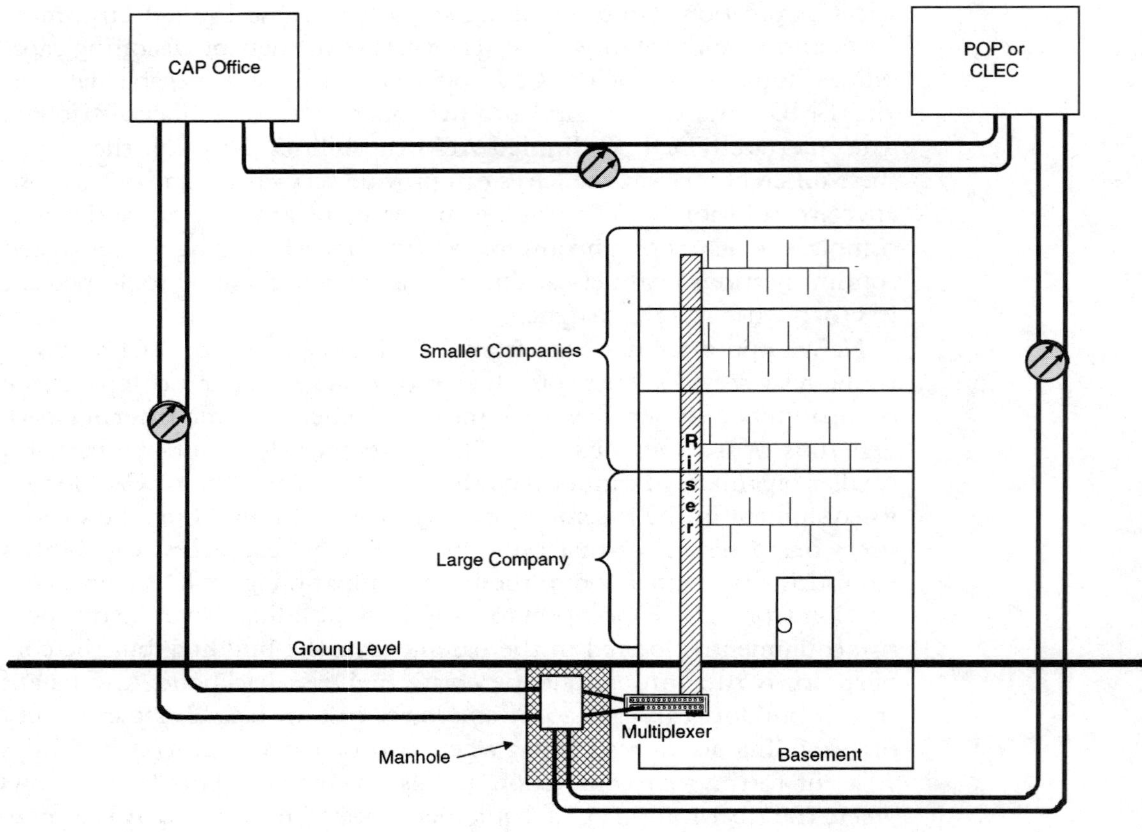

Figure 8.1 The CAP can serve both large and small companies when the equipment is located in the basement.

cable TV companies now have available to them. Using this fiber backbone, they can now support the high-speed ISDN, frame relay, SMDS, and ATM capabilities on the same fiber backbone cable system. Their cost is limited strictly to the new equipment necessary. The cable itself and the services rendered by that cable pay for the delivery mechanism (the cable). Therefore, any new service being added on is strictly a marginal, incremental cost. Customers will see significant discounts in a competitive marketplace. Moreover, the cable companies will reap huge profits based on this reuse of the existing cable system.

One caveat to this whole environment is that the cable companies must use a two-way communication system. An alternative to using fiber optics

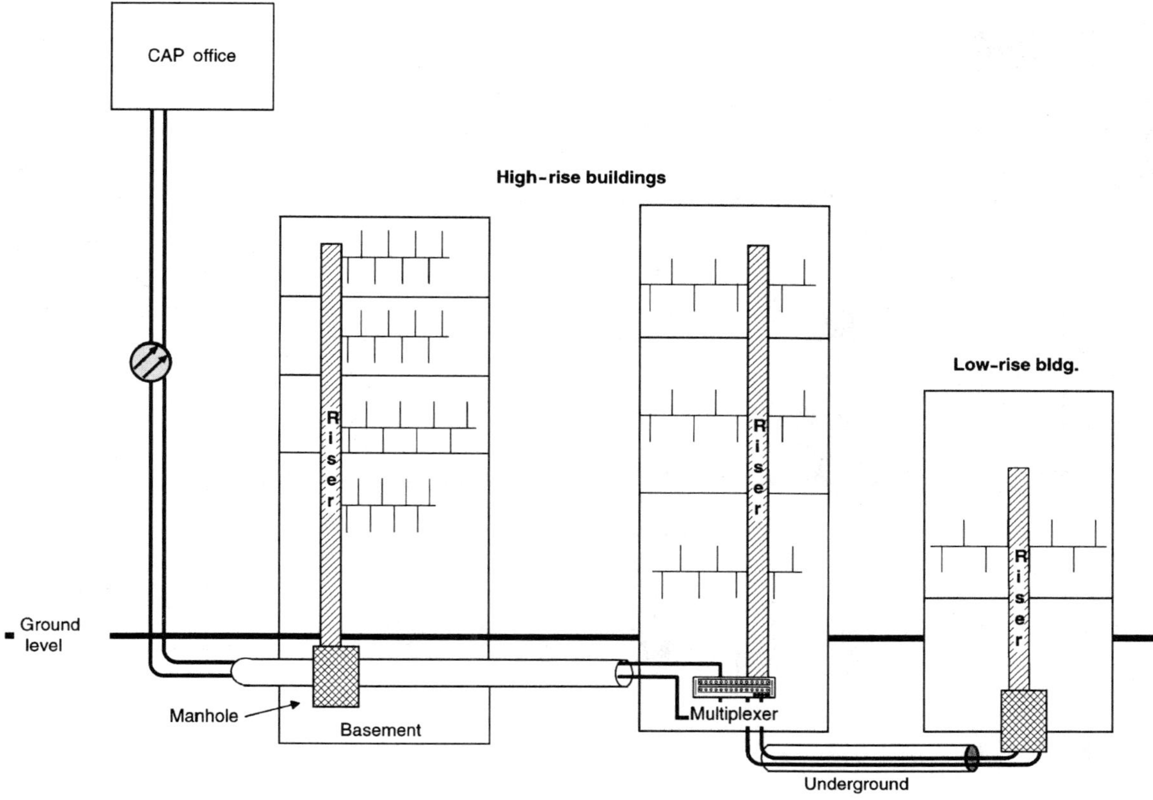

Figure 8.2 The CAP can serve adjacent buildings via an underground conduit.

is the ability to have a dual fiber system, allowing transmission and reception of data across the individual fibers. Now the cable TV companies can deliver significant amounts of services and capabilities to the end-user community. Users and internetworking managers can now look at the different options for some of these higher-speed, fast-relay services.

Frame Relay

One of the hottest topics in the industry today is the emergence of frame relay service. As a fast-relay technology, frame relay is a modified

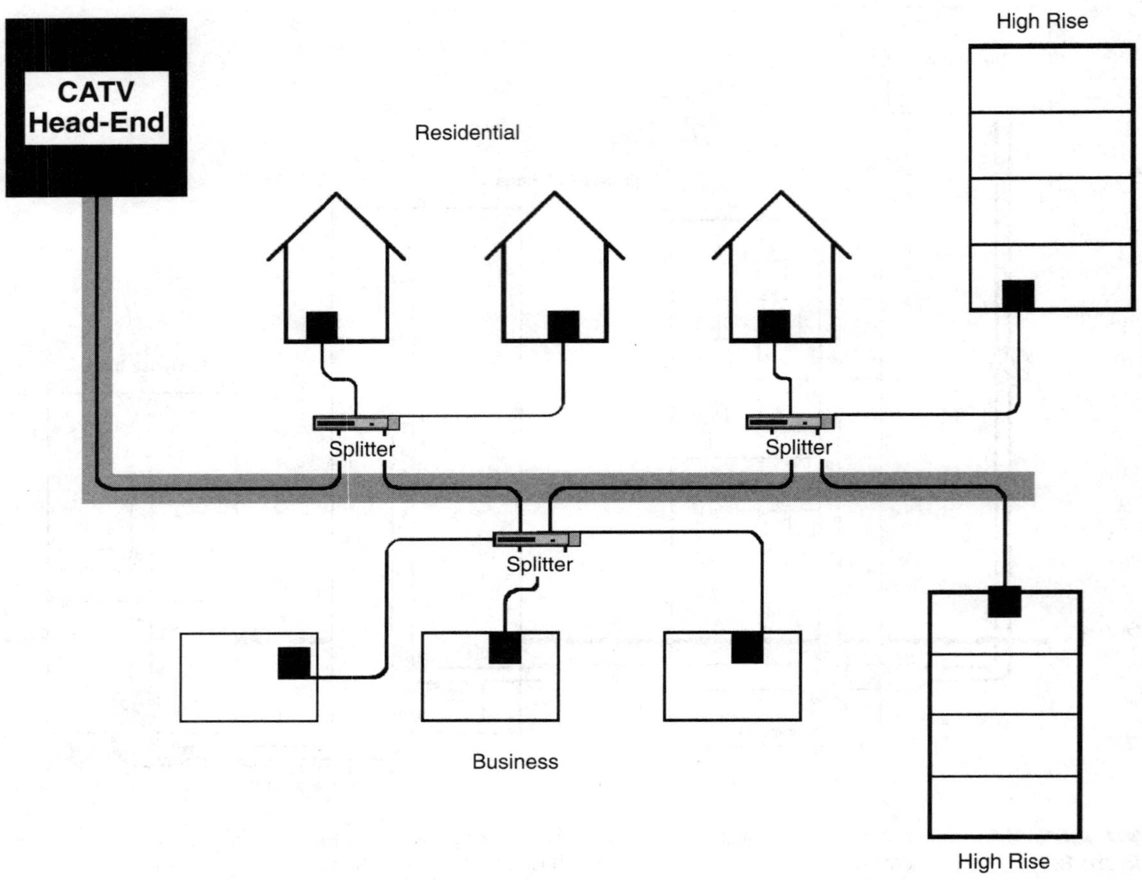

Figure 8.3 CATV companies install high-capacity connections to residences and businesses.

version of packet switching. As a matter of fact, many carriers call the service a fast packet-switching service. Introduced in 1989, its use emerged slowly. Prior to 1994, not many organizations were excited about frame relay services. What happened in 1994 was phenomenal, with nearly a 400 percent increase in the number of users. 1995 and 1996 followed suit. This technology caught on in its own time. One should remember the service was actually created and defined in 1989, but the first commercial implementation did not occur until late 1991. Only the leaders and the testers of technology who were concerned about high-speed communications services were willing to experiment with frame relay. So this technology has been a slowly evolving implementation. The carriers had a sleeper application in the use of client/server internetworking, but they failed to realize it early on.

As new client/server networks are deployed, users are quickly discovering that frame relay is a natural fit. Instead of leasing multiple circuits in support of a new network, a single access link can provide a highly robust means of connectivity. What would normally require a meshed or semimeshed leased-line network can now be done on the virtual network. This eliminates the need for several links, using an asymmetrical data transfer rate at whatever speeds are necessary, up to the speed of the access link. Where many organizations were spending hundreds of thousands of dollars to provide the necessary connections to their various sites around the globe, the access on a single link and the use of a permanent virtual circuit (PVC) can reduce the monthly charges by as much as 40 to 60 percent.

Looking at this on the surface one might ask, "What's the catch?" Yet when analyzing the nature of frame services, the answer is fairly straightforward. Using the best features of the OSI level three (network layer) and the reliable framing of data onto the data link level (layer 2), a combined and reduced overhead can be used for the client/server needs. This technique eliminates a lot of the overhead associated with the older X.25 packet-switching systems. Further, by using the services of a frame relay network, a *breathable* networking system can be employed. What is meant by breathable is that when additional bandwidth is necessary, the network will allow the customer-premises access equipment to increase its output across the link at speeds in excess of one to two times what is actually being paid for. This expandability fits nicely with the frame relay service where a client/server architecture may, in fact, have very bursty data. Due to the nature of a client/server network, it is imperative that enough capacity exists during these bursts. Frame relay allows that to happen. Moreover, this service also incorporates the ability while bursting (using more than what you bought) to allocate or dissipate specific traffic types based on a priority routing scheme. Typically, data that is going to the server is held in high priority and therefore marked as discard-ineligible. However, when data is burst across this network to a less critical application, that data can be discarded. These are some of the benefits of a true client/server internetworking capability using the burst rates of frame relay.

In Fig. 8.4, the actual frame is shown. Note the part called the DLCI (data link connection identifier). This DLCI designates the addressing

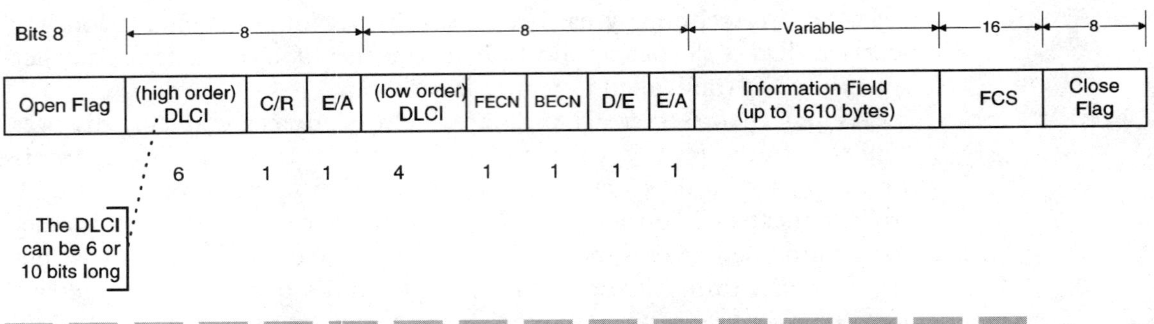

Figure 8.4 The frame used in frame relay uses little overhead, whereas the data field is variable.

information that uses 10 bits of information for an address. At 10 bits, the addressable number of devices per permanent virtual circuit equates to 1024 (not all are available to the customer). Beyond the address, located in the second byte of the DLCI are three separate and distinct fields, each being a single bit. The first includes what is called a forward explicit congestion notification bit (FECN). The next bit is the backward explicit congestion notification bit (BECN). The last bit is the discard eligibility bit (DE). This bit is the one that was referred to in terms of the eligibility or ineligibility of the data frame to be discarded. When bursting, that is, exceeding the capacity actually rented, frames in excess of the committed information rate (CIR) are eligible for discard. However, using the flexibility of a frame relay service, specific frames can be marked ineligible for discard, thereby making others eligible for discard and allowing the prioritization of the application, protocol, or specific frame itself. This brings a lot of flexibility to the use of a client/server network. Moreover, pricewise, it allows a significant decrease in the overall cost while still increasing the robustness of the network.

Figure 8.5 shows a frame relay network connecting the three-computer architecture of a client/server network. Note that routers are used extensively in this particular network, but other devices, called frame relay access devices (FRADs) could be used. A FRAD is used when connecting to leased-line services or other application-specific capabilities. In this particular network, the server is used as a single entity in a corporate environment. The additional application servers are attached to this network on an FDDI ring, acting as traffic cops for access to the high-end server. These application servers provide and spawn processes into the host for access to databases, word processing, or other applications that reside on the server.

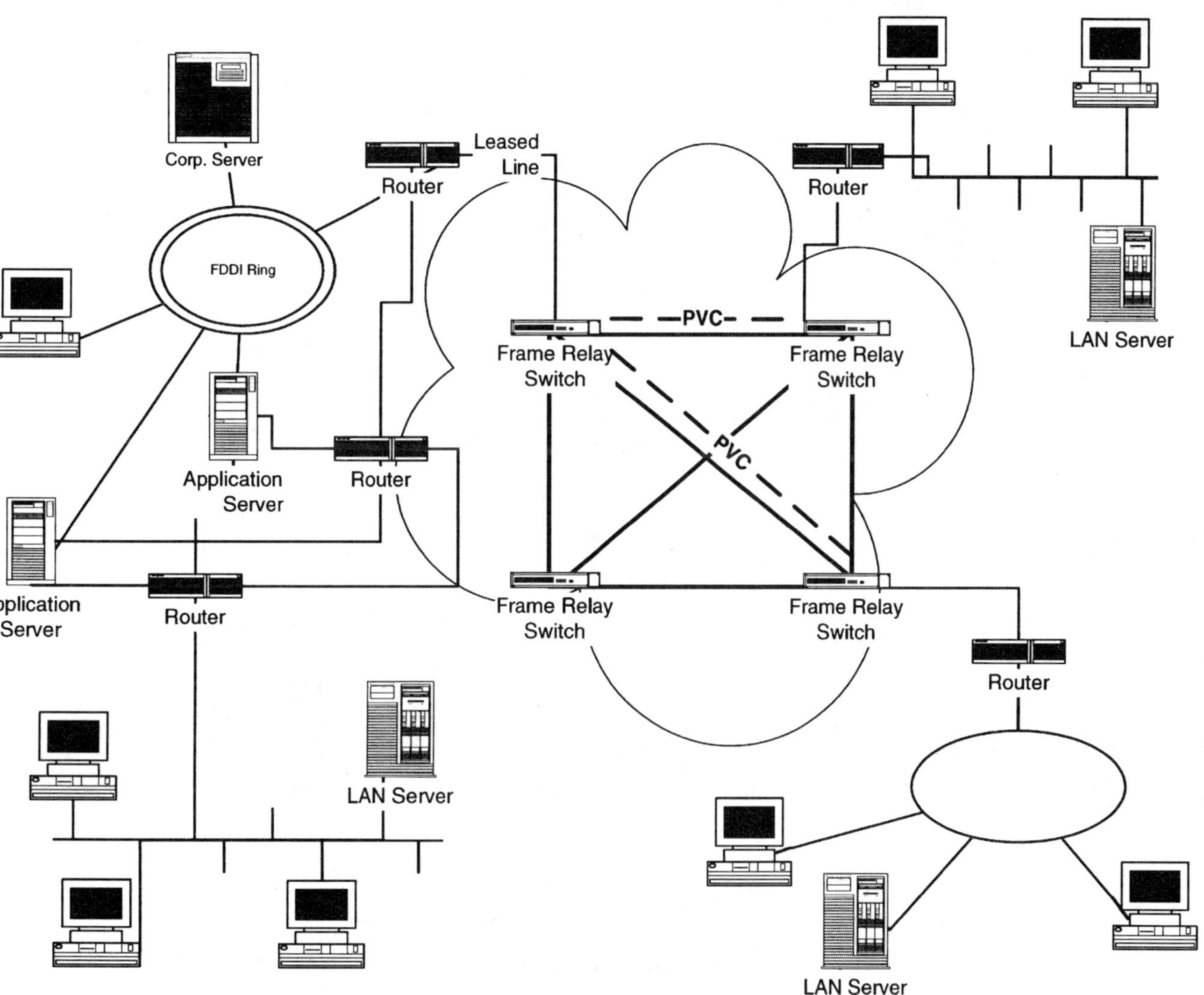

Figure 8.5 The frame relay three-computer architecture for an internetwork.

Frame Relay Benefits

For a client/server networking capability, the use of frame relay brings a lot to the forefront. Essentially, the client/server network is a series of computers linked together using this three-computer architecture. In a local network, these computing systems are linked together over common cabling infrastructures. When dealing with an internetwork, however, the connection will now move across the wide area network. To gain access to this wide area network, a high-speed digital access link is used. A single interface can be attached depending on the speeds needed. Figure 8.6 shows a traditional leased-line, high-speed network. In this figure, several connections are run from the major corporate location to each of the subsets or subnetworks that are attached across the

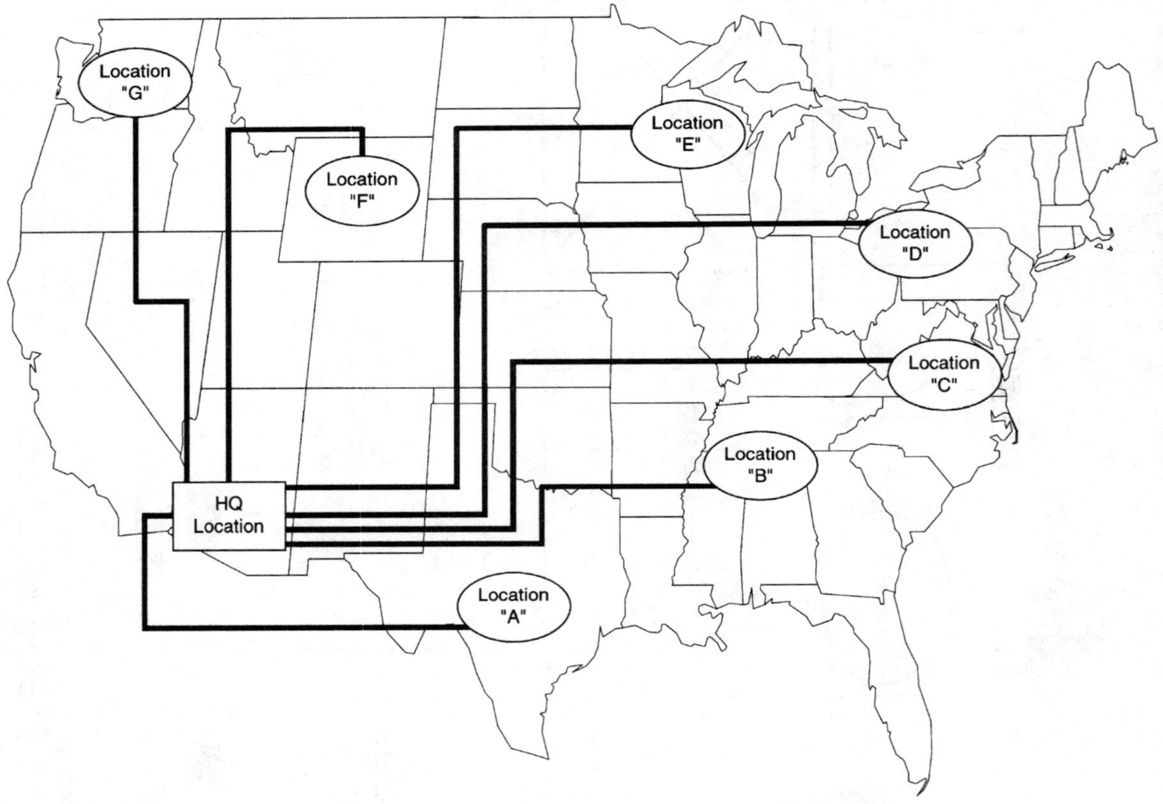

Figure 8.6 The traditional leased-line network required separate links to each location.

TABLE 8.1

Comparison of Leased-Line Costs and T1 Costs to Several Locations

Location	Cost of Leased-Line Access				Cost of T1 Access			
From/to	Local loop	IXC	Total	Speed	Local loop	IXC	Total	Speed
AZ/PA	912	1,668	2,580	9.6	1,500	17,500	19,000	1.544
AZ/SC	917	2,468	3,385	1.544	1,817	15,500	17,317	1.544
AZ/NM	442	1,164	1,606	9.6	1,440	5,500	6,940	1.544
AZ/TX	853	796	1,649	9.6	1,200	7,500	8,700	1.544
AZ/NV	734	1,294	2,028	9.6	1,440	5,500	6,940	1.544
AZ/MO	540	870	1,410	9.6	1,300	8,500	9,800	1.544
AZ/NE	127	498	625	9.6	1,200	9,200	10,400	1.544
AZ/CO	594	1,163	1,757	9.6	1,400	7,500	8,900	1.544
Total	$5,119	$9,921	$15,040		$11,297	$76,700	$87,997	

domestic United States. These connections prove to be quite expensive because the consolidated grouping of these T1 links is excessive. Note that each of the connections provides, however, the dedicated throughput and capacities needed for each of these locations to transmit back to the corporate facility. The cost associated with these links is therefore a detriment to the rollout of a client/server internetwork.

Table 8.1 shows a comparison of the cost of the links to several locations around the United States. This table compares the leased-line facility to the cost of using high-speed digital access in the form of a T1 to each of these sites. One should recognize, however, that not all sites would need a complete T1. Fractional T1 can also be used. In many cases, when more than five DS0s are used, the cost of the fractional piece makes the price difference negligible. Therefore, organizations typically install the full T1. This network becomes cost-prohibitive, negating some of the benefits of the client/server internetwork. One can imagine justifying the costs shown in this table to senior management. When dealing with senior management and attempting to justify this interconnectivity, it is always difficult when the costs exceed the tangible benefits.

Frame relay, on the other hand, allows for a single high-speed, digital-access link, usually in the form of a T1, into the frame relay cloud. This single access link can sustain and support multiple simultaneous

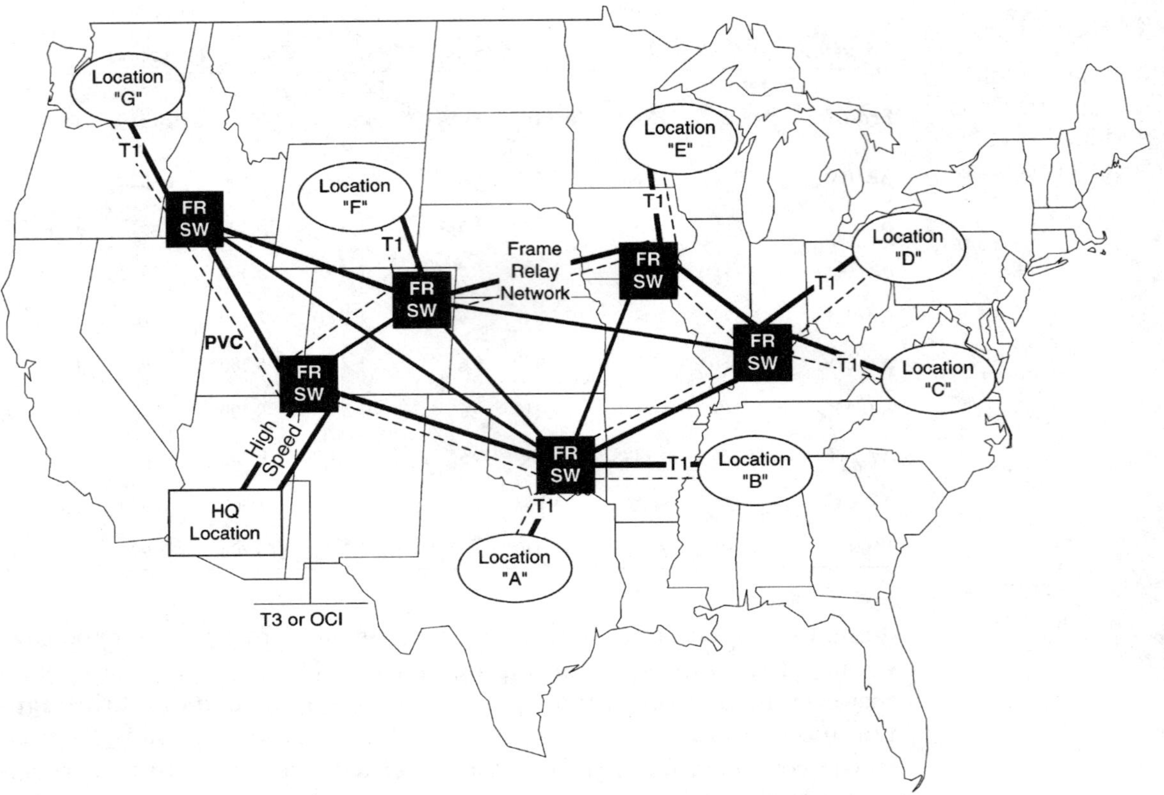

Figure 8.7 The simplified frame relay network uses a single access link and a PVC instead of a dedicated link.

sessions on that single link. Therefore, instead of having to draw specific dedicated circuits to each of the locations as shown in Fig. 8.6, a separate network (Fig. 8.7) limits the amount of connections needed. In this new scenario, a single high-speed link is used to access the frame relay network. Each of the subnetworks stretched around the United States is also using a single access link into the frame relay network. Where the difference starts to show is in the use of the PVC, a logical connection but not a physical dedicated link, which eliminates the need for high-speed communications channels to each of the sites on a permanent basis, reducing the overall monthly cost. Using permanent virtual circuits, the frame relay network provides the capacity when needed and releases it when it is not. Using the link access procedure—D channel (LAP-D) protocol, the PVC is activated and ready for transmission. Once transmission begins, the two sites are connected for the duration of the transmission. When the data is transmitted and no more is to be sent, the LAP-D message is then used to release the circuit.

Aggregating all of these individual circuits, the PVCs can be established at fractional T1 speeds. By using the fractional pieces, a user can now establish PVC at 384 kbytes per second (kbps) and, using just the 384 kbps, transmit data from the site to the corporate headquarters hosting the server. However, if more than one simultaneous transmission is required or more than 384 kbps is needed, the frame relay network allows the breathability to expand the capacity for short durations. The two-second burst periods allowed by the carriers give the end users the capacity to transmit at speeds of an additional 192 kbps. Further, if even more data is required, the excess burst rate (Be) is allowed at an additional capacity of between 96 and 192 kbps. What this essentially means is the end user can be transmitting data at speeds of up to 768 kbps. By not having the dedicated T1 access link on a point-to-point basis, the cost of the 384-kbps PVC is significantly less. The client/server network manager would therefore be able to reduce costs on a monthly basis, allow for increased speed and capacity, and provide the transparent connections for the multiple users needing access to the single corporate server. Table 8.2 shows the difference in cost by comparing the

TABLE 8.2 Comparison of Frame Relay and T1 Costs for 384 kbps

Location	Cost of Frame Relay Access					Cost of T1 Access			
From/to	Access	Port	PVC	Total	Speed	Local loop	IXC	Total	Speed
AZ/PA	912	658	453	2,023	384	1,500	17,500	19,000	1.544
AZ/SC	917	2,468	2,227	5,612	1.544	1,817	15,500	17,317	1.544
AZ/NM	442	658	453	1,553	384	1,440	5,500	6,940	1.544
AZ/TX	853	658	453	1,964	384	1,200	7,500	8,700	1.544
AZ/NV	734	658	453	1,845	384	1,440	5,500	6,940	1.544
AZ/MO	540	658	453	1,651	384	1,300	8,500	9,800	1.544
AZ/NE	450	658	453	1,561	384	1,200	9,200	10,400	1.544
AZ/CO	594	658	453	1,705	384	1,400	7,500	8,900	1.544
Total	$5,442	$7,074	$5,398	$17,914		$11,297	$76,700	$87,997	

access cost on a frame relay network to that of dedicated point-to-point T1 circuits. This is where frame relay excels. It is not uncommon for a client/server internetwork to see cost reductions in the range of 40 to 60 percent over the leased-line costs, as shown in this table.

Not all costs are associated with just the leased-line services, however. In some cases, the use of high-speed routers must also be included into the equation. Many sites can get by with a single router using a single high-speed WAN access link. Routers could cost from $4000 to $75,000 each, depending on the configuration. Yet with a frame relay network, many of the carriers offering frame services also provide a totally managed networking capability, including the router, in their monthly costs. Once again, in a client/server network, using the carriers' communications equipment on a monthly basis can help to limit expenses. Table 8.3 compares the costs of using a fully managed network and purchasing a router with renting or leasing the router from the same network supplier. Also shown is the cost of managing these routers on an individualized basis versus having the network supplier provide that service. Here again,

TABLE 8.3 Comparison of Purchase and Vendor-Provided Router

Location	Cost of Frame Relay Access				Cost of Router		
From/to	Access	Port	PVC	Total	Router	Vendor-provided	Total
				Circuit	One Time	Monthly	Monthly
AZ/PA	912	658	453	2,023	15,000	225	2,248
AZ/SC	917	2,468	2,227	5,612	15,000	225	5,837
AZ/NM	442	658	453	1,553	15,000	225	1,778
AZ/TX	853	658	453	1,964	15,000	225	2,189
AZ/NV	734	658	453	1,845	15,000	225	2,070
AZ/MO	540	658	453	1,651	15,000	225	1,876
AZ/NE	450	658	453	1,561	15,000	225	1,786
AZ/CO	594	658	453	1,705	15,000	225	1,930
Total	$5,442	$7,074	$5,398	$17,914	$120,000	$1,800	$19,714
5-Year Depreciation				+ →	$2,000		
Grand Total					$19,914		$19,714

the costs are diminished by 40 to 60 percent on a monthly basis by using a turnkey package with frame relay services. Moreover, by using the frame capabilities, not only do we get reduced cost and increased capacities due to the bursting capability of frame relay, the network can also be as resilient and robust as necessary. New sites can be added relatively quickly. Without redesigning the whole network, the carrier can also handle sites that would be closed or downsized.

In a leased-line environment, as shown in Fig. 8.6, a star-and-spoke-type network is often used to accommodate the capabilities and hold down the cost. Using the frame relay services and the permanent virtual circuits, this is no longer a necessity. Each PVC is literally a point-to-point circuit yielding a star network from the corporate headquarters, without the star. One caution on the use of this frame capability: If a star network of this sort is used, the client/server network manager essentially has a point-to-point network, which means that if a site on the East Coast needs to communicate with another site in Dallas, all data would have to be transmitted back to the router at the corporate facility (in Phoenix) and then retransmitted on the outbound link on the frame relay services. In reality, a dual transmission has taken place. If, in fact, enough data is transmitted between the East Coast and Dallas, a separate PVC might well be installed, building a form of meshed network. This, of course, adds to the cost of the overall client/server internetwork. However, the demand or the need to communicate between these two sites might mitigate the overall cost. It would not necessarily be prudent to have all transmissions routed to the corporate environment only to be retransmitted a second time.

If used this way, this connection would increase the latency and propagation delay of all data sets working between the East Coast and Dallas because of the need to reroute the data through the single high-speed corporate communications link. To prevent this delay, dedicated PVCs between these two sites could be used. Another choice would be to use a frame relay star and spoke again. Perhaps in this environment, a star network could be installed from the corporate facility to the major divisional or regional offices spread around the country. In this case, PVCs would be pulled to the five locations shown in Fig. 8.8. From each of these regional sites, separate PVCs would be extended to the lower-end branch or divisional offices spread out behind the regional offices. What this arrangement does is limit the number of PVCs necessary to run all the way across the country back to the headquarters. Every site, however, would have to transmit its data sets to its

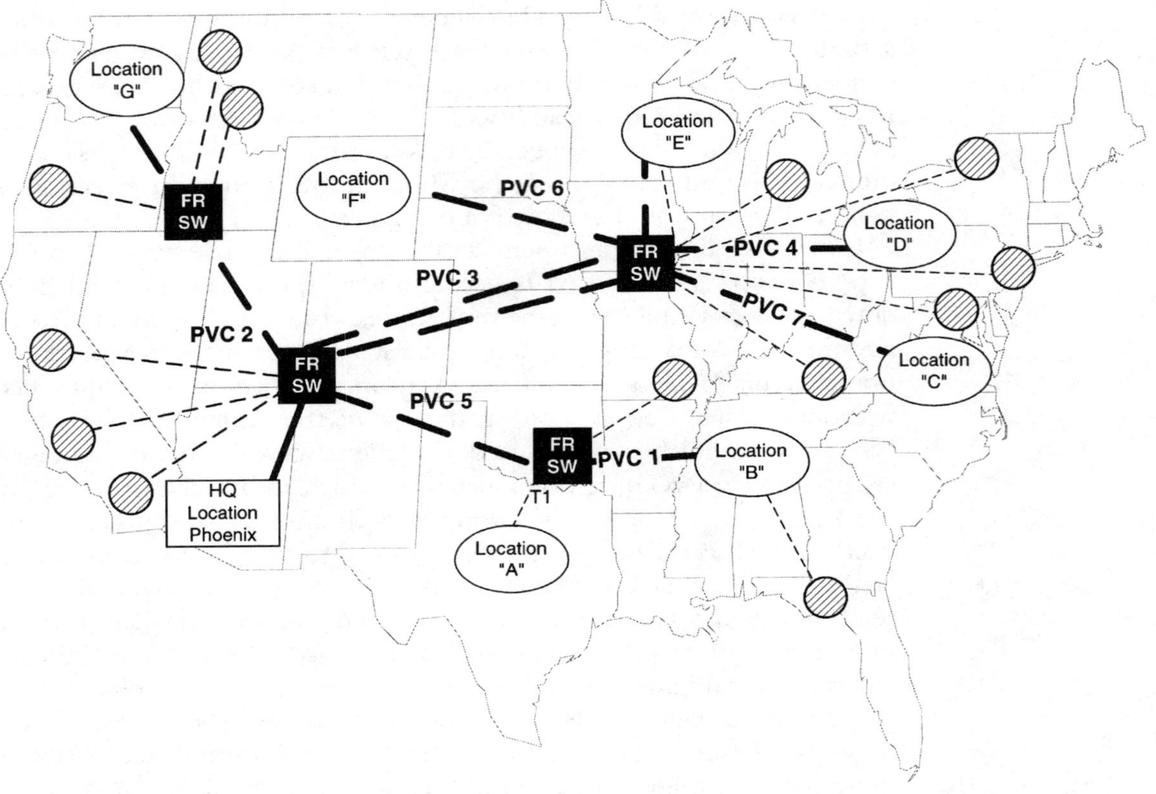

Figure 8.8 The heavy lines are the major PVCs to corporate headquarters; the light lines connect branches to the regions via PVCs.

regional office for retransmission to the corporate office, and, on the reverse flow, all data sets coming from the corporate office must be processed through the regional office and then to the originating site. Again, this setup can produce increased latency while yielding lower costs. Rather than showing the costs associated with these examples here, the client/server network manager should review the data needed for site-to-site communications. This newer version of the star network allows for communications between sites within a given region; however, it still allows access to the rest of the corporate environment as needed by rerouting through the corporate headquarters. Latency in the frame relay network can be very low, or it may be moderately high, depending on the nature and design of this network. Therefore, the client/server network manager must very careful in choosing the committed information rates and the speed of the PVCs necessary to each of these sites. This setup does increase the complexity of the network design while at the same time simplifying the network design, which is somewhat of a paradox.

There is no right or wrong decision in using this frame relay capacity; however, many managers of these internetworks have a propensity of installing more capacity than necessary. After two or three months of usage, they go back and modify the capacities based on actual usage. Doing so serves a twofold purpose: First, it prevents demands from exceeding capacities because excess is already in place. Second, it eliminates many of the concerns and frustrations of having too little right up front. The reverse of that whole equation means that when the fine-tuning takes place after a review of two or three months of data, the network may have been dynamic. Static networks very rarely exist in a client/server architecture. More data is generated on a regular basis, yielding more and more demands on a frame relay network. These newer demands are satisfied with the bursting capabilities. If, in the fine-tuning process, the network is tuned down while the volume of traffic is increasing, an inverse relationship becomes evident. Figure 8.9 shows this relationship as an inverse curve. Note that as the traffic increases and the capacity decreases, a certain threshold is achieved. This threshold, or break-even point, occurs at some level, depending on the nature of the traffic. What then happens is that the network manager is constantly tweaking and fine-tuning this network to raise the level of performance while lowering the overall frustration and delays in this network. Consequently, as the network is being fine-tuned on a regular basis, it consumes more of the client/server network manager's time. Unfortunately, time is very precious, and most managers have little of it. The use of this time in constantly monitoring the network is a direct opposite of what frame relay was essentially designed to accommodate. Frame relay was designed to be robust and resilient without all the fine-tuning on an ongoing basis. It is easy to fall into a trap. In constantly trying to tweak the network, the users are exposed to more frustrations and less confidence in the client/server internetwork. This loss of confidence manifests itself in user frustrations and complaints to senior staff or senior management. Therefore, the client/server network manager is put in a position of constantly justifying the equation between cost and benefit and trying to protect his or her decisions in the network design.

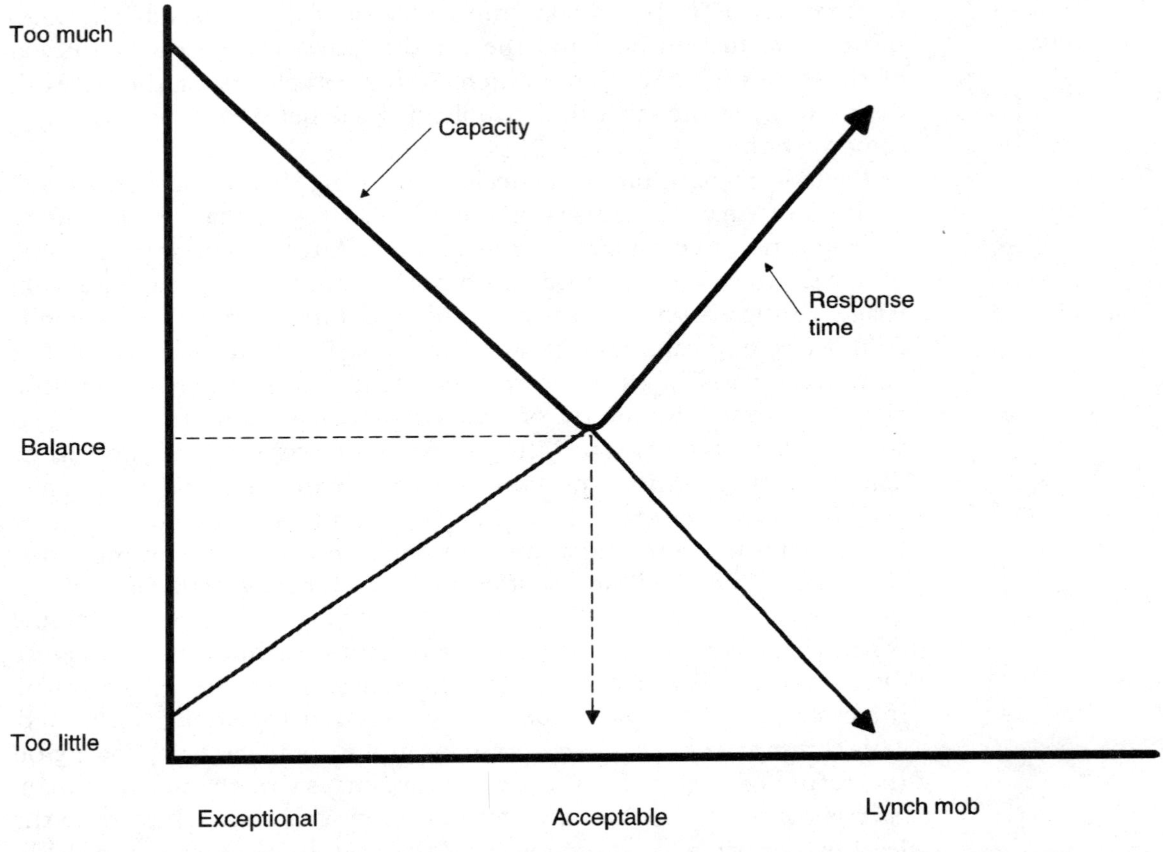

Figure 8.9 *As capacity decreases, the response time increases, yielding unacceptable performance.*

Carrier Support

The client/server network manager could rely on the network suppliers and carriers to assist in the design and rollout of frame relay capability. Unfortunately, this reliance has not met with great success. The carriers are learning themselves and are not yet fully familiar with all the benefits of frame relay capabilities. Frame relay was not readily deployed and accepted, so the carriers did not have a lot of user experience. For example, at about mid-1995, only about 5000 frame relay customers existed on a worldwide basis. Considering that the technology and the concept were initially rolled out in the early 1990s and became available commercially in mid-1991, there were not a lot of endorsements for the use of this service. Thus, as frame relay users were coming up to speed and learning about the capacities, the carriers were still trying to determine their best strategy in supporting these capabilities. By 1996, approximately 100,000 ports were installed worldwide. Although 100,000 ports may sound like a lot of services, in viewing a worldwide network, the number is insignificant compared to the total number of leased-line facilities and public packet-switched services available today. As the vendors are learning, they will design networks using various protocols.

In many cases, client/server networks rolled out across a worldwide basis were installed using older routing protocols. Routing information protocol (RIP) was used extensively by many of the carriers to support TCP/IP and IPX traffic in many local area networks. Unfortunately, RIP is overhead-intensive and delay-sensitive. Moreover, the routing tables using RIP become overwhelming. Using defaults based on standards, service advertising protocols (SAPs) are broadcast across the network in default of 30-minute increments. Twice per hour every router broadcasts its entire routing table to every other router as it cascades through the network. In many client/server networks of any significant size, these RIP broadcasts consume 10 to 20 minutes of what is called convergence. This slow convergence based on RIP means that the typical user network has only 30 to 40 minutes of available time to broadcast actual data.

Open shortest path first (OSPF) relieves some of this congestion by eliminating the need to broadcast in a slow convergence methodology. OSPF uses a fast convergence process that broadcasts only updates to tables instead of the entire routing table, reclaiming a significant amount of broadcast time. However, it does not support all of the routed protocols that are used on a network. IPX, for example, is typically not supported in OSPF. However, there are ways around this problem by using IPX traffic tunneled into an IP packet. By tunneling, we tend to add additional overhead; therefore, we must constantly be aware of the overhead associated with the combined TCP/IP and IPX tunneled traffic. One must compare the benefits and reclaimed time to the added overhead that would detract from total data throughput. Beyond that, the carrier community offering frame relay services does not typically understand the routing and routed protocol formats. In many cases, the carriers support and install RIP. With the overhead associated with the frame relay network and the RIP broadcasts, the frame relay network must be overdesigned to carry the actual data. Unfortunately, this has been the fate of many frame relay installations. Once a network on a frame relay service has been deployed and all routing tables have been built, it is very difficult to go back and reconfigure. Each router would have to be installed or reconfigured with the newer protocols (i.e., OSPF) at the exact same time. If this cannot be done, a dual protocol stack must be run during the transition from an older RIP to an OSPF environment. The amount of memory required in each of the routers would double or triple in size. Unless the routers had been configured with a significant excess capacity of memory, this is not an easy task. Therefore, one must make the decision up front on which protocols to support and run on a frame relay network. One should note that this discussion does not get limited to frame relay services. The same applies whether any other network technology is used.

Beyond the OSPF and RIP decision, there are several vendor-proprietary protocols being used in the industry. Many carriers offer these proprietary protocols based on the product lines that they support. An example includes carriers that offer Cisco routers as part of their overall offering. Cisco has developed the enhanced internetwork gateway routing protocol (EIGRP) as its primary offering. When a vendor has this service and offers the Cisco routers, it likely will steer the client/server network manager toward the use of EIGRP. Although it is not necessarily an unreasonable decision, it does limit the possibilities and the options to that specific vendor's products. In a mixed router environment, where a user may have many manufacturers' routing products, like Bay Networks, ACC, and Cisco, the use of EIGRP is not supported by the two competing vendors. What EIGRP does bring to the table, however, is the ability to support TCP/IP, IPX, and several other protocols, including the ability to run SNA/SDLC traffic in a tunneled fashion. This selection probably incorporates the bulk of the protocols that organizations are using, but it has a price. The memory capacities, as well as the vendor-specific products, tend to bear a higher cost from the carriers.

When the decision to use a protocol across a frame relay network is made, it must be made very carefully. Once a frame network decision is made, the change-out of routing and routed protocols is very, very complex. To change out, for example, from RIP to OSPF or from RIP to EIGRP, every router across the network should be changed at exactly the same time so that the new tables can be built instantaneously. It must be done during an off-hours cycle because of the network traffic that is generated by the routers as they initially set the tables across the network. However, in a global frame relay network or any form of wide area network supporting client/server internetworking, there is no such thing as off hours. Time zone differences on a global basis always have users trying to communicate to the server, no matter what the hour. Depending on the diversity and the spread of different sites, one therefore has to select the lightest use cycle. A second option would exist whereby a dual protocol stack could be used in routers. For short periods of time, OSPF could used in some routers and RIP could be used in others. This complicates the situation because many of the routers would have to support the dual protocol stacks simultaneously. Unless the routers were selected with enough additional memory available to support two separate sets of routing tables, the increase in memory in each of the routers is both cost-prohibitive and very complex. Carriers rolling out one set of protocols therefore could limit the options to the vendor-specific products they offer, which may not be in the best interest of the end user. Moreover, when this convergence must take place, a data set being routed across the network in a dual stack mode may well have to go through protocol conversion. An end user at a local area network might transmit data across the frame relay network back to the corporate headquarters on one set of protocols, where it then would have to be converted and retransmitted to another router that operates on a different protocol. This conversion process adds to the overall latency, delay, and cost of the frame relay service.

Chapter 9 discusses the various routing protocols and equipment; however, it behooves each client/server networking manager to understand the potential drawbacks and risks before proceeding and installing a set of tables and a set of protocols that could ultimately become detrimental. Although the carriers are neither deliberately sabotaging the end users' requirements nor trying to drive up the demands of data throughput, that is the end result. To support these higher-convergence protocols like RIP, excess capacity in the PVCs must be installed to support the entire overhead necessary to run this network. This excess capacity is wasted strictly as a result of the routing table updates. For now, one must just appreciate that the design and rollout of a client/server internetwork is not a simple task. The improper design, the wrong protocols, or the wrong vendor choice could significantly impact the overall effectiveness and acceptance of a client/server internetwork. Barring these issues, the cost savings that could have been achieved on frame relay may well be mitigated or totally reversed to a more expensive proposition. These are the risks that users must face as they choose the appropriate networking topology.

In any frame relay network supporting a client/server application, there are occasions when multicasting of data sets or frames of information is required. If the vendor has not used the frame relay specifications that support multicast services and full internetworking capabilities between different carriers, other problems could arise. An example in the United States stemmed from the unacceptance or reluctance of some of the long-haul carriers to provide a network-to-network interface (NNI) between the local exchange carriers using frame relay services and the wide area network carriers. Many customers are forced to select a sole source to provide their networking services, which again may not be to the best advantage of the end user. More of these carriers supporting wide area networking services are now getting into a network-to-network interface capability, providing full internetworking services. However, it is again a slow rollout and acceptance. The frame relay user must therefore understand exactly how the carrier selected will support these different capabilities. Where frame relay reduces the cost of a meshed network and provides the reliability and resiliency over what a private line does, these lower costs can be offset by having to use a single network supplier if the NNI is not available. An example might well include the local exchange carrier offerings providing 64-kbps frame relay services at flat-rate pricing. Where an LEC may offer a flat-rate 64-kbps frame service for $30 to $40 per month per site, the wide area networking suppliers may well have been offering the same speed and services for costs in excess of $200 per month. This cost disadvantage impairs the ability to provide global connectivity on a ubiquitous basis. Once again, the end user designing the client/server internetwork must understand where the data must go and at what speeds. It would not be uncommon to use several network suppliers, each providing a different regional offering or a different global offering, and mix and match these services. Separate network links may well be required at the WAN side of the router. Adding additional WAN ports to these routers incrementally increases the cost.

This discussion is not designed to scare the client/server internetworking manager away from frame relay or from the carriers. Many successful implementations have been achieved over the past five years. Furthermore, many carriers have been supportive and assisted their clients in designing the networks to be fine-tuned while performing internetworking architectures. The true benefits of frame relay services include the following:

1. Savings of the on-demand services over a private-line, point-to-point circuitry
2. More flexibility in the design and change of a network versus the private-line facilities
3. Higher expected robustness and resiliency in the network
4. Lower costs and, hopefully, better utilization of the bandwidth and speed throughputs available on frame services
5. Multiprotocol support consolidating local area and wide area networking capabilities, including IBM's SNA architecture
6. Simplified network designs and overall network performance
7. Reduced costs and higher application-performance capabilities

Frame relay therefore should be considered as one of the viable alternatives for designing the client/server internetwork. Its capability overcomes the past limitations of time division multiplexed T1 networks and point-to-point circuits by using a statistical multiplexing capability with the option of higher-speed bursting. Moreover, the average traffic load is what is considered when designing frame relay, as opposed to trying to overdesign just for peak performances. This negates the need to have far more capacity for the average transfer of information. Profits will follow. Alternatively, the ability to use multiple protocols and support multiple data sets of different manufacturers' systems and products gives the client/server internetwork manager far more options and less complexities than having separate data networks for an IBM architecture, a Novell architecture, and an NT network. Using standard products such as routers, bridges, and FRADs, as mentioned earlier, the device can handle varying payloads of different links, give the greatest throughput, and minimize the overhead where possible. Consequently, frame relay provides a very robust solution for internetworking in a client/server environment.

ISDN Backup Capabilities

An addition to frame relay access in a client/server internetwork is the ability to provide automatic alternate routing or dial backup capabilities using ISDN basic rate interface (BRI) as a backup facility in the event of a leased-line failure on the local frame relay access link. Routers, bridges, and FRADs now have the capability of automatically dialing into the

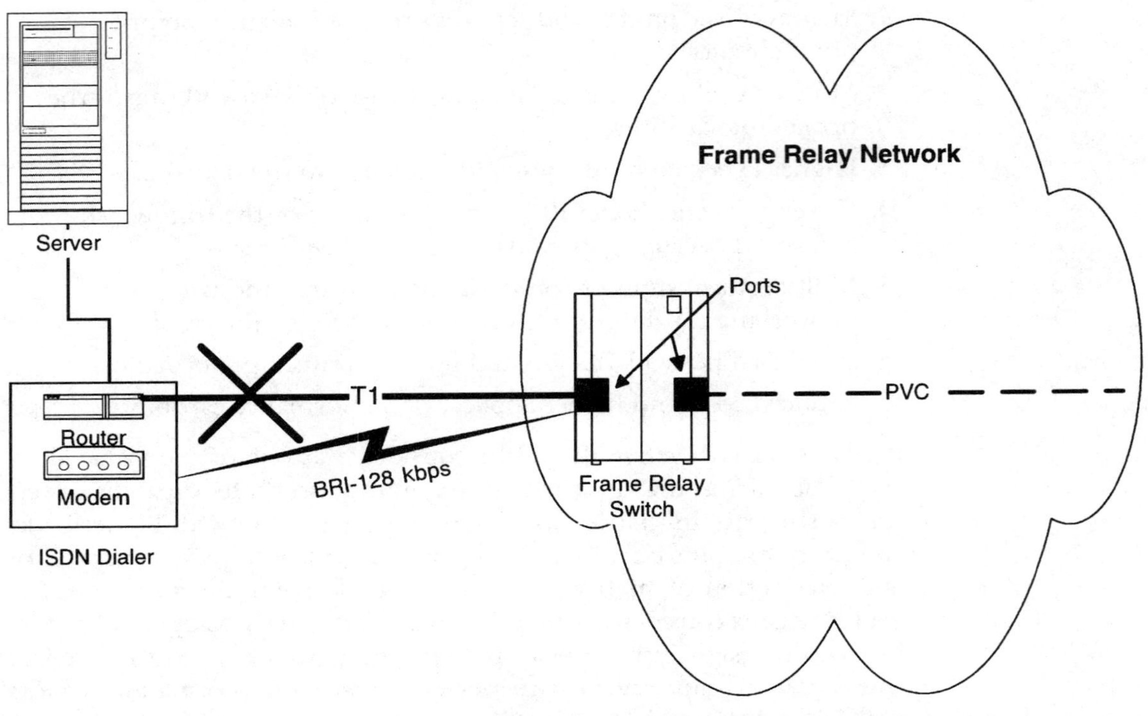

Figure 8.10 With ISDN dial backup (BRI), the router can auto-dial into the frame relay switch port if a leased line fails.

frame relay network in the event of a link failure, as shown in Fig. 8.10. Although it may take some time to activate the ISDN link, dial up the connection to the frame relay port, and reestablish a connection, it is much faster than having to wait for the LEC or PTT to repair a downed link. Moreover, in the event the frame relay network is down, an alternative dial backup plan can be used whereby the ISDN link can dial directly point-to-point to a communications server located back at the regional office. Figure 8.11 represents this alternative to provide the connectivity in the event of a link state failure. The use of this dial backup capability can be incorporated into the client/server internetworking contract with the carriers.

An alternative is to convince the carrier that if the frame relay network is down, it is highly likely that their entire dial network serving a particular location is also down. Therefore, by using an ISDN BRI pro-

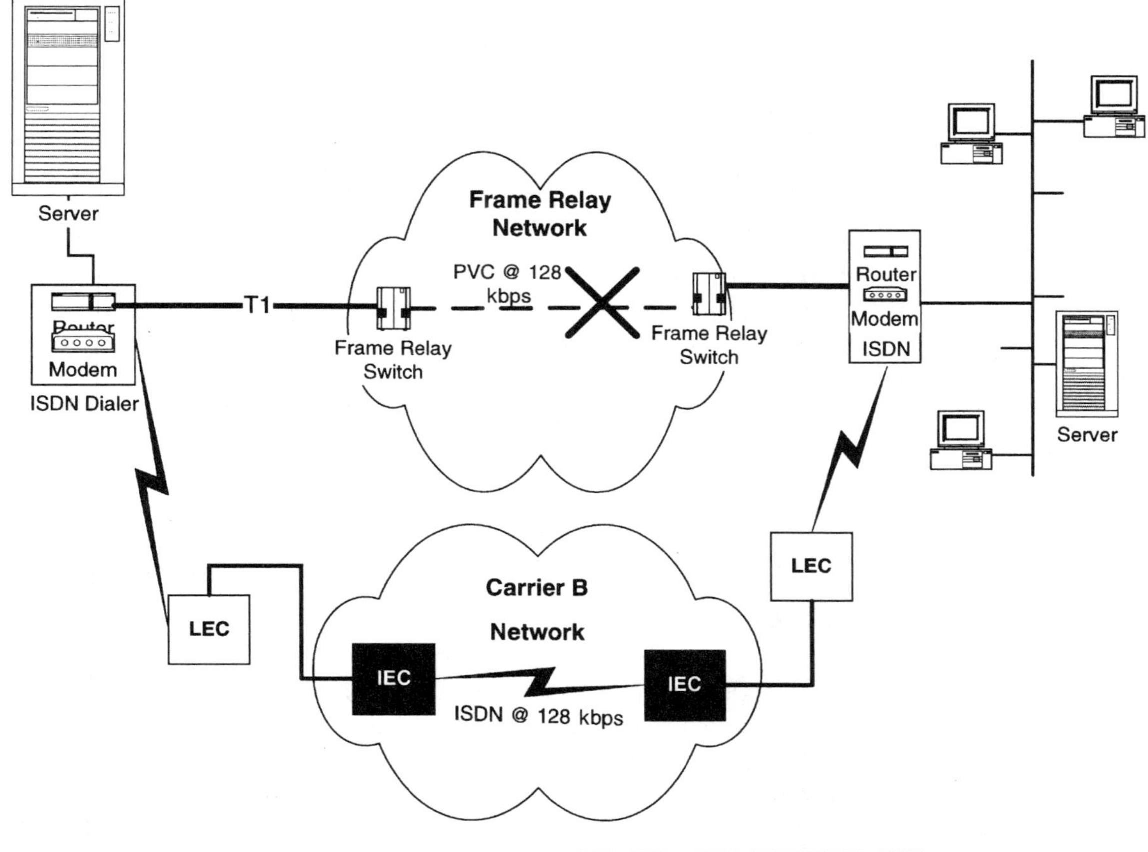

Figure 8.11 An ISDN direct dial can be used around the frame relay as an alternative.

vided by the LEC as opposed to the wide area networking carrier, the ability to steer the dial backup across a competitive network exists. This alternative is not popular with the carriers, because it steers traffic to competitors. However, it does provide incentive for that carrier to guarantee network performance and assurances rather than to route traffic to one of its competitors. An obvious but unstated position here is that the carrier should absorb the cost for each of the dial-up connections that occur when a link state failure or a frame relay network failure occurs. There is no reason the client/server networking manager or the client company should have to pay to recover the network during short periods of time, albeit at reduced rates of speed when it becomes evident that the network is down. This is a carrier responsibility and should be considered as such. Many client/server networking managers have been able to negotiate this form of a deal. It is not easy, nor do the various carriers readily accept it. However, the goal is to provide high availability, high performance, robustness, and assurances that the data will go through when all of an organization's data resides on this single networking architecture. Therefore, the carrier, although negatively responding to this proposal, can be convinced that it is in both its and the client's best interest to provide this ubiquitous connection. One can imagine the support that could be achieved when a network link failure occurs and traffic is being routed to a competitor. The incentive and the drive rests strictly with the carrier whose network is failing to get service back up and running quickly and efficiently to minimize the amount of money it has to pay a competitor.

Integrated Services Digital Network (ISDN)

Another service that is available to client/server managers is integrated services digital network (ISDN). ISDN is a technology that has been considered for approximately 15 years, but it never really made it big in the industry. Although the concept is sound, carriers and vendors alike could not produce a product or a service that was ubiquitously available to all users. Moreover, the use of ISDN was implemented differently from carrier to carrier, thereby causing total confusion throughout the industry. As users were experimenting with ISDN, they discovered that inconsistencies and incompatibilities existed between network suppliers. This in turn caused the user to hold back or withdraw acceptance of ISDN. Now standards exist. As a result, users can look to ISDN as an integrating tool to link their client/server networks together. Since ISDN was designed as primarily a raw pipe, it allows the user to place any voice or nonvoice circuit-switched capability on this pipe. In a client/server network, the user can integrate ISDN into and around higher-speed communications needs. An example might be the branch office use where dedicated point-to-point circuits cannot be justified. As a result, using a router with the ability to do circuit-switched connectivity, the branch office or remote smaller office can easily be accommodated. Costwise, the use of

ISDN eliminates the point-to-point circuitry that would be needed otherwise. By using on-demand circuit-switched communications or a programmed time-of-day routing capability, a local site can automatically initiate a call between its location and the headquarters hosting the server. In the basic rate interface (BRI), the ability to bond two channels together at 64 kbps gives the router at the remote site the ability to move up to 128 kbps. Using the ISDN BRI and the timed sequence, a network service can provide fairly decent performance. However, one should realize this is not a real trunk but a preprogrammed connection that could cause some delay or latency. Looking at the smaller branch offices, however, one can assume that the LAN user will typically be accessing the capabilities of the localized server; therefore, the connection to the host server in a client/server network may not be needed on a full-time basis.

Another option would be to have the router programmed at some threshold that data generated on the LAN would automatically dial-up to the server even though a time sequence has not arrived. This capability may well be used with either a protocol-specific application or a threshold of buffers that accumulate and, upon filling, automatically generate a dial-up connection. The BRI is a relatively inexpensive solution connecting to the circuit-switched dial-up communications network. As an all-digital service using clear channel capability (64 kbps), a network supplier can provide 64 to 128 kbps to the remote office. Taking this one step further, larger sites may well look at the primary rate interface (PRI). The PRI is really nothing more than a T1 link on a circuit-switched basis using 23 channels of 64 kbps for data transport, plus a 64-kbps channel for signaling and control. In either case, the use of ISDN can add some flexibility and cost-containment ideas to the client/server network. Figure 8.12 shows the ISDN BRI. It is a two-wire circuit brought to the user's door by the local supplier or whoever is providing service. Through this two-wire connection, the user is given circuit-switch capabilities at two channels operating on 64 kbps plus an out-of-band signaling channel capability at 16 kbps. This figure shows what the user sees and gets. At some point in time, this may well be rolled out to the end user or be used by the carrier in supplementing its network services.

Figure 8.13 shows a typical configuration with a router using an ISDN BRI connection. Here the routers are connected into the circuit-switched portion of the network as opposed to the frame/packet-switched network. As the access is used on a dial-up basis, the communications channel can be routed to any addressable location. Using standard telephone numbers makes the connection more robust in that regard.

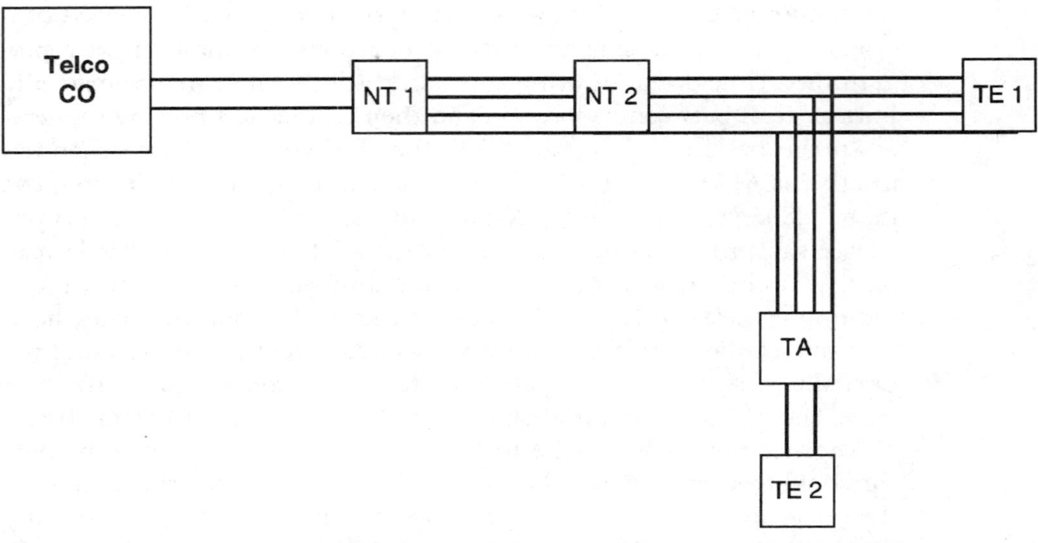

Figure 8.12 The ISDN BRI model. NT1 = network termination type 1 (demarcation jack). NT 2 = network termination type 2 (PBX, router, LAN, etc.). TE 1 = ISDN terminal equipment type 1 (ISDN terminal). TA = terminal adapter (analog/digital converter). TE 2 = terminal equipment type 2—non-ISDN (modem, fax, etc.).

However, one must also consider that ISDN dial-up communications bonding two channels together at 128 kbps will draw a significant penalty: cost. The routers shown in this figure are merely using a circuit-switched connection capability. In the event more capacity is needed, the primary rate can be brought in, as shown in Fig. 8.14. In this case, the router can automatically activate or deactivate the circuits necessary, depending on the degree of speed needed, on some preconfigured routing table that activates capacity as necessary, or as certain thresholds of buffering are achieved. The PRI also allows for the capability of preconfiguring by using multirate ISDN services. In this case, specific locations may always be addressed at 384 kbps and others at 128 kbps. What this option gives us is something similar to what the frame relay services offer without having to pay for a predesignated or committed capacity. One merely has to program the router to automatically switch circuits as necessary. When not used for data communications in the client/server network, the PRI channels can be used for circuit-switched voice or dial-up video conferencing capabilities, allowing more flexibility in smaller, more remote offices that do not consistently transmit data all day long in bursts but burst perhaps once or twice a day.

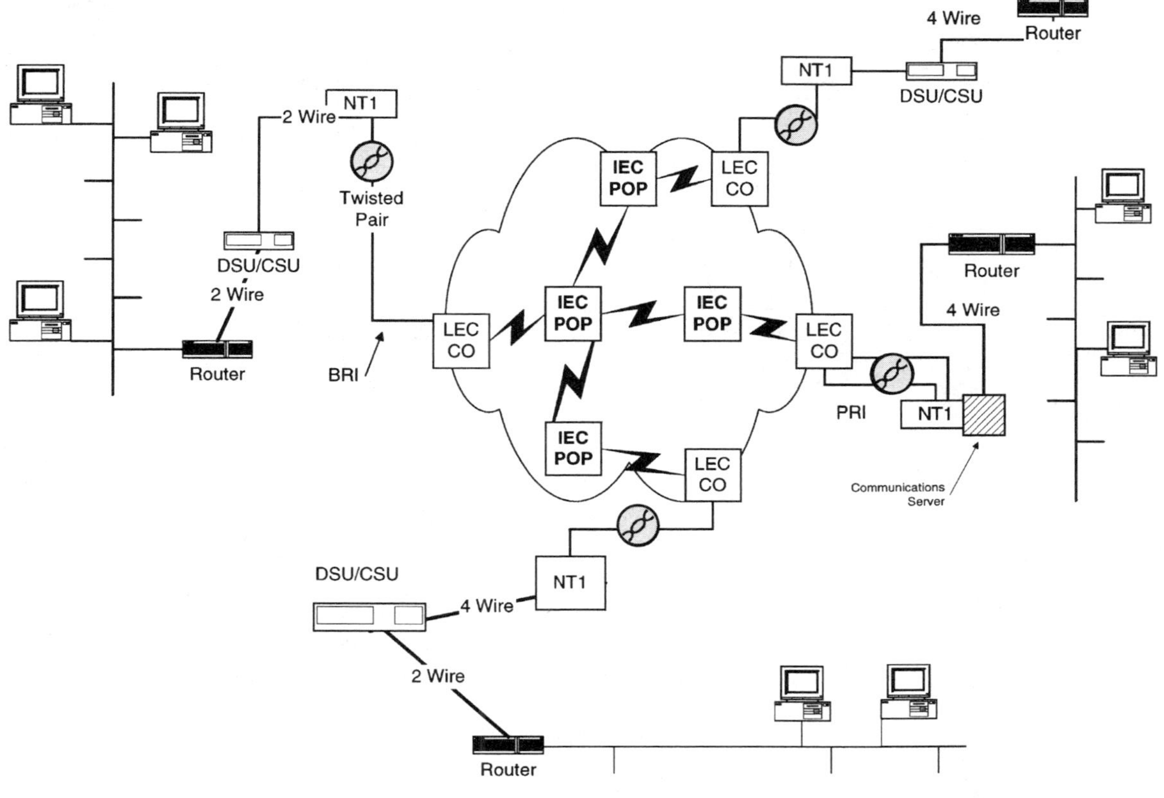

Figure 8.13 A typical ISDN dial-up connection with routers allows any circuit-switched location connectivity.

ISDN will also be used to connect with bridges and routers. Figure 8.15 shows a router network. This router network, using leased-line capabilities or some form of frame service, now has the ability, through ISDN, to add capacity as congestion begins to build. In the event a certain buffer parameter is exceeded, the router automatically activates a 64-kbps channel. If that addition is not enough, the router can add channels as necessary. Through this whole process, as more and more channels are added, the router keeps track of the circuit-switch connection. One must assume that the receiving end also has the ability to receive these calls at the designated speeds. From there, as the traffic is handled and the congestion subsides, the router releases the channel-by-channel capabilities in 64-kbps increments until the link is back to its

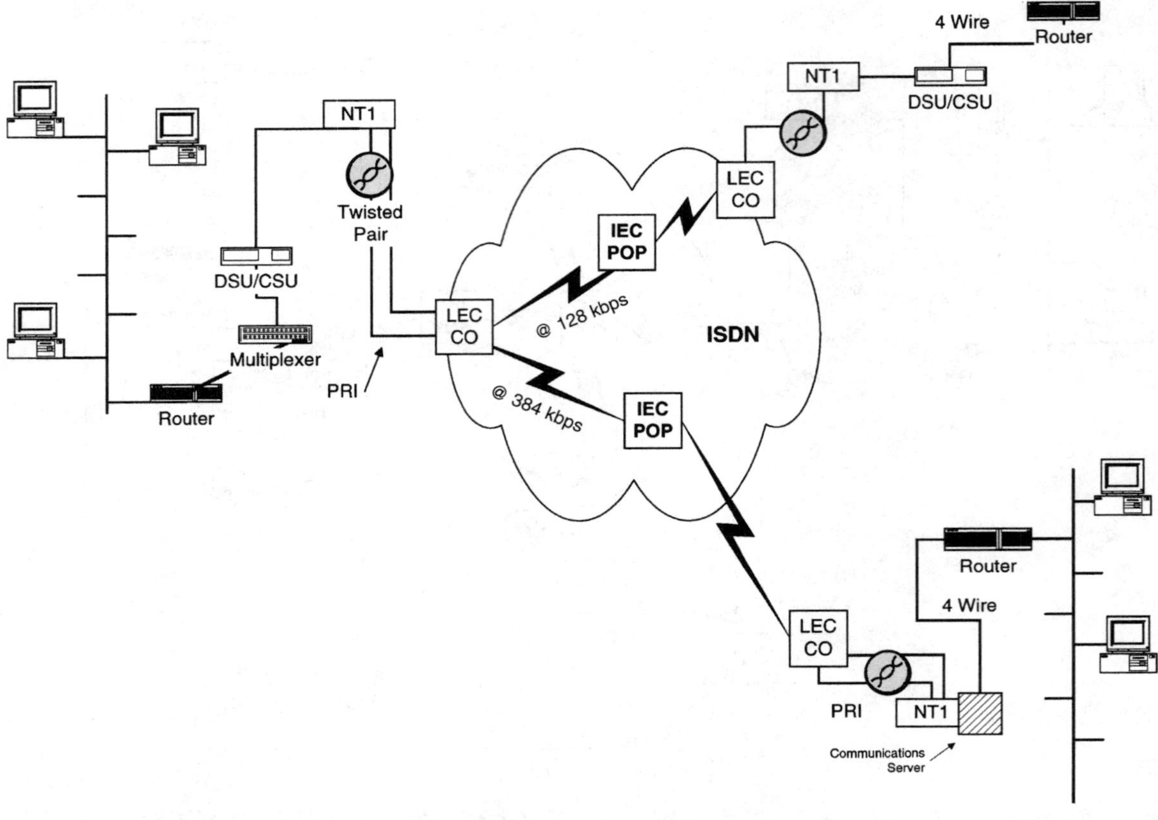

Figure 8.14 The router can activate as much capacity as needed up to 23 channels on the PRI.

original state. This setup allows a lot of flexibility and robustness in a client/server network, as well as another choice. By using the ISDN circuit-switched capability, sites can be added or deleted on the fly. When a new site is needed, ISDN on a dial-up basis is an alternative for quick communications connectivity while waiting for a PTT or a local exchange carrier to provide the local connection. It is only the confusion and the incompatible connections that have held back ISDN in a client/server network for so long. Now ISDN is starting to yield a resurgence in both popularity and availability, which will change the way the client/server internetwork is being used. Bridging techniques—linking two sites together directly on a dedicated point-to-point circuit—are no longer needed. Where needed, these techniques can be used; where not, ISDN

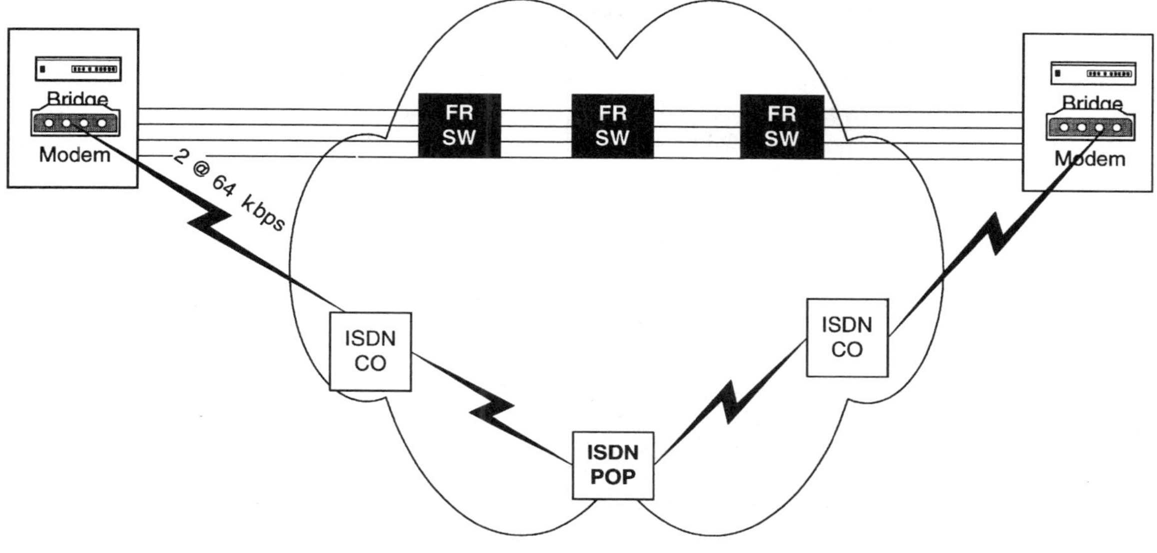

Figure 8.15 The additional capacity can be added on a dial-up basis using ISDN dynamically. When demand decreases, the 64-kbps channels are released.

can offer some choices. As more and more client/server internetworks are built, the server-based platforms with demands of circuit-switched voice, data, multimedia, and video capabilities to the desktop may well be satisfied through the use of high-speed ISDN services.

ISDN is but a precursor of future networks called broadband ISDN (B-ISDN). B-IDSN will bring to the table even more capacity and speed to achieve all of these services on a circuit-switched, cost-per-minute, call-by-call basis. What then is available to the end user includes the capabilities of any type of voice or data communications across any network service, anywhere in the world. Client/server network managers should definitely spend time reviewing the abilities and capabilities of ISDN in their overall network designs.

For primary service, as well as backup service and a robust short-term solution to local loop problems, ISDN brings much more to the table than one would have once expected. A problem with ISDN that should be addressed is the price issue. Where this book has been considering the variations for typical communications channel capabilities, ISDN should not be excluded. One must look at what a local exchange carrier or PTT offers in terms of pricing issues. In many parts of the

United States, LECs are basically supportive of ISDN and, therefore, reflect that in their pricing. For example, an IDSN link using BRI in California can cost as little as $30 per month using the two bearer services and the data link channel capability for call setup and tear-down. At this price, ISDN is reasonable; however, if one were to look a mere few hundred miles to the east, U.S. West offers the same type of service for $75 a month with usage-sensitive pricing. Under this pricing arrangement, one could expect to pay in the vicinity of several hundred to thousands of dollars per month. The price is not competitive and users are typically shying away from it. Interestingly, when dealing with the PRI, the carriers are inverse in their pricing arrangements. They are charging more yet delivering slightly less. One must consider the access link at T1 speeds versus PRI speeds and determine what might be a better alternative. There is no one single solution that any end user can choose. Each network will be different, configured differently, and priced appropriately. ISDN should be considered as a potential alternative or primary service.

Switched Multimegabit Data Services (SMDS)

Another service that LECs can bring to the table is switched multimegabit data services (SMDS). This is another part of the fast-relay (fast packet-switching) family. In 1989, BellCore developed SMDS for local exchange carriers as a means of providing a high-speed communications channel capability within a geographic area (the metropolitan area). SMDS is a public packet-switching concept that links together LANs in the MAN. As a high-speed communications capability, SMDS offers rates of speed for client/server internetworking that were not possible before. In this particular case, a client/server manager can select high-speed communications channel capabilities across a metropolitan area at speeds of 4, 10, 16, 25, or 34 megabits per second. At these speeds, the client/server network can be interconnected at native-LAN throughput capabilities. One must merely rent a high-speed communication access link from the LEC into the facility, as shown in Fig. 8.16, typically at speeds of T3. Although T3 has always been an expensive proposition, when dealing with SMDS, the LECs are very creative in providing this access pipe. In many parts of the United States where SMDS has been rolled out and deployed well within their domain, LECs have offered it at lower than T3 prices. In many cases, a T3 access link to a site may well have been in the range of $6000 to $8000 per month, but the same access pipe for SMDS service could cost as little as $1000 a month. This LAN connection across the metropolitan area allows for native throughput in a packet-switching concept. SMDS uses a distributed queue on a dual bus (DQDB) architecture concept. By using a queued service or a shared

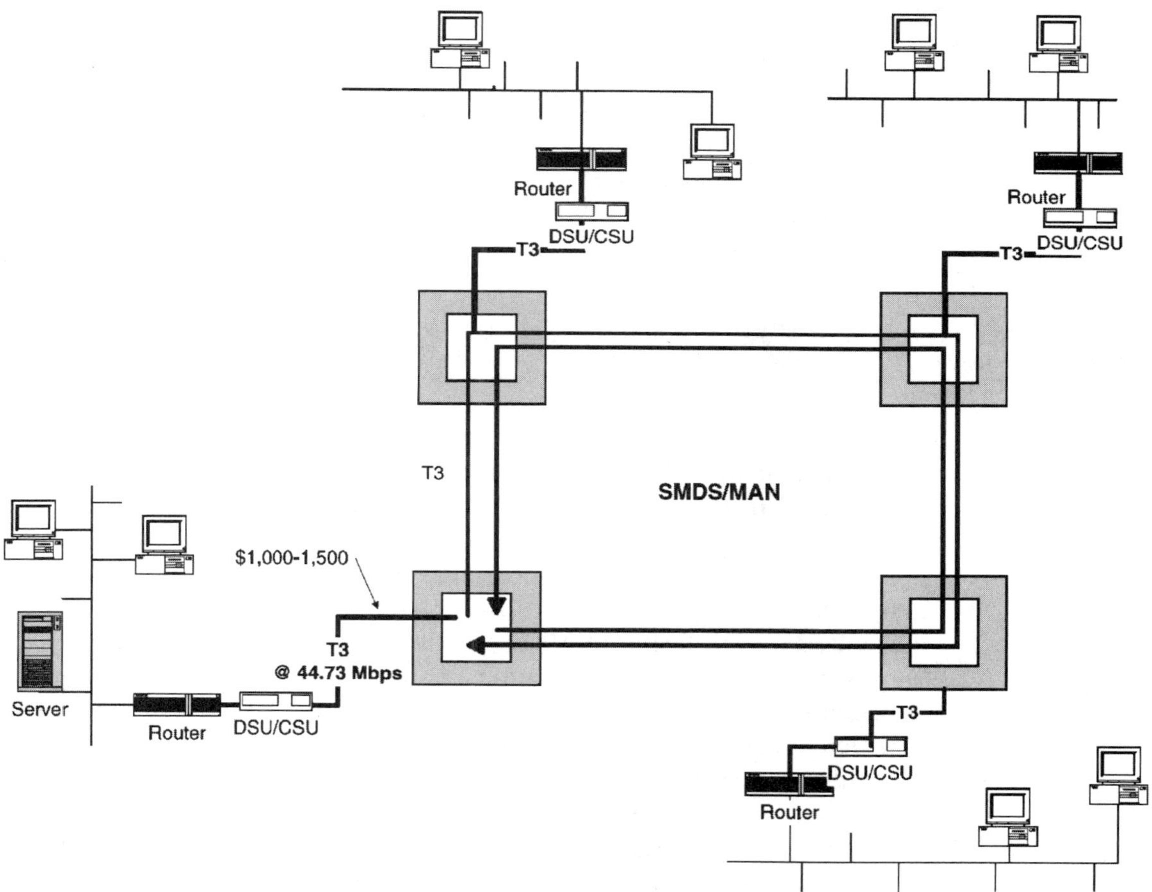

Figure 8.16 A single high-speed T3 link is needed into the metropolitan area network (MAN) at each site for SMDS access.

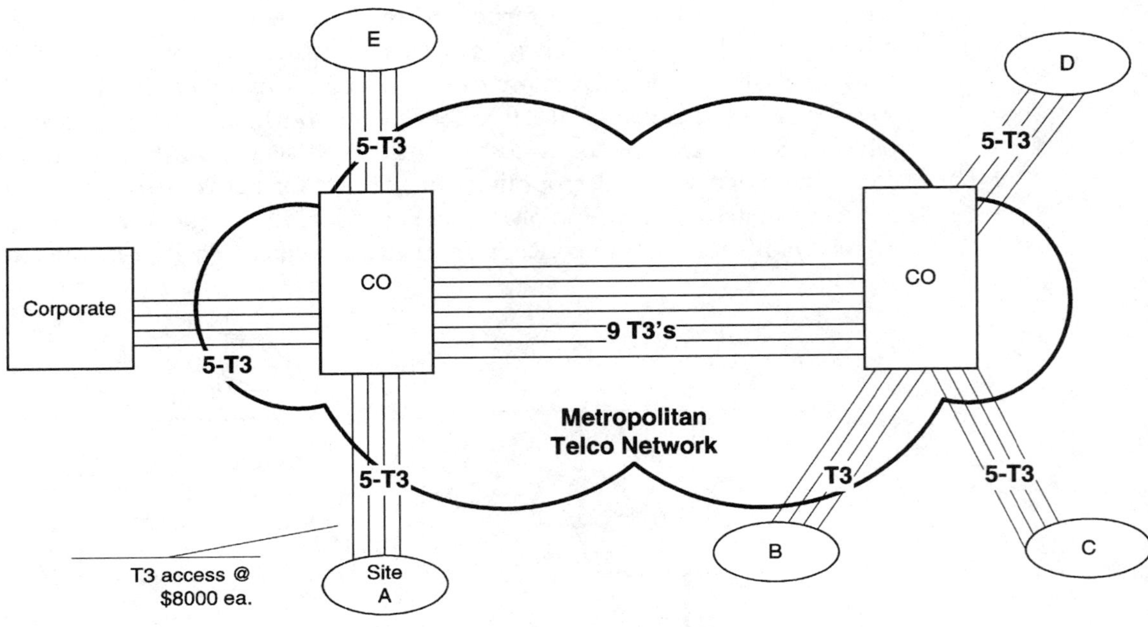

Figure 8.17 In a fully meshed network, the total number of circuits becomes exponential and cost-prohibitive.

resource across the links, the LECs offer competitive pricing. Instead of buying a dedicated point-to-point circuit meshing all of the sites together, as shown in Fig. 8.17, the end user must only buy a single access connection into the dual bus and provide connections there. SMDS using DQDB is a fast packet-switching concept, but it actually produces a 53-byte cell that will be used on this network. Perfect! High-speed routers are used to link LAN to LAN across the MAN. In many cases the carrier provides these high-speed routers. In a metropolitan area, reasonably priced services at native LAN throughputs are becoming more prevalent, which means higher-speed connections and happier end users in a client/server access method.

When a client/server network is being distributed throughout a major metropolitan area, this SMDS service can offer some highly robust and highly reliable services. Figure 8.18 shows a network using a distributed queue on a dual bus. In this particular case, the network can be provided using what is called a closed architecture. In a closed architecture, although it is a bus topology, it strongly resembles a ring topology. As a result, in the event of a link failure, the network can heal

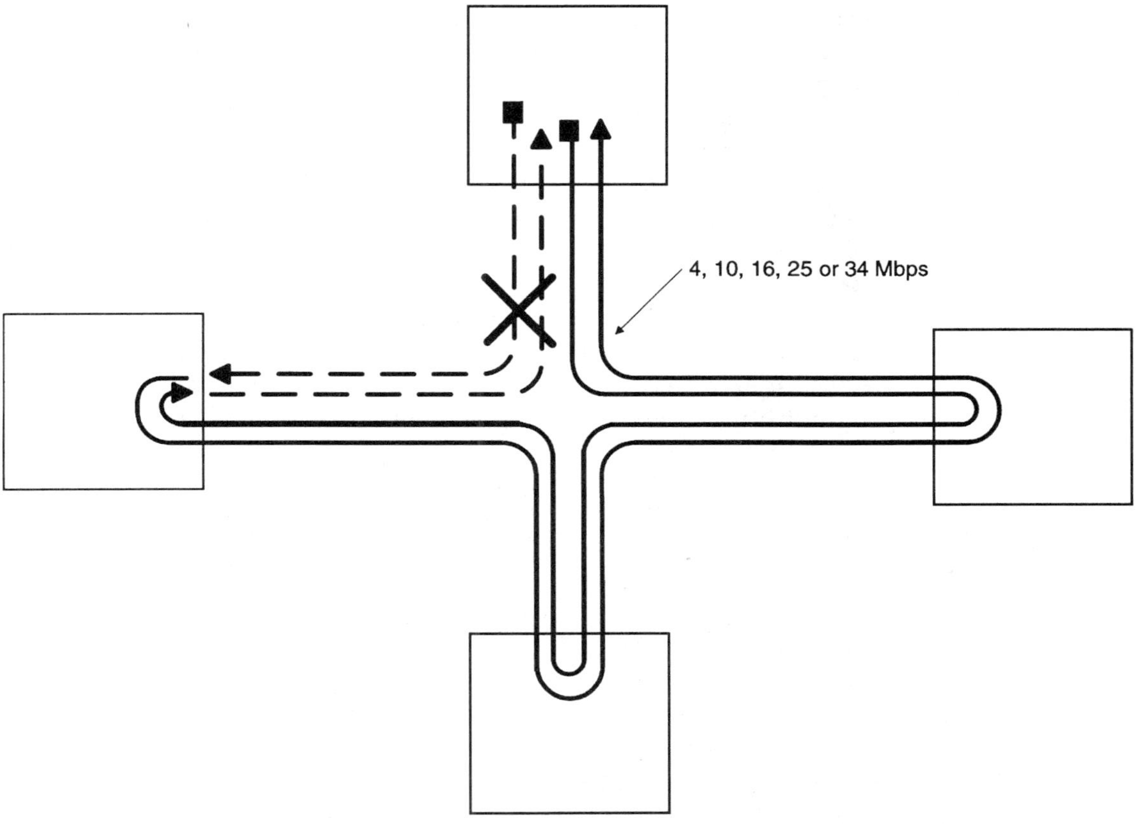

Figure 8.18 The closed architecture on two unidirectional bus systems allows the network to heal itself after a link failure.

itself, reversing the direction of the cable communications system and restoring itself immediately. When dealing with this kind of throughput at up to 34 Mbps, one needs to have assurances that the network will be highly available. Pricewise, LECs have provided the services at almost a give-away proposition.

On an international basis, SMDS is delivered by the PTTs using a different terminology. In this particular case, connectionless broadband data services (CBDS) are what the carriers offer. Regardless of its name, they both are functionally the same. In a CBDS environment, the international community delivers 4, 10, 16, and 25 Mbps, not yet the 34 Mbps. That difference will likely disappear in the very near future. While the industry was waiting for high-speed communications in the wide area networks scenario, the PTTs and LECs decided to roll out their connections, at least within the metropolitan area. As a fast packet service, SMDS can support the client/server network very nicely. Regardless of the protocols used, the topology used at the LAN environment, or the application that is being run, the SMDS network is protocol-independent. Therefore, as the data is prepared to be shipped onto the cable system, the high-speed communications router merely encapsulates it into a 53-byte cell and prepares it for transmission. In its independence, protocolwise, the network can deliver the data transparently across the network at very high rates of speed. This ability yields better throughput, reduces cost, and allows more flexibility within that geographically bounded area called the MAN. The LECs have been giving this service away at very, very inexpensive prices. It would not be uncommon to hear of an LEC providing the service and the router as part of the DCE/DTE (data circuit/data terminating equipment) instead of the customer-premises equipment. This gives the LEC better control of the network by providing the router as the interface to its network service. While using this capability, it can therefore configure and control the bandwidth use across the high-speed fiber channels throughout the metropolitan area. Some locations have been noted as offering these same kinds of services, including the router, for as little as $1000 per month per site with no charge for the usage or the cells. These prices have been unheard of in the past and yet now are more readily available and viable as an alternative connection capability within that area. Resiliency, robustness, and price competitiveness have all been delivered through this service. It becomes evident that the client/server manager must analyze the possibility of using SMDS. Not all carriers in the LEC community or PTTs offer this service. However, where it is available, one may well look at the possibilities of deploying high-speed communications at native LAN throughputs across a geographic area such as a city or a major campus environment. Moreover, some of the IECs offer the connection between SMDS in the metropolitan area to the wide area network. An example of this is the MCI (now British Telecom) network throughout the United States. In the United Kingdom, British Telecom (BT) offers CBDS. These services are readily available in the areas where they are well deployed, but they are not ubiquitous, as already stated. SMDS can offer some high throughput capabilities at very reasonable prices for a client/server internetwork.

Asynchronous Transfer Mode (ATM)

While the industry was busy looking at some of the other services already mentioned, such as frame relay, ISDN, and SMDS, there was another movement afoot to produce a high-speed communications structure to deliver greater throughputs. The result is asynchronous transfer mode (ATM), introduced in 1992. Although not yet ready for prime time, when it becomes fully available, this one technology offers the high-speed capabilities for which client/server network managers have been looking. Slated to start at 50 Mbps, ATM takes up where all other transport systems leave off. ATM delivers to the client/server internetwork the capability of linking all services to include LAN to LAN, LAN to WAN, LAN to MAN, and LAN to CAN. This one transport system is designed to work from the desktop all the way across the wide area. What ATM brings to the client/server networking strategy is the capability of merging voice, data, video, and multimedia services to the desktop and across all the other networking strategies. Figure 8.19 shows the ATM cell. As part of the fast packet-switching family, called cell relay, ATM uses a fixed cell size to deliver all of the capabilities discussed here. The important part of ATM is not the data or transport that is being carried, but the header information and the fixed cell size. In a client/server network where several protocols will be run both at the desktop and across the wide area, ATM is protocol-independent. This independence allows a client/server manager to link sites remotely on a PVC today, which allows the header information to be the primary concern with routing the information. Whether a client/server network uses RIP, OSPF, or EIGRP, the network will still transport in an encapsulated 53-byte cell format. The industry is excited about the use of ATM and aggregated throughput capabilities. Client/server networks can now draw upon native

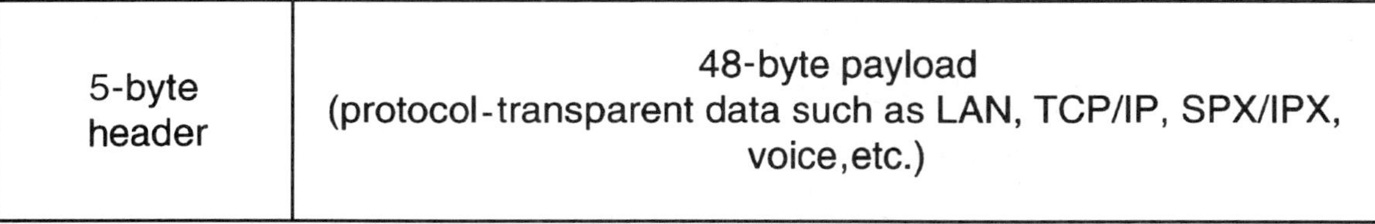

Figure 8.19 The ATM cell is fixed at 53 bytes (5 for the header and 48 for payload) and carries any form of data.

LAN throughput across a wide area regardless of any other intermediate steps. Whether at the desktop, the backbone infrastructure of a high-rise building, across a city, or across the entire domestic United States and international sites, ATM brings to the forefront a single transport system that will allow total transparency and high-speed communications. Although pricing is not yet a given, client/server network managers can negotiate with their carriers and discuss long-term pricing agreements to bring this technology to the forefront. One can assume that by the turn of the century ATM will be ubiquitous (or closely so) and that the pricing methodologies and congestion-management systems will all be in place. However, for the short term, the client/server manager still has options for negotiation with the carriers.

This transport capability will allow for an early release of data through network nodes across the complete domain of the wide area. Once the header information has been transmitted to a switching system, either at the LAN or WAN environment, the data is all ready to be transported to its next location. This differs from older techniques, where the entire frame had to be received and buffered before anything could be done with the data. By reducing this step, latency can be reduced or totally eliminated as the network proliferates. In Fig. 8.20, the ATM network is shown as an aggregation of bandwidth, at speeds ranging from basic voice, using 64-kbps digital transmission systems, up to 622 Mbps of information. In this drawing, one can see how the various pieces can be pulled together to allow the client/server network to aggregate as well as to bring together all of our transport systems onto a single high-speed communications link. Figure 8.21 shows the permanent virtual circuit connections.

By using a constant bit rate (CBR), which is the frame relay equivalent of a committed information rate (CIR), the end user can establish links that will provide high-speed communications throughput between multiple sites. Although not really called a CIR, ATM uses some of the basic strategies of frame relay. In fact, today's infrastructure frame relay is used by the end user and then repackaged as ATM cells in the wide area by the IECs. Therefore, what we really see today is a combination of ATM and frame relay working harmoniously together across the wide area. Frames enter the cloud, as shown in Fig. 8.22, and the carrier then reduces the frame into cells at 53 bytes each. Output from the far end of the cloud is now repackaged into frames operating at whatever speed the frame relay is rented. This synergy between ATM and frame relay will likely remain in place for the next three to four years.

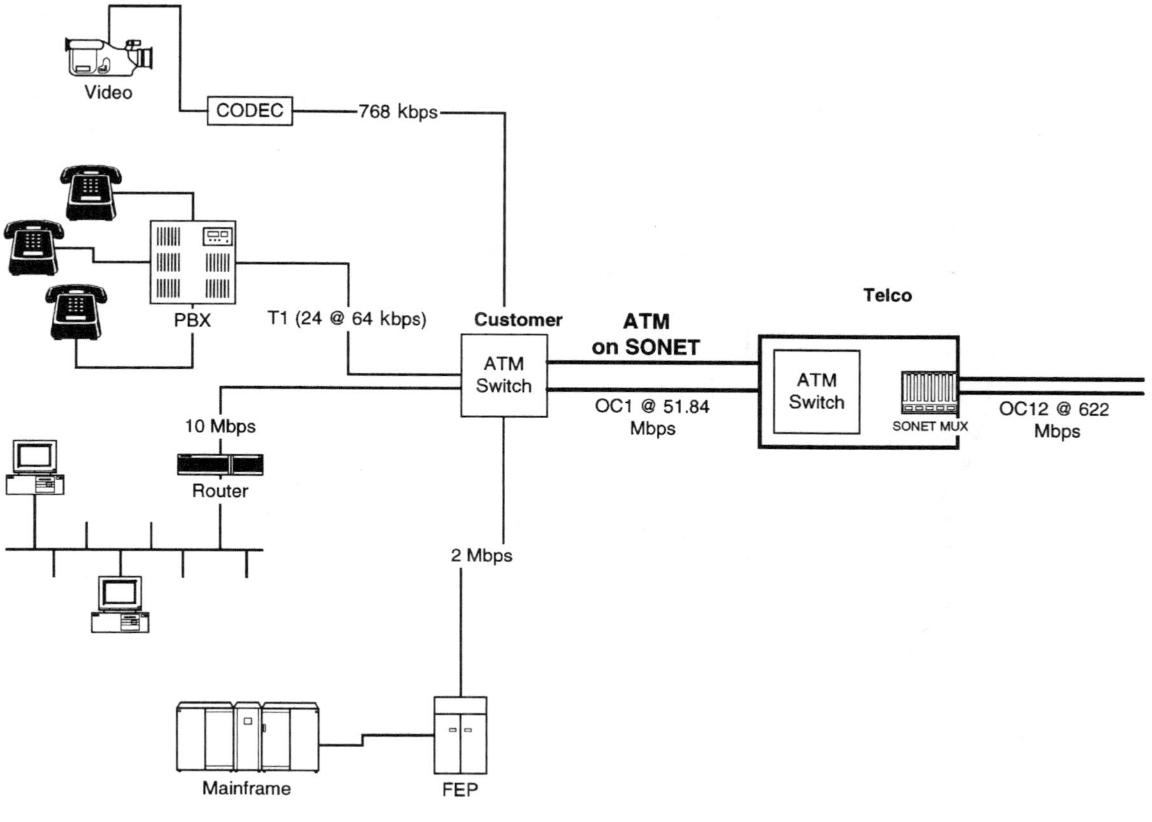

Figure 8.20 ATM aggregates bandwidth to support all types of data and voice.

Many organizations cannot afford the throughput and input demands at 50 Mbps and above. As a result, ATM can be run on T1 access lines, or frame relay can be used at up to T1 speeds where it is then packaged as ATM on a higher-speed backbone network. It is through this combination of both T1 and frame relay that ATM may well satisfy many demands of the client/server network. One must be aware of changes in technologies and transport offered by the carriers on an ongoing basis to avoid wasting or overcommitting budgetary monies. Through these techniques, ATM will become the transport system of the future. As stated earlier, ATM is not ready for prime time. Many issues are yet to be addressed and resolved, including congestion management, committed information rates, pricing mechanisms for on-demand circuit-switched capabilities, and maintenance and diagnostics.

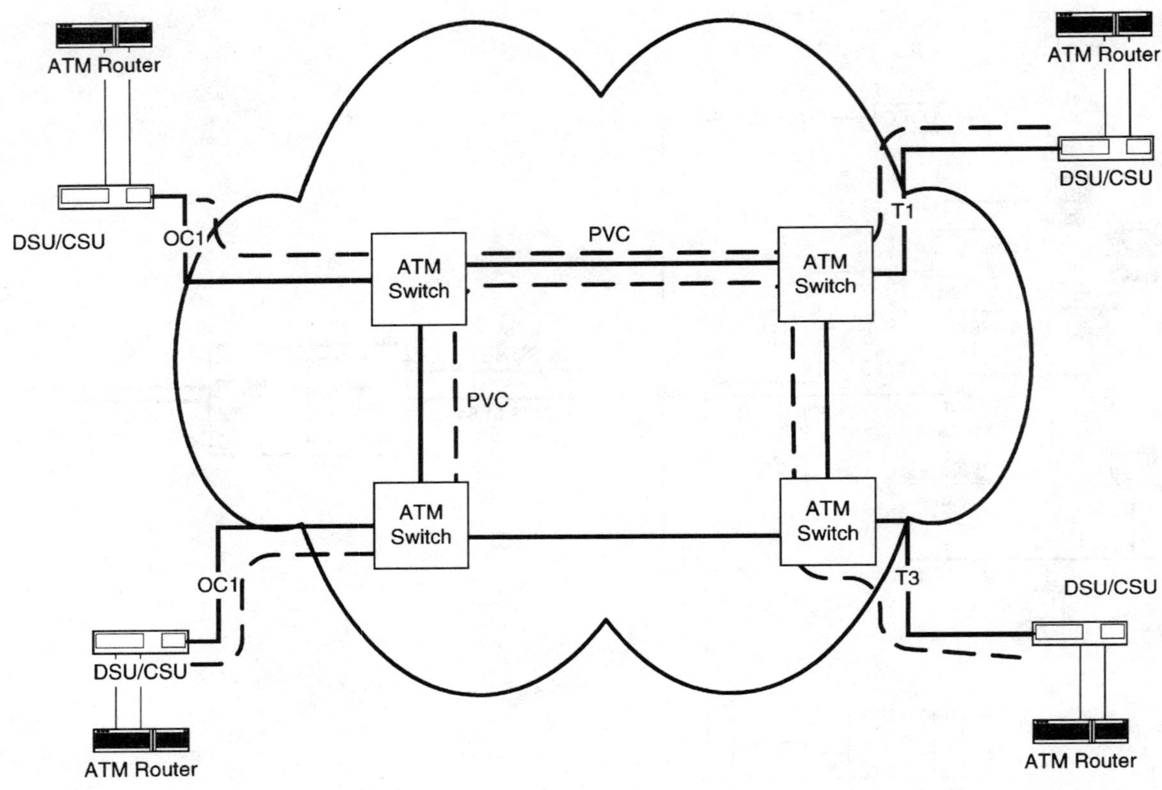

Figure 8.21 ATM uses a permanent virtual connection between locations. Switched connections will come later.

Another issue that has been worked on and is nearly solved is the compatibility and interoperability between network suppliers. Figure 8.23 depicts a network showing ATM at the desktop, at the campus area, across the metropolitan area, and into a wide area. ATM allows for a single topology to be used in a client/server network. In this figure, a network-to-network interface called the intercarrier interface (ICI) is shown linking two different carrier ATM networks together. This link will be very useful in an international network environment where an enterprise network is pulled together. Once again, issues must yet be resolved before all the pieces come together cleanly. However, significant work is being done through the ATM Forum, the International Telecommunication Union (ITU), and the International Standards Organization (ISO) to resolve these issues as quickly as possible. Furthermore, when the ICI is finalized, the use of network-to-network interfacing can make a transparent, seamless client/server internetwork appear to be one close-proximity environment. Using the high-speed demands of the client/server internetwork combined with the ATM carrying capabilities, the client/server network manager can eliminate multiple different networks. Instead of having separate voice networks, data networks, video networks, and finally, internetworks for client/server architectures, a single transport mechanism can be used at very high throughputs.

With all of the changes that have been taking place in the telecommunications industry, cost and availability for this type of service is now becoming readily acceptable. The changes in the local exchange environment, which is now becoming competitive in the United States, as well as what is

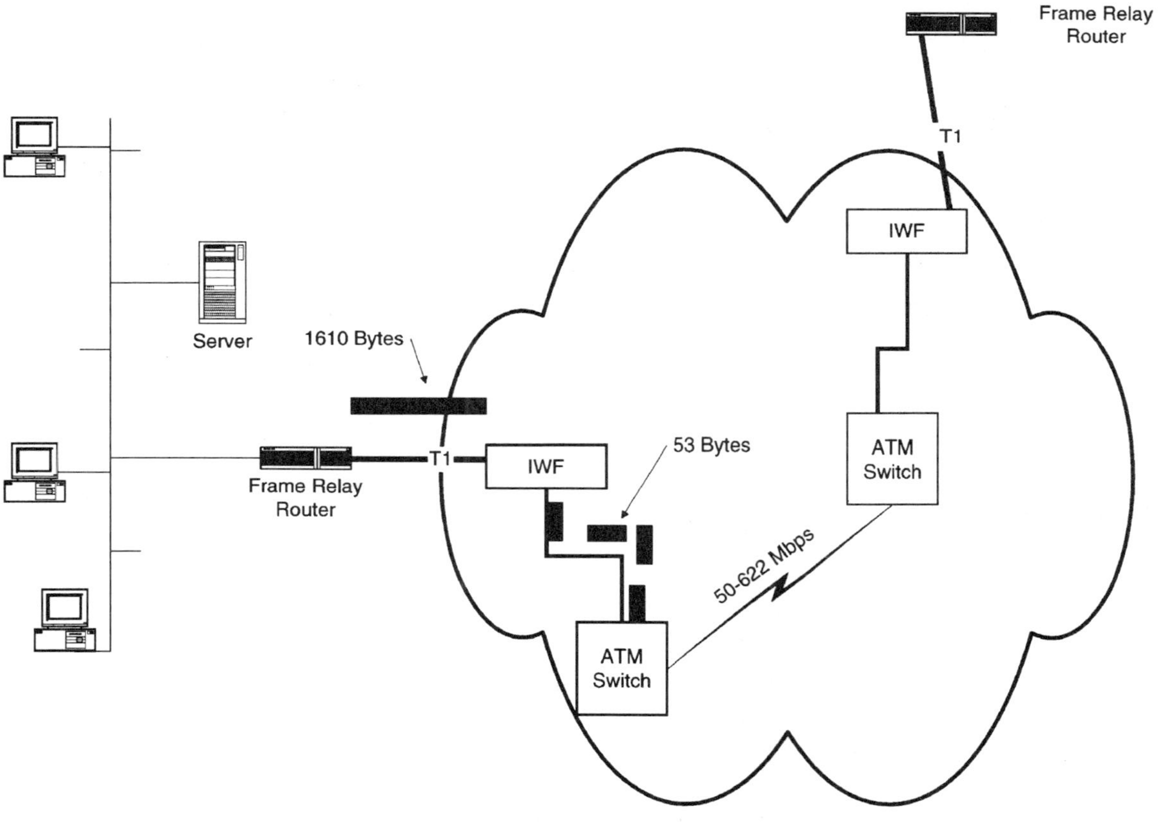

Figure 8.22 The internetworking function converts frame relay frames into ATM cells.

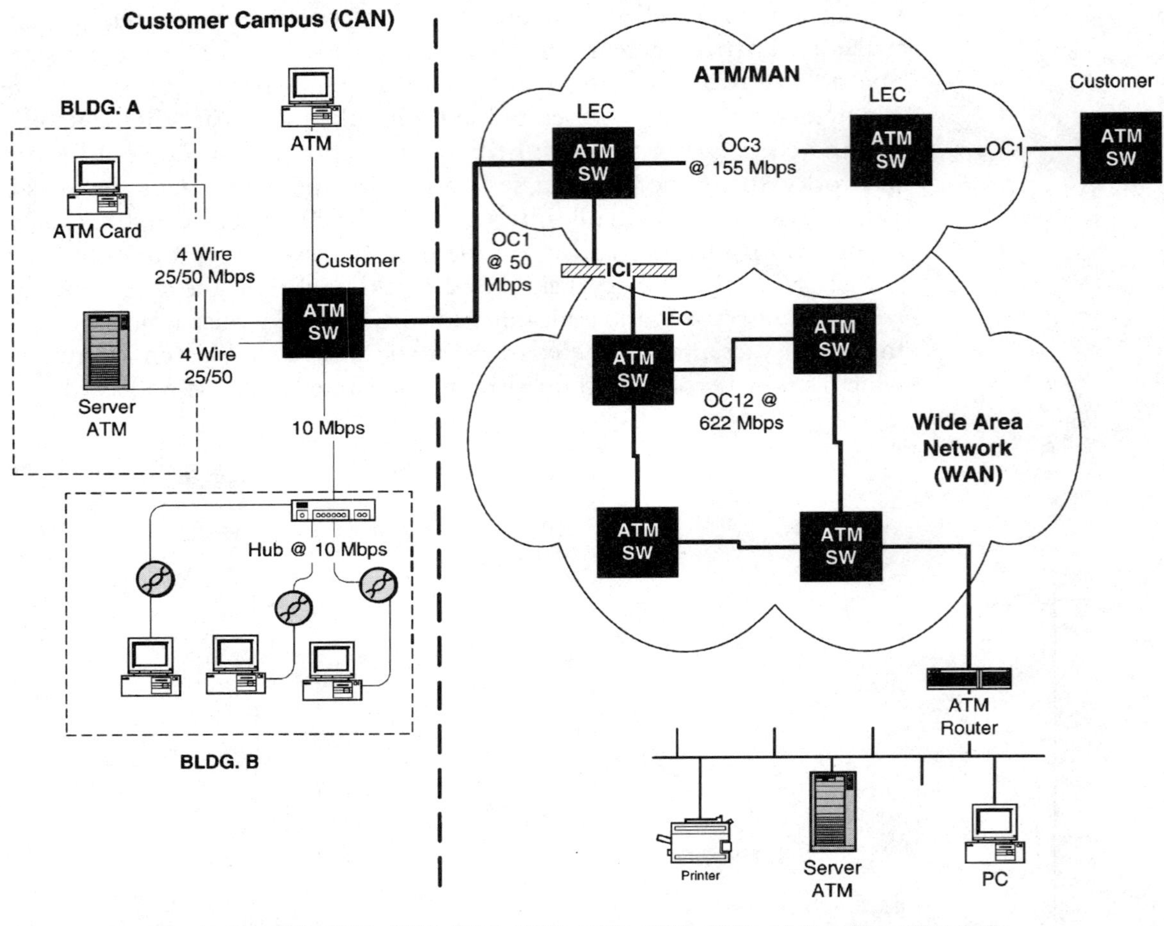

Figure 8.23 ATM at the desktop, the campus, the MAN, and the WAN, all at different speeds.

going on internationally, allow for many players to break into these carrying capabilities. Upon completion of a basic infrastructure, these newer players in the local loop will offer ATM services and ATM switching services as a means of high-speed transport into the wide area. Alliances between the LECs [or competitive local exchange carriers (CLECs)] and the IECs will offer more availability of ATM to the end user. One can see how a strategy linking these different services together can clearly meet the high data throughput capabilities and needs of a client/server network. Instead of network managers trying to fine-tune networks and manage them so tightly that it is all time-consuming, ATM will allow the aggregation of throughput on an as-needed basis. As long as the high-speed communications channel and a high-speed switching system or router are available, the ATM platform can clearly meet these demands. Once fully deployed, ATM will be the transport system for the turn of the century.

In the meantime, permanent virtual circuits are available on a point-to-point, leased-line basis today or, in some cases, strictly as PVCs from the long-haul carriers. Later on, switched virtual circuits (SVCs) will also become available, allowing remote sites and nomadic users to access the client/server network from anywhere. SVCs are still not resolved to date, but work is being done to resolve this issue quickly. Through the use of the SVC and the PVC, the client/server network manager will be able to transport just about any service necessary. One can assume that ISDN dial-backup will become B-ISDN as an on-demand, high-speed dial-up, circuit-switched capability in the future. As long as the price is reasonable, there is no reason not to consider and pilot such a transport system. In satisfying some of the higher demands for this client/server architecture, such as imaging systems, data warehousing and mining, as well as some of the graphic-intensive data needs of a client/server infrastructure, ATM can help to solve many of the problems. If, in fact, it is not available, special arrangements can be made with various carriers that are looking for pilot programs and applications that can run on these networks. Pilots are ongoing throughout the world and are very prolific in a client/server architecture.

One can see that the various service offerings from the carriers now give us many choices. It is through a single infrastructure or a complex infrastructure using pieces or parts of these technologies that the client/server network can be internetworked across the entire globe. Prices do not have to be excessive, demands are not that great, and transport is now available that will satisfy these needs. Through these different technologies, a client/server network can offer seamless connectivity, high-speed throughput with low latency, and price-competitive offerings to satisfy the demands of the enterprise. Linking all of these services together is no longer the insurmountable goal that it once was. Using the high-speed transport systems, a network manger can pave the way for the high-speed data transport demanded to keep an organization competitive and on the move. It is merely a matter of creativity and thorough research on the different transport systems. No one solution will solve all the problems.

CHAPTER 9

Internetworking Components

Regardless of the transmission capabilities discussed in the previous two chapters, another decision must be made in internetworking connectivity. There are several ways to provide the forms of connectivity that are necessary for a client/server network. These include

1. Bridges
2. Routers
3. Brouters
4. Gateways
5. Switches/hubs
6. CSU/DSU connections

In this chapter, each of these components is looked at to determine which might have the best possibility of providing the necessary connections. When dealing with the local area network and a client/server interconnection, some of the easier pieces include such things as bridges, switches, and hubs. In this particular chapter, the intent is not to dwell on the individual components but to look at the connectivity needs to link the client and the server together.

Bridges

In using a bridge, one looks at the LAN connectivity solution. Although bridges can be used to link both localized and long-haul communications needs in a client/server network, their typical position does wind up in a localized environment (the LAN). Bridges, using the OSI model, work at layer 2 (data link layer) and are used to provide LAN-to-LAN interconnection. At this data link layer, the bridge is typically used between common or similar networks. Therefore, when linking two networks together, such as Ethernet to Ethernet or token ring to token ring, the bridge has a very suitable place. In the internetwork, bridges can be used at the data link layer across leased or dedicated lines. In this scenario, using a leased-line connection, one would typically use a dedicated digital communications channel such as a 56-kbps up to and including a full T1 connection. There are some situations that best suit the bridge, including segmentation of collision domains on an Ethernet or the segmentation or subnetworking of token rings. Bridges typically are used with LANs that operate using the same layer 2 protocols, not disparate protocols. Bridges come in three basic categories:

1. Transparent
2. Source route
3. Source route transparent (SRT)

The bridge is designed to provide connectivity between and among LANs within the client/server world.

A reason one would use a bridge is to improve performance on the actual LAN in a client/server architecture. For example, when dealing with an Ethernet carrier sense multiple access/collision detection (CSMA/CD) that operates at 10 Mbps, the average expected throughput is approximately 3.3 to 4 Mbps, and for a 100-Mbps LAN, the average expected throughput equates to 33 to 40 Mbps. When dealing with a token ring network, the average expected throughput on a 4-Mbps ring will be 3.3 Mbps, and for a 16-Mbps ring, approximately 12 Mbps can be expected.

This 3- to 4-Mbps throughput expectation is established by looking at a series of connections that would exist on the LAN regardless of the topology. One can assume that on a 10-Mbps LAN or a 4/16-Mbps LAN, 25 to 30 PCs performing mostly text and a little bit of graphics will consume the capacity, yielding only 3.3 Mbps on the higher-speed networks. Ten desktop publishing devices, such as PCs using laser printers, result in the same throughputs. Six CAD/CAM workstations or two minicomputers will draw the network's performance down to these expected throughputs. This estimation essentially gives the client/server manager some idea of the actual throughput that can be achieved using these LAN topologies. One can also look at the total throughput capabilities based on these limited throughputs and recognize what must be done. Therefore, bridging would be used to split or separate collision domains in a CSMA/CD network. The bridge assists in separating or segmenting the collision domains to prevent bottlenecks or degradation of the service. In Fig. 9.1, the initial local area network is shown without a bridge. In this particular case, with multiple workstations attached to a bus topology, one can see that collisions will obviously draw down the total throughput and performance of this network. However, as shown in Fig. 9.2, using a bridge, the collision domains can be separated into much smaller subnetworks, improving the performance of the network.

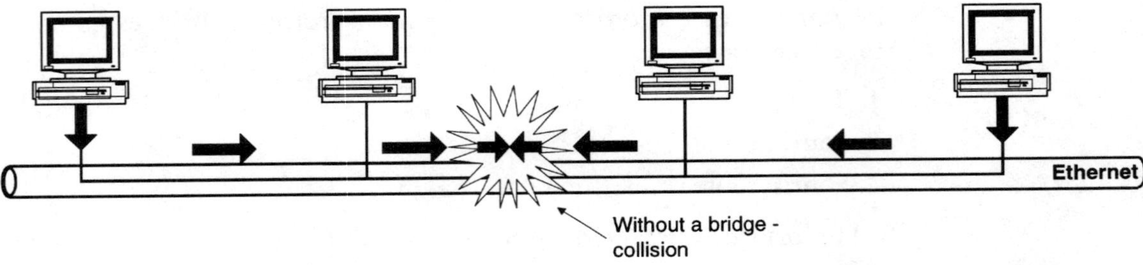

Figure 9.1 Collisions occur without a bridge.

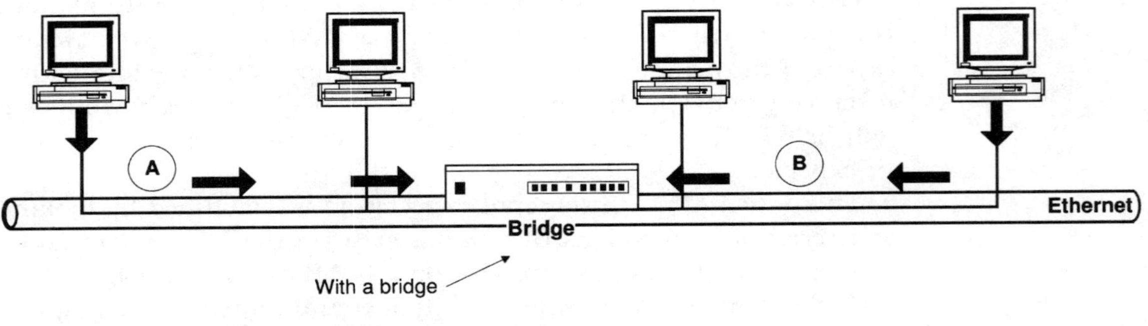

Figure 9.2 Bridging techniques split collision domains.

Transparent Bridging

Transparent bridging is a process that allows nodes on LAN A as shown on Fig. 9.2 to send frames of information to nodes on another LAN (B) in one of the following situations:

1. The frame of information is unicast (single address), and its destination MAC[1] address is on LAN B, while the originator or source MAC address is on LAN A.
2. The frame is unicast, but the bridge does not know where the destination address is located.

1. The media access control (MAC) layer address is a 6-byte address on LANs.

3. The frame is multicast, and some nodes on LAN B are assigned the multicast address.
4. The frame is a broadcast frame that will go between both LANs.

The bridge filters all frames and forwards only those that meet one of the above criteria. This process is shown in Fig. 9.3, where frames are being transmitted on LAN A. Essentially, when the network node begins to transmit the frames, the bridge receives the frames and blocks any messages that are addressed to a device that is on LAN A from proceeding across the boundary to LAN B. However, the bridge forwards the frames that are destined from a node on LAN A to a node on LAN B. This figure represents how the bridge can conduct a filter-and-forward capability.

The process described is called *transparent* because the nodes on LAN A transmit the frames to nodes on LAN B as if they all resided on the

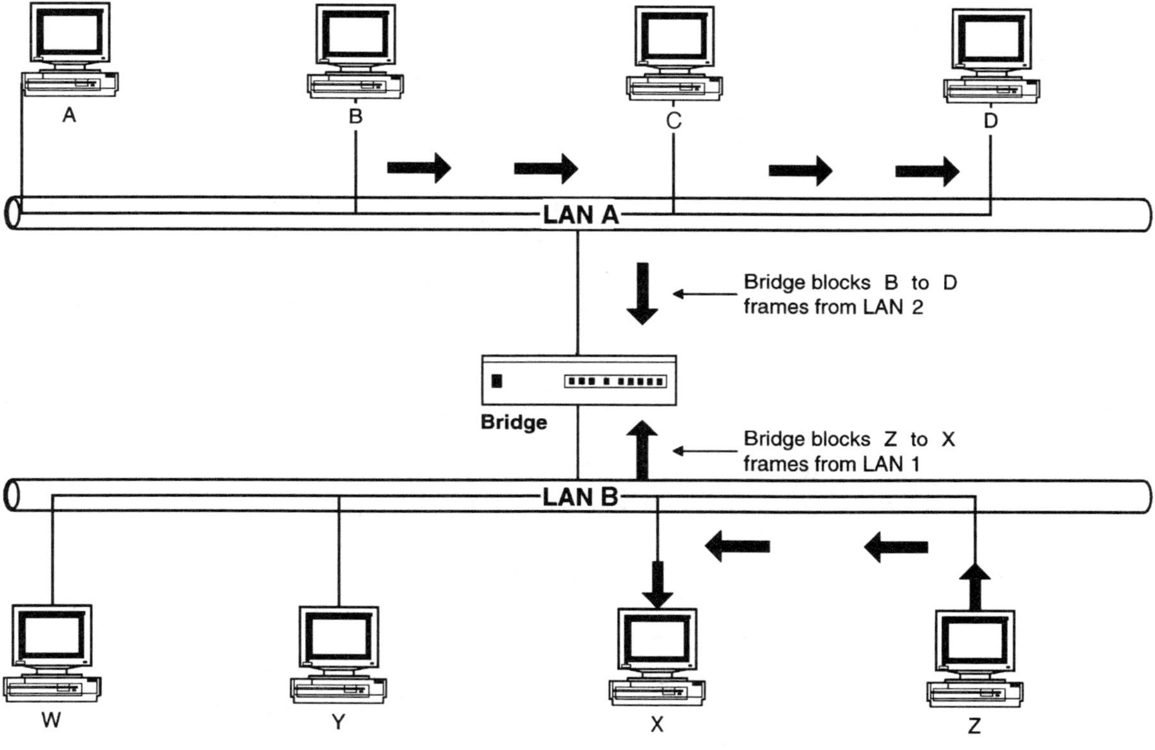

Figure 9.3 In transparent bridging, the bridge filters frames from going across but allows frames between LANs when necessary.

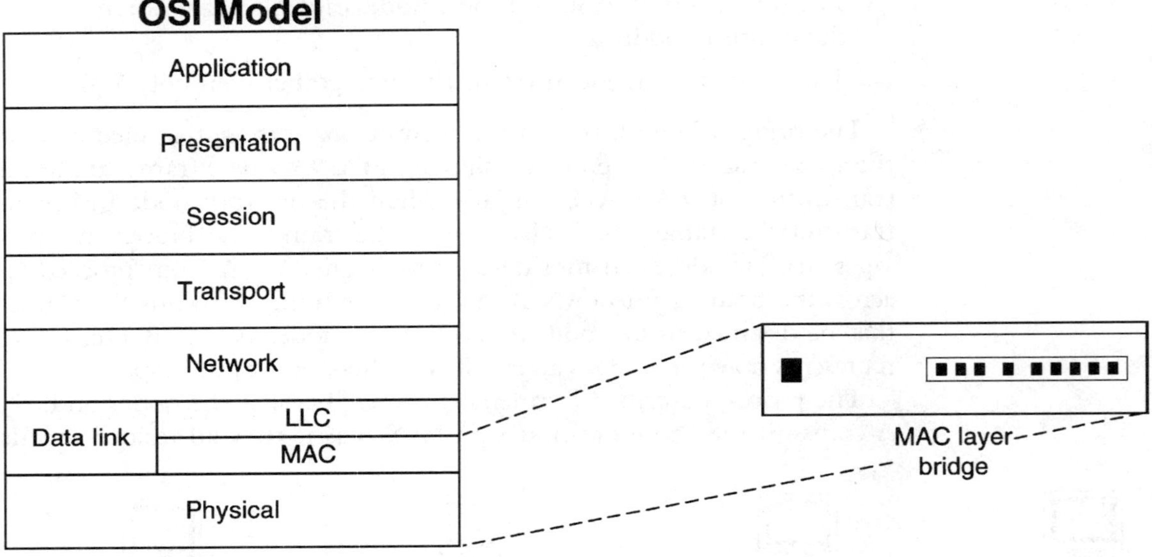

Figure 9.4 The bridge works at the MAC and physical layers.

same network, i.e., the bridge is transparent to the end user. Bridging is done based on the MAC layer address, and this is why such bridges are typically referred to as MAC layer bridges. During the filtering process, some of the frames may be prevented from crossing the bridge based on some of the filtering criteria other than the MAC address. These criteria could include specific protocols, specific application information, or specific users who would be restricted from forwarding information across the network. In Fig. 9.4, the transparent bridge is continually referred to as a MAC layer bridge. In this particular figure the representation to the OSI model indicates that the bridge works at both the physical and the data link layers only. The data link layer is divided into two parts in this drawing, showing the MAC layer address, which again is the MAC layer bridging location address, and the logical link control sitting above it.

The bridging process splits very large contention domains into smaller ones, allowing for increased throughput while maintaining connectivity.

- For CSMA/CD networks, the bridges split collision domains.
- For token-passing networks, the bridges split token access domains.

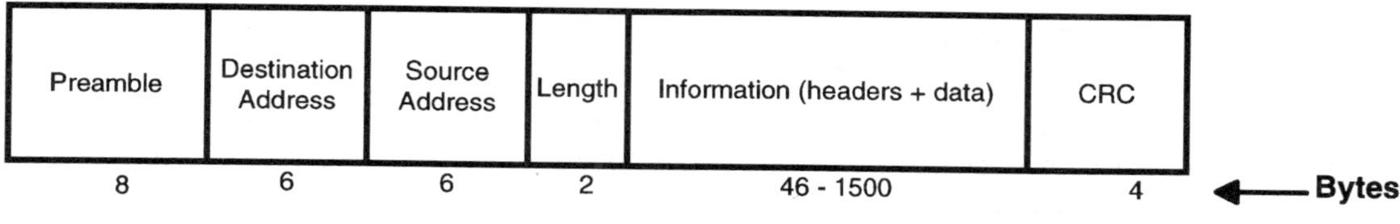

Figure 9.5 The 802.3 frame, as approved and adopted, uses CSMA/CD.

A transparent bridge learns the MAC layer addresses that are associated with each of the ports on it. It does this by listening to all the frames that are being broadcast across the network and updating a database and forwarding its address tables based on source MAC addresses. What this also means is that an inactive node, one that never transmits or receives information, may never be learned by the bridge. Figure 9.5 is a representation of a CSMA/CD frame format or, in today's standard, the 802.3 frame. Note the destination and the source address in this particular frame. These addresses, consisting of 6 bytes of information, are used for the bridges to learn both the source and the destination addresses of all nodes on either side of the network. It is through these addresses that the bridge can build the table and keep it updated as active devices broadcast their information.

Filtering and Forwarding

Each unicast frame transmitted across a LAN is examined for the following:

1. The port number associated with the source address
2. The port number associated with the destination address

If the port source and the port destination are equal or a filtering condition is not met, then the bridge blocks the path across the links, meaning the bridge has filtered the packet off. If this does not happen, then the packet or frame is forwarded across the bridge.

In the case of a multicast frame, each frame is examined for the filtering condition. If the filtering condition is not met, then it will either block the path across the bridge or forward the frame across the bridge.

Learning

Whenever data is moved across a network, as shown in Fig. 9.6, the learning process occurs. Each of the bridges associated on the multiple LANs shown in this figure will build a table. Each table will consist of the three different entities in this drawing. This table will consider what is local or what is locally attached on a particular LAN and what is on the other two ports that are connected to the bridge. Consider LAN 2 and LAN 1: As data is transmitted across the localized network, the bridge accepts the frame, examines the address, and determines the next step. If, in fact, the bridge cannot determine the address because a device has not been addressed in the past or has not broadcast in the past, the bridge will then forward the data frames to each of the two ports associated with it. At that point, the bridge will then listen to the device that is basically responding or accepting the data frame. Once that listening has taken place, the bridge will then recognize where the particular device is located. In this particular case, in LAN A, device X is transmitting information to device W. The bridge not recognizing where that address is located will transmit the frame to both of the attached LANs, 1 and 2. Once W responds or receives the packet based on bridge number 2 forwarding the data frame to that particular device, bridge number 2 will recognize that device W is local and device X has communicated with device W from LAN A. Subsequently, bridge number 3 will also have heard the message and now knows that device X is located off of its port number 2. The learning process has begun. This makes for a very simple means of communicating using bridges. As the bridges learn, they will be able to continually build tables that will be aged to the point that as new devices come onto the network they will be added to the table, but as devices become inactive, their entry will be dropped off the table. As a result, the network remains continually updated through this learning process.

Transparent Bridging Loops

It is possible, however, that things can go awry. When designing a client/server internetwork with bridges, one must be aware of bridging loops. In Fig. 9.7, frames of information will be broadcast from LAN A through a bridge. In this particular case, device X is transmitting again to device W. Because all of the bridges associated with this particular

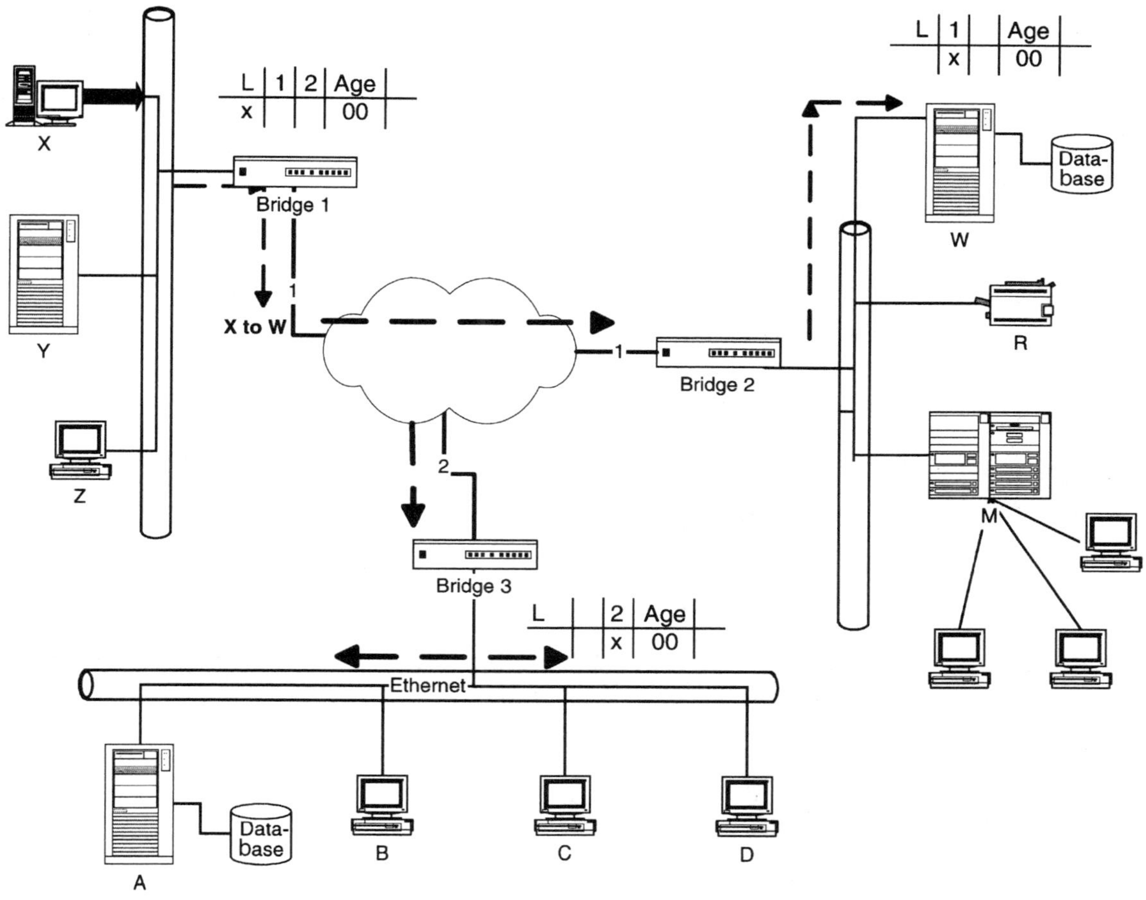

Figure 9.6 The self-learning process with bridges.

network are now learning the location of each of the devices, when bridge 1 receives the frame that is addressed to device W, it sends data out across its ports. In this case, however, it is highly possible that the bridge will send the data frame to the two downstream bridges, 2 and 3. Therefore, the frame might be sent in two different directions at the same time. It is highly possible that addressing can begin to roll between bridges. As they look up their tables, they all start to realize that device X is not only on their first network (LAN A) but also has been recognized as a passthrough or tandem frame from bridge number 3. Now different addresses exist in the table for the same location or same node.

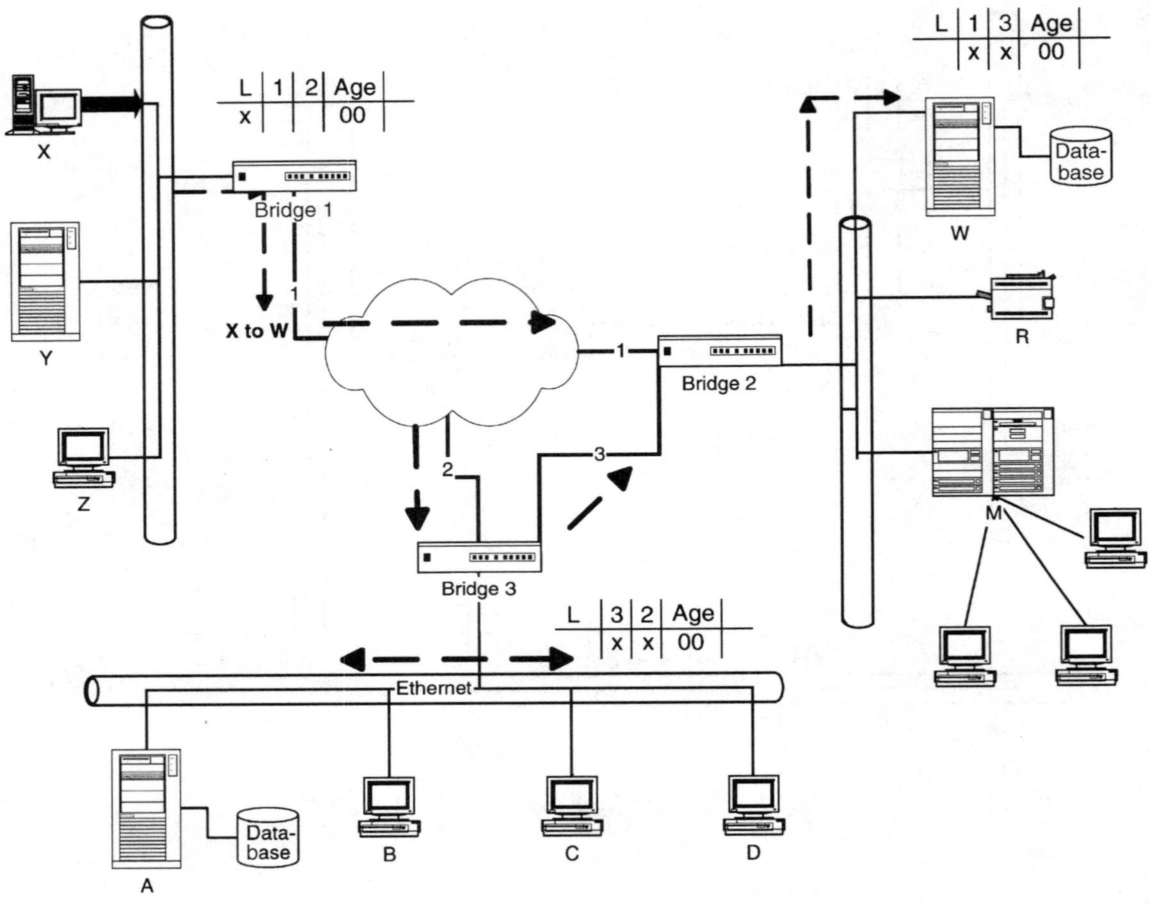

Figure 9.7 A loop can be created with transparent bridging.

As data is transmitted between these devices, the possibility exists that a loop can be formed. When device X needs to be addressed, all of the devices would then try to use the associated ports on each of the bridges to communicate with X, causing the data to continually roll around the network from different locations as it is moving around. To prevent this from occurring, a spanning tree protocol was established. The IEEE developed the standard 802.1d (which allows for internetworking with bridges) and decided that loops in a transparent bridging environment are illegal.

Unfortunately, although this was a noble decision, loops are necessary for resiliency across these networks. In the event a link fails between two LANs, an alternate path can exist between any two points by using the alternate route. Therefore, resiliency is one thing that should be considered. To prevent this from occurring, some links will be blocked from passing data across them. However, in the event an active links fails, a blocked link can be taken over to deliver the message. This would only happen if, in fact, an active link fails and the bridges know about it. The network configuration is conducted or reconfigured by the bridges after the network manager sets up each bridge in preparation by selecting a spanning tree protocol. This spanning tree process is shown in Fig. 9.8. Note that when a link fails, the network is capable of rerouting all traffic across the network. To accommodate this spanning tree protocol, the LAN network manager or the client/server internetwork manager would follow certain steps:

1. Bridge identification numbers are used with the lowest number considered the root. Thinking in terms of a tree, the root would be the base.
2. Port numbers and network numbers would then be assigned based on each of the network adjacencies.
3. Port path costs or some other metric would be built into this spanning tree protocol to select the priority of a designed root.
4. Bridges, multicast-group-addressed at the MAC layer, are assigned.
5. Turn on spanning tree protocol.

Roots build a spanning tree database and then send all of their addressing to all other bridges downstream. The downstream bridges then choose the active links, considering the least-cost path, the lower number port numbers, or the smallest of the bridge identification numbers. This sequence allows the bridge to take one of three choices in selecting the preferred route between two bridges. Bridging is then conducted between the devices. The bridges exchange their configurations and set up information with the root (the lowest number in the whole sequence). They exchange information such as acknowledgment notes back and forth between each other periodically using both their active as well as their inactive links. These messages constitute the bridging protocol data units and are used in a spanning tree protocol. In the case of any form of failure, the spanning tree is then recalculated. If the root fails, the bridge with the next-lowest ID number assumes

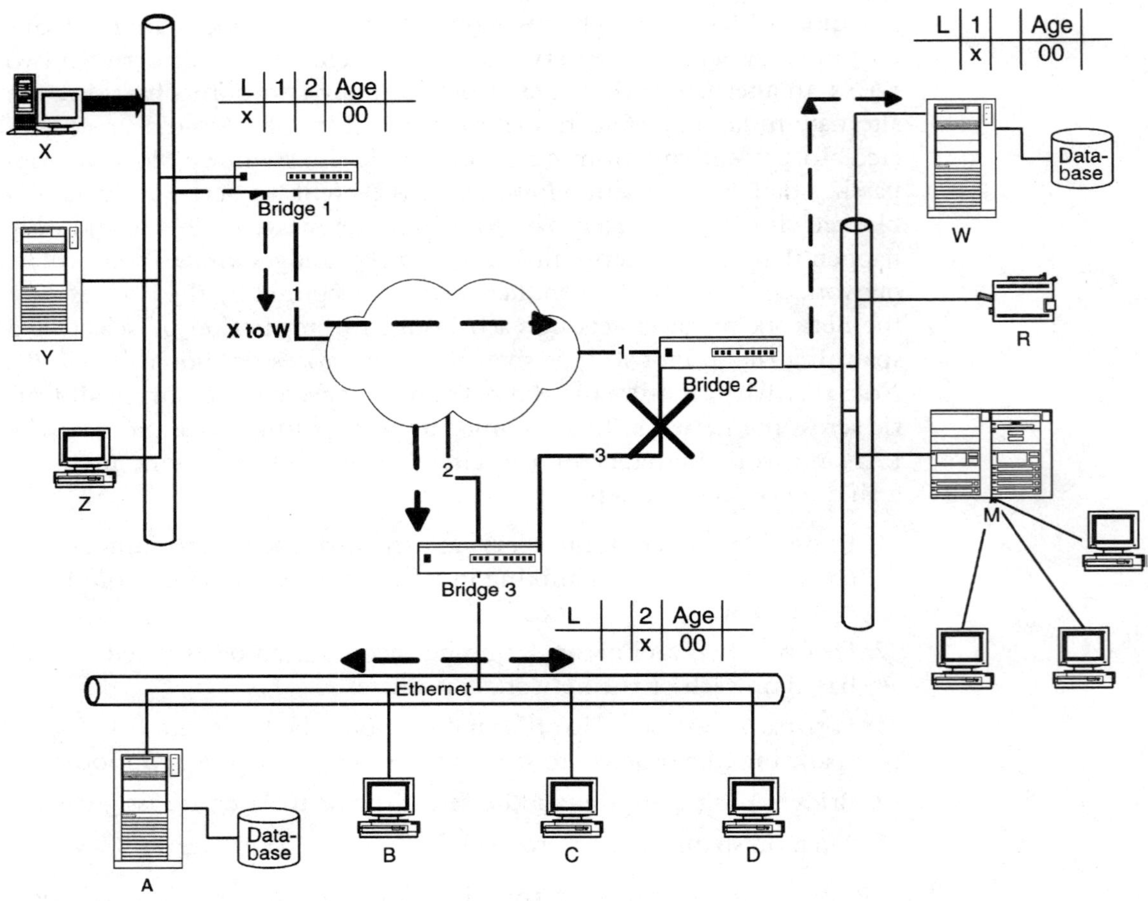

Figure 9.8 The spanning tree protocol prevents bridging loops.

its role, allowing for robustness and resiliency in the event of a link failure or a bridge failure.

The advantages of using a spanning tree protocol include the elimination of broadcast storms due to loops that can be formed on a bridging network. However, there are disadvantages as well, including additional traffic overhead in the bridging table updates, as well a waste in terms of cost by providing expensive links for redundancy. One must decide when dealing with the spanning tree protocols what is the actual goal: resiliency and robustness or budget efficiency. It is through this decision that one can decide what level of spanning tree protocol to use and what redundancy to provide throughout the network. Typically, the spanning tree protocol would be used in a form of a tree network environment. If a pure star network is used to internetwork multiple sites from a single common location, point-to-point, spanning tree protocols are not needed.

When using bridges between two networks, whether localized or across the wide area network, one must consider the use of the traffic capabilities of the interconnection. In Fig. 9.9, the use of a link between two networks, in this case Ethernets, can range from a leased line at 56/64 kbps up through a T1 connection. Using this connection, one must understand that the data rate on the Ethernet will be approximately 14,400 frames per second, whereas on a link at 56 kbps to T1, the link

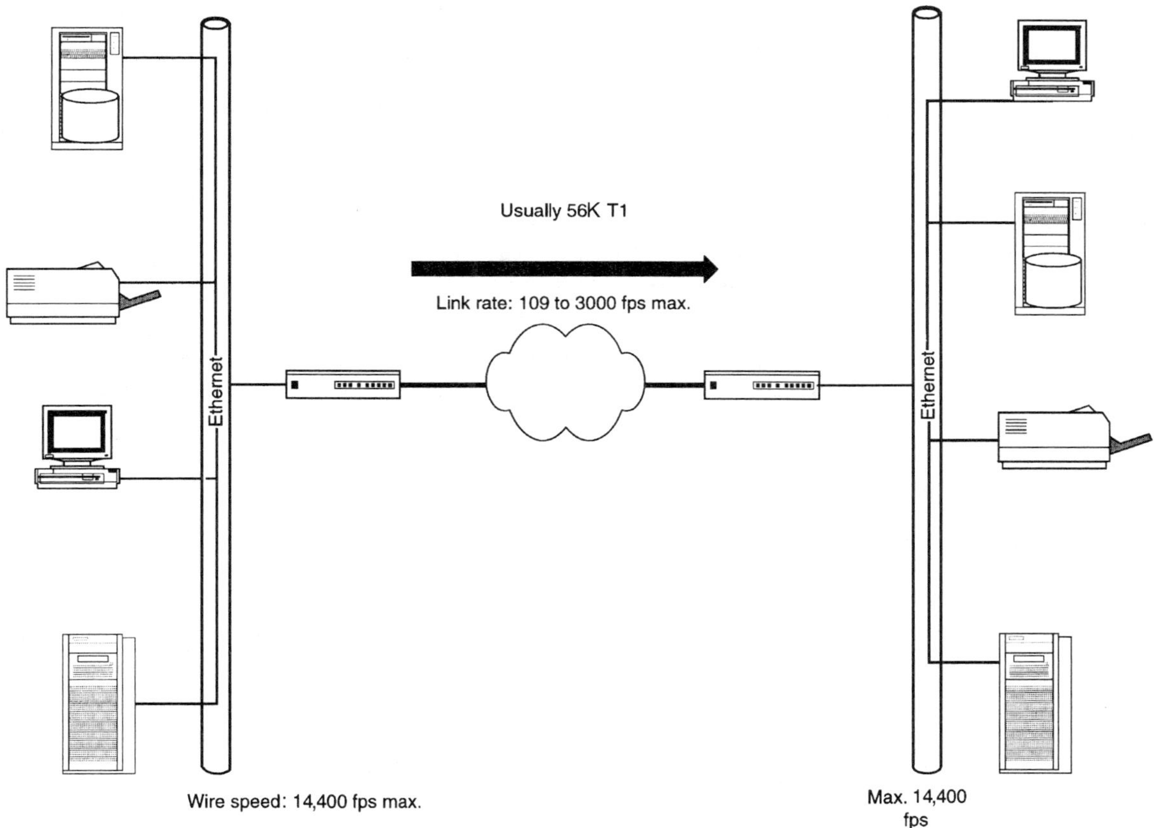

Figure 9.9 Traffic analysis is necessary with bridging.

rate between these networks only operates between 109 and 3000 frames per second. This can create bottlenecks between the two local area networks, of which the client/server manager must be aware. Considering the link rates and the cost associated with renting these facilities, one must evaluate whether throughput or price is the issue. In this particular case, a T1 in the domestic United States from the East Coast to the West Coast might cost in the vicinity of $20,000. Can one justify that expense to link the two networks together? Ultimately, the data rate is what is important and if, in fact, this is a client/server network, the link rate must be as high as possible to support the demands of the end-user devices. If too low a rate is selected because of cost, the users will not be satisfied or happy with the expected throughput capabilities. Consequently, one would see an unsuccessful client/server internetwork because of unnecessary and excessive bottlenecks.

To accommodate these lower data rates between two networks operating at 10 Mbps, Fig. 9.10 shows an example where specific types of information might well be generated across the network. In this figure, different types of data protocols are being used; for example, e-mail, inquiry response, and file transfer are all shown. The bridges use fair and equitable treatment on this network. Therefore, the traffic is just interleaved as it is generated, causing e-mail to have an equal priority with file transfer, for an example. This means that mission-critical data operating on this client/server internetwork may have to play second fiddle to other less mission-critical information, such as e-mail or inquiry response. One may not want to do that. Therefore, the implication leads us to believe that, using the bridging techniques, the Ethernet overhead, for example, will also have additional overhead applied to it. This overhead includes the WAN protocol overhead, such as high-level data link control (HDLC), frame relay, or another transmission system. Again, this network deals with the ability to move voluminous amounts of information in a client/server architecture. This additional overhead only serves to congest the network even further. One must consider the alternatives or capabilities of some of the bridging functions to smooth the traffic or to prioritize specific application traffic as necessary. To improve upon the traffic capabilities through the bridge, one should consider some of the alternatives:

1. Frame compression
2. Data compression
3. Protocol prioritization

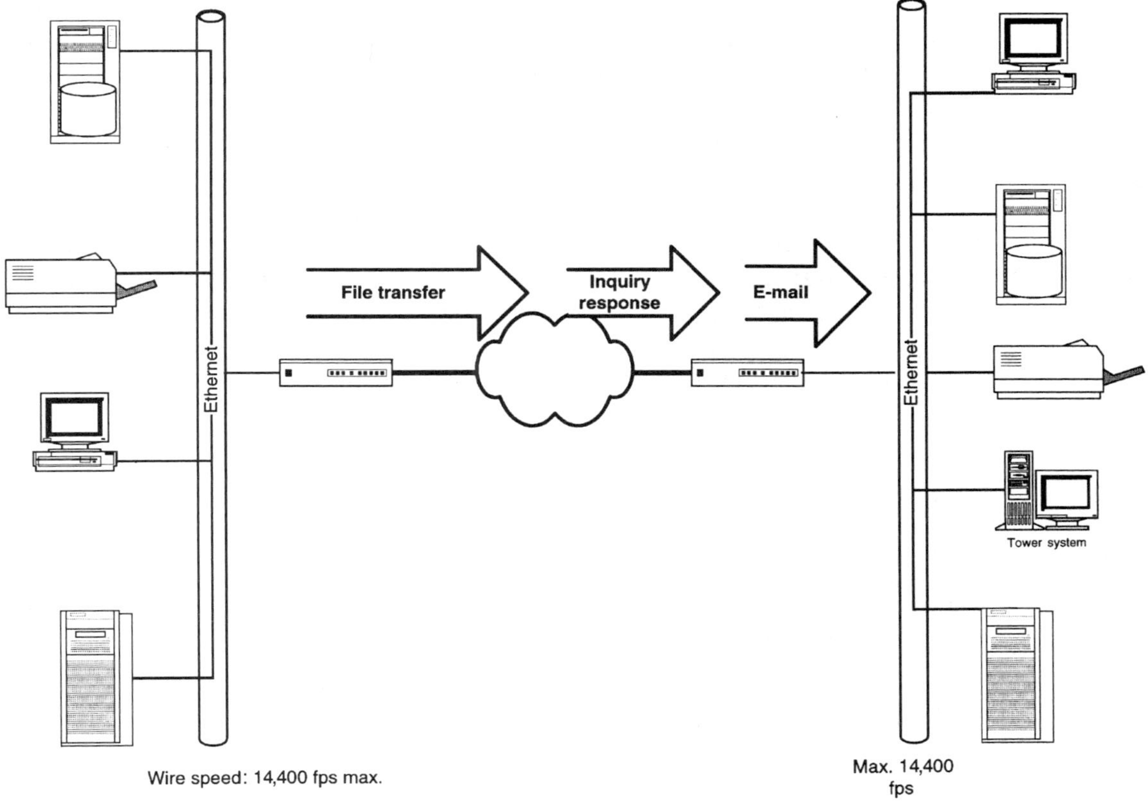

Figure 9.10 The bridge can provide various frames for different applications.

4. Protocol emulation or spoofing
5. Fair queuing techniques
6. Inverse multiplexing
7. Bandwidth on demand

In frame compression, the ability to strip off all of the overhead that would be contained on the Ethernet can be accomplished by removing pads and the MAC layer CRCs, the MAC frame headers and data, and any other associated subnetwork access protocol information. What can then happen is the actual data can be compressed and the WAN protocol overhead assigned or applied by the bridges as the data moves across the link.

As shown in Fig. 9.11*a* and *b*, it will be highly compressed as it moves across the wide area. At the reverse end, the bridge on the receiving side will remove the WAN overhead, uncompress the data, and reattach any pads or MAC CRCs as well as the MAC frame header and data. This allows approximately a 4-to-1 compression. The data compression inside this frame can also be compressed by assigning shorter codes for any repetitive data combinations. This would be constructed dynamically by learning from both sides of the WAN. Therefore, using these combined techniques of both frame and data compression, the compression ratio could reach 8-to-1, depending on how redundant the data is and how well the compression techniques work. This process could achieve some significant benefits in the client/server network because the compression and the overhead

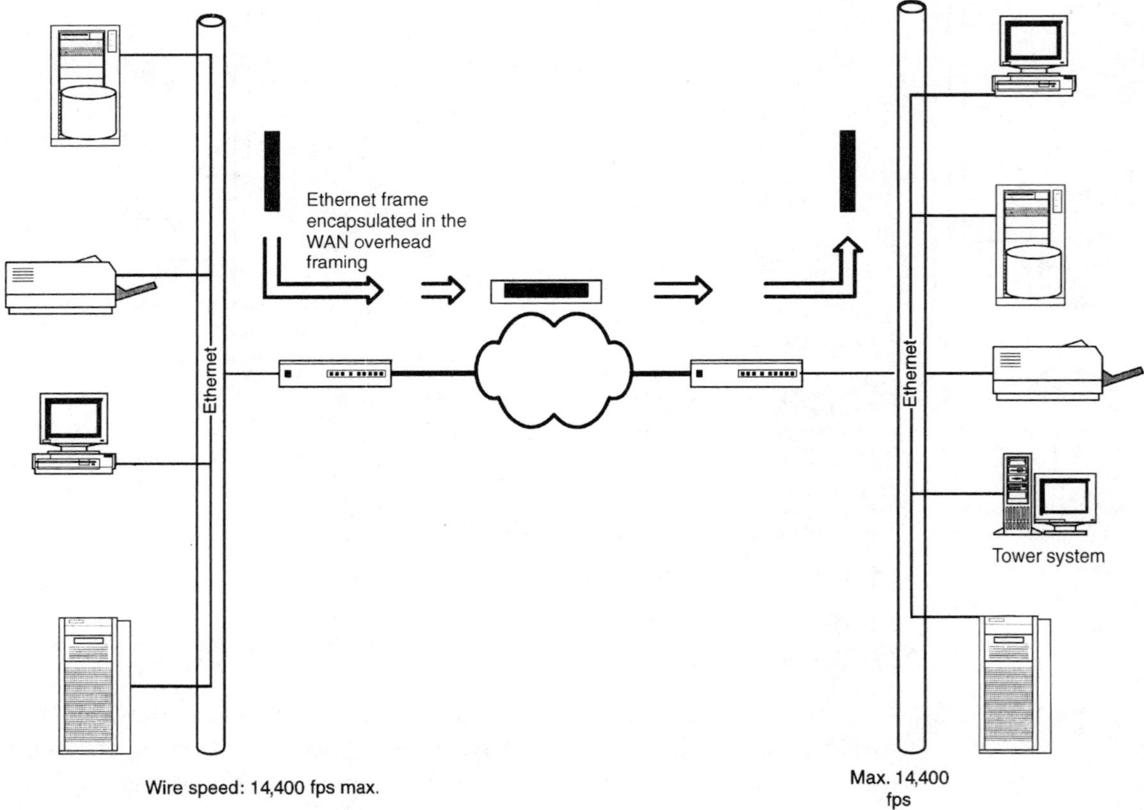

Figure 9.11a The Ethernet frame is encapsulated in the WAN overhead framing.

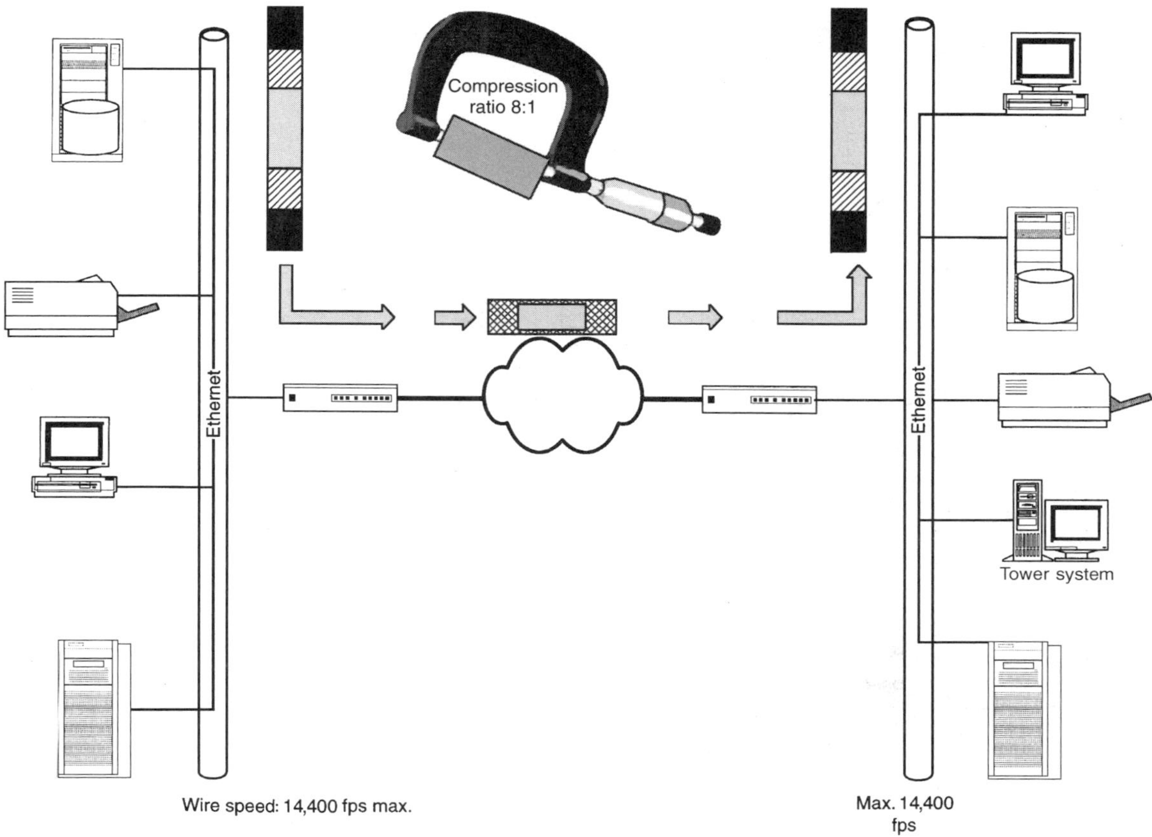

Figure 9.11b Frame and data compression can achieve up to 8-to-1 ratios.

removal could emulate much higher throughputs. Although one is only using a T1 link for the example by doing an 8-to-1 compression across the data network, this could represent native LAN throughput as far as Ethernets are concerned. This is not really true data but is compressed data, and one must look at the actual repetitive nature of the data before assuming such ratios could be achieved. If successful, however, by achieving an 8-to-1 compression technique on the LAN, the client/server network manager can achieve what appears to be straight or native throughput, satisfying the demands of the end-user applications as well as holding the cost to a minimum. The goal of the client/server internetwork is to provide the service, achieve the cost results, and provide satisfied users access to their data in the performance of their mission.

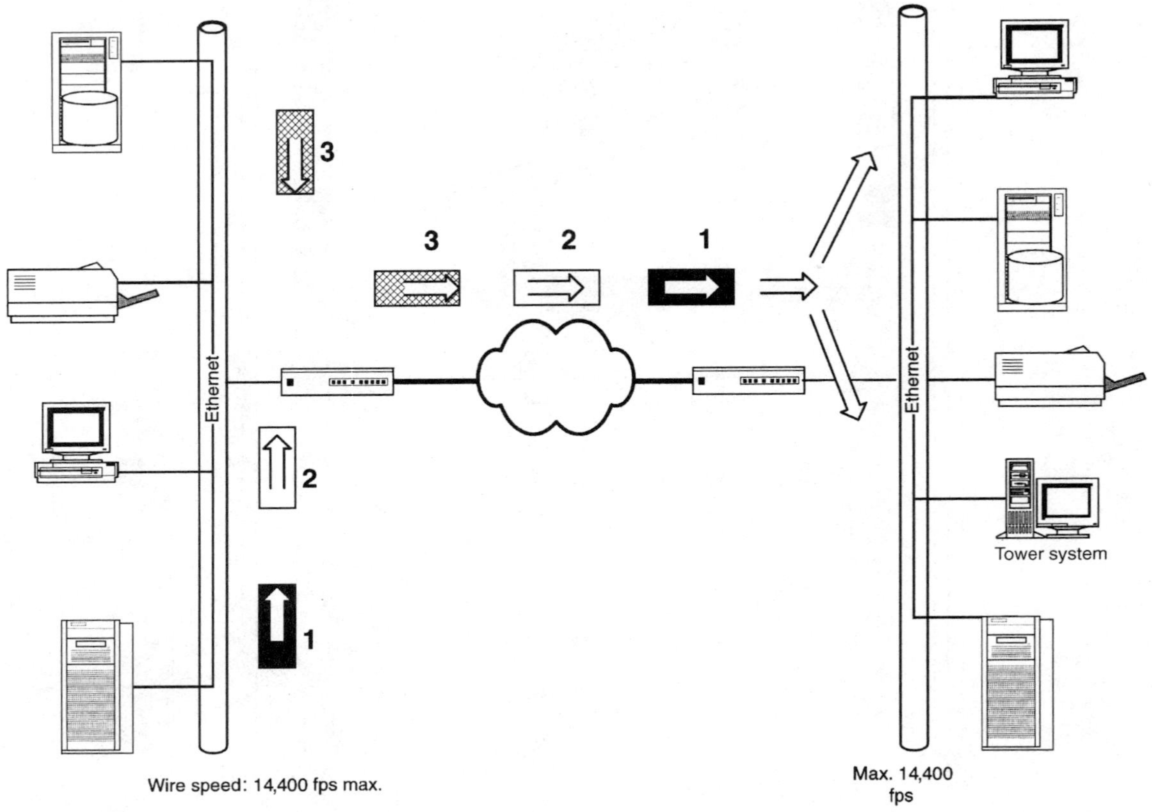

Figure 9.12 *The bridge prioritizes the WAN output queue based on protocol types.*

In the protocol prioritization technique shown in Fig. 9.12, the bridge can place a regulated order in the data flow across the network by building queues and then prioritizing the data to be transmitted based on the protocol types being used. For example, e-mail may have a lower priority than inquiry response, and inquiry response may have a lower priority than file transfer. By using this protocol prioritization, significant improvements can also be achieved by giving the service where necessary to the client/server applications while still allowing some capabilities for routine traffic to traverse this network. Another opportunity, however, would be to use protocol emulation, in this case some form of spoofing.

Using the two networks as the example and continuing this thought process, the protocol emulation would allow the bridges to advertise the services available on each of the local LANs on behalf of the servers located on the remote LANs. The data traffic or the service-advertising protocols (SAPs) would not need to be transferred across the network on a regular basis. The bridge, in its table based on a learning protocol, would be able to recognize where the devices are and handle the data transfer smoothly. Eliminating all the advertising protocols from each of the networks on a continual basis allows the network to carry real data as opposed to advertised data. This concept is shown in Fig. 9.13, where the bridges are basically advertising or spoofing the protocols. Each of

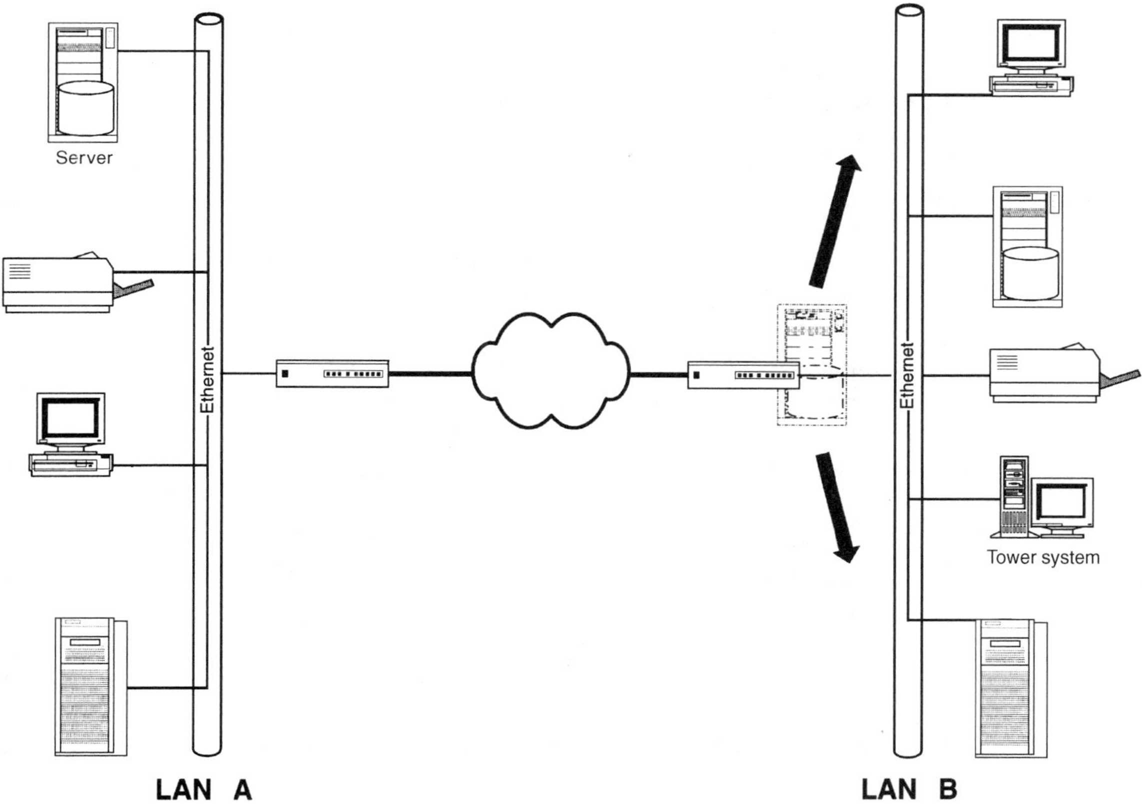

Figure 9.13 Spoofing allows the bridge to advertise services to users on LAN B on behalf of servers located on remote LAN A.

the devices on the LAN is aware of the existence of servers, print services, communications services, or disk farms, even though they are remote. Allowing this application to take place again eliminates the overhead between the two bridges or between the two servers on the different LANs. The third alternative is to use fair queuing, in which the bridge is responsible for providing messaging capabilities of different lengths between the different services, such as on a time division multiplex network. This way, shorter messages can arrive first at a destination. In the fair queuing technique, the bridge actually takes larger data frames from the individual service capabilities on the LAN and breaks them down into smaller and smaller messages until all messages are equal in size. Because they are broken down into the same-size frames and transported across the wide area network as the capability or the service is delivered, the receiving bridge reassembles the data frames. Of course, the shorter messages arrive in a sequenced basis much faster. This improves a lot of the performance characteristics of the client/server internetwork while still satisfying some of the routine and administrative traffic demands. Fair queuing is a technique that has always been used, and yet it is not necessarily understood. The shorter the message, the more performance characteristics one can expect.

Another technique that could be used in improving performance between client/server internetworks, still using our example of the two LANs linked together through bridging, is the technique called *inverse multiplexing*. Using inverse multiplexing systems, shown in Fig. 9.14, what happens is the bridge allocates more traffic capabilities by dialing up a remote site, literally using additional linkage between the two sites or the two end points. As traffic demand increases, the bridge adds additional capacity by using a 64 kbps dial-up (ISDN BRI), and, as the traffic begins to decrease, the bridge releases the links. There are some cost penalties associated with this method because the dial-up traffic can be expensive over time. If this inverse multiplexing technique is used on a continual basis, and short bursty messages are dialed up, the initial-minute costs of dial-up by ISDN can amount to a significant dollar value by the end of the month. The client/server internetwork manager must be cautious and aware of how this technique works. One does not want to see a huge, unanticipated bill at the end of the month. Although the traffic was satisfied, the cost benefits were not achieved, and management may lose faith in the ability of the client/server network to support the demands of the organization at a reasonable cost. Inverse multiplexing can be a valuable asset to a client/server network

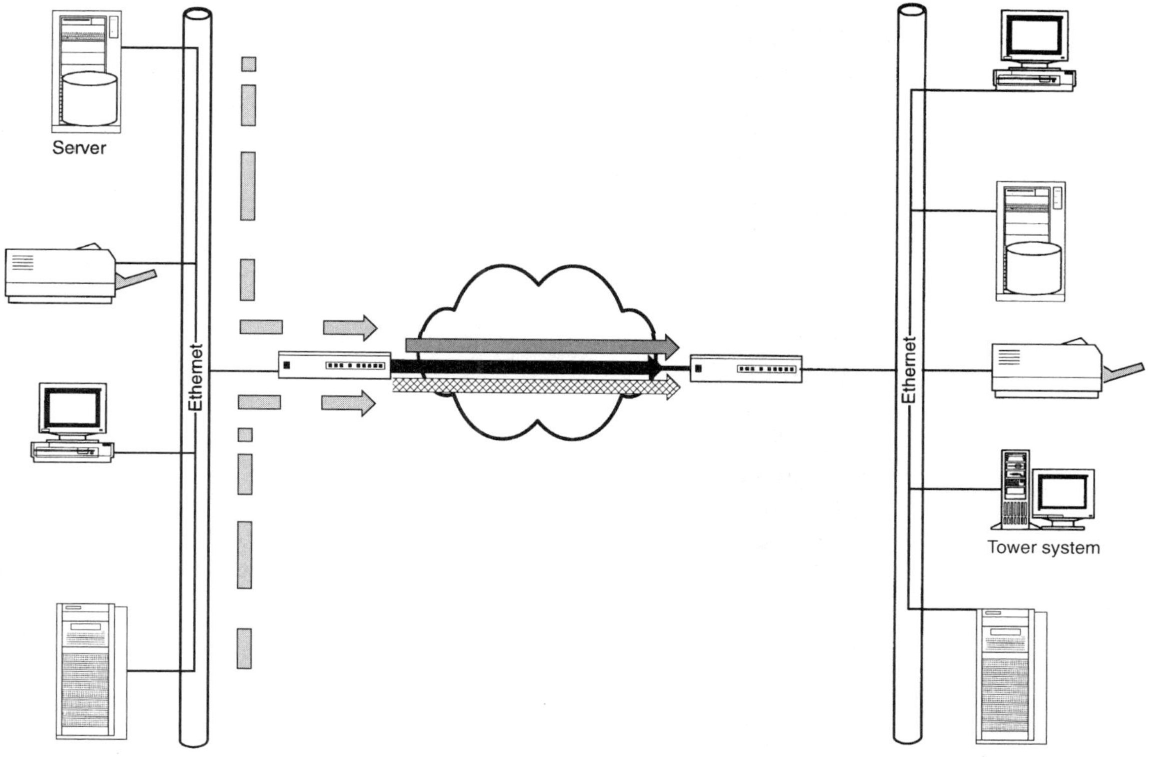

Figure 9.14 Using inverse multiplexing, the bridge dials over additional ports for additional links between the same end points. As traffic decreases, the bridge releases the links.

when bursty traffic occurs at certain periods of the day. If, however, these bursts occur all day long, this dial-up inverse multiplexing technique may not be the best choice.

As frame relay and ATM become more readily available within a client/server architecture, the bandwidth-on-demand concept may prove to be another beneficial asset. Frame relay today is one of the current technologies being considered by many client/server network managers. As traffic increases, bandwidth is allocated by the network on the same physical link as it is required. There is a certain committed information rate (CIR), as discussed in the previous chapter, that can be a guaranteed data flow rate. However, during the day and during periods of peak traffic demands, the burst committed rate and the burst excess rate can be used to increase the capacity without dial-up but using just the bandwidth-on-demand allocation provided by the frame relay network. Assuming that the carrier is not charging extra for this bandwidth on demand, the client/server network can be satisfied with some fixed cost rates. One must be aware of the committed rates, the expected burst rates, and the overall cost associated with this type of network connection. Using these high-speed communications links and the capabilities of frame relay, one can usually achieve 40 to 60 percent reduction in costs over the dedicated point-to-point leased lines. This is particularly true when T1s are used between the sites.

When ATM becomes readily available in the marketplace, its ability to support these on-demand bandwidth allocations can also satisfy the need. However, as mentioned in Chap. 8, ATM is not ready for prime time. In the interim, frame relay may well provide the capacity we're looking for. Frame relay operating at speeds of T1/E1 and later growing and evolving to a T2/E2 and soon T3 can add some depth and breadth to the client/server network. One must be aware that as frame relay evolves and ATM backbones continue to proliferate, the use of frame into the interexchange carriers' networks will be the primary means of achieving the access. However, in the backbone, the interexchange carrier may well segment the frames into cells and carry them as ATM on higher-speed links. At the receiving end, the carrier switch would then reassemble the cells back into frames and deliver them to the client/server network as a frame relay technique. In the interim, this method gives the user the best of both worlds: lower-speed access at the local loop and higher-speed access across the WAN. These alternatives continue to raise the issues and the awareness of how important client/server internetworking will be in the future. One cannot assume that these services will be ubiquitous, spread across North America or even internationally in a reasonable period of time. Therefore, a contingency plan should be to consider frame services as an interim solution with a migration plan to ATM as it becomes more readily available.

Source Route Bridging

Up to now the discussion on bridging dealt with the transparent bridging techniques used primarily on Ethernets and the capabilities of learning and spanning tree protocols to support these needs. In a token ring environment, however, additional bridging techniques, called source route bridging, are used. Figure 9.15 shows the token ring frame. In this figure, beyond the typical header and addressing information is an additional field called the routing information field. It is this routing information field that is used to determine the specific techniques of bridging between token rings. Note that this information can be used to determine the means of getting from point A to point B across the network. The source route bridge is also a MAC layer bridge working at the bottom half of the data link layer of the OSI model.

Source route bridging is designed around a source, that being a device, a PC, or a node on a ring assuming that a destination to be addressed is on the same ring. In this particular case, the data will be transported

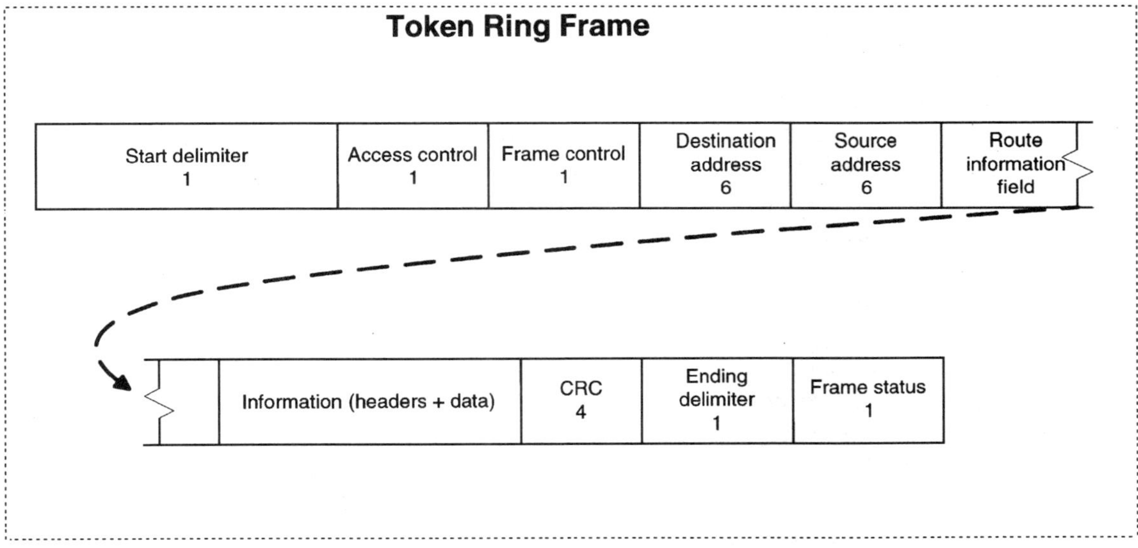

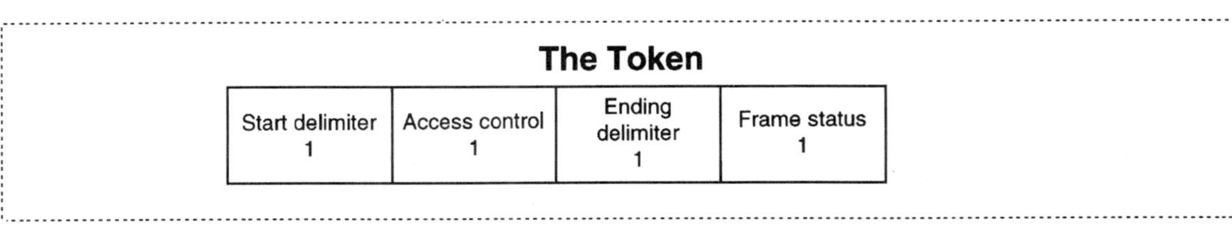

Figure 9.15 The token and the token ring frame used in source route bridging.

around a normal ring in a normal sequence. However, no address control or copied bits (A and C) will be used by any device on the ring, indicating to the source device that the address that was used to transmit the information is not local. The destination must therefore be on another LAN. What occurs is that the source location will switch to what is called a *resolve protocol*. The resolve protocol (basically what the source will do) transmits the data to all bridges associated or attached to this particular ring. The data is therefore transmitted across multiple paths from the source to the destination through the various bridges attached on the network and across the various links. Consequently, multiple packets or frames of information arrive at the destination location. The destination responds to all queries over all the respective prerecorded routes that were used to get the data from source to destination. Multiple responses come back to the original source, indicating the primary and alternate routes on how to get from source to destination. The source device then chooses one route to send the data from the location to the desired destination, typically the shortest or first response received. One can assume that the first response came across the shortest route. Therefore, the source will basically use that as its desired route. Once this has occurred, the source and the destination exchange information during a session over the chosen route. This process is shown in Fig. 9.16.

In source route bridging, the routing information field, using a discovery method, can basically assign the addressing methodology in a three-number sequence. First is a ring number, second is a bridge number, and third is the corresponding ring at the far end of a bridge (Fig. 9.17).

When dealing with source route bridging, the actual source device (a PC, server, or any other device) chooses a route that it will take based on the responses that it receives from explorer frames sent across the network and proliferating across all the bridges. This route is chosen as follows:

1. By default it selects the first response it receives.
2. The source could be programmed to pick a specific route with the smallest number of hops out of all the responses that came within a specific time period.

Bridges may be programmed to accept only packets or frames that did not exceed a maximum number of hops, for example, hop count equals less than 7. The maximum number of hops does not include any intermediate WAN links; for example, the data between two consecutive rings, no matter how complex, is considered one hop.

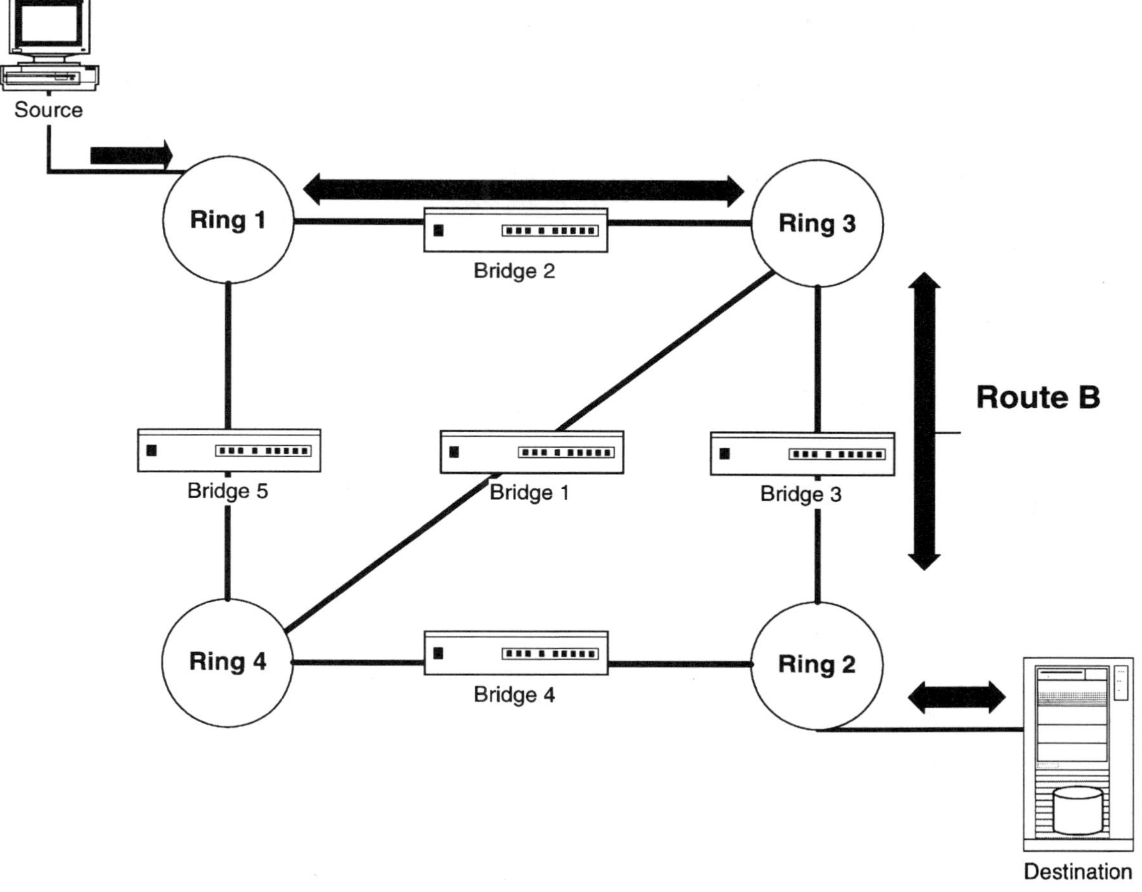

Figure 9.16 Source route bridging involves source and destination exchange frames during a session over chosen route B.

The resolve procedure, that is, the address resolution, works only if the source knows the destination MAC address. If not, a discovery procedure is followed. In an IBM token ring, a query is sent to all local NET BIOS stations. If no response is received, then the address will go into a query that is broadcast to all rings across the WAN. Source route bridging software must be loaded on all nodes and bridges on the network for this to work.

Source route bridging is not sensitive to network topology changes or any workstation movement. The bridges have no knowledge of the network topology (the layout of the ring). They only know the two rings to

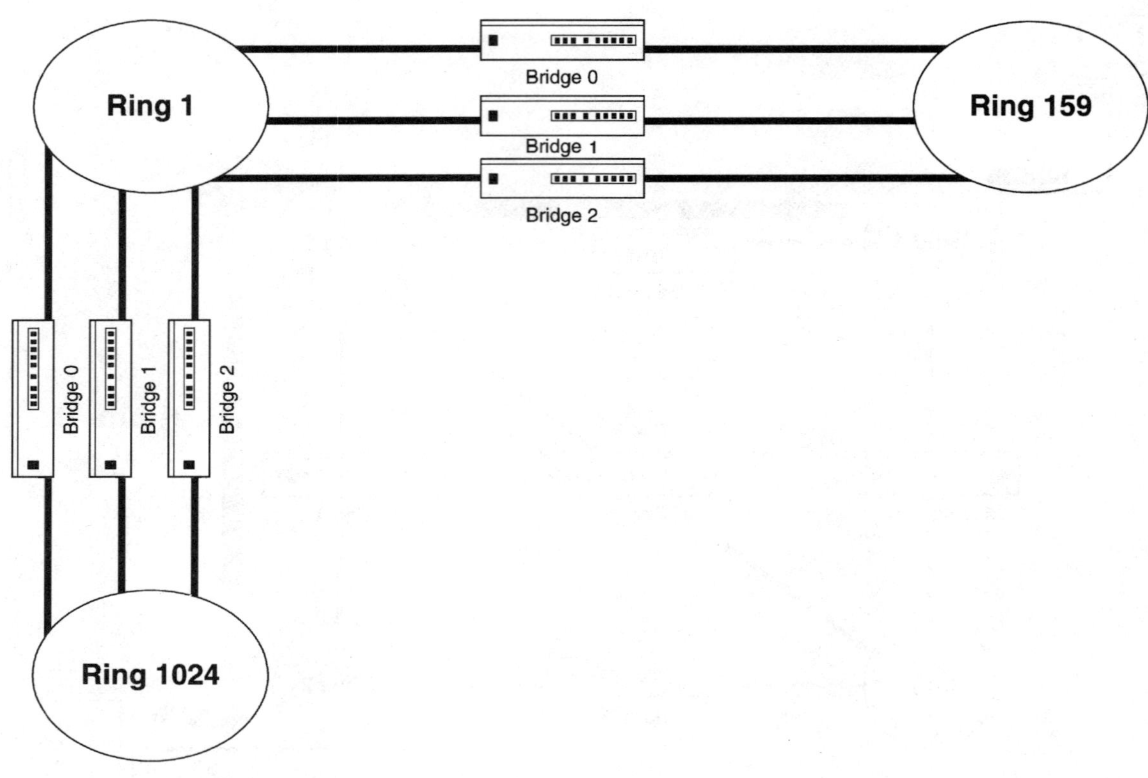

Figure 9.17 The components of the routing information field use rings, bridges, and ring addresses.

which they are connected. One condition that must be understood is that source route bridging is nonadaptive. Once a session is established, the root is fixed.

Source route bridging cannot reroute around a failed component or any congested links without breaking a session. As the network has defined the route to be chosen with a bridge, that same route will be used over and over again. In the event this connection is established between the source and the destination address and congestion occurs, the client/server network will obviously degrade. Until the congestion is cleared or until a new session is established between the client and the server, all traffic will proceed across this link regardless of the performance characteristics. For this reason, one must be very cautious when determining how to use source route bridging.

One method used for source route bridging is to actually transmit across a frame relay network. In this case, the frames generated across an SRB (source route bridge) can be encapsulated inside a frame along the frame relay network. Many organizations using a client/server architecture have chosen to do this because of the nature of their network. Rather than go into complex rerouting techniques and so on, the use of a source route bridge run across a frame relay network can easily satisfy their immediate needs. However, using this route information field and the frame relay network could cause some additional latency that in turn equates to delay. The performance overhead in a client/server internetwork can therefore be affected by overhead associated with this source route bridging technique. When planning the client/server network, one must be aware of any associated or undocumented types of overhead in latency that could subsequently be implied on the network. Often it is too late after the network is up and running to go back and reconsider this option. When the network has been fully deployed across the span of the wide area, it is very difficult to update all nodes and all locations simultaneously. Therefore, the consideration of what routing or bridging technique to use is of paramount importance.

Source Route Transparent Bridging

In some mixed environments, the same bridge can change its role of operation from transparent to source route bridging by simply examining the first bit of a source MAC address. If a bit is toggled to 0, the frame is to be filtered and forwarded transparently. If, however, the first bit is toggled to 1, the frame is then to be forwarded according to its recorded route in the route information field.

A source route transparent bridge has a dual stack of software loaded in it. It cannot connect a source routing workstation with a nonsource routing workstation. Instead, it must act like a traffic cop directing the frames between compatible workstations for a source route to a source route bridge or a nonsource route to a nonsource route bridge. This means that options exist in the use of bridging technologies.

A minor commentary here is that bridges tend to be very simple in operation between similar networks. If two Ethernets are used, then bridging can be used very efficiently. If two token rings are used and internetworked, then bridges can also be used. What typically does not happen is the connection of an Ethernet to a token ring network through bridging technologies. Although this can be accomplished, it is typically not the function of a bridge to accomplish these goals. Simplicity may be part of the goal in achieving a client/server network. Therefore, the client/server internetwork manager must always look at the options available and determine what is the best choice to link locations or networks and subnetworks together in this client/server architecture.

Routers

In this section, more complex yet robust devices called routers are categorically considered. Where bridges typically link different networks together via a single network connection and a hard-wire connection, such as a leased line, routers can use multiple mixed links to provide the connectivity. Therefore, routers tend to be more robust and allow the ability of mixing links such as leased-line, dial-up connections, packet-switching networks (X.25 services), etc. Routers can also support multiprotocol environments. This introduces layer 3 of the OSI model (network layer). Routers are more complex, more sophisticated, and more robust than bridges. With a router, we introduce an additional layer of global internetworking capabilities and addressing very similar to the addressing schemes used in a postal service. Where the post office routes information based on city, state, and zip code (the zip code being what they really route on), the router can do very similar things. The router uses the network layer as its universal and global routing technique. However, the router also covers both the data link and the physical layer below the network layer on the OSI model. In routing techniques, the capability to address universally across a client/server architecture provides for the added depth that would not be available in bridged connections. It is through this robustness and resiliency and the added dimension of having multiple different wide area network transport capabilities that the router brings more to the table than a bridge. This statement does not mean that the bridge is not reliable or sophisticated in its own right, but the router can deal with multiple protocols working between different LAN topologies and different protocols where a bridge typically does not.

In a routing technique, a global addressing scheme is adopted. Each node is distributed and assigned a logical address coded by the network, followed by the host address. Figure 9.18 shows a typical routing net-

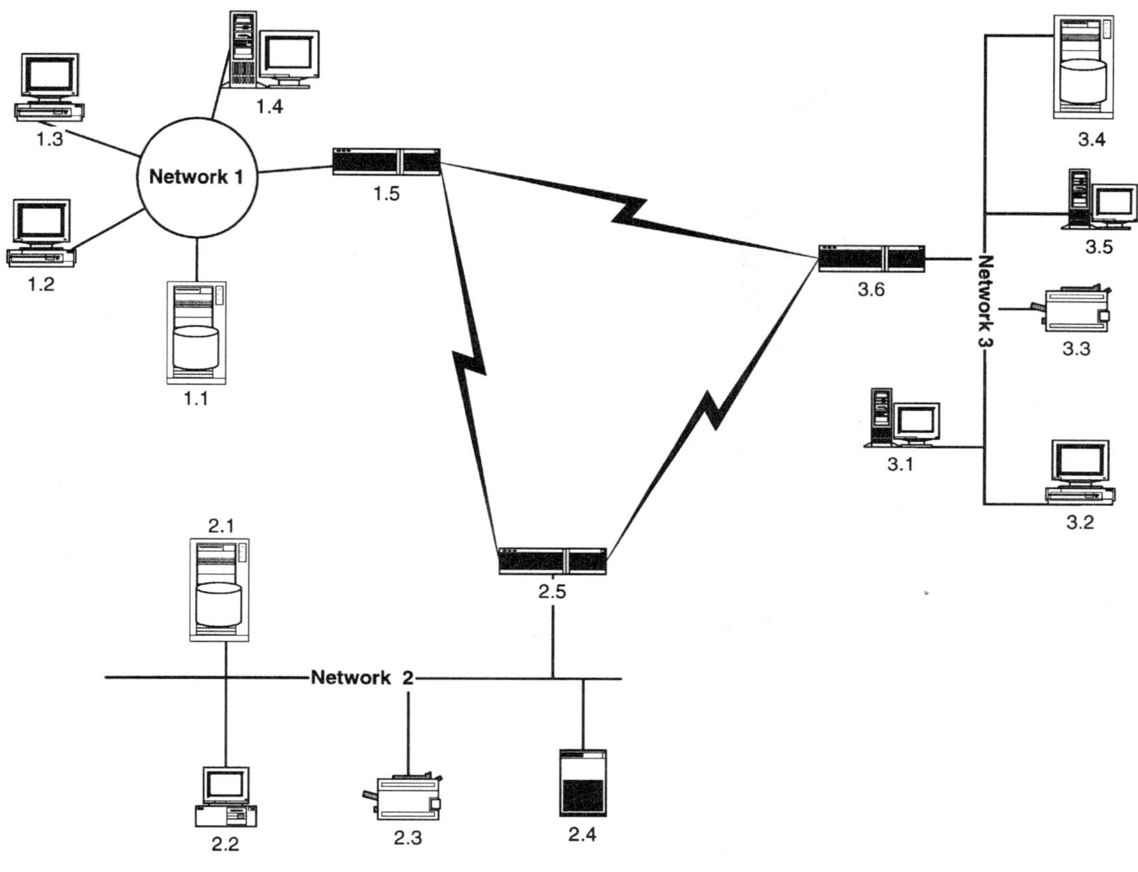

Figure 9.18 A typical routing network uses addresses by network and host.

work. In this particular case, a very simple network topology is laid out. Each network is numbered. Following the network number will be a node or host address. Included in all of the node addresses for each of the PCs or servers on the network is also an address for each of the routers. Each router associated with an individual network therefore uses a gateway-type function (*gateway* in this reference means more of a traffic cop role as opposed to a high-level operational system that addresses higher-level protocols on the OSI model). As data is prepared on a network node, for example, a PC or a server on one of the networks, the packets and frames of information change in scope as they are moved from network to network in this client/server architecture.

The enveloping that takes place requires various stages. In Fig. 9.19, this addressing is shown where the overhead and addressing schemes continually change as they go through the various steps across the wide area network. The only thing that does not change in this global addressing scheme is the actual data itself. The data should be transparent to all of the routing schemes being used, and the only thing that should be changed is the address.

Figure 9.20 shows a typical routing protocol. In this particular case, a node attaches a network header to the data that needs to be moved. This network header consists of destination and source address. This node then sends its information in packet form over the token ring shown in this figure to a default router. The router now sets the A and C bits and retransmits the packet over the token ring. The A and C bits indicate that the address was recognized and the data was copied. Next the router examines the destination network number and looks in its routing table for the best path or the least expensive route or whatever routing table parameters that have been set. Upon assumption or selection of the path, the router drops the token ring information and builds a wide area network envelope. The router then ships the data with the enveloping information out over the WAN. At the destination network, the information is now examined for the network address as sent from router to router across this platform over the best or selected route according to whatever the routing table indicated. At the receiving end, the router there recognizes the destination address of one of its own. This router strips off the WAN envelope, builds an Ethernet frame, and sends the information to the destination-addressed node, in this particular case, a server. The server recognizes the destination address as its own and strips off the Ethernet frame and forwards the information to its upper layers. This procedure is a typical routing scheme used in most wide area networks and concurrently with client/server architectures.

In the scenario described, the sending device requires the MAC address of the immediate destination (the final end point); otherwise, it cannot send its packets over the token ring to the remote Ethernet. To solve this problem and eliminate some potential pitfalls, either of the following ideas can be implemented:

1. The MAC address is computable or directly derived from the network address.
2. The sender will broadcast a query message over the LAN requesting the MAC address corresponding to the known network address of the immediate destination.

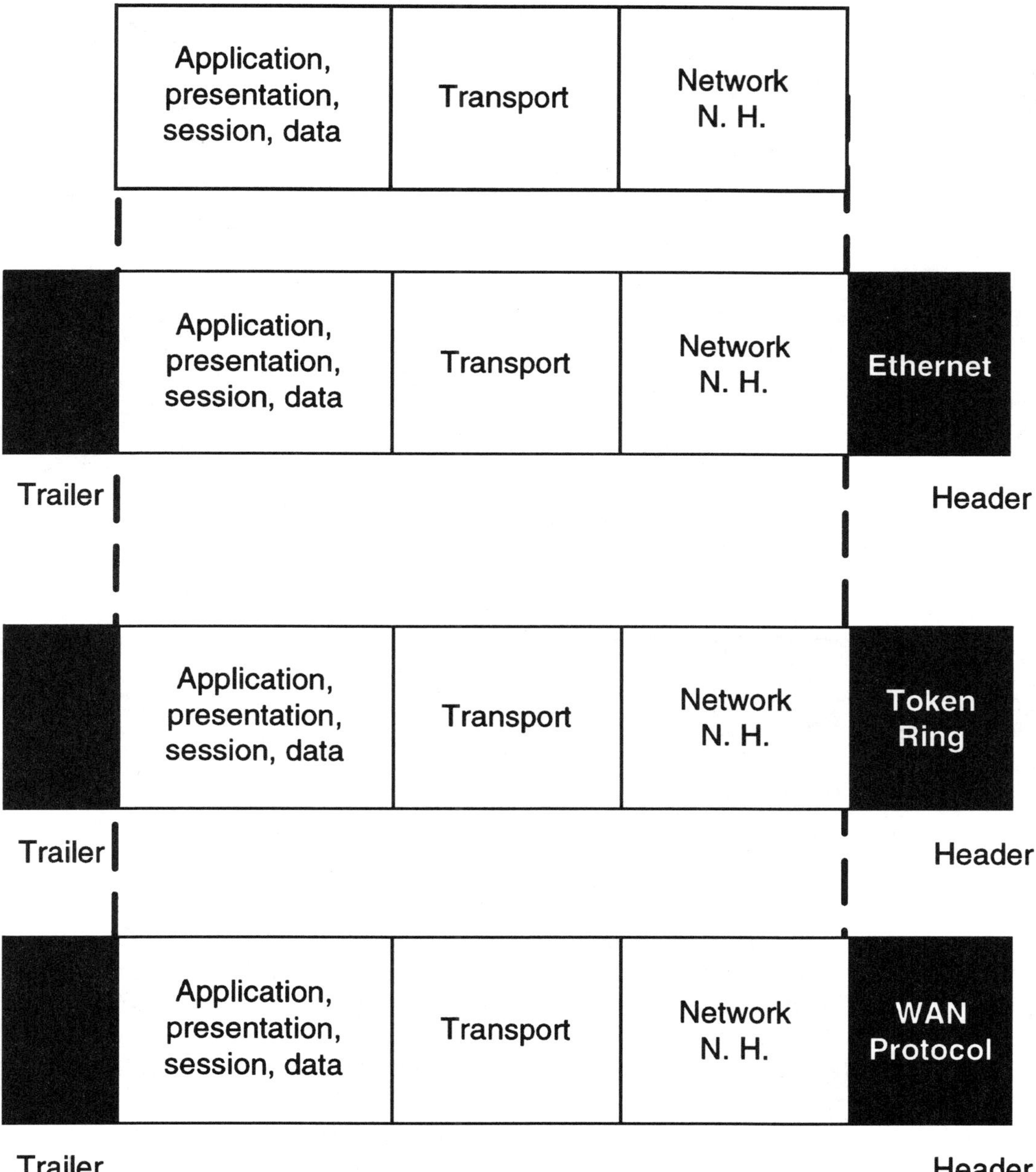

Figure 9.19 Packets in the network change envelopes as required by various stages.

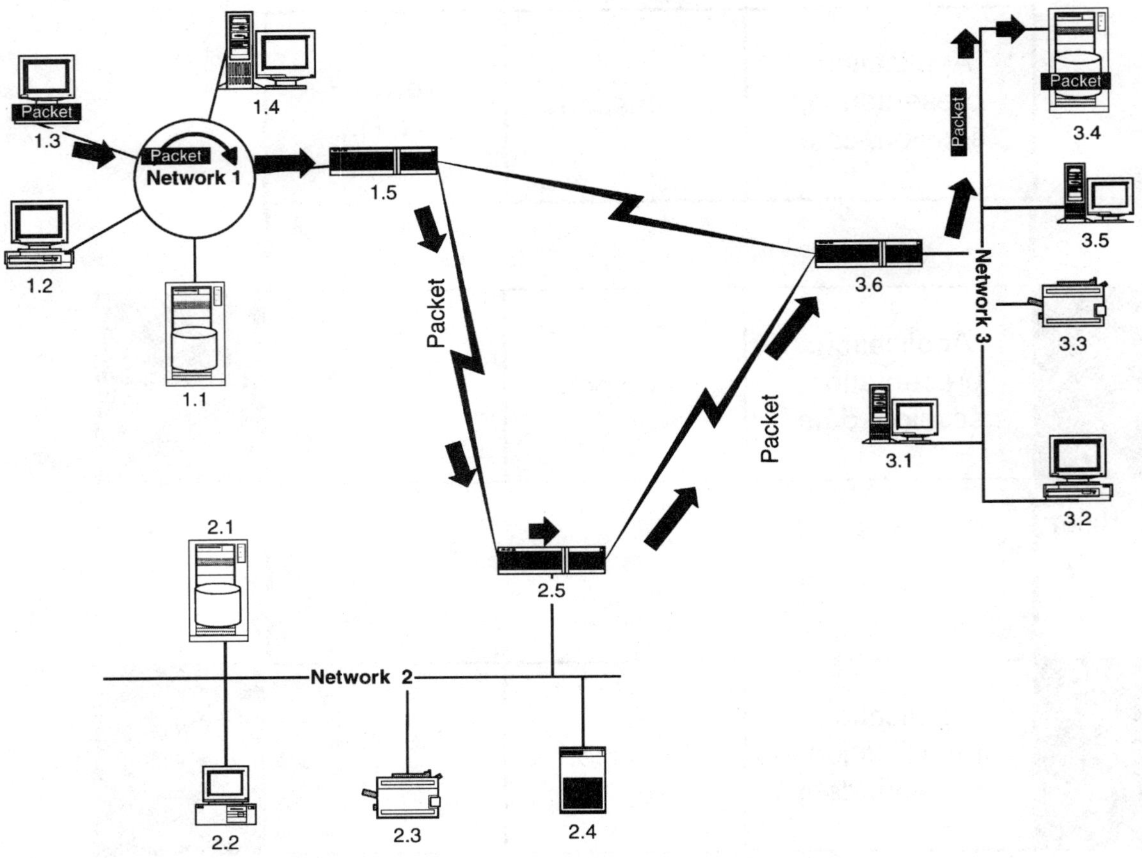

Figure 9.20 A normal routing scenario: The end node 1.3 sends data to end node 3.4.

The destination or some proxy agent responds with a message containing the MAC layer address and its network address. The protocol used for this identification process is called address resolution protocol (ARP). ARP messages are always localized. They are transmitted by bridges but blocked by routers. This blockage helps to eliminate some chit-chat or the overhead associated with wide area networking protocols.

In an alternative for diskless workstations or diskless PCs (or even some of the new net PCs) that only know their MAC layer address, they may find their assigned IP address from a server by exchanging by what is known as a reverse ARP. The reverse address resolution protocol (RARP) is used to request and reply. This scenario basically describes the way a diskless workstation would go out and ask a server or another device on the network, "Who am I?" and that device in turn would respond by giving the IP address of the individual device. This assumes that static IP addresses are being used on the particular network. In the event a dynamic host control protocol (DHCP) is being used, each IP address is assigned as the device is logging on to the network. In a DHCP, upon bootup the host server in control of the network, such as a primary domain controller (PDC), assigns an IP address to each station as it logs on to the network. DHCP allows for better utilization of IP addresses on an existing network because the IP address can change from time to time. It is this PDC that controls the identity and the addressing methodology on the fly.

Routers, particularly in a client/server architecture, are being used in many applications utilizing an IP addressing scheme. Earlier chapters discussed the use of TCP/IP as the protocol of choice and the middleware of most client/server architectures. Other protocols can be used, of course, but TCP/IP has been accepted as the de facto standard for many client/server networks. Using IP as the routing scheme allows a lot of flexibility and a unique addressing capability for every node on this wide area network and the client/server architecture. The IP address, using current technology, is a 32-bit addressing capability that again is broken down by network followed by a host address.

Several different formats are being used for TCP/IP addressing schemes, including the following classes of address: A, B, C, D, and E (which is used for special projects for Internet access). Because of the robustness of the TCP/IP protocol, a client/server network can use subnetworking concepts and mask the TCP/IP address. Then, in a subnet, typically more than 16 bits of this 32-bit address are used for the network number. Figure 9.21 shows a typical design or diagram of a multinetworked environment using a client/server architecture. In this particular case, a class B address is used for this major corporation's network. Each of the subnets is then masked into a 16-bit network number, which allows for resiliency and robustness in assigning the IP addresses by each department, as shown in this figure. IP masking here refers to the ability to assign a value associated with each IP address, which is configured by the network manager, and allow the nodes and routers to read the portion of the IP address that represents the network (or subnetwork) number. One complexity with this whole situation is that the mask is represented in decimal, although it really represents a binary value that has a 1 in every bit position corresponding

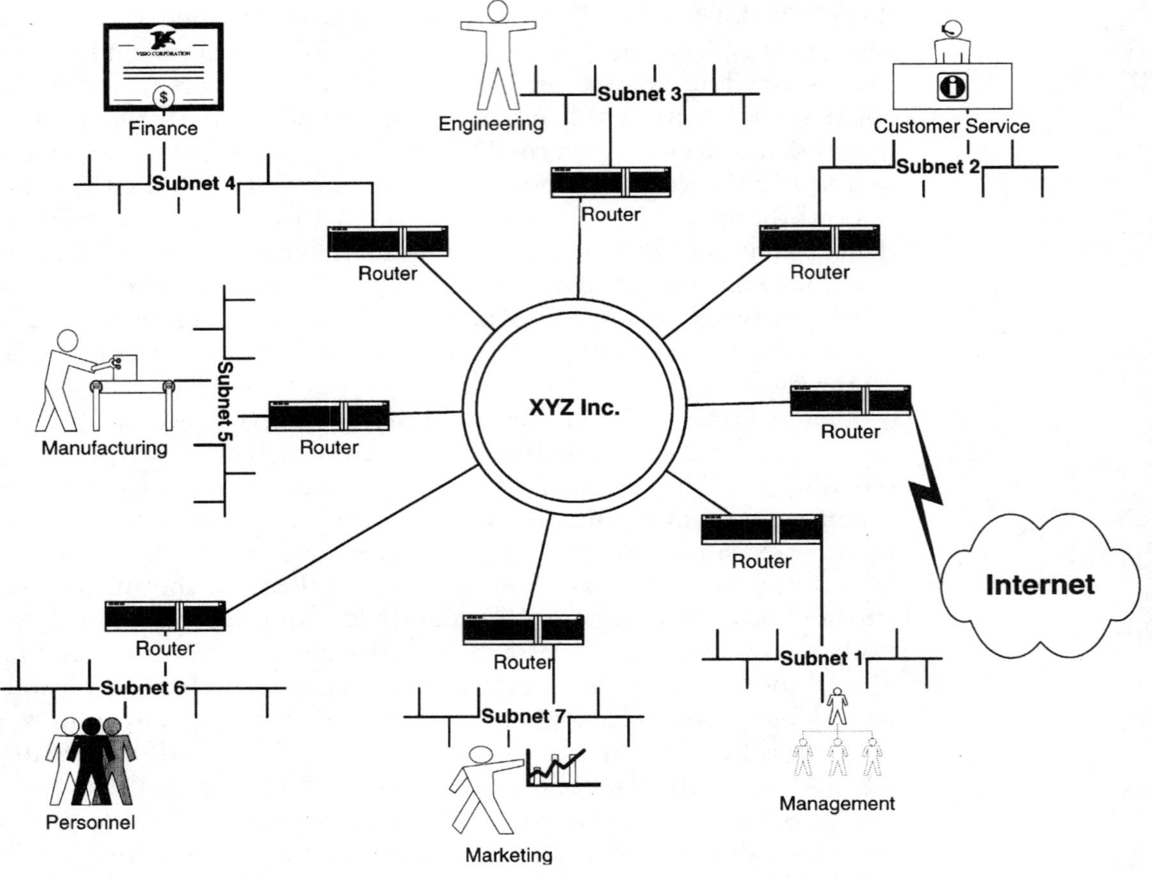

Figure 9.21 The main router uses 16 bits for the network address (class B) and 24 bits for each subnetwork (class C).

to a network number and a 0 in those bits corresponding to a host number.

One of the constant complaints of network managers in dealing with TCP/IP is that the overhead associated with IP itself is extensive. Individual client/server managers must be aware of certain tradeoffs. Using the IP system and the routing capabilities that allow for very robust and dynamic allocation has an overhead price. Typical overhead caused by the segmentation of the information can range from 20 to 30 percent or more. Using lower-speed communications channels in a routing network would therefore cause additional congestion or overhead associated with this IP addressing scheme. However, the robustness you get in an IP address more than compensates for the overhead. Using compression techniques and dynamic allocation of bandwidth type networks, the IP overhead can become ancillary.

Figure 9.22 is a representation of an IP header. In this particular header, several things are at work. First, the version number of IP that is being used allows us to evolve through different layers of the protocol. The next idea, or the next grouping of bits, is the Internet header

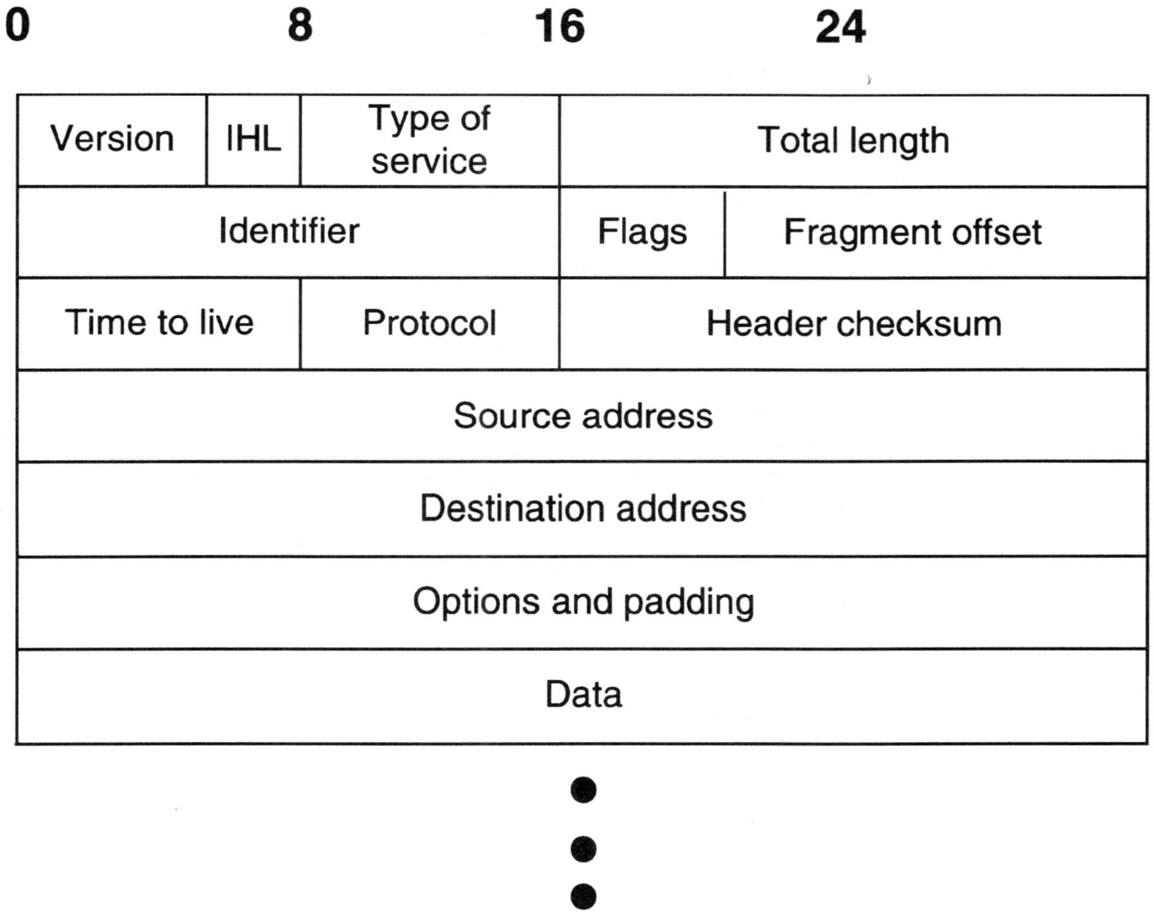

0		8	16		24
Version	IHL	Type of service	Total length		
Identifier			Flags	Fragment offset	
Time to live		Protocol	Header checksum		
Source address					
Destination address					
Options and padding					
Data					

•
•
•

Figure 9.22 The IP header uses a lot of overhead, and new addresses will be 128 bits long.

length (IHL), the length of the header in 32-bit words. The minimum number of header is five words, or 20 octets. The next portion of the header shows the type of service. The type of service being used can include such things as the point-to-point protocol (PPP) and can have several different precedence capabilities that allow for various prioritizations of the data packets. Following that, the type of service can also include *delay throughput and reliability* (DTR). The D can be set to specific or normal versus high or low delay, the throughput can be used for either high throughput or normal throughput, and the reliability can be set for either high or normal. Using the DTR capabilities in our header can establish certain priorities based on protocol, application or user-specific designated routines, which allows some flexibility when setting up the type of service in an IP network.

On the third line of this figure is also one byte of information that refers to the time to live. One of the situations with IP, as already discussed, is the fact that a decrementing counter is used when an IP segment is shipped out across the network. As the segment is being shipped out, it can take many paths across the wide area to get to the end point. Assuming that each node must process the information and pass it through based on various links that are available, it is possible that the IP segment (packet) may take a very diverse or convoluted route. As it processes this packet of information, each node decrements the counter starting at 15 and working its way down to 0. If by chance the information has not reached the destination address by the time the counter has been set to 0, the IP packet is discarded. Although this may sound harsh, the last thing one wants is to have IP traveling the network in circuitous routing and not making it to the end point. Therefore, by allowing a 16-count sequence, the IP scheme only allows the packet to stay on the network for a designated period of time. It is therefore up to TCP to be the responsible agent to know that the data did not arrive. IP does not care whether the data arrives at the end point or not; this is a role of TCP. For the client/server network manager, hearing that data may well be discarded while en route could cause consternation. Fear not; this is the way IP works. For the most part, the routes will be established and the data will be delivered within a reasonable amount of time. However, in those rare cases where the data is going in circuitous routing, the intent is to make sure that within a reasonable amount of time the data has arrived, or if not, it is discarded. This is a price one pays when using TCP/IP, although it is a small price to pay when all things are considered.

Routing Information Protocol (RIP)

As discussed in Chap. 8, the routing information protocol is a very popular and dynamic routing protocol because it is included with all of the Berkeley UNIX packages. The basis of the routing information protocol is always to take the shortest route in metrics (hop counts). The maximum hop count is restricted to 15. This is where *time to live* is established in an IP header. Any change in the wide area network triggers table updates, and each of the table updates that are being changed must propagate throughout the network. The stage when all routers have exactly the same view of the network is a very slow approach. The process to reach that stage of a single view is called *convergence*. RIP is a slow-convergence protocol. RIP routers forward their entire routing tables to their neighboring routers. Each of the receiving routers processes these new tables by comparing each entry with the entries in the current existing tables. This operation is repeated every 30 seconds by default. The client/server network manager can reset that default value to longer periods of time, such as 30 minutes; however, if the routing default is used, every 30 seconds the tables are broadcast. One can imagine in a client/server architecture with multiple nodes and hosts spread around the country or around the world what this would do to the potential throughput across a network.

The routing information protocol is an interior gateway protocol (IGP) for building and maintaining the routing tables within an autonomous system. To route between autonomous systems, an exterior gateway protocol (EGP) is required. RIP is what is known as a *distance vector algorithm table*. The result is a routing table with an entry listed for each target network that contains the following information:

1. The destination IP address
2. The metric to reach that target (the hop count)
3. The IP address of the next downstream neighbor (router)
4. The identity of neighboring routers that supplied this entry
5. The amount of time since this entry was last updated

Tables are broadcast periodically as mentioned. A route entry times out at six times the broadcast timer interval, meaning that if the default is set to 30-second increments, the time entry actually times out at 180 seconds. Updates are triggered automatically in the event of any link failure.

The reference to neighbors means routers that share a common network. Routers use their neighbors as both upstream and downstream serviceability environments. Neighbors can be bridged, meaning the two routers can be bridged together across a wide area network. Although this might sound complex, the routing information protocol is fairly robust and widely accepted by many organizations in the deployment of their client/server network memory. Oscillation can occur in this situation. Figure 9.23 shows networks where the routing scheme lists how data traverses this network. In this particular case, three routers are shown linking four different networks together. If, by chance, the link from router 1 to router 2 fails, router 2 times out the route to the target location through router number 1 and forwards all of its traffic to the target through router number 3. Router number 3 then forwards all of its traffic back to router number 2 heading towards the target located at router number 1. This routing creates a loop that is called *oscillation.* Oscillation, or loops, causes significant overhead and bogs the networks down to the point that no data would be allowed to pass. The solution to this oscilla-

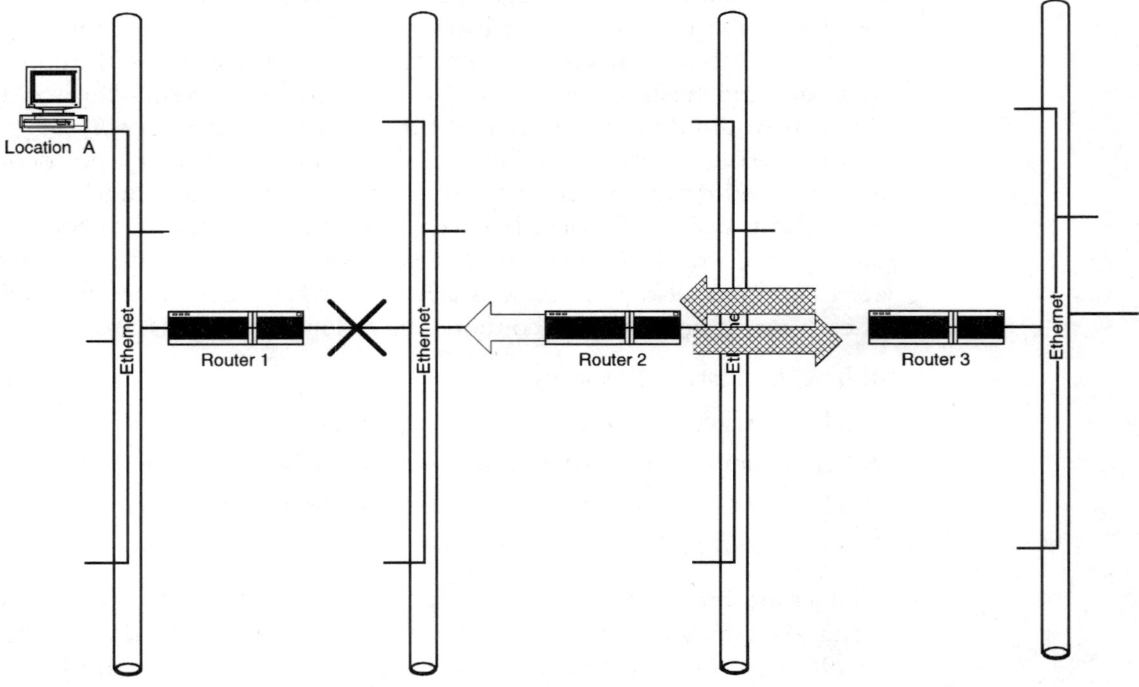

Figure 9.23 If a link failure occurs, a routing loop, or oscillation, can occur.

tion problem is a technique called *split horizon*. In the split horizon scenario, a router does not propagate a route to a target over a port that actually supplied the same route to the same target. Where oscillation is turned on, data arriving on a specific link to a router designated to some other location cannot be redirected across the same link and back out to the network. However, in Chap. 8, using the discussion of frame relay, the idea of having a single connection out to the frame relay network indicates that data coming from one frame relay source and destination to still a second source may have to pass through an intermediate node. This node may be the corporate headquarters, where the data is sent to the corporate location and then redirected back out across the network to another location. Unfortunately, in the split horizon environment this would not be allowed. The client/server network manager must be aware of this potential risk. Two choices emerge to prevent this from happening:

1. Turn off split horizon. Turning off split horizon, however, would allow the risk that oscillation could be encountered.
2. Use a different PVC to connect between the different locations. Although we are using the same circuit, different PVC numbers can be assigned, which in turn fakes the router into believing the data is actually traversing a completely different link. This solves the oscillation problem and allows the data to pass through an intermediate node on a single connection into the frame relay network.

Open Shortest Path First (OSPF)

Open shortest path first (OSPF) is an interior gateway protocol that is intended to be used within an IP network under common administration, such as a corporate headquarters, a campus, or a regional network (autonomous system). This protocol requires the administrator to assign a cost to each circuit between routers. The cost is actually based on the speed of the given interface—the higher the speed, the lower the cost. Aggregate costs on this type of environment are cumulative. OSPF does not calculate route cost on a hop-count metric system as you would see in RIP; therefore, it is not restricted to the 15-hop maximum. However, if the client/server network administrator does not assign a cost, the route selection is based on a hop count. This assignment of cost is actually a discretionary value that is placed on the cost of the circuit. For example, if different protocols and applications are being used, the network manager can assign specific metrics for specific applications across different routes so that the traffic routes across different paths. Therefore, in the environment with a client/server network, the lower-cost route, which would be the first selected, would be assigned for client/server network traffic. Yet, when e-mail is used, a higher-cost value would be assigned to that same route. To accommodate the e-mail application, a different route with a lower cost would be assigned for that particular metric, which allows for some robust solutions to the competition or the contention for the bandwidth on the OSPF protocols.

In OSPF, the messages that are sent between the routers contain a change statement that must be propagated to the tables or a no-change statement can be broadcast. Information exchange between the routers includes information about all links in terms of their status—whether they are up and down, the link speed, and the link ports (what are they connected with?). These messages are exchanged between the routers within a defined area and a designated router for that area. This way, the broadcasts used with RIP are eliminated, making OSPF a potentially better choice in a client/server network. OSPF maintains a complete synchronized link-state database in every router of an area. Therefore, OSPF is a fast-convergence protocol. To prevent accidental misconfigurations of a network and to allow the existence of multiple OSPF networks in the same autonomous system, authentication keys are used in the OSPF packets. OSPF works well with the IP type of service feature, because the routers are specified to build up to eight different routing tables of the same area with different link costs associated with each different type of service.

One can imagine the capabilities and the strengths of using OSPF in a client/server network architecture. The lower overhead, the elimination of the broadcasts associated with RIP, and the ability to provide a type of service can all enhance network management. Using OSPF is a decision that must be made, but cannot be made lightly. As already mentioned, if the environment includes the IPX/SPX traffic on a Novell LAN being connected into the client/server network, one must consider the consequences of having to tunnel the IPX traffic into IP so that it can then be routed across OSPF. This process could add to some of the overhead, yet eliminate other associated overhead at the same time. The tradeoff must be evaluated closely and carefully so that the wrong decision is not made. Newer techniques will come from the industry that will probably incorporate the capability of including IPX in an OSPF path. However, another alternative could exist. Novell may well abandon its IPX protocols, which are proprietary to Novell, and go to a fully supported TCP/IP suite. If this becomes reality, the network manager's decision-making process becomes simpler. TCP/IP is the protocol of choice in the client/server architecture. Therefore, if this particular vendor begins to support TCP/IP and abandons its proprietary protocols, the job becomes that much less taxing.

Dial on Demand

In some cases, routers have the ability to use a dial on-demand feature. This feature was discussed earlier in Chap. 8 when looking at ISDN as a dial backup facility to provide additional capacity in the event of congestion. It was also shown in the bridge discussions earlier in this chapter. By using this dial on-demand feature, expensive WAN bandwidth can be used only when needed. The cost of a circuit-switched dial-up connection using either ISDN or some other circuit-switching technique can become prohibitive. One would only use this option when excessive demand exists or a link-state failure occurs. It is better to have a connection, albeit a slow connection, instead of no connection at all. The use of the dial on-demand capabilities therefore requires some form of a switched connection. It may be based on a destination IP address, typically to more than one address or destination. The dial on-demand feature may well be used to a single circuit-switched connection to various locations, but only one at a time. This dial on-demand capability may be based on any LAN traffic (a MAC address) to a single address. The switched facilities may include such things as circuit-switched dial-up communications, ISDN/BRI, switched 56/64 kbps, X.25 packet switching, frame relay, or cell relay.

Point-to-Point Protocol (PPP)

If, in fact, a switched on-demand service or some form of a fast relay service is used for dial on-demand capabilities, a different protocol may well suit the need. In this particular case, the point-to-point protocol was designed to establish communications over a point-to-point link. The originating entity would first use a link control procedure to configure and test the data circuit. The link is established and optional facilities are negotiated on an as-needed basis by this link control procedure; then the originating PPP sends its network control protocol packets to choose and configure one or more of the network layer protocols. These network layer protocols may include X.25 circuit switched, dial-up communications, ISDN, or other. Once the configuration is completed, datagrams from each of the network-layer protocols can be sent across the link. This link remains configured for communications between the two entities until some external event occurs or an explicit packet is issued to close down the link. This external event could be user intervention (human error) or some activity timer timing out in an expiration period. Using the PPP, any form of a DCE/DTE interface can be used, including EIA232D, RS449, V.35, or others. The PPP is designed around a duplex circuit only for dedicated or circuit-switched, asynchronous or synchronous communications, without great restrictions, and it may be used for greater control and performance. The physical layer is transparent to the data link layer of the PPP. Many organizations now use Internet and intranet capabilities that involve circuit-switched dial-up communications across the public switched network, circuit-switched capabilities, or ISDN. In this environment, when the client/server network is operating with TCP/IP protocols, the PPP protocol is used to establish the connection between the calling and the called location. Upon establishment of this PPP link, the network control protocols then establish the ability to begin routing IP packets.

Hubs

In many of the discussions already, the issue was a client/server network spread across a wide area. However, not all client/server architectures involve wide area networking solutions. In some cases, the simplest client/server internetwork would work inside a campus or localized environment. In these particular cases, a hub might well be used as an internetworking tool.

Hubs allow for a collapsed backbone environment in a high-rise office building, a campus area, or some other spread-out area that is still localized within some geographically constrained boundary. Essentially, this hub is the backbone in a box. This hub also acts as a switch, taking care of the switching of traffic from one local area network in a geographically bounded area to another one. The hub forwards traffic on a high-speed communications bus architecture within its backplane. In many cases, it deals with the MAC layer address and does not need wide area networking such as IP or other associated addressing schemes.

For all intents and purposes, what the hub brings to the table is a local internetworking solution. In Fig. 9.24, a hub links many different network segments to a single infrastructure. In this particular case, all

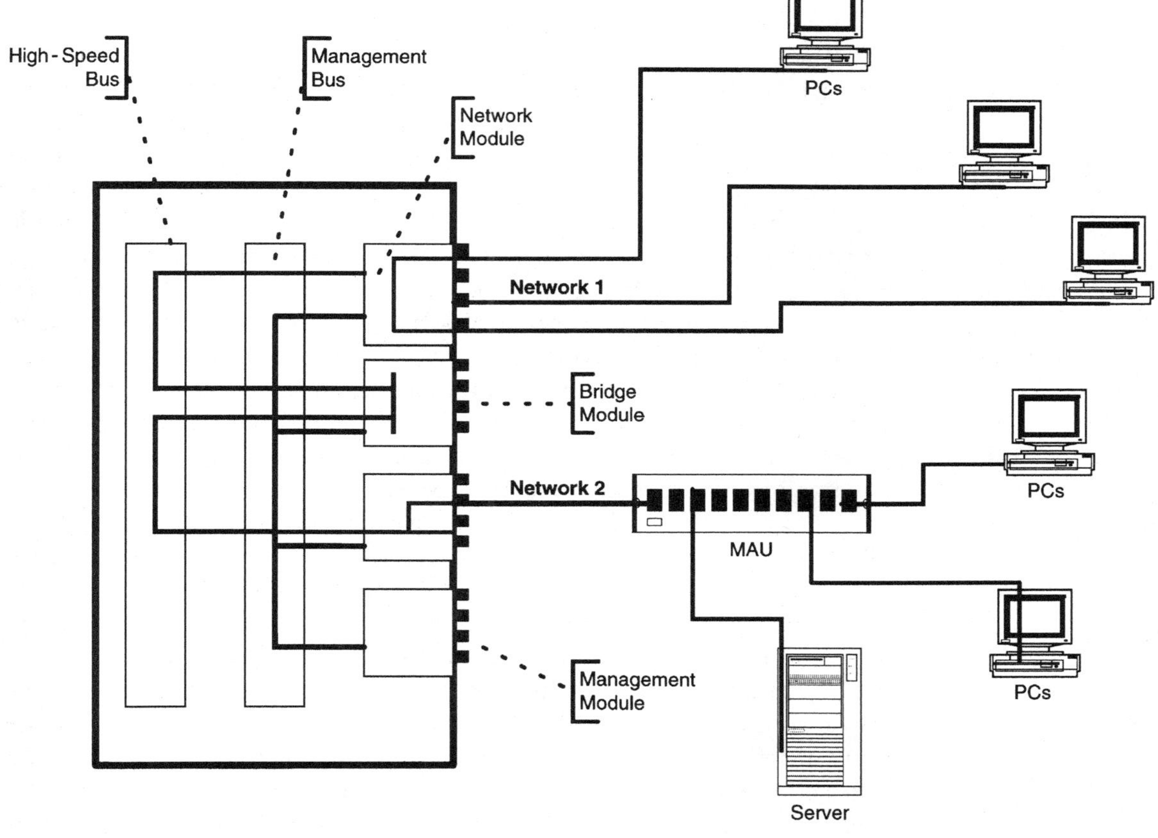

Figure 9.24 *The hub links many LAN segments together into a client/server network.*

of the components that have been discussed previously for localized services can be included. Note in the figure that individual, stand-alone, high-end workstations or PCs can be attached to a network module inside the hub. Standard high-speed communications links, such as dedicated 10-Mbps links or dedicated 100-Mbps links, can provide a twisted-pair solution within a local building. When these high-end workstations are plugged into the network module, they each have their own capacity to switch the information from the workstation to the server in this client/server world. Moreover, the figure also shows a network. In this particular network, a connection to the network module can support a localized token ring or Ethernet. Depending on the topology layout, 20,

30, or more stations can be attached to the individual network, which now has a single high-speed pipe to the network module.

In the center of this figure is the hub. Located in the backplane is a management bus and a high-speed data bus. The high-speed data bus carries the data traffic from port to port. The management bus is responsible for the internetworking capability across these high-speed links. A bridging module is also associated with this particular hub environment. Therefore, the high-speed data buses are connected from the data module to the bridging module, which, in turn, cross-links or bridges between one bus and another where the server is located. Using these high-speed hubs, an additional network can also be attached, for example, with a token ring through a multistation access unit (MAU). The server can be plugged into that MAU, allowing total access to each of the workstations regardless of its physical location by using the switching hub to provide the connectivity.

The address is based on the MAC layer; however, it can also be based on some other addressing system, such as IP or IPX. This decision is up to the user. In the high-speed hubbing environments, which run from $20,000 to about $80,000 or more, one makes these decisions carefully. However, each of the vendors in the marketplace is now producing stackable high-speed communications hubs. The hubs, acting as a collapsed backbone environment, can pull high-speed 100-Mbps links into the high-speed data bus and allow for some very broad bandpass capabilities. Traffic should be minimized through the use of the bridging and the switching architectures built into these hubs. If more traffic is positioned onto the network, then additional backplane hub capabilities can be installed at a price. Not all client/server networks must span the globe. In the case of a specific building, a client/server networking manager may need just to transmit data from floor to floor. Using the hub, life can be simple. One does not necessarily assume that by just using a hub all of the problems associated with the client/server network disappear. Using this type of architecture does, however, mean more simplified management and simplified configurations for moves, additions, and changes. Thus, the client/server networking manager should consider all of the options available. Hubs are but one option, albeit a very simple option.

Switches

Another option within a geographically bounded area is to use stackable hubs or LAN switches. More environments and client/server net-

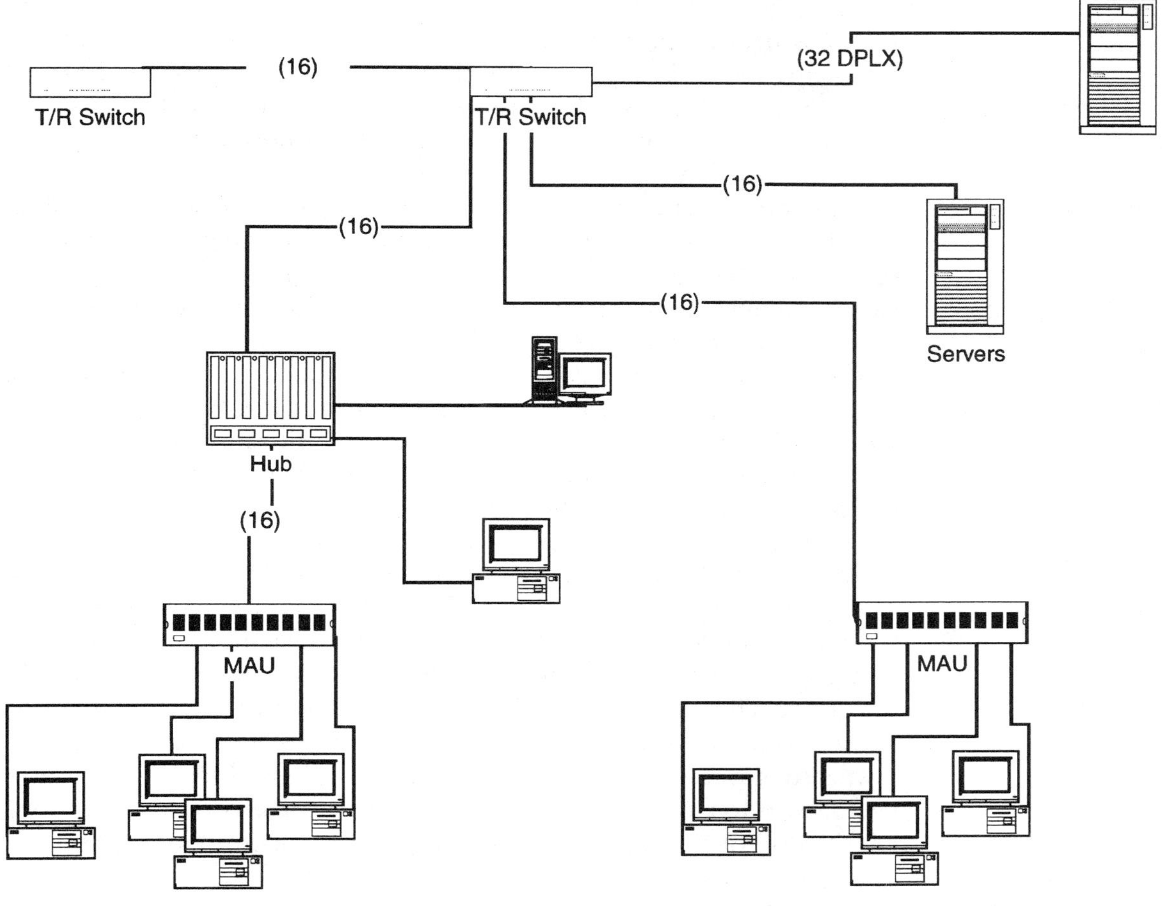

Figure 9.25 Switches can add port-to-port connections and increase throughput.

works are being established through some form of a switch. This switch can take on the form of an Ethernet switch or a token ring switch, as shown in Fig. 9.25. In a switched environment, for example with token ring, a switch can be positioned in the middle of a building. The high-end servers can use high-speed communications channel capabilities, for example, the capability of having dual server connections, or dual cards, at up to 32 megabits of information per second operating in a duplex environment. These switches allow full duplex capability for send and receive simultaneously on a 16-Mbps ring. The cabling infrastructure supports this function as the switch adds the dimension.

Still other servers that operate in strictly a half duplex at the higher 16 Mbps may be hung off this token ring switch. Coming out of this token ring switch in Fig. 9.25 is another link at 16 Mbps that is connected to a port on a MAU. In that regard, the MAU is then the logical extension out to the loads running to each of the workstations at 16 Mbps. Note also in this token ring switching environment there is a high-speed communications link between the switch and a high-end hub as depicted in the previous paragraph. In this regard, a high-speed communications hub or collapsed backbone can be plugged into the token ring switch, allowing access from multiple workstations attached to the hub to the servers that are on the backbone switch.

Token ring switching doesn't always gain much throughput. Because the nature of token ring is fairly deterministic, switching does not bring significant improvements over the bandwidth utilization. However, what switching does bring is the ability to do port-to-port switching for connections to the various different servers. Therefore, in this client/server internetwork, on a localized basis, multiple devices spread throughout a high-rise building can access the servers regardless of their location in the building. The creation of a switched environment can also produce the virtual LAN (V-LAN). Using port-to-port switching on these token ring switches loads and nodes attached on one ring creates another virtual LAN. This virtual LAN starts to add additional dimension to the client/server network. In the past, devices that may have been subnetworked due to congestion or constraints on a physical location can now be attached to a token ring port and appear to be part of a subnetwork, which was not possible before. By so doing, the client/server applications can be within reach readily. One should consider the use of switches in a localized environment to serve local users. When dealing with remote users, the issues of bridging or routing can be used; however, in a localized environment, hubs and switches are more important. Switches are not all that expensive, making the cost of connectivity far more reasonable. Using unshielded twisted pairs throughout this environment can be an inexpensive yet robust solution for the provisioning of the client/server network. Figure 9.25 shows many, many connections that all have an operational need and meet a demand for the client/server world to be able to access corporate data instantaneously. By using the switches, one can reconfigure the network fairly quickly.

The components listed in the previous sections—bridges, routers, switches, and hubs—are all just pieces that can be put together to provide this client/server internetworking capability. No one solution solves all needs. It behooves the client/server network manager to do the necessary research on the various applications and configurations that can serve the need easily. Using these various techniques and paying attention to the protocols that would be required, along with the protocol encapsulation or translation needs, the client/server network manager can provide a fairly robust interconnectivity solution.

With the onset of the broadband communications discussed in Chap. 8 and each of the components discussed in this chapter, the client/server networking architecture becomes far more readily achievable. Learning from those who have traveled this path before and discovered the components that could be internetworked to link a homogenous network together, one can feel comfortable in assuming the role of the client/server network manager. This does not imply that the task will be simple or that all of the protocols are readily available and ready to roll out. One must see the application, the protocol, and the components in action before making the final decision. In many cases, vendors will offer products and services that are still vaporware. Unfortunately, in this industry, changes are dynamic. Day-to-day operational needs must be satisfied while the architecture is being built. Therefore, while trying to satisfy day-to-day needs, it is easy for the client/server network manager to lose sight of what was initially to be implemented. Only through keeping a focused approach on longer-term interconnectivity solutions can this network actually come to fruition. Look at the alternatives, prove the results, test the results again, and double-check every step along the way. Find the tools that allow for protocol analysis, traffic analysis, and management reporting capabilities so that bottlenecks or problem protocols can quickly be isolated. Without these tools on all of these components and all of these network capabilities, one can get into trouble very, very quickly. In many cases, client/server internetworks started by other organizations have met with unsatisfactory results strictly because the tools were not in place. Today they are available if one takes the time to do the homework. Using foresight, budgetary constraints, and changing user demands, the client/server networking manager can assume that this network can be built and work properly. But this assumption goes hand in hand with the old adage: Show me.

CHAPTER 10

Deploying the Architecture

At this particular point in time, it appears the pieces are finally coming together. Each of the previous sections has outlined a specific topic that deals with the client/server internetwork. What still remains to be completed is an implementation plan to pull all of the pieces together. Hopefully, throughout this book several areas have pointed to using caution as the operative word for the client/server networking manager. One must always remember that when dealing with this architecture, nothing is as simple as it seems. Each and every one of the sections has discussed some of the variations that can be selected throughout the whole process of implementing a client/server internetwork. From the very beginning, looking at the server side of the business, a comparison was made among the different types of servers. Remember from earlier sections that the client/server internetwork, as defined in this book, involves a three-computer architecture. These three computers included the main server, which in many corporations and organizations is a mainframe. In other organizations, that server could be as simple as a PC-based application server.

Creating a client/server network is not as simple as looking at one significant architecture; it involves developing a strategic plan on how one might migrate from various computing platforms to a single-server environment. As we've said before, no single solution is appropriate for all organizations. At every step along the way, this book tried to facilitate and point out the variations and the differences between protocols, networking components, servers, and operating systems. If it was a simple as selecting one solution, there would be no need for this or any other book dealing with the client/server architecture. One must always remember when starting this process that several other demands and targets will emerge while looking at all of the pieces. Murphy is alive and well.

User Demands

In various organizations where a client/server architecture was deployed, each of the individuals responsible for the development of the planning process, the strategy for future computing network services, and the overall internetworking function has learned one basic rule. This rule should always be kept in the forefront of the planning process: *Users will always ask for more, faster, better, and cheaper.* What this means is that although a plan begins with certain target markets or target work groups, several other things will take place. Time has a way of changing each and every one of the goals that were established in the beginning of the process. When users are first approached about the services and access they need, their demands may well be very limited. But, as time progresses and they begin to get a flavor for the access capabilities and the availability of organizational information, they will certainly demand more data or more access.

As connectivity decisions are being made, the developers might approach the users again and describe how they might access the network. In most cases, the users agree to either a limited amount of capacity and speed or their demands are very, very moderate. However, as the system begins to roll out several new and emerging systems, accesses and capabilities automatically start to bog down the network. As the network begins to slow down, users begin to demand a higher-speed communications infrastructure. Therefore, we must keep in mind that the demands placed on a network (or an internetwork) will continually create new pressure to speed up the communications process.

As the users begin the process of evaluation and experimentation, they will demand a much faster communications capability. If you have a single network, a subnetwork may be necessary to separate the collision domains. On the other hand, if you have a token ring environment, the ability to bridge two rings at 4 Mbps may well be necessary. Inevitably, however, you will need to speed the network up to one of the higher-speed capabilities. Even though subnetworking will work for a short time, eventually the higher-speed networks will still be needed, particularly in the backbone. Thus, 16-Mbps rings may well be the suit of the day. Figure 10.1 shows a 16-Mbps high-speed communications ring (token passing), with feeder subnetworks bridged together using a 4-Mbps departmental connection. Hybrids, of course, will emerge through this process. In Fig. 10.2, a hybrid approach is being used. In this particular approach, departments also have 16 Mbps for the high-end users while the moderate users are supported by a 4-Mbps ring. These will then be linked onto a 16-Mbps ring for individual departments as well as the backbone. Continuing this thought, in an Ethernet environment, the same approach can be used. Where a 10-Mbps shared resource is used, several other approaches can be implemented to provide different capabilities, including switching, virtual Ethernets, and 100-Mbps Ethernet capabilities. One or all of these approaches can be used, depending on the application and the user demands. Clearly, the industry is leading us to a higher-speed thoughput-demand capability, such as the gigabit Ethernet. This capability is beyond the scope of this particular book; however, one should be aware that new demands and new services are on the horizon.

A third choice to speed up some of the communications facilities and capabilities to the end-user departments would be to mix the 100-Mbps and the switched Ethernet capabilities, as shown in Fig. 10.3. In this scenario, using hubs for 10-Mbps shared Ethernet, the hubs are linked together with a 100-Mbps backbone network, 100 Mbps to the desktop for certain users, and a switching hub stacked inside a closet, which can all be combined to provide the various capabilities and services needed

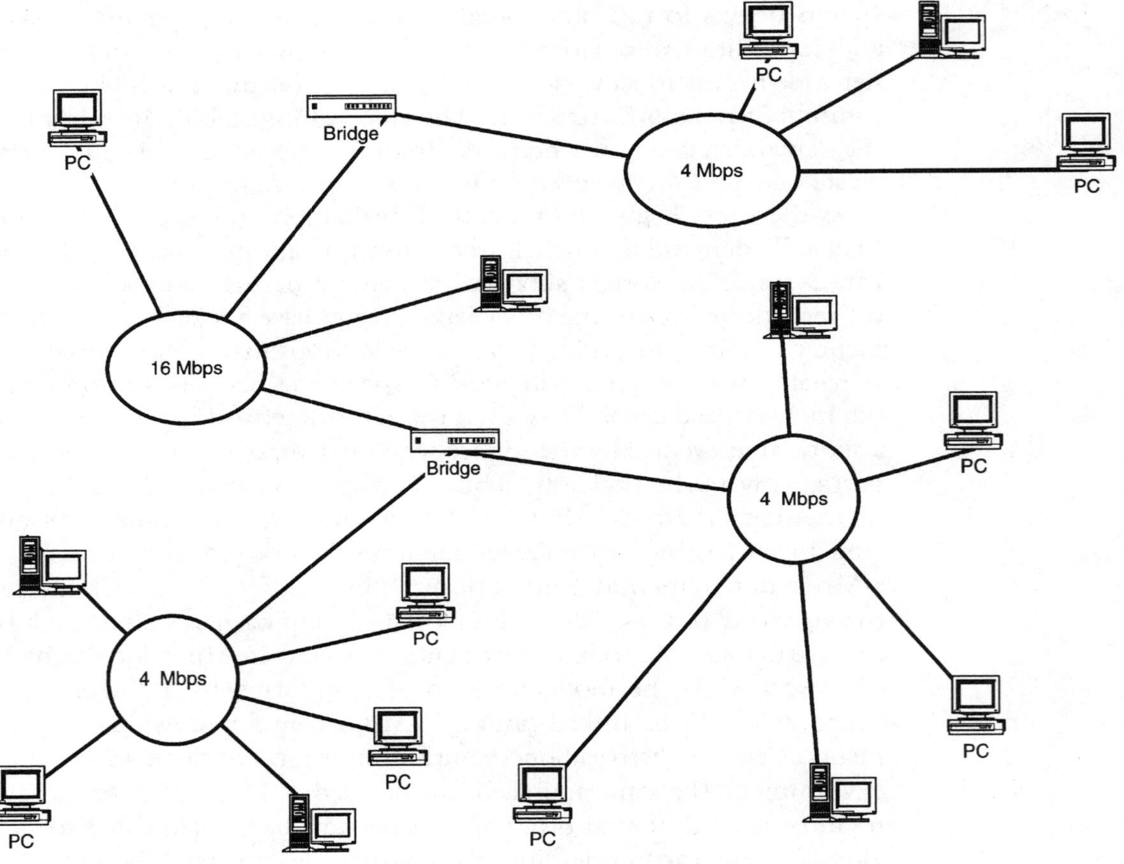

Figure 10.1 The departmental connection at 4 Mbps to the 16-Mbps corporate network.

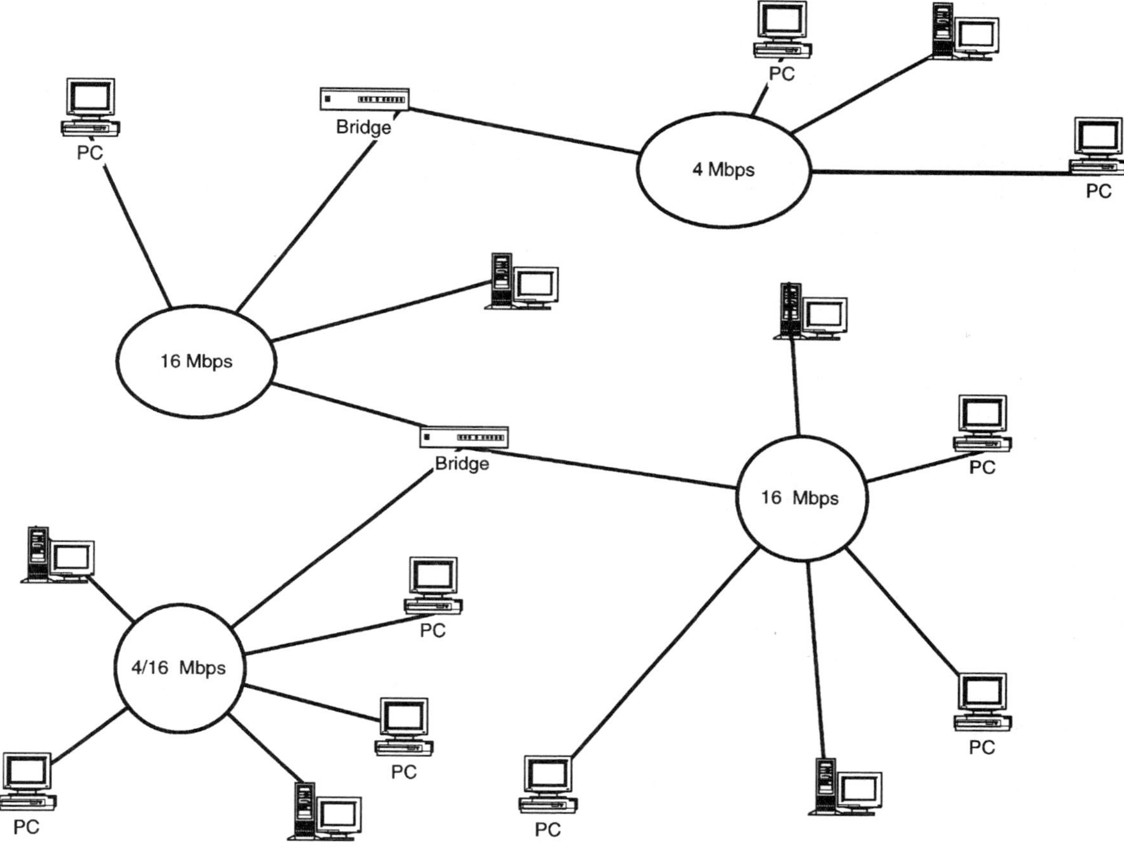

Figure 10.2 The departmental connection at 4 or 16 Mbps to the 16-Mbps corporate network creates the hybrid.

by a user department. The services will vary depending on the user, the application, and data needs as the network is being deployed. These considerations all become part of the planning process before deploying the architecture. Missing any component or ignoring specific needs and demands that the users may have is a sure blueprint for disaster. No matter how much you provide, they will not be satisfied. Plan for the inevitable! Keep in mind that although they may say they do not have a demand, it will surface as the network begins to roll out.

When users begin to see the services and capabilities that can be deployed on a client/server internetwork, they immediately begin to

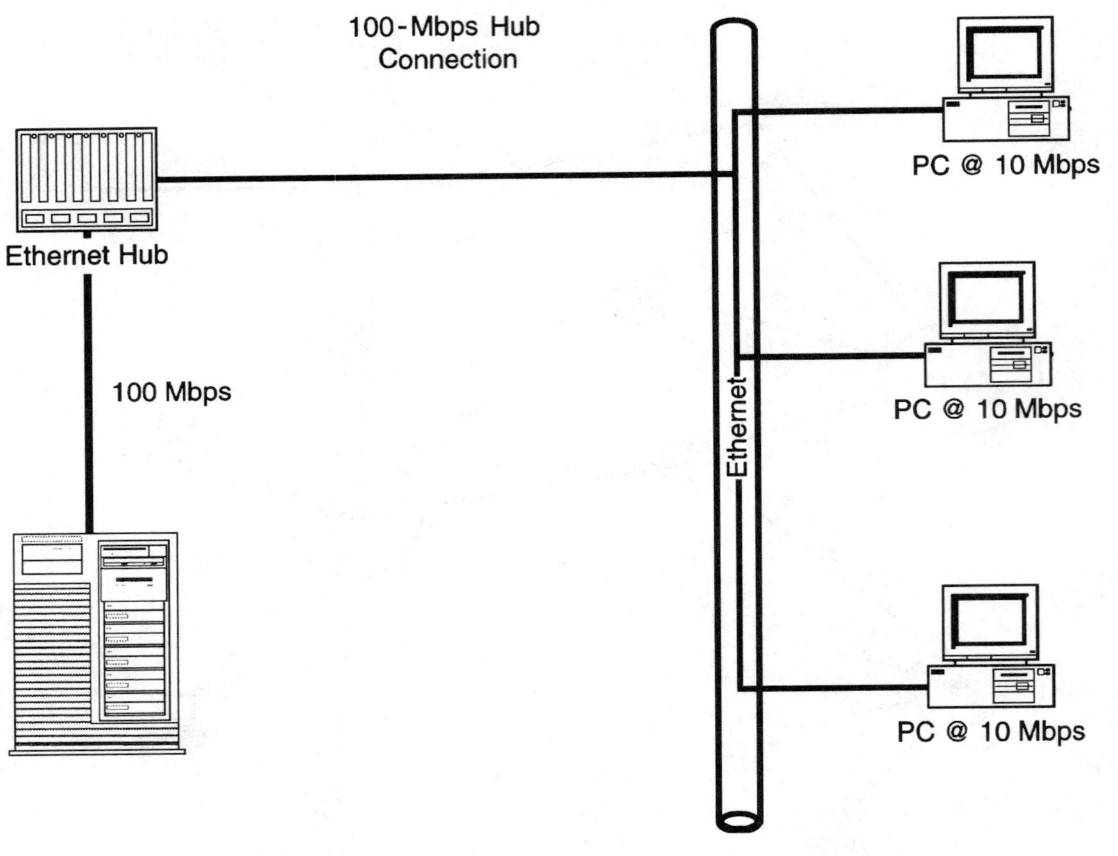

Figure 10.3 The 10/100-Mbps Ethernet connections.

demand even better service. In the past, they may have been satisfied and accepted less service. However, once the network begins to roll out on a wide area or even a localized area basis, the users will start to want more. By more, they want better. Things that never worked before should automatically be resolved in this client/server architecture, or so they will think. Consequently, in dealing with all of these different variations, one must clearly keep in mind a focused approach to deploying the architecture. Always plan for more. More is better, according to the user. In each case, regardless of what their demands and needs are, if users do not see a significant improvement or a significant effort to meet their needs, their first stop will be in management's office. Management will then be put under pressure to determine what to do next. Unless the right plan is in place, management may well have to make a decision that goes against the grain of the original plan, which could be devastating for the network.

The last issue is that users want it cheaper. Clearly, when dealing with an architectural rollout that takes years to accomplish, users begin to feel stress in their budgeting process. Unless a significant amount of funding is recognized and planned for, the plan could fail. Whenever the goals are laid out to the user, it should be clearly stated that what they can expect to achieve is based on what they are willing to fund. It is not uncommon to have a user department hem and haw about the funding needs or to withdraw and hold back funding to which it originally committed. In addition, management starts to lose focus the longer the plan takes to roll out. What might have been fine a year ago might well be a pressure point for management in terms of budgeting and constraints today. If downsizing, market slippage, or just a business decline of any sort is evident, management will start to curtail funds. Without funds, the plan stalls. Therefore, a contingency must be built in to deal with this situation. One cannot forget that without the funds, the rollout of an architecture of this nature cannot take place. Consequently, a mutual arrangement between users and management must be agreed to right up front.

Timeline

Figure 10.4 shows the structure of a time process for planning. This structure is not the be-all or end-all. However, it is an approach to at least provide the structure that one might see in the normal planning and design process for a client/server internetwork. This stack basically tries to highlight some of the overall steps or stages that will take place as the client/server internetwork is being deployed. The numbers next to the stack reflect the approximate time, in months, on average. Clearly, each organization must determine its own timing sequences as well as its own demands, for no one solution fits all. Note that in the four phases, the stack takes the following course:

At the bottom of the stack is the needs assessment. The needs assessment is very, very critical in getting everything started but must be accomplished over roughly a one- to three-month period. The reason for

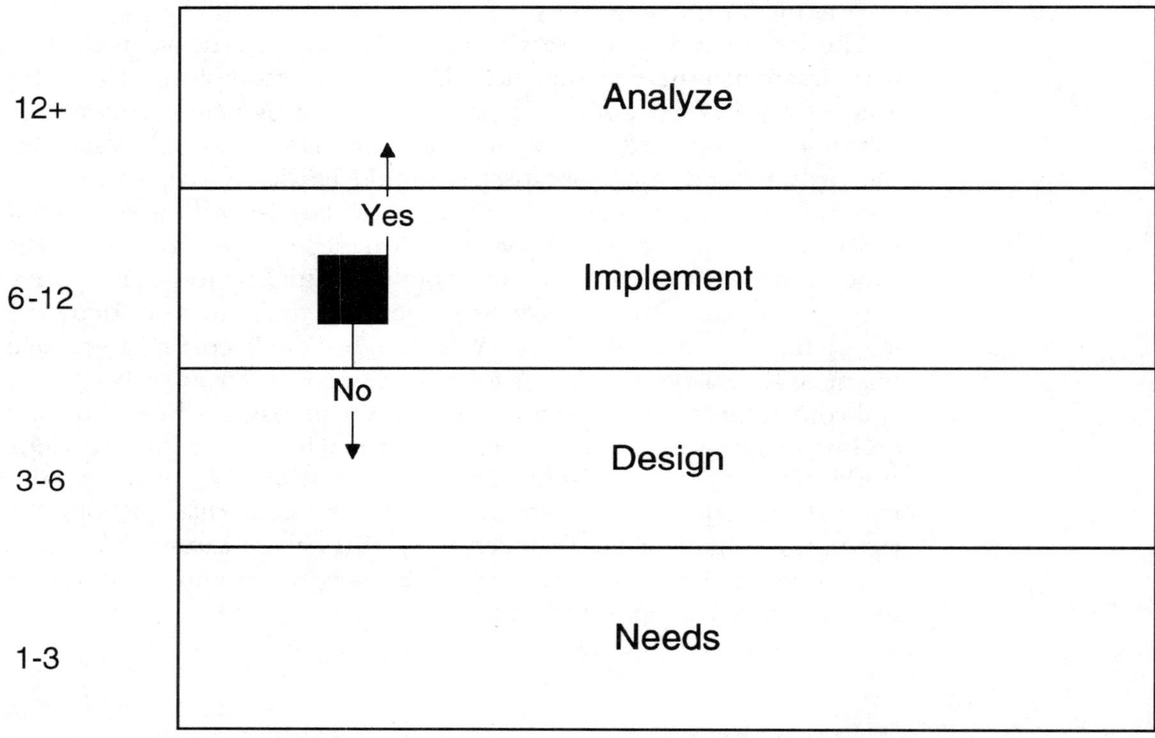

Figure 10.4 *The timing process for planning.*

the short duration is that the longer it takes to do an assessment, the more complex and difficult it will be to get to the next step. One cannot analyze needs forever; certain points in time must be established based on what is trying to be accomplished. Using the three-month target in this figure, one must also be careful to recognize that needs are ever-changing. The overall process is a quite lengthy one; therefore, targets are constantly moving based on business situations, profitability indices, market plans, or any other variable that might well change the needs and demands for information processing. In each case, as the target moves, one must be aware that the needs might also change or restructure, which could in turn affect the overall planning and design process.

Therefore, it is imperative to pick a base or pilot group. This pilot group should be selected based on each of the demands necessary to meet the business need. What might initially start out as a small population of users that will accept and be willing to ride out the implementation could change very quickly. Getting to a resolution in terms of the needs to be met is an essential requirement. A caution here: Keep the aspirin handy. Start with a small pilot group. Remember to define what you are trying to accomplish. Start small! A small group in the needs assessment and development will help in the developing of the overall structure of this planning process. Go through the entire process of what currently exists, what the user demands are, and what their expectations are. From that we deduce what it is we can and are willing to deliver. Seek out and find the problems that currently plague the individual user departments. Finding these problems gives us a base to develop the solutions that will meet these needs. Necessity is always the mother of invention. Use that idea while developing the overall plan.

While conducting the needs analysis, estimate the degree of exposure to which all parties are willing to commit. Should this be an application that is mission-impacting? Or should the exposure be mitigated to a non-mission-critical function to start? Target your base. Look at the exposure and determine what penetration level will be used. By *penetration,* we mean that one has to decide how deep into the organization these changes will be deployed initially. Keep in mind, this pilot is part of the needs assessment and commitment stage. After completing this initial needs assessment, one must develop a solid team of expertise. Use every resource available to you. Include in these resources any internal integrated technologies (IT) personnel that are available, communications departmental personnel, vendor resources, and users. One of the biggest mistakes that most LAN or client/server network managers make is the exclusion of the user in the whole process. All too often these managers believe that they can assess and decide what the user really needs. Nothing can be farther from the truth! To assume so begs disaster. If the user is not involved, there is no buy-in. Without buy-in, there will be no support over a long period of time. Remember from Fig. 10.4 that the total process will take a minimum of 24 to 36 months, and, in many organizations, it can take significantly longer.

Be careful what commitments you make. All too often users' expectations are incorrectly set due to misstatements or overcommitments by the LAN or client/server manager. When dealing with the user, make only commitments on what you know is achievable within a reasonable period of time. Be prepared to sift through the rubble. A lot of debris and a lot of clutter will be available for users to throw in your path. What they may well do is overstate their needs or overstate the limitations of the existing network. That puts the client/server manager in a position of trying to accomplish or commit to more than what might be originally necessary. Beware—ignore the pie-in-the-sky syndrome. Users will want everything under the sun while the client/server network manager tries to promise just that. Start with a close definition of the project, but remain flexible throughout. In many cases the users really don't have an idea of what they really need, and that is why we do what we do. Take heed to double your estimates:

1. Double the time that you think it will take.
2. Double your estimates of the funds that will be needed over the entire course of the project, keeping in mind that this will be broken down over several budget years.
3. Users to be served will always increase at least twofold or even exponentially during the pilot as well as the final stages of a plan.
4. Applications that never before existed will appear, and the number of applications and operating systems that you will have to support will at least double.
5. Bandwidth will become a limitation, so if your estimate indicates that you have sufficient bandwidth, double your estimate. You may even want to double that again.
6. Storage requirements for the data will immediately increase once all of the graphical user interfaces (GUIs) are installed and in use. No matter how much storage you believe you need, double it again.

This list comes from experiences and stories of existing as well as past installed networks from myriad users. No one industry has a monopoly on the problems or the pitfalls that have existed over the past. Regardless of the business segment, each and every one of these listed items will become a reality.

One must plan to set the expectations or else the result will be as shown in Fig. 10.5. In this particular case, no one's expectations matched. The user has one set of expectations and management another, and the client/server administrator is caught in the middle with a completely different agenda. This scenario describes how many implementations have already taken place. Over the past three to four years, several organi-

Figure 10.5 Expectations must be set realistically.

zations that have undertaken a client/server networking architecture and the ensuing internetwork have all faced the same problems. Learn from their experience.

Design and Planning

Upon completion of the needs assessment and working with the users, one must then design how the entire network and the applications will all come together. The basis for this entire network design is what was determined by the needs assessment. Therefore, it is imperative to continue to work with the users very closely. Do not lose sight of who is being served. The client/server internetwork is being positioned as a corporate resource to serve the end users in the accomplishment of their mission. Therefore, in the design stages, one must keep in mind what the users must do to perform their mission. Is it a global information system (GIS)? Or is it strictly an individual organization expansion?

Determine the size of all of the servers that need to be put in place. One cannot just look at the main server, the high end of the three-computer architecture; also look at the application servers that sit just underneath the main server. Consider the size necessary by capacity for each of these computing architectures. Also consider the desktop device. All too often, when rolling out a client/server internetwork, designers tend to miss the overall desktop need. What computing architecture will be supported at the desktop? How much memory will be required for each device (client)? Further, one must also consider the actual bandwidth needs to support the high-speed data throughput that will follow. Keeping in mind each of these issues, the client/server network administrator must always be prepared to meet the demands of this new computing architecture. Understand also that the client/server implementation adds overhead of its own. Therefore, whatever capacities and bandwidth demands were previously necessary will be increased by additional overhead. This overhead may include using various routing or routed protocols, bridging architectures to link these services altogether, or the internetworking services of both leased-line as well as delay-sensitive network services. The plan in this design is to accomplish the needs and demands and meet the future expectations of the organization without being unrealistic. Therefore, one must continue to watch what these capacities and sizes might be. How fast a computer is necessary?

Estimate a realistic and workable budget. Remember from earlier discussions that at each and every step along the way, the users and management must be constantly reassured that their budgetary funds are being spent wisely. If, in fact, they are not convinced, they will withdraw that support and funding. All too often client/server internetworks begin, but the administrator or network manager fails to meet this goal. As a result, several client/server architectures have been scrapped halfway through the process. How unfortunate and wasteful! Most of this could be avoided as long as the user is kept advised, the needs are met, management is kept apprised of progress, and the overall focus is never lost.

Develop evaluation criteria for what will constitute success or failure. Undertaking a project of this size, or the magnitude that could ultimately unfold, requires some expectation setting as well as benchmarking. What would constitute a success? Or, conversely, what would constitute a failure? Most network administrators never allow themselves to ask these questions. They automatically believe that their project will go according to plan, or they are misguided into believing that nothing will change. Therefore, the only factor that they consider is success. Unless success or failure is measured, there is no way to determine whether or not the project is moving according to the plan or whether the actual original goal has been achieved. Here again is where the user will continue to move the target and what might appear at first to be unsuccessful (failed) may well be a very successful program. However, without some means of benchmarking or evaluating what was really expected, there is no way to prove it. This evaluation must include two different categories: quantitative and qualitative results. In most cases, the evaluation criteria usually only assess a qualitative result, which is usually extremely difficult to measure. Qualitative is subjective; quantitative is objective. Although both are needed, one should place more emphasis on the ability to quantify or show measurable, tangible results. Be cautious, however, that the quantitative analysis or results expected are not oversimplified. One must be very careful in determining what exactly is to be accomplished and how it will be done. If, in fact, the organization is looking for a 10 percent increase in market growth as a result of this client/server network, this result is quantitative. On the other hand, another issue creeps in. If the 10 percent increase is the direct result of improvements due to the client/server network, then the success was there. However, if a 10 percent sales growth or market share growth was inevitable with or without the client/server network, then nothing has been achieved. Keep very close adherence to what the commitments are and what the demonstrable results are. All too often, a simple little mistake can be challenged in a management decision or in an end-user decision. In either case, it could mean disaster for the entire project. Select your pilot carefully. Make sure that as you look at the pilot group, it is a limited audience who might show demonstrable improvement or an increase in productivity. Next, using that pilot group, make sure that everything is documented up front. Set the rules. Live by the plan! Both goals are easily achievable if one keeps focused on what is trying to be accomplished.

Agree to and settle on the applications that will be supported. In many cases, a client/server network may well be developed to support one specific group of applications, which might include transaction processing or front-office automation. In either case, it is not uncommon to have the user try to mix and match the applications. What started out with a defined set of goals quickly evolves into more and more demands on the part of the users to integrate *all* of their applications. Therefore, as the applications are being selected and as the tools are being rolled out, make sure that the agreement continually meets what the users expected.

Work with vendors regarding the system demands. In past installations, many client/server networks have been installed on the basis of improving performance, speeding up application support, or even just changing management and control. In each case, the users were led to believe that the use of the client/server internetwork would provide all of these services. This idea may have come from the vendor in an indirectly misleading representation, or it may well have been a software provider that has provided business information. Regardless of where the ill is created, the client/server network administrator must be aware that new demands and new services will constantly place stress on the current server and the existing applications. Be aware that these changes could create bottlenecks, giving the end user the perception of a failure. When working with vendors, have them map out the exact amount of processing time that is required to provide their particular brand of service or their speeds and capabilities to support this network. An example is shown in Table 10.1. In this particular table, an application that existed prior to a client/server architecture consisted of a user accessing three screens of information. Each transaction with three screens of information, using an IBM/SNA/SDLC architecture, required 750 bytes

TABLE 10.1 Comparing the Data Sets before and after Client/Server Implementation

Users	Screens/trans.	Bytes/trans.	Trans/hr.	Hrs./day	Total bytes	Difference by users
			With SNA before Client/Server			
20	3	750	8	7	2,520,000	
30	3	750	8	7	3,780,000	
35	3	750	8	7	4,410,000	
			After Client/Server Implementation			
20	7	2000	8	7	15,680,000	13,160,000
30	7	2000	8	7	23,520,000	19,740,000
35	7	2000	8	7	27,440,000	23,030,000

of data per transaction. In the second section of the table, the architecture has changed to a client/server application. In this case, the use of the client/server software, the centralized database, and all of the GUIs surrounding the data adds up to place new demands and burdens on the computing architecture. Therefore, in the second section of this table one sees that now seven screens are necessary, each screen requiring approximately 2 kbytes of text, and with all of the GUIs, the file has now tripled or quadrupled in size. Was the vendor able to predict this increase, or did it just slip in unannounced?

Decide on how to serve the user. Should it be done with a locally attached server, or should it be done through a distributed architecture? The client/server internetwork implies that the distributed architecture is the way to go. However, this is not always the case. In deciding in how to best serve the user, keep in mind the demands for speed, capacity, and the overall throughput to be achieved. In a distributed architecture, which is typically the goal, a different set of parameters would be evident. What is locally attached can usually achieve direct computer speeds and use a high-speed serial connection as opposed to using the WAN or the LAN. Distributed architecture, on the other hand, would be just the converse. As you decide how you are going to serve the users, consider also where are they located, such as centrally or remotely.

Establish the timing. Back in Fig. 10.4, the model shows 24 to 36 months of timing overall; however, one has to maintain as much flexibility as possible. This flexibility includes the ability to recycle or restart if necessary. Do not be so rigid in the plan that allowances are not made for restarts or false starts. If the plan is that rigid, it is destined for failure. The timing has to be realistic, neither too optimistic nor too pessimistic. One must understand that even if users are demanding faster and better, realism must be applied. All too often when a rollout of an architecture begins, everyone tries to escalate the procedures or the steps necessary to get to closure, which can be a fatal mistake.

Select the connectivity to be used. A lot of information in the earlier sections of this book was devoted to the connectivity needs. Now comes the true task. How does the network get attached and built upon itself to provide the overall connectivity? Should the decision be made to bridge, to route, or to use dial-up access capabilities? In each case, significant consequences can come with each decision. One must be aware of both the pros and cons of these decisions. Do not lose sight of the fact that high-speed interconnectivity bears a price; however, low-speed interconnectivity bears an even tougher price. One cannot make the wrong decision or the results could be devastating. The decisions must also take into account whether we are dealing with a LAN or a WAN in terms of this interconnection need. Bridging is better used when dealing with a localized area network, although it can be used across a wide area network. Routing, on the other hand, has a tendency to be used more in the wide area. Neither of these can be mutually exclusive or selected as an either/or decision. Consequently, the decision is not a simple one, but it may be far more straightforward than one anticipates. Connectivity is important; access is more important. Using a bridging or routing technique may well suffice for those fixed locations where users need access. However, other factors must not be overlooked, such as smaller branch office locations or nomadic users. These nomadic users could be traveling sales personnel or traveling executives who need access from a variety of different locations. In this particular case, they may well need the particular ability to have dial-up access (dial-in access). These decisions go hand-in-hand with what need we are trying to serve.

Estimate the transmission speeds. When dealing with bridging, one typically tries to accomplish some lower-speed interconnectivity service; however, dealing with a 4-, 10-, or 16-Mbps LAN often places some other burdens on the issue. For example, if we are dealing with a wide area network connection and our transmission speeds cannot be achieved, then an overall bottleneck will degrade performance and disappoint users and management alike. Other issues must not be overlooked either. For example, looking at the overall connection and speeds required might still deal with far less throughput than what the actual LAN or WAN can carry. One cannot always afford financially to install a high-speed interconnection at the rates of speed similar to the line speed on the LAN. A 10-Mbps channel capacity may be far too expensive to internetwork different locations. Using the estimated transmission speeds, add some overhead. Depending on the protocols to be used on the LAN and the client/server architecture, overhead will mean further complications. Take an example of a TCP/IP network. When dealing with TCP/IP, one must be aware that the overhead associated in using these protocols on the LAN or a WAN can be significant. Often these overheads amount to between 30 and 50 percent additional demand for data across the network. This demand comes in the form of retransmissions, segmentation, inquiry and response, and acknowledgments. All of these factors can bog down the network if they are not anticipated.

Select the routing protocol. Whether one uses RIP or OSPF or some other set of routing protocols (of which there are many), a decision still needs to be made. It may well be that the internetwork involves many protocols. One can imagine that both routing and routed protocols on a single network can amount to as many as 29 or more. Some users implementing a client/server internetwork were appalled when they learned just that situation. How did 29 different protocols get introduced onto their networks? What they failed to realize is that for each and every application and operating system, routing and routed protocols are needed. It is through this multiprotocol environment that one should be aware of some of the possibilities that complicate the overall throughput and demands of the client/server network. Each and every protocol in use on the network has its own demands for framing and formatting of the data as well as overhead associated with the transmission and the segmentation of the data. Therefore, when dealing with this framing format and protocol selection, one must be aware of what each of the demands are.

Select the access for the internetwork. At this point in the overall client/server internetwork, one must decide how the wide area pieces will all come together. In earlier chapters, the discussion centered on the variations of the older leased-line, point-to-point circuits or myriad new opportunities that have been introduced, including frame relay, SMDS, ISDN, and ATM. Once again, no single solution satisfies every demand. A hybrid may well emerge. One might imagine that in a localized environment such as in a metropolitan area, SMDS might be used to link the client/server internetworking devices together. On the other hand, to the desktop and in the backbone networks, ATM might be a beginning stage of what is deployed. Moreover, on the wide area network, frame relay might be the choice to support the national and international interconnection. These protocols can further be supplemented or complimented by ISDN. Now complicating the overall network beyond all of the protocols for both routing and routed, we have the ability to use various new system tools. Those tools all bear with them their own overhead and subsequent latency that might well change the way the network works. Is the decision going to be financial, or is the decision going to be based on speed, throughput, and capacity? Regardless of the decision, one must work through the scenarios and try to match to service capabilities. The network cannot be frivolously used for expensive communications, but the throughput and demands must be met in the overall performance. Therefore, some decision must be made on how to internetwork between and among the various corporate locations, which starts to constitute the full client/server internetwork.

Order the pieces. Assuming each of the preceding steps has been followed, adhered to, or at least used as a model, the pieces must now fall in place. When dealing with a client/server internetwork, it is imperative to understand that things take time. Unfortunately, the timing involved also includes lead times that one must be very aware of. It would not be prudent, for example, to order all of the wide area links and not order the interconnection devices (such as the routers). In many cases, some pieces may take longer than others, and it would not be prudent to have some pieces sitting around for many weeks or months while waiting for others to arrive. Therefore, one must estimate how long it will take to build this internetwork. How long will the links take to install? This is a variable; each vendor will provide certain timing arrangements according to its normal guidelines. A wide area network provider (IEC) may still depend on the LEC or PTT to provide the local connection at the far end. It could very well be this local connection that becomes a bottleneck, even though the wide area could be put in place very quickly. One does not want to spend money to have idle links sitting around when the local area is not available.

Be aware of the timing of delivery. Coupled with the links comes the componentry, such as bridges, routers, and gateways, that might be used. One must take into account whether sufficient memory is available, whether the vendor can support the memory requirements, and how long it will take to provide this service. In a router or bridge, for example, how many wide area network ports are available versus how many local area ports are available? Many users do not fully understand exactly what they are buying. Consequently, they make wrong decisions. It would be imprudent to buy into a technology only to find out that it is either obsolete or that it doesn't work in your environment. Be aware, work with the carriers, work with the vendors, and find alternative solutions that might fit. One example is to search out a lease/rent arrangement from the carriers. This puts that componentry on the to-do list of the carrier instead of the client/server network manager. The onus, now shifted to someone else, is also something that must be supported on a lease basis over the life of a contracted period. Let's face it, most of the internetworking services will be in existence for at least three to five years, so it would be prudent to lease or rent the equipment for three to five years. This, of course, comes with the caveat that if technology changes or the network grows or declines, the carrier will change-out the equipment as necessary and either increase or decrease the cost appropriately. It becomes a win/win situation for the client/server network manager. Also included in this entire architecture is the installation of the hardware—servers, workstations, and the high-end server. As the links and the pieces are being ordered and planned, one must consider how long the lead times are to bring in the desktop devices or the application devices and, finally, the main server. How long will the application take to install? In this regard, also include how long it will take to actually get the application to work. In one of the earlier examples, the client/server internetwork was based on a SAP architecture. This SAP architecture took a total of three and a half years to implement, a good portion of which involved the conversion process. The conversion was hastily implemented, much to the detriment of the overall network. One cannot force-feed these installations. Converting data, implementing and installing operating systems, upgrading databases, and finding the front ends all require time. This timing may well be three years long, both in the conversion as well as the build-out of the whole new implementation process. Therefore, when ordering the services, one must be aware that the wide area network need not be there until the local network is there, unless a dual network will be run. This scenario has been successfully used in many other cases, where an existing network was run onto the new internetworking architecture while the new client/server applications were being built. This allowed for a smoother transition and a selection of the multiprotocols that were going to be used. Breathing room was achieved, and the network manager felt more comfortable with the installation and implementation. Do not lose sight of all of the applications needed to run on the system.

Plan the installation process, but expect the unexpected. It probably goes without saying, but the old rule of thumb is, "if something is going to go wrong, it will." In planning the process of installing a whole network environment and internetwork, one must be aware of any complications or any drawbacks that might ensue. For example, if an entire network were taken down over a weekend and could not be brought up by Monday, the impact could be devastating. Contingency planning as well as resource availability should be considered in this installation. All too often in the past, client/server internetwork managers assumed that these pieces were all taken care of by someone else, only to find out that they were not. Carriers will do what they are asked to do, sometimes as part of the installation contract or for a fee. If they are not contracted to do something, however, they are not likely to do it. So make sure that while performing the installation process, resources such as spare facilities, dial back-up, additional people, and spare parts are all available no matter what the day or week of the installation. This installation may also be spread out over multiple weeks depending on the size and complexity of the network. It is incumbent upon the client/server network manager to be aware of what the complications could be. The spread of two to three weeks may mean the two networks are up and running side by side, causing confusion for the user on which side of the network the data should be sent or accessed.

Train the support staff. As all of the different pieces are coming together, the installation process is about to take place. The links are being installed, and the applications are being or have been installed, fine-tuned, and tested. Now comes the important part to ensure that the staff has been fully trained on how to operate and maintain the network. The support staff should be trained in advance, obviously, of the whole installation. This cannot be done too soon in the process or the trained personnel may not have a need to use their training and consequently forget what they learned. In a protracted environment, then, it would be best to try some training at various times during the process, with various benchmarks to refresh or update the training. Also take into consideration the fact that the training cannot be done at the very last minute. If done at the last minute, the staff will not be in a position to assist with applications that don't work correctly, to troubleshoot physical or hardware problems, and more importantly, to support the help-desk function for the end user who will perceive something is not right. Therefore, be aware that the training is an important part throughout the whole process that must also be considered and timed accordingly. This training can come from a combination of two different sources: from the vendors that provide the products or from independent training that is provided elsewhere, such as in training houses/seminars or computer-based training (CBT).

Install the hardware. Hopefully, test and acceptance procedures have already been developed by the vendor. These test and acceptance procedures should include a detailed list of what would take place before, during, and after the installation. As all of the hardware pieces are being installed, the vendor should know how the pieces should be implemented, how they will be tested, and how they will be accepted. Accept no item that does not work properly! Most vendors, although honorable in their intentions, when it comes to the final conclusion will always try to get the customer to accept even a marginally operating system. They assure the customer that they will fine-tune and fix the problems after the fact, but they need a signature now. Do not fall into that trap. Many networks have gone in working marginally and sent an immediate alarm through the organization that all was awry. As things performed marginally, the users placed more and more demands by retransmitting or regenerating requests for information, placing further burdens on an already overburdened network. Of course, everything came to a screeching halt. Be aware that if something is not working properly in the test and acceptance procedures, it should not be accepted—no ifs, ands, or buts about it.

Once the hardware is installed, the next set of sequences would probably follow suit.

1. Install the operating system.
2. Install the network operating system.
3. Load the application and maintain control.
4. Load some test data.
5. Get preliminary check-off from each of the users that the data is there and that they can use it.
6. Run some test reports.
7. Train the end users, not the support users (assuming the support users are already trained!).
8. Add the pilot group to the overall network. Don't let these users run away with new goals.
9. Run the parallel systems, if that was the plan.
10. Be sure to synchronize the data from the parallel systems.
11. Monitor the progress at every step along the way, keeping well-documented records.

12. Fix immediately what doesn't work properly.
13. After completing these steps, migrate the users in the pilot group department slowly.
14. Monitor the progress of the new users.
15. Provide management with initial results.
16. Keep everyone informed on all progress and all delays. No one likes surprises.
17. Select a remote access test.
18. Run the test.
19. Analyze the results. Fix what doesn't work.
20. Verify that all communications systems capacities are in place.
21. Publish your results, keeping management informed.
22. Select the next group of users.
23. Have the original pilot group meet with the new users to discuss successes or failures. Let these pilot users be your best public relations and sales agents.
24. Validate everything; document everything.
25. Verify all costs in relation to the budget. Keep track of the money.
26. Benchmark the results for all future implementations.
27. Continue to seek out and gain management and end-user support.
28. Select the next site or the new application to be added to the test.
29. Start over. Treat every new site and every new application as a new project and a new set of challenges.

This list is a type of linear transition through the process of the installation of the client/server internetwork. It is not all-inclusive, because every network is different; however, as a general guideline and a general set of rules, it works very nicely. Remember certain characteristics that have already been stated: Not every organization needs a client/server network, nor does it fit every application. Understand also that in the deployment of client/server internetworking architecture and interconnections around a local geographic area, around a city, across the whole country, or across the whole world, mainframes are still going to be here for quite some time. The mainframe may well be the server, and you therefore just have to develop the client interface. The mainframe will be here because millions of lines of code that have been developed over the past 30 years are not easily converted or migrated onto a new platform. The cost to do this would be horrendous, and there isn't enough time or enough staff to really make it happen. Therefore, the internetworks may involve both the mainframe and the application server environments for quite some time.

Realize also the fact that the demands on your networks and staff will be extremely intensive, because both environments in a mainframe and a client/server world must be simultaneously supported. Unless duplicate staff is provided, which is highly unlikely, then the stress levels will go up significantly for all staff members within the organization, particularly in the IS and LAN departments. Understand also the complexities of supporting multiprotocol networks, which will be the norm. The support staff and the help desk have to recognize in a dual environment what protocols or what applications are running on which portion of the network that may be causing the problem. Consequently, it is imperative to understand that the fine-tuning of this network is also going to be a high-demand item on staff time. Until real-time scalable networks become a reality in this industry, the fine-tuning of the network, subnetworking, and overcommitment of bandwidth will all be the norm. This doesn't paint a very rosy picture, which was exactly what this section was intended to do. Do not be lulled into believing that a client/server internetwork is an easy project that will go in like cake. Too many departments have been totally displaced or replaced as a result of an improper installation. Too many organizations have scrapped their plans to move ahead halfway through an implementation. Still other organizations have been pushed to the brink of bankruptcy. One cannot encounter a client/server internetworking project and run the risk of pushing the business out of business. This is not the intent of the information services or the internetworking process. The internetwork was designed to improve productivity, reduce costs, and provide an overall strategic posture for the organization. Unfortunately, these goals have met with very mixed results through the various implementations.

Training Requirements

Earlier, training was discussed as being a necessity to provide for the support staff, the help-desk staff, and, more importantly, the end user.

Some organizations that have moved to a client/server architecture rudely discovered that not only were several days, weeks, and even months of training required for their support staff, as many as 80 different training programs were needed to train the end users on how to use the new client/server architecture as well as the internetwork. It was a shock when they discovered just how much training was actually necessary. Much of this training involved not a mere one or two hours, but days of training just to get people up to speed. One cannot overlook the importance or the demands to train on the new client/server internetwork. Even with GUIs and the simplicity that they bring to the table, additional training is always a must. When moving to a full client/server internetwork, the database engine that is running all of the corporate data may well involve some intricacies that users are not familiar with. Therefore, as the training is being developed and the training plan is evolving, one must include all of the various pieces. Looking at the training requirements for the network, such as the wide area and the local area, one should understand what training is available from the vendor or what must be provided internally through self-developed training programs. One cannot assume that the network carriers and vendors will always have sufficient types and details in their training program to bring the staff up to speed.

Looking at additional middleware, such as TCP/IP, one then needs to know what training would be required. TCP/IP is not a simple technique for a lot of people to use. Although it is transparent or invisible to the end user under normal conditions, the support staff and the help-desk function will need significant training in this part of the network. Again, one must be very cognizant of just how much additional training will be necessary to bring this network up to speed.

When applications are involved on a client/server internetwork, additional training may be required to optimize the network traffic. If not, what other tools are available to help with the optimization of the actual traffic? This training may involve strictly CBT or off-site courses provided either by vendors or other seminar houses. In either case, whenever this training is being made available, one must be aware that after the training, the end user or the support staff needs to get hands-on, real-time interaction with the network from that point forward. All too often users have been trained only to be delayed for several weeks or months before they finally get to use the applications.

In as much as the internetwork is concerned, for example, the SMDS or frame relay environment, one also needs training on the optimization and tuning of this type of network. Some of the conditions, such as what frame size should be used, are very critical in the layout and operation of the network. Given this particular type of internetwork, if the wrong frame size or packet size is selected, the network may well bog down. One should be aware that the transmission of many empty packets or frames across the internetwork causes a lot of excessive overhead. Coupled with this type of training, one needs to understand not only the frame size, but also the overhead associated with the routing protocols. If fiber optics is used in the backbone or across the internetwork, the support team may need additional training on how to handle as well as how to terminate this type of linkage. These people must be aware of the complications and the intricacies of putting together a fiber-based network. It is not the same, nor is it as simple, as using a copper-based twisted pair or coax-cable network.

Beyond the training of how to operate the network, a series of network management tools are required. These tools go hand-in-hand with additional training that will be needed so that the network manager will understand how to catch the information and how to analyze it. One may look at the addition of simple network management protocol (SNMP) or remote monitor capabilities (RMON) to help in supporting this network. To use either SNMP or RMON, the user will need extensive training on understanding and interpreting the management data. These tools are a necessity, however, and should not be overlooked. Beyond the network management tools and training, additional training may also be needed when dealing with various protocol suites. In a client/server internetwork, for example, if Novell NetWare is used, training on SPX/IPX is another requirement. Furthermore, in a mixed environment, TCP/IP or OS/2 protocols may also be required. In these mixed environments, the user must be available to learn how they differ and how they interwork with each other. These training demands are not unique. In many cases organizations discover through a series of interruptions or oversights that additional training is necessary. Only through some of these oversights and by stumbling into situations does the organization finally realize what the vendor should have explained. This is not to say that vendors deliberately hide information from the client/server internetwork manager, but in many cases, they just don't understand what the organization needs. In addition, it may well be that the user was told of the additional training requirements but chose to ignore or defer this type of training. This only leads to the detriment of the installation and operation of the client/server internetwork.

Final Deployment and Ubiquity

Once the pilot program is up and running, based on all of the steps that have been outlined here, it then becomes imperative to set the stage for additional rollout. This added rollout or the migration of many other sites as needed will be benchmarked on the model that has already been used. Using the guidelines, results, and documentation that have all been amassed during the initial stages of the client/server internetwork, the next steps become somewhat repetitive. One must therefore start planning a phased migration site-by-site or application-by-application. This migration depends on how the rollout will take place, the number of sites involved, or the specific applications that are common throughout the entire network.

It is still possible that during the rollout and the phased migration to the client/server internetwork from the various locations that disparities will exist. One may have to mix the services or levels of service based on what is available in the given area. It would be ideal if all sites could be brought up in exactly same way, but in reality, this will not happen. Looking at the internetworking portion, one will find the following:

1. 384 kbps is not always available everywhere, and in many parts of the country, or the world for that matter, digital services may be significantly limited.
2. T1 may be far too expensive to deploy throughout an entire network, which in turn, would make the network too costly to implement. Therefore, T1 and fractional T1 may become an issue by not being viable by price or by availability.
3. Consequently, transparency may not be ensured. Various sites may have different operating speeds that offer different levels of service based on their access means.
4. In many cases, the only high-speed digital service available (56/64 kbps) may be far too slow to accommodate this internetworking need, thereby causing additional complications.
5. ISDN is still a very complex service and may not be readily available in a usable fashion in many parts of the country or the world.
6. Leased-line, point-to-point analog circuits may be the only alternative, albeit a very expensive alternative.

It is incumbent upon the client/server internetwork manager to be aware of what is available and what is not and to be somewhat patient in the rollout of the goods and services across the country or across the world. Most client/server internetworks being installed today involve multisite, multicountry locations. The goods and services available from the LECs, PTTs, and the IECs are all different, which places an additional burden on the client/server internetwork manager to understand these differences and the pricing differential before proceeding. It is not prudent to just assume that everything will be totally ubiquitous. Many times the rollout in client/server architecture may span several years. Be patient, continue to probe your vendors, and keep management informed in terms of the progress and the process that is required. End users also must be kept aware every step of the way. Only through this coordinated and concerted effort will the entire network really begin to take shape.

Keep good documentation; do not assume the vendor or the carrier is doing it for you. Keep records of all equipment and components used in the internetworking site, circuit numbers, telephone numbers, and vendor contact numbers for each and every site or each and every circuit attached to the internetwork. These pieces of information will ultimately be the salvation for the client/server internetwork manager. Many organizations that did not preserve this information have discovered the hard way the complexities of restoring a network when it is down and no documentation exists. They were sadly and rudely awakened when the vendors suggested that they provided the information along with all the associated training, and therefore it became a customer responsibility to maintain it. Routing tables that had been updated or pieces of information that one would have expected the vendor to support and hold were no longer available. One must be aware of these pieces in the implementation of a client/server internetwork.

CHAPTER 11

Variations in Access Methods

Up to now the discussion in this book has centered around the client/server internetworking capability from primarily localized and wide area networking bases. Despite the variations, certain truths hold for either access method. As already discussed in this book, the variations can include a strictly local area network environment where various LANs are internetworked for client/server access, a campus area network (CAN) with localized networks internetworked, or an internetwork that spans the globe. Internetworking involves everyone from the local user, the remote user, and even the legacy users who are attached to mainframe platforms or to a host/terminal-based environment. In every facet of the implementation, the client/server internetwork spreads from the desktop across a global or enterprise environment. One cannot forget that the internetwork starts with the major server in this three-computer architecture, through the application server, and right to the desktop user. This chapter, then, looks at building the pieces together to form a true client/server internetwork. It starts at the very beginning with the localized environment and works out to the wider area connections.

In many past instances, users attempting to implement a client/server internetwork have made the mistake of trying to attach disparate LANs around the globe, further complicating their implementation procedures. It is much easier to begin on a localized basis, work out problems, and be able to control both ends of the internetworking function before rolling it out across the globe. Think, if you will, of an implementation where a client/server network would start with two locations—one in the midwestern United States and a remote site halfway around the globe, say in the Far East. Think of the strategic implications of working in this environment. Further compounding this problem would be the logistics involved in controlling the installation and rollout of various products and services in support of this widely disparate connection. This is not to imply that it cannot be done this way, but for control purposes, it may be easier to implement the localized end first. If a problem occurs and support staff need to be able to work around the problems or implement the procedures differently, complications arise when the sites are so distant from each other. Here in the United States the time zones are completely different from those in the Far East. Should a problem arise, one of the sites will be inconvenienced when workaround situations are required. For example, during the business day in the States, the Far East implementers and IT workers would be required to work at some very odd hours. Depending on where these sites are located, it could be worked out that both sites are in a similar-type position without the difficulty of covering very early morning hours. But this would take a lot of additional coordination that would not be required if both sites were in the same time zone. Therefore, the idea of beginning the client/server internetwork on a more localized basis makes more sense.

After determining how the networks will link together and ensuring that all of the applications, protocols, and connectivity devices can all coexist and work harmoniously, then reach out to other sites across the globe. These ideas are not new. In many cases, organizations that have already attempted to implement the client/server internetwork across such disparate and distant locations have all said in retrospect that they may have done it differently had they had realized the implications and the potential problems. Coordination becomes one of the crucial and key points in a successful or unsuccessful implementation. The localization and rollout of the client/server in fairly close proximity may add to the success ratio of a total implementation procedure. One can imagine, for example, if management were to approach the client/server network manager to ask about the progress, and the client/server network manager had to postpone answering the question until such time as the remote site staff came to work and returned an answer. Remember that success is not always perceived in just installing equipment on time, bringing up the applications that work, and staying within budget. Instead, success may well be a perception on the users' side of the equation as to the friendliness and the usability of this client/server internetwork. If users experience problems, and the remote site cannot reach the client/server network manger within a reasonable amount of time due to time-zone differences, the perception is that it is not working. This perception will generate user dissatisfaction. When users are dissatisfied, the information or feedback to management is negative. No matter how successful the actual implementation is, management is hearing a completely different feedback. One must consider then what the best means of implementation will be. In no way shall this book try to dissuade your current plans for implementation, but rather its aim is to point out the potential pitfalls that could arise in the event the wrong choice is made. In reality, there is no right and wrong choice, just a group of different decisions that are being made. It is how these decisions are accepted and received that really constitutes the actual success of the client/server internetwork.

Local Access through LANs

In Fig. 11.1, a group of LANs are linked together across a backbone network. This figure can be the model for the client/server internetwork using a localized structure to provide the necessary access for users. In this particular case, a mainframe, or legacy system, is used as the main server. Other servers shown in this illustration are being used as either local application servers that in turn spawn a process off to the host, or as just localized applications that are not provided by the main server. The departmental LANs, whether token ring or bus topology, can all be

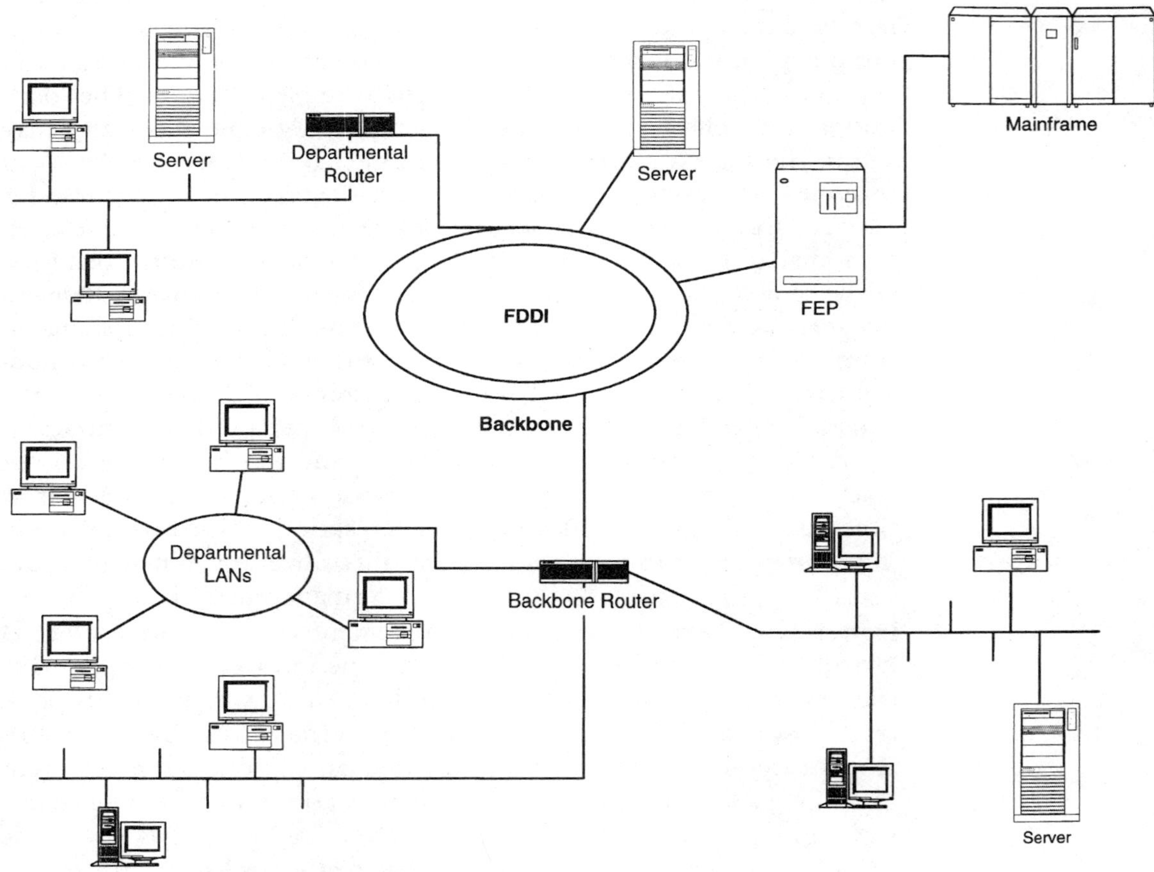

Figure 11.1 Local access through LANs is one way to implement the client/server network.

linked through a series of interconnection capabilities. A high-speed backbone network is shown in this illustration as a high-speed ring. This ring can either be a high-speed, 16-Mbps token ring or an FDDI at 100 Mbps.

Two routers are also shown. The routers would be used as departmental routers, allowing access to the backbone network so that access can be provided to the main server. Because routers are being used, the routers can handle the various multiprotocol capabilities necessary to support the variations in the departmental LANs. For example, a combination of ring and bus topologies is shown in this illustration. These routers allow for the encapsulation or the translation as though a wide area network access was available. Therefore, the MAC-specific protocols, such as 802.3 and 802.5 (IEEE standards), can be translated or encapsulated into the wide area networking protocol such as a TCP/IP network backbone capability.

In this particular illustration, the linkage and the internetworking capabilities exist where additional servers are mounted on the backbone network, allowing for the spawning of a process to the front-end processor (FEP) connected to the host. One can imagine the complexities that might exist on a simple local network like this one. The different physical topologies used, operating at different speeds and protocols, and the differing routing techniques and routed protocol capabilities, combined with a legacy host system, introduce all of the complexities needed for an internetwork. A server might well be used as a gateway function to allow the conversion process from TCP/IP or SPX/IPX or whatever other protocols are being run on the LANs to access a 3270 emulation mode in accessing the host. Here, if a client/server application is being run at the host level, the desktop users have to go through a protocol converter to be able to access and use this information. This is exactly what a client/server internetwork is all about. Because of the locality and the proximity of all the devices to the host, any problems that may surface are easily traceable across the backbone network and the individual local area networks should be able to troubleshoot and solve problems quickly. One need not go halfway across the country or the world to be able to map and capture information that is required on this network. Therefore, using local access capabilities through local area networks may be a very good starting point to provide the methodology for the client/server internetwork.

Figure 11.2 shows the access in a localized area across LAN boundaries. Here, multiple token-passing rings are being used at variations of 4 and 16 Mbps. Note in each case the departmental LANs may or may

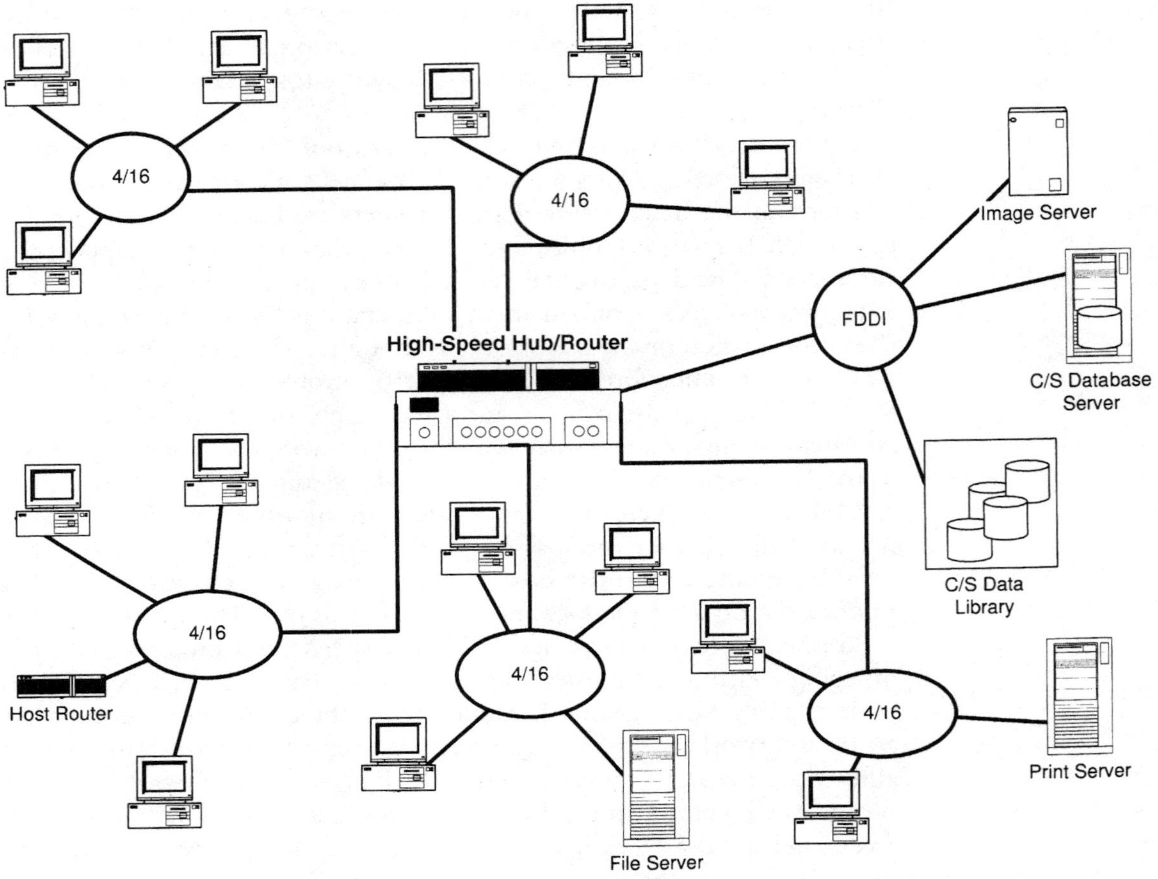

Figure 11.2 Local access across the LAN boundaries still meets the access criteria.

not have their own specific serving functions that provide localized services. Instead, each of these LANs are connected to a high-speed hub/router capability. As a hub, the device in the center of the illustration can act as a token-to-token passing device, allowing user-to-user communications across the LAN. However, when things need to go beyond an individual LAN structure, one may have to route across a network. Note the high-speed communications capability being attached from the hub/router to an FDDI ring. On the FDDI, the high-end services are readily available to any one of the users. Some of the capabilities shown in this figure include such things as image servers, database servers, and data libraries. Print services or local application services can still be provided at the localized level while the higher-end services can be accessible across the internetwork through the hub/router.

One of the advantages of using such a hub/routing capability is the functionality of the hub in general, acting strictly as a port-to-port switching function. Moreover, with a high-speed router card installed, a high-speed serial interface can be used to attach to the FDDI. What this means is that a local user sitting at a desktop device can access file services and print services locally and still internetwork to the higher-end database image servers. Routing across this backbone provides the capability of translating the MAC-layer addressing from each of the LANs into the FDDI-layer addressing on the backbone network. From there, one can assume that the image servers and database servers are client/server compatible. In this particular case, the hub/router can become fairly accessible and easily installable by using a localized barrier. Yet the access is still working across boundaries, and it is the boundaries that establish the internetwork.

Where necessary, remote sites or other LANs even in a localized area can be brought into connectivity through a router, for example, as shown on the bottom left-hand side of Fig. 11.2. This router may well act as the interface to the client/server internetwork by passing through an individual token-ring network operating at 4 or 16 Mbps, passing through the hub/router onto the FDDI, and ultimately reaching the final destination at the database engine. Although this process may sound complicated, and it can be, it is still fairly straightforward in determining the access methods, the routing protocols, and approximations of latency as well as deliverability of information. By the nature of the different speeds on this network backbone, one can also see that certain amounts of buffering may well be required. On the way from the individual user device to the high-end server devices, the speeds will be at lower throughput capabilities at 4 or 16 Mbps. However, in packaging and preparing the information to move across the FDDI, the data will move at the 100-Mbps rate. This poses no great problem because the higher-speed network can obviously process the information across this FDDI backbone much quicker. Where the potential problem and pitfall may exist is on the backside. When the database server or image server is delivering data back down to the desktop device, some buffering will be involved. A 100-Mbps output from a server working its way through this backbone network back down to the desktop device that can only receive at 4 Mbps will create some latency and buffering. This situation gives the client/server internetwork manager the ability to test the latency and the variations in delivery in terms of the overall performance across this network. It happens to be a good test bed before determining how far out to take the network. If, in fact, the client/server database or image server is very data intensive, then one may have to consider how to speed up the localized cable infrastructure to be able to support more reliable and faster data throughputs to provide the user with high-speed interfacing and data accessibility. In no way, shape, or form does this constitute a major problem. This is the way many client/server internetworks have already been built, with great success. When looking at the variations and the capabilities available to an end user, the client/server network manger has control on a localized basis, crosses the LAN boundaries, uses the various multiprotocol support capabilities, and still can see a true throughput need across this platform. This would be an exceptional test bed for a small organization whose needs are localized with internetworking capability still demanded. When dealing with larger networks, other choices may well be available and considered to support this total environment from a true client/server world.

Figure 11.3 shows a new variation as a means of interconnecting the legacy-type host environment with the lower-speed application servers that would work across boundaries similar to those in Fig. 11.2. However, in this particular case, a direct attachment may well be used for channel extension services. Note in this figure, a campus environment may be employed as opposed to just a local area network environment. The introduction of this campus area places new pitfalls and challenges on the network. This change would allow the client/server internetworking manager to determine throughput needs and accessibility across different types of cabling, medium, and protocol supports to be able to provide the necessary access.

This particular illustration shows three different building environments all internetworked through high-speed routers and servers to be able to provide the services that we've been discussing. On the left-hand side of the figure is the main building with the main server installed. Again, this main server may well be a mainframe (legacy system) or a midrange platform such as a RISC processor or a midrange AS400. Note that in front of that server a channel attachment to a NetWare server is provided. This particular server providing the SNA-to-NetWare gateway functionality will provide the necessary access into the host. The channel attachment then would operate at different speeds with a high-speed host communications capability, possibly at the multimegabit ranges. In

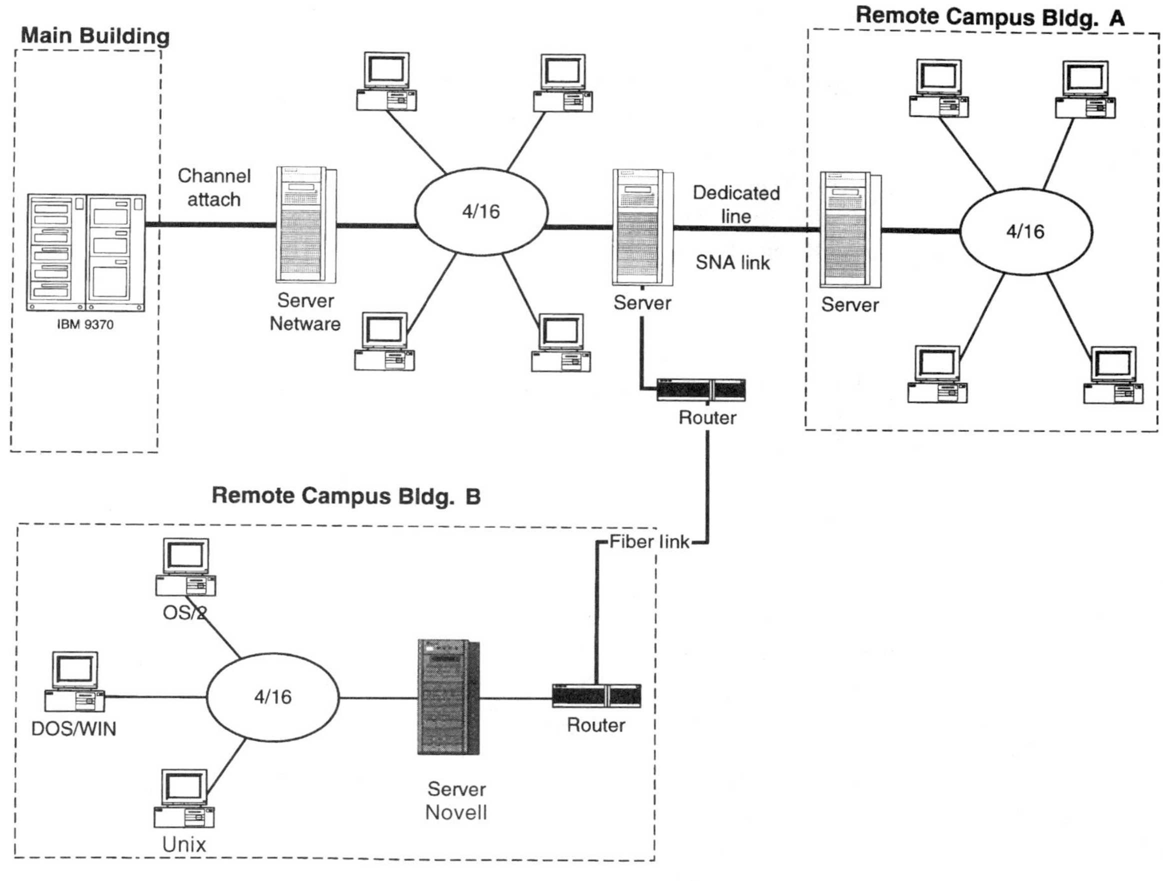

Figure 11.3 Local access across LAN boundaries using a direct attachment.

some cases, this connection may be up to 45 Mbps; traditionally it has been at a LAN speed at 4, 10, or 16 Mbps. In this particular illustration, the 4- or 16-Mbps speeds are being used because the token-passing ring networks, those of the 4- and 16-Mbps ranges, are the preferred route into a host environment. One must take into consideration the vendors that are being used to provide this attachment.

Directly behind the server that has the channel attachment to the mainframe, the 4-Mbps ring is connected to an application server on the right-hand side of this particular ring. From that server, direct attachments would be used on a dedicated line running SNA/SDLC, for example, to a remote server located in Campus Building A. Here the server is an SNA/SDLC server function. This server in turn is attached to a 4- or 16-Mbps token ring serving the particular Campus Building A. From the user's perspective, how the access is actually being provided is transparent, as it well should be. One of the successes of a client/server internetwork is the ability to make the entire process transparent to the end user. All the user should care about is accessing the data and using the data on the fly. In this particular case, it will be somewhat transparent and therefore the user does not have to be concerned with the internetworking functionality.

Another attachment off the application server providing the SNA linkage across the campus area is a router sitting behind the server, located in the center of the drawing. This router has a fiber-optic link that operates at 4, 10, or 16 Mbps, or higher, as needed. Connecting to Campus Building B, the fiber link terminates into another router. This router sits directly in front of a Novell server. On the Novell server, a dual stack function can be run—TCP/IP and SPX/IPX. In reality, this Novell server provides access just to a gateway function through the server located in the Main Building. To the left of the Novell server on a 4- or 16-Mbps token ring, several different applications and operating systems may exist. Think of the multiple protocols that are being supported on this one token ring. For example, a DOS or Windows platform may well be run on one of the PCs (clients) while on another it may well be UNIX, which in turn uses the services of TCP/IP. A third choice is to run an OS/2 operating system that provides the access, again running either TCP/IP or a Novell SPX/IPX protocol stack. Regardless of which operating system or which protocols are being supported on this token ring, it is the function of the Novell server to receive the data packet requests, package them for the router, and transmit them out across its output card to the server providing access to the host. What better way to show a client/server internetwork than to link multiple protocols, multiple operating systems, multiple network operating systems (NOS), and multiple hooks, such as fiber and channel extension, all on a single platform. This direct access with attachment capabilities should provide fairly high-speed throughput capabilities and somewhat transparent services for any one of the end users.

Figure 11.4 shows another local access methodology that can be used. In this illustration, two buildings are linked together through high-speed communications channel services on a ring. In this case, hubs are used in various locations around this campus. High-end, high-speed

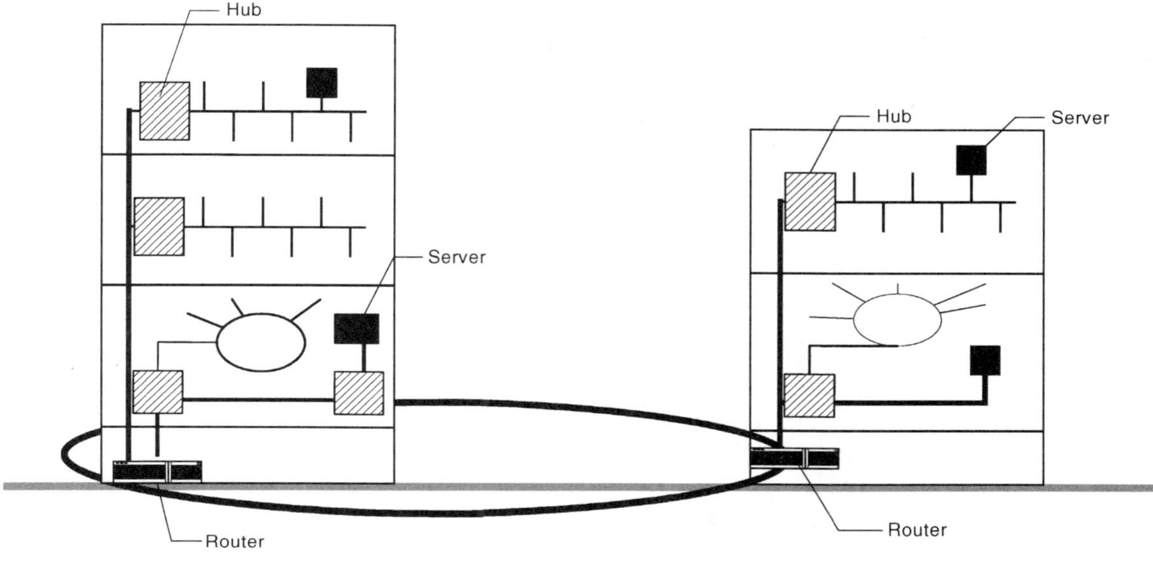

Figure 11.4 Local access via hubs extends the client/server network access across a campus or town.

communications hub services supporting both Ethernet and token ring networks on a localized basis can provide access to a high-end server regardless of where it might reside. In this figure, five high-end hubs are used, which can be stackable or stand-alone hubs. On many of the token rings and on Ethernet servers, localized servers may be attached. In this particular case, these localized servers may be strictly departmental, application-specific functions that are needed by individual user departments. Or, as an alternative, the servers may be distributed computing platforms that are used by all users regardless of their locations within the building.

One might look at this drawing and come to the conclusion that the mix and match between the specific token ring and Ethernet topologies may be a misfit in terms of providing access. This is a natural first reaction when looking at this type of network; however, one cannot assume that all networks will be built upon the same topology at the same operating speed. LANs evolve over time and may also evolve with different topologies. In the past, local area networks were built by departments or LAN administrative personnel who were not totally aware of the differences or the variations in these technologies. Consequently, a series of different LANs at different operating speeds might have been installed. Once this installation occurs, it is far more difficult to go back and displace or replace existing technologies.

The client/server internetwork must address these variations as they exist in the current building structures. The particular hubs, although not vendor-specific, can provide high-speed backbone access for communications channels on a fiber running through the riser closets from floor to floor in each of the buildings. With these high-speed backbones, one may be using either 4, 10, or 16 Mbps, or an FDDI network that would still provide 100-Mbps passing capability. The hubs located in the basement of each of the buildings can provide the method of accessing of the router and the server, regardless of where it exists within the internetwork. Note also that, from time to time, hubs may just serve as a connection for an individual server, a stand-alone, or a departmental server. This allows for some fluidity throughout the network so that one specific topology is not a requirement. The high-speed backbone that connects the two local buildings together may be FDDI, or it may just look like a WAN operating at some other operating speed. Again, this allows both flexibility and connectivity at the same time. One must really consider where the internetworking function might be achieved. In each of the cases shown in the four previous figures, variations for localized distributing of computing architectures, the interconnection through various topologies and techniques, and the variations and speeds have all been considered. This allows for a fully flexible client/server internetwork but still gives the networking manager the ability to move between buildings or between floors and solve and resolve problems as they arise. It is only through this local access that more attention can be paid to the immediacy of the demands for the pilot as well as the working groups. One should consider very carefully how this might be done in one's environment.

Remember, no single solution fits all organizations or all networks. Therefore, hybrids or variations of these figures, as dispersed and as varied as we may try to portray them, may still emerge. Working with the vendors of the various products, services, and applications, a client/server internetworking manager can find still more opportunities to provide the connectivity without sacrificing response time or service. Bear in mind, we are discussing strictly the rollout on the first attempt. Later the distributed computing across the wide area network will still be necessary. In that particular case, bridges and routers can be used across a wide area network through the various high-speed IEC and LEC connections, as already discussed in previous chapters. In no way will this book try to force-fit a network to every single client. Instead, variations and options continue to pop in and out of this discussion so that the client/server network manger can see the differences and imagine the differing ways in which connections can be attained. If one is working with a vendor and only a single approach is being provided or suggested, one may have to solve the problem himself or herself. For that reason, variations will continue to be shown in this book.

Remote Access Capabilities

Once the local access has been provided or at least determined, the next step is to provide for remote access. By remote access, we mean providing nomadic access from a dial-in or dial-out service. We still are not into the wide area networking at this particular point; we're taking a more localized approach for users who are not physically located in the same building. The reason for this approach is to determine from a more localized environment how the users will provide or gain access to their data while residing or traveling around the domestic areas. Several options come up as we take a look at the differences in remote access capabilities, including such things as circuit-switched dial-up modem communications, ISDN access methods, and other variations that may be available to a traveling individual, although one may look at the approach here and wonder why one should not take the wide area network immediately out across a frame relay or ATM platform rather than provide for remote access services on a dial-in basis. The attempt is to look at localized control before deploying across very wide area. Remote access users, although remote, still access a localized service across the wide area. It is because they will be using variations and modem communications capabilities as opposed to fixed-function, high-cost facilities that the approach is to look at this section first.

Figure 11.5 shows remote access across a dial-in capability. In this particular case, two differences are used. First and foremost are dial-up modem communications from remote sites or from traveling salespeople who are located in hotels, customer locations, or anywhere else that is typically not hardwire-connected. The second variation here is the use of ISDN dial-up communications, which may imply the telecommuter. In most cases, ISDN is not readily available to the traveling individual at

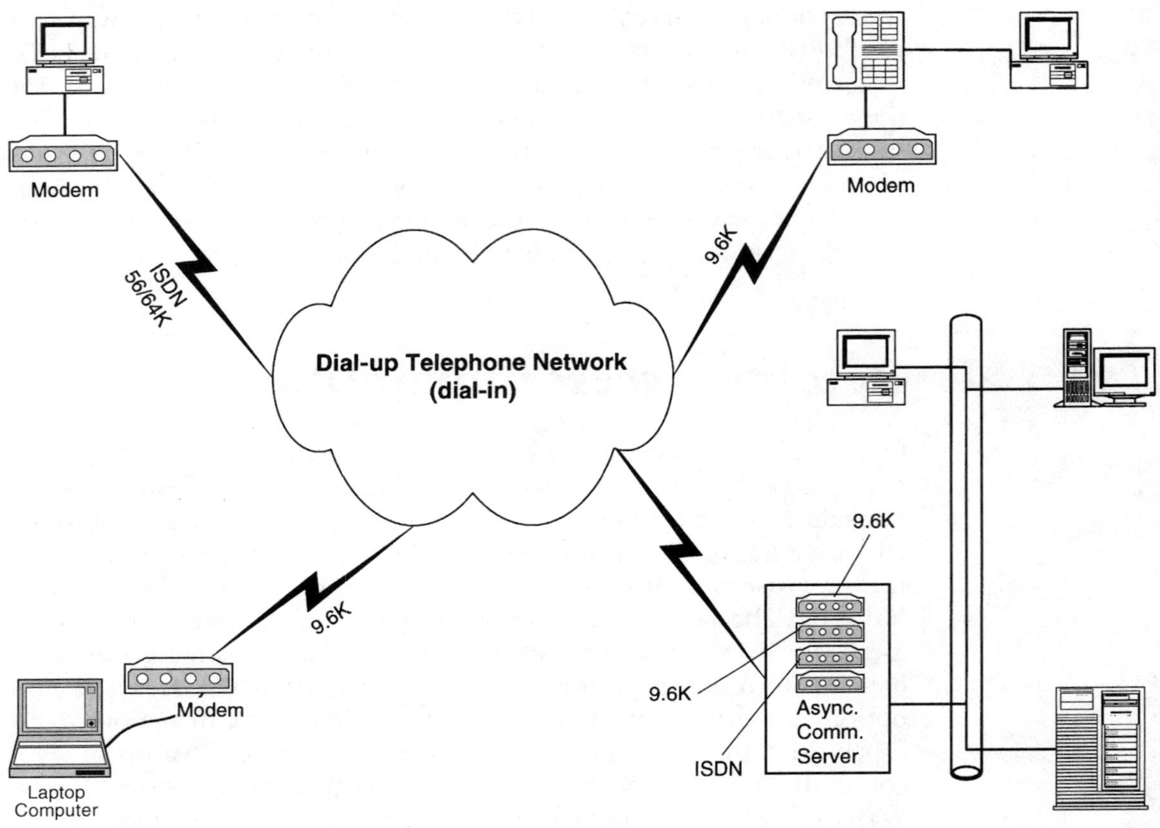

Figure 11.5 Remote dial-in access across the public switched network.

hotels and other client locations; therefore, the differences must be shown. When using this capability, an asynchronous communication server function, such as a modem pool attached to an asynchronous server box, can be attached to a local area network. In this particular case, the asynchronous comm server serves as the gateway onto the LAN. The LAN hosts the server. The LAN also hosts a group of clients. The LAN must also accommodate the access to the host from the remote PC-based users. Therefore, the circuit-switched dial-up telephone network is a very effective means of providing this access.

In this figure, two locations are shown using some lower-speed dial-up communications capabilities at speeds ranging from 9.6 to 28.8 kilobits per second. These modem communications can support the fixed-function communications or the laptop/notebook user traveling around the country. Using attached modem communications on a circuit-switched, dial-up connection, remote users will dial into the asynchronous communications server. At this point, these devices will then be challenged, authenticated, and allowed access to the server. Remote users can then download files, upload files, and access e-mail or other functions. These services may be limited in comparison to what is available at the desktop devices in a permanent location. The reason for these limitations is the data sets that are accessible to the users as well as the amount of information that can be uploaded or downloaded off the network. Many organizations limit the amount of information that travels back and forth across this type of network. A remote user at a customer location, for example, may be able to access a database to determine availability of products, price lists, or inventory control procedures for order placement via high-speed communications. On the other hand, users in telecommuting environments, working from home or other rented space, may well use ISDN services from a local exchange carrier. In this particular case, the LEC is a recommended solution as the means of providing the local loop and the ISDN access so that the end user can pick and choose the IEC to be used to carry the network call. Nothing is changed in terms of a telecommunications environment, so this end user or telecommuter can steer the call across different networks depending on problems or throughput needs specific to a carrier environment. An example might be a user who would normally use one network, say AT&T, but experiences problems with the connection and can still use a 10XXX dialing plan to a second carrier (MCI or Sprint). Had the ISDN link been brought in by the IEC (AT&T, for example), then the only way the call would be placed would be across the AT&T network. By providing the service from the LEC, the flexibility for equal access gives the end user the necessary choices. Note this ISDN user may well be using 64- to 128-kbps dial-up services across a basic rate interface (BRI). At the receiving end, the comm server, an ISDN access link at the BRI, will also be provided. Therefore, ISDN-to-ISDN services can be used across the dial-up telephone network to access a client/server internetwork. A telecommuter's needs may be greater than those of a traveling nomadic user. These telecommuters may need to be able to upload and download much larger files, more frequently, than a nomad traveling around the country. As a direct consequence, the client/server internetworking manager must provide various speeds and access methods to the server to meet the demands of the organization.

Another alternative for remote access to the client/server internetwork involves a third application, for example, from a small branch office or a fixed-site location other than a telecommuting environment. This alternative is shown in Fig. 11.6 with remote access via dial-up routing capabilities. The dial-in router would still provide the means of connection for the smaller branch offices that perhaps only require access to the server occasionally. This technique has several advantages:

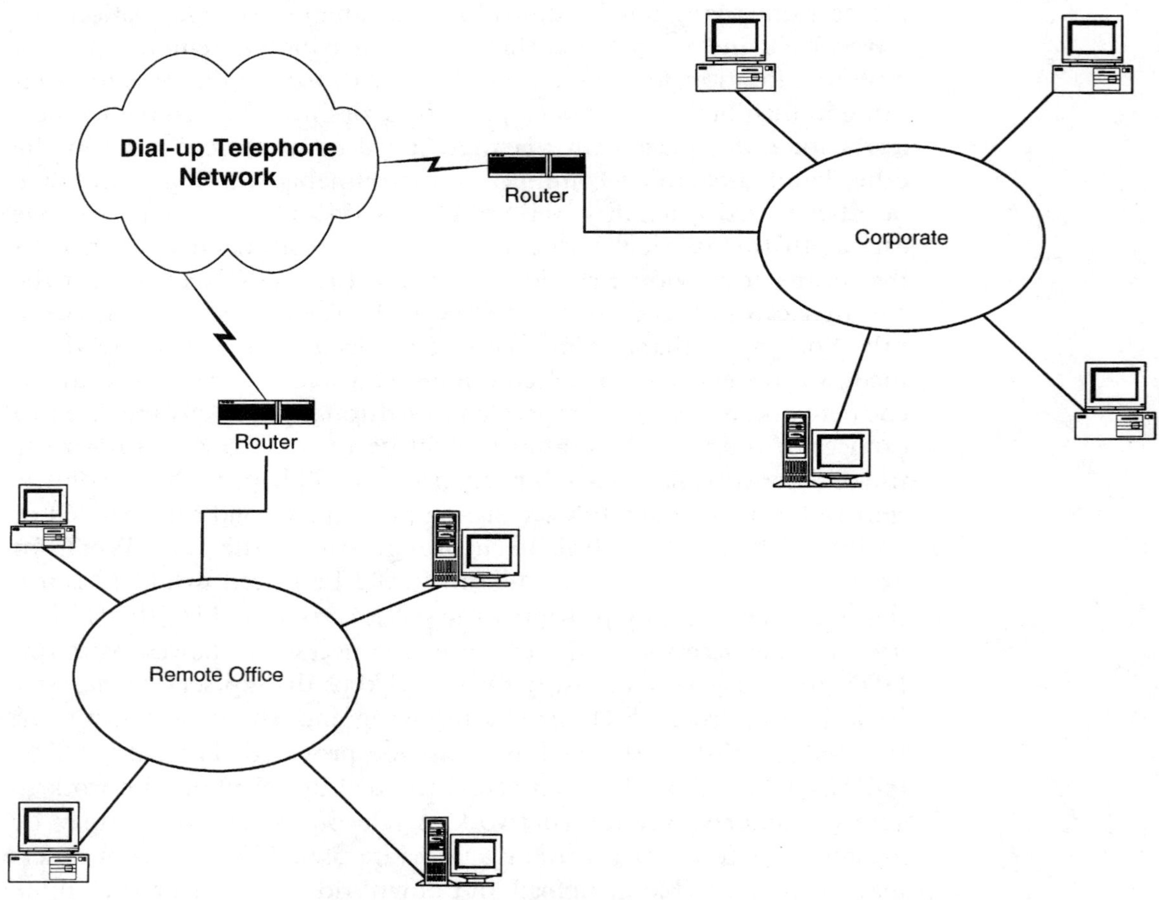

Figure 11.6 Dial-in access using branch-office routers extends service to remote locations.

1. Cost advantages based on the pricing of the routers
2. Use of dial-up instead of higher-cost, leased-line circuits (depending on the traffic between the two sites)
3. An exception use for remote access where fixed sites and fixed facilities are not always used
4. Multiple protocol support (IPX/SPX, NetBios, LAT, and TCP/IP)
5. A wide variety of usable interfaces (X.25, frame relay, SMDS, and ISDN)
6. Dial backup capabilities in a small branch-office environment in the event of a failure

Just about all of the router manufacturers provide branch-office routers that take advantage of the lower-cost, circuit-switched network topologies at a reasonable cost. These advances have provided very flexible arrangements for client/server internetworking that were previously unavailable to the manager. By considering these new options, one can see some of the benefits of controlling the budget and still rolling out the demands and the access needs of the user. Open-mindedness and flexibility are some of the key items that must be considered when rolling out this client/server internetwork. Keep in mind the ability to use a dial-in capability from the smaller locations that only need occasional access. Consider such things as the ability of getting service and support from the vendor. These branch-office or remote-location routers may be in inaccessible areas or very suburban areas. Additionally, when selecting a router for this remote access, the client/server internetwork manager should conform to the standards for routing capabilities, meaning the ability of the router to conform to the normal routing standards and protocols, as well as the interfaces to the LEC and the IEC environment. Several brands of these products are on the market. One must be aware that the mixing and matching of a branch-office router connecting across the wide area network or metropolitan area network should be compatible with other devices already on the network. It would be extremely embarrassing to buy a group of these low-cost, branch-office routers only to find out that they will not pass the information to the corporate router at the main server environment. One never knows until the equipment has been tested, proven, demonstrated, and finally installed at both ends. Although these are not major concerns, they are essential and must be considered.

Throughput on a branch-office router is an additional concern and criteria in terms of the selection process. While dealing with throughput one must take into account the throughput expected out of the router, the ability of the router to pass the information without a lot of overhead, and any network overhead that would be applied either in the routing or routed protocols given this particular router. Throughput essentially involves the capability of passing data through the network between two LANs to interconnect to the server environment, but it also involves the dollars expected in terms of a budgetary constraint. These routers are typically inexpensive, but buying a router that does not give the same kinds of throughput as a traditional router may cost more in the long run. Overhead on a client/server internetwork can amount to 30 to 40 percent, which can cause latency or delay across the internetwork. One must therefore use benchmark tests to consider the aggregate throughput versus the actual and expected throughput on the link. By comparing these numbers and the total throughput capability of the router, a better selection can be made.

Although it is not totally discussed at this point, another concern in using a branch-office router is the ability of providing for network management protocols. The simple network management protocol (SNMP), discussed later, is a desirable feature. Many organizations claim that they fully support and are compliant with SNMP, but when asked what it means, they hedge in terms of an actual answer. It is incumbent upon the client/server internetworking manager to determine just what support and capabilities using network management can be achieved through the branch-office router. While this router may be used on a dial-up basis, it is still imperative that the SNMP management information can be passed to the main server environment or the network management protocols that are being run on the client/server architecture. As long as the data can be derived and proactive performance management can be applied, the router should suffice. SNMP is not a given, so the router must be checked completely before a final decision is made. Once again, it is incumbent upon the client/server network manger to determine what the vendor has to offer and what is actually produced.

Beyond network management, standards, service, and support capabilities on these branch-office routers, one must also take into consideration the ease of use. Because these routers are placed at remote locations, someone at the local end (the end with this particular router) has to be responsible for gathering information or rebooting from time to time. Unless this function can be done across the network, someone at that branch office must be trained to use and support this router. When things go wrong, such as a line hang-up or a downed line, someone must restart the router or be able to determine wherein the problem lies. Because this is not a day-to-day event, it is more important to have an easy-to-use, possibly menu-driven system, so that a person who normally does not get involved with the routing systems can easily take action. This might also involve remote access from the client/server headquarters location to log onto this branch-office router to determine its current state. Can remote diagnostics and restarts be accomplished? Does the vendor offer these services in a user-friendly GUI approach?

While these branch-office routers are being connected primarily to remote locations, they still need to have access in some regard to the WAN service. One must be able to move up from just a dial-up arrangement to a leased line to a fixed-point arrangement if the situation warrants. Locking into a technology that does not allow growth or new services can be a frivolous expense that should be avoided. The networking manager has to be very careful in selecting a device that locks the network into a specific access method. In the use of WAN services, the ability to upgrade as upgrades become warranted to frame relay, ATM, or SMDS is a must. The wide area network link currently being used as a dial-up arrangement would therefore have to see a permanent virtual circuit connection and be able to use it without the dial procedure. One must be aware of whether this can be accomplished. In many cases, these branch-office routers tend to be priced very competitively, but they lock you into a specific type of service. Unless the network is fully dynamic and new sites are being added all the time so that routers can be moved from office to office, etc., one must consider upgradeability and scalability. A typical branch-office router that may be configured for 128 kbps dial-up ISDN connections, for example, should also have the ability to support a full T1 architecture if in fact that need is evident. Beyond the T1, one might also look for multiple ports to the WAN access. In view of the routing protocols that are being used, one should also be concerned with the availability of multiple input ports or multiple PVCs on a single circuit so that oscillation and split horizon do not become major issues. For information on oscillation and split horizon, refer back to Chap. 8.

Given these selection criteria, Fig. 11.6 shows the dial-in access using a branch-office router that allows the use of the circuit-switched, dial-up communications network to the fullest extent. Servers or client/server architectures can still be supported from remote, smaller offices, which typically would not be achievable through leased-line facilities due to cost. A hybrid of both private-line, PVC, and circuit-switched, dial-up connections can emerge into the client/server internetwork. This hybridization will sustain and support the localized branch offices regardless of their locations. Going back to the original discussion in this chapter, the intent was to show a localized arrangement. The use of this branch-office router may be selected within some geographically localized area so that, in the event problems do occur, the client/server network manger can easily get to the site within a reasonable amount of time. The typical configuration for this pilot or test would be a branch-office connection within a 50- to 100-mile radius of the client/server network headquarters. This is particularly true when the branch- or small-office location does not have a trained, suitably knowledgeable individual to perform any of the maintenance, diagnostics, or restarts that will be necessary. One could also consider the use of a vendor in this particular situation. However, using the vendor to provide this type of support, on an on-call basis, can be expensive. The purpose of this discussion is to point out how these intricacies may involve multiple parties, as well as the possible complexities that could emerge in the event a problem does arise. By using a mix of services, the budget can still be met.

Another option is shown in Fig. 11.7. A dial-in server with modem communications capabilities can be provided. This setup again allows for the remote access from either a local or a wide area where users can dial into a modem server. As shown in this figure, the client at a remote site using either a PC, a notebook, or even a LAN arrangement can use client/server remote software for both uploading and downloading information on demand. Using asynchronous dial-up communications connections or synchronous dial-up communications connections can be alternatives here. In this particular case, a server-based platform located at the corporate entity or headquarters running server software will allow the connection of eight asynchronous communications links. The difference here is the client-end server software that would reside at the varying devices.

This figure also shows a gateway function that sits between the mainframe environment (the server) and the application server that is providing the remote access software. This gateway function, represented as a PC sitting between these two computing platforms, provides merely the protocol emulation and gateway function as opposed to actually being the client software. It is through this arrangement that the remote dial-

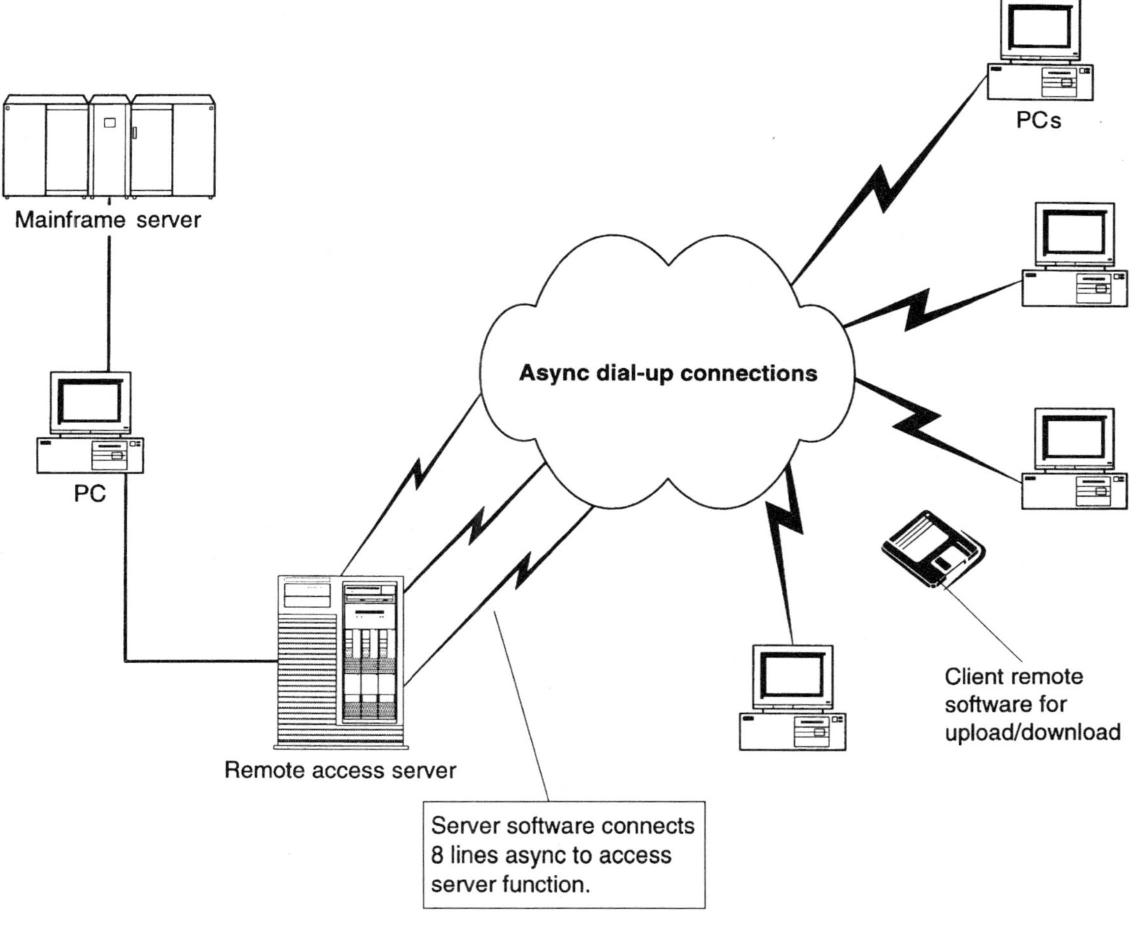

Figure 11.7 Dial-in server modem pools are heavily used for remote access.

up users can access the major network from fixed locations or from traveling locations around the country. This would provide a good test bed for remote-dial access capabilities in a localized area. The client/server internetworking manager could even serve this function from a local site or from home, for that matter. The difference between this particular graphic and others that have already been shown is the remote client and server software being run. In the other cases already shown, this remote client and server software was not being used, whereas in this illustration it is. One should talk to the communications providers as well as the software providers that are building out this client/server network. They can recommend the software that will best work in their environment.

Dial-out Access

The discussion so far has dealt with the ability of remote locations being able to access the client/server network. If the data needs to be sent out from the client/server network, rather than into the network, a different choice might be in order. Figure 11.8 shows one option: a dial-out modem pool. In this figure, a client/server networking architecture, for example the file server, can still pass data down to remote sites via dial-up, circuit-switched communications capabilities. This dial-out capability would be done through a communications server. The concerns and the issues in this particular case place the burden at the localized site as opposed to the remote site. Across a dial-up, circuit-switched network, this asynchronous communication server (or synchronous communication server) is under the direct and local control of the client/server network manger. Through the use of a dial-out capability, high-speed circuit switching can be provided for four to eight dial-up connections at a time, which can be incremented as needs dictate. This dial-out service would provide for specific capabilities—to download files, to download upgrades on software, or finally just to respond to inquiries in a database environment.

Not necessarily just for LAN-to-LAN communications, the dial-out capability can also be used to stand-alone PCs at a telecommuter's home or at an office location if the telephone number can be precoordinated and arranged. A different choice would be to use a specific dial-back facility that allows the end user to dial in on one server and the client/server architecture would then respond on an outbound dial system. In this particular case the remote user might call in and give a call-back number. One must be aware, though, when dealing with hotels and client locations, it is not always possible to dial into the communications system at the distant end. For example, if the server were trying to reach someone staying as a guest in a hotel, it would be extremely difficult to reach that person due to the PBX sitting at the front desk. The PBX attendant answering the call would receive the modem tone and most likely hang up! There would be no way for the information to be passed

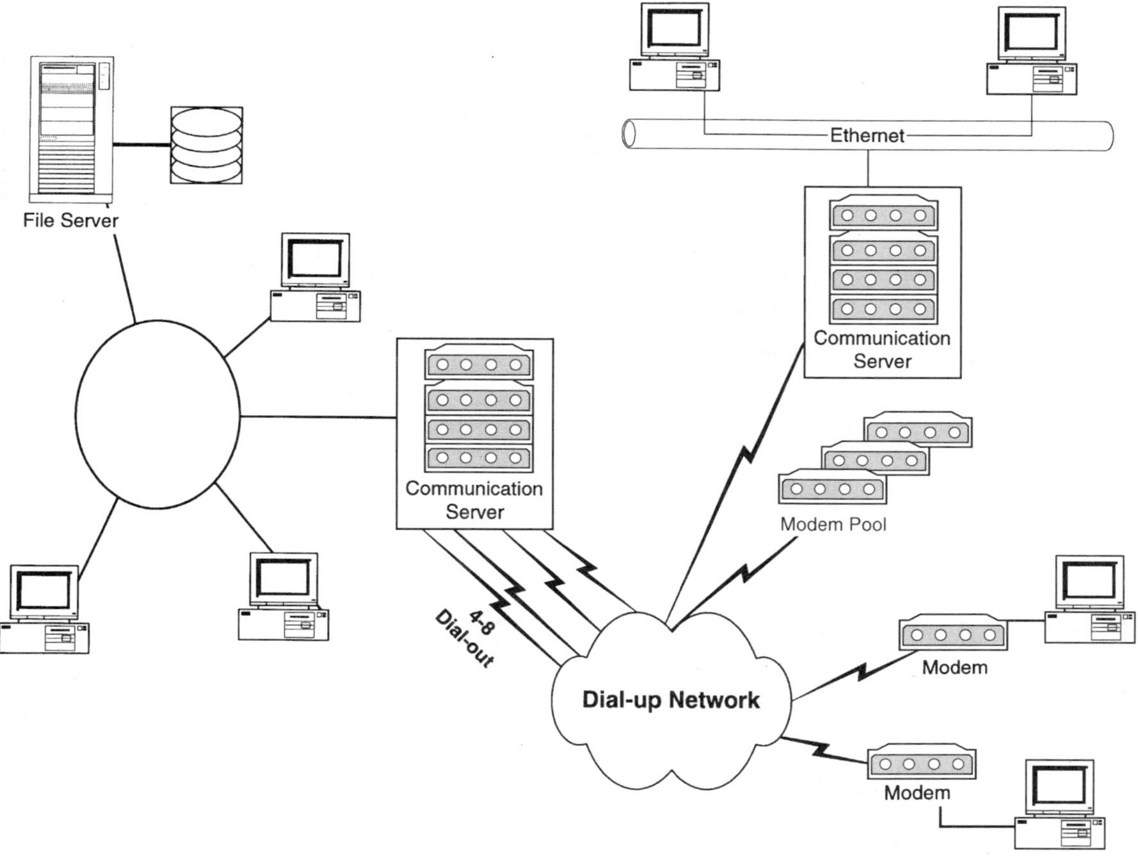

Figure 11.8 Dial-out access also allows for the logical extension of remote access.

down to this PBX operator so that the extension could be connected. Therefore, this application is one where specific locations are being used on a prearranged and precoordinated basis. The intent, of course, is to show the variations that could be used in a given client/server internetworking architecture. Whether it is inbound or outbound services, each can have and fit a specific niche. One just has to look at the options and the software that is available to provide the given services.

Still another variation of accessing the client/server internetwork by nomadic users is shown in Fig. 11.9. In this particular case, one can assume that some nomadic users are using a wireless connection. It might be a cellular phone, the new PCS communication systems, or

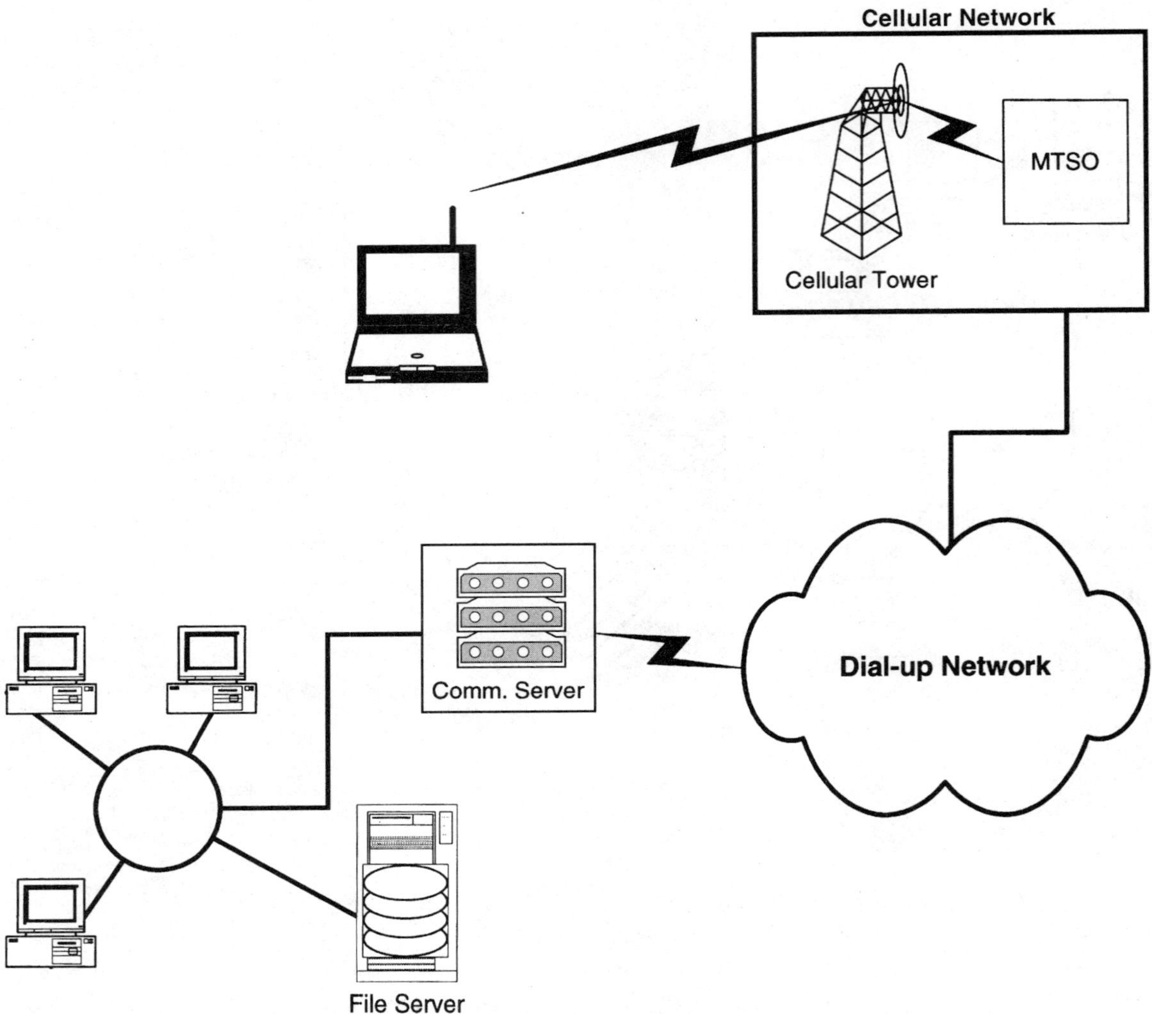

Figure 11.9 Mobile remote users can access the internetwork via cellular communications.

some specialized mobile radio provider. The illustration shows a simplified client/server internetwork connected across a communications server to the dial-up telephone network. As the mobile user travels around the country, or for that matter anywhere else, a connection is made through the cellular network back to the dial-up telephone network. In this particular case, a mobile user using a cell phone or a special PC card that might be installed in a notebook or laptop computer can provide this access. Using the cell phone, the caller would communicate through the airwaves to the closest base station serving the area. In the airwaves, clearly, the data moves much, much slower. In today's technology, a client/server internetworking user accessing the network across cellular-based networks can expect to achieve dial-up communications at approximately 9.6 kbps. Once the connection is made through the base station, the base station then relays either via airwaves or via a dedicated hard-wire link to the mobile telephone switching office (MTSO). The MTSO then establishes a trunk connection to the dial-up telephone network. What then happens is the dialed digits for the comm server would then be passed along through the dial-up network and a circuit-switched connection would be established. One must be aware that when using this arrangement, it might not be plain vanilla. In some cases, using the circuit-switched mobile communications capabilities may require special drivers or special communications software that allow for the interconnection running the protocol support necessary to sustain a connection in a client/server internetwork. In some cases, specific gateway software may also be used, allowing for point-to-point protocol (PPP) or serial line Internet protocol (SLIP) to provide the connectivity. The remote user may well be stationary, in a fixed location such as a hotel room or customer location. Using this circuit-switched, dial-up communications capability through the wireless networks, one can extend the services and capabilities to these remote users to allow a file transfer or a database query.

One should not expect to be able to sustain the operations of a high-speed communications channel capability on a full-time basis using this communications infrastructure. First, it would be far too expensive to sustain a wireless connection through the cellular network when the connection through a cellular provider costs approximately 35¢ per minute local or 65¢ per minute roaming. The cellular networks are not inherently reliable, although improvements are continually being made. For the occasional user who needs access to the client/server architecture, this method can provide quick, easy communications for casual access. It would be imprudent to believe that all users roaming around the country or the world could automatically log onto the client/server network and get all of the services they would normally have in their office environment. As already mentioned, it can be quite expensive. Moreover, this arrangement may also be prone to a lot more data errors than one would see on a permanent connection through a wire facility. There also may be the possibility of more cutoffs on the connections due to overburdening of the cellular networks or some other disruption of the airwaves, which can prove to be a frustration for some remote or nomadic users. They must be trained and made aware of the possible risks of data transmission across a wireless facility. Things will improve over time, as they do on a daily basis, which may provide for compression and higher-speed data throughputs across some of these cellular networks. For now, one must accept what can be reasonably anticipated in terms of total throughput, which, as already mentioned, is about 9.6 kbps.

Mobile users are a funny group. When their demands and needs for access to the client/server networking architecture are first discussed, they are usually fairly acquiescent in terms of the throughput and reliability of the data transfer. They acknowledge that they understand that problems can occur, connections can be poor, or that cutoffs can happen on a more frequent basis. As they are first brought into the network connection in the beginning stages of their activity, they are ready and willing to admit that they can deal with the potential problems. Over time this acceptance erodes. After having file transfer capabilities or database query capabilities from a remote device, they tend to become more dependent on this service. As their dependency increases, their willingness to deal with potential communications problems starts to wane. It doesn't take too long for these users to become chronic complainers about the connections or the services that they are not able to sustain. They may constantly demand better service or faster communications capabilities where none may exist. Again, it is important to train the user and set expectations right up front. If users become dissatisfied with a service, two things might happen: First, they will start to move toward a wired-type infrastructure using a modem, which means they will now have two separate devices with which to use the network. Second, they may begin to complain to management about the lack of service or ability to perform their jobs. In either case, both of these situations create unique problems for the client/server internetworking manager. Peer pressure and senior-level pressure continually mount, causing the client/server internetworking manager to seek out new sources of connectivity. Unfortunately, when dealing with nomadic users, it is difficult to provide reliable and guaranteed service when one does not know where that nomadic user may be next. Consequently, in setting the stage for the client/server internetwork, the client/server network manger should choose a selective group of nomadic users who are willing to work with the problems. By selecting this elite group of communicators, a test bed and service expectation criteria can be established. Using the established criteria, the client/server internetworking manager can set a benchmark or guideline for all new users who ask for this type of connection.

At the 9.6-kbps transmissions rates across the cellular network, one must expect that the cost of communications will be significantly higher for this group of users. Budgetary responsibility is always a concern for the client/server network. One other strategy is to determine who will pay for the cost of communications. If this cost becomes part of the client/server budget, the users will have no qualms about driving the costs up or staying online an inordinate amount of time. However, if the costs are passed through to the users' budgets, they tend to be more selective about the amount of time and the amount of data that they need to transmit. On one hand, if the budget is being paid by the client/server internetworking department, the users will be more willing to use the data transmission capabilities and subsequently proliferate more data and more access to the data. On the other hand, however, as the budget is being passed through to the user departments, this group of users may well start to complain that they cannot get at the data due to the cost. Here again is a dilemma for the client/server internetworking manager. The service is being provided in support of the organization's mission. Yet due to costs and constraints, the user tends to pull away from using the service, which in turn defeats the whole purpose for building this client/server internetwork. Therefore, careful decisions must be made when selecting the methodology for users to access this network. One cannot assume that no connections will be made via a cellular or PCS network. What one can assume is that a hybrid mix of services will always be a requirement. Careful considerations and response capabilities from a help-desk function or from the vendors providing these communication services must be considered right up front.

Another alternative to the circuit-switched, dial-up communications capability would be to use a specialized mobile carrier service, which may be provided by any of the cellular companies or through specialty companies. As shown in Fig. 11.10, mobile users can access a packetized data communications network using wireless transmission facilities. Several different alternatives exist here, including cellular digital packetized data (CDPD) as provided by all of the cellular companies or specialized mobile radio (SMR) applications from companies like Ardis or RAM Mobile Data, providing a packetized arrangement for data

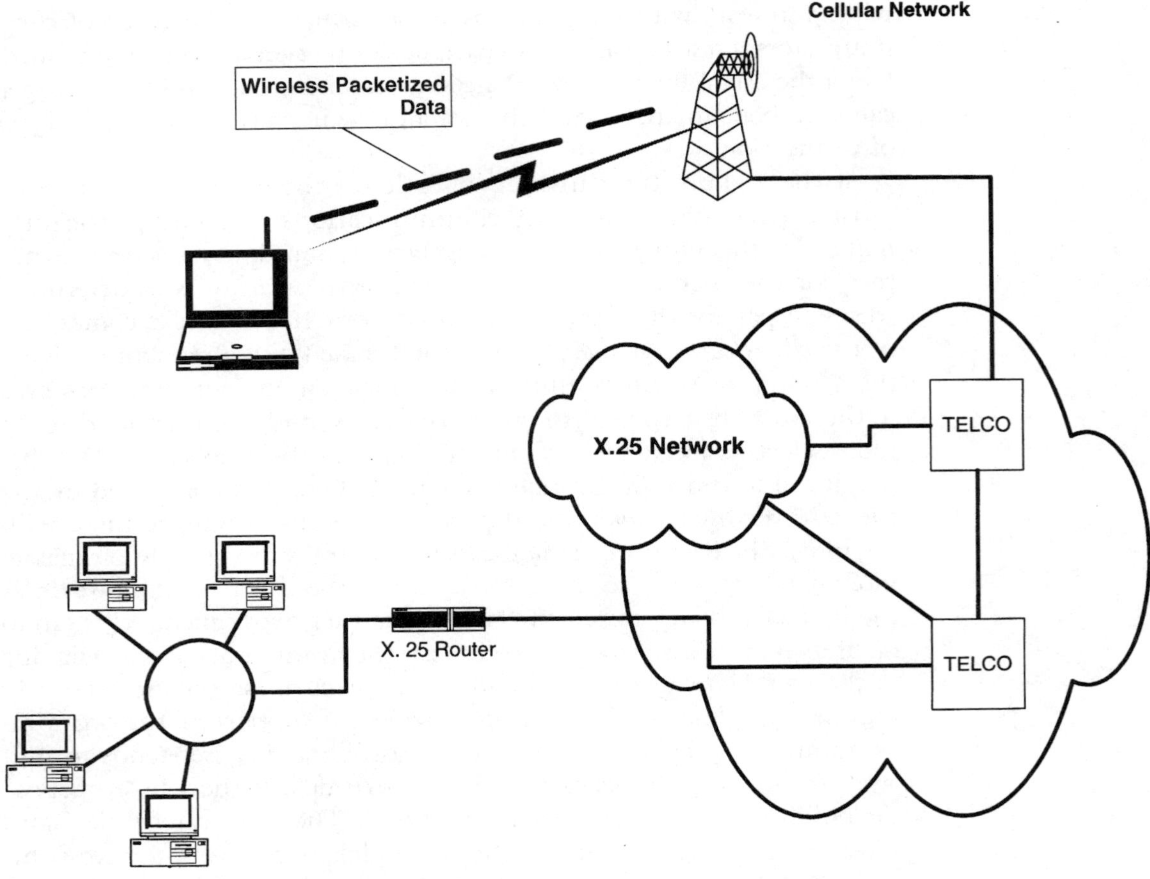

Figure 11.10 Mobile users can access the network through a wireless X.25 connection.

transmission. In this regard, each of these specific applications and services are provided to accommodate data needs as opposed to circuit-switched voice needs. In the figure, the wireless user would access the network remotely through this wireless packetized data arrangement, communicating either through a wireless database station that is hard-wired back to a telephone company WAN or a cellular base station providing packetized data that is then wired back to the MTSO. The user is given the options to provide for the interconnection back to the corporate environment in a structured organization. Note in the illustration that as the connection is provided from this wireless base station with a hard-wire facility back to a telephone company central office, it is then attached to the packet-switched data networks provided by the value-added suppliers. Here the X.25 network provides for packet-switching capabilities. By using this capability, one can combine the nomadic users' needs with an X.25 packet-switching network environment to provide the facilities that would also be available to users who are hard-wire-attached to the localized networks. An X.25 router can be used to provide these facilities, allowing nomadic users to dial in on the switched services of a packet network, as well as the outbound services with a dedicated connection to a packetized network from a router located at the client/server network itself.

Packet switching can be both inexpensive and expensive at the same time. If one strictly uses X.25 services, the old reliable packet data networks that were built in the late 1970s, one can expect inexpensive communications. These services can operate at speeds of 9.6 to 64 kbps, either analog or digital. However, on the reverse side, when coming from a mobile application, the packet-switched environment can be very expensive. If, in fact, a CDPD environment is used in the wider area, with connection back through an X.25 or a special CDPD receiver at the fixed location, the costs are based on a per-packet environment. One must compare the costs versus the data applications that are going to be served by this arrangement. When dealing with shorts bursts of data, such as a quick database query, an e-mail, or perhaps even a quick data transfer, the use of CDPD can be very effective. However, if large file transfers and sustained data throughputs are needed, the CDPD environment would be extremely expensive. Some analysis must be provided in advance of servicing these types of applications. There have been comparisons that have been run whereby a CDPD connection using mobile access for file transfer combinations and e-mail could cost as much as $1500 per user per month. This solution is extraordinary, but it must be weighed against the value of what the data provides. For example, if a normal user generated several million dollars worth of sales activity or sales leads, the $1500 cost would not seem that extraordinary. However, if the user is strictly an administrative user who does not generate new revenues or who is in a sales support function not generating new revenues, this cost could be extraordinarily high.

Moving away from the CDPD world, another alternative is the SMR application provided by these specialized providers. The entire goal of these specialized providers is to provide for short, bursty data transfer capabilities, again at varying speeds. Although many of the vendors offering this service claim speeds of 19.2 kbps or better, reality states that the actual throughput approximates between 9.6 and 12 kbps in today's technology. A significant amount of overhead may well be involved when dealing with some of these SMR applications. Overhead costs money but does not provide usable data. One can assume that at least 20 to 30 percent of all the data transmitted across these networks will be in the form of overhead. Fixed or reduced prices can be arranged through these specialized carriers, which may help lower the cost per bit or cost per transmission for nomadic users. These carriers provide for data transmission in the form of packetized or special packets of data. However, the overhead associated with this data is strictly as a transport medium, as opposed to other overhead that is also required. For example, if the client is using a TCP/IP architecture, additional overhead may well be required that would again reduce the total amount of data on a packet-by-packet basis. The additional TCP/IP overhead could generate an additional 20 to 30 percent overhead in total, meaning that for every thousand bits of data being transmitted across the network, as few as 400 to 500 bits are actual data; the rest are overhead. Careful selection must be determined before choosing one of these solution sets. Some of the services available through these SMR devices and carriers, however, include a very robust set of protocols and gateway support for SNA/SDLC architecture TCP/IP or other variations of major client/server applications. This discussion is not trying to be negative, but to point out there are both risks as well as benefits when choosing to connect mobile and nomadic users in the client/server world. As an internetworking protocol, the use of TCP/IP is almost inherently adopted and accepted as the standard. However, this TCP/IP information would have to be encapsulated inside an X.25 packet. Therefore, other sets of operating systems, other drivers, and other software components may all be required both at the client environment as well as the server environment to be able to support and sustain the connection for these remote users. One needs to be very cautious when building out these connection solutions.

Security

Regardless of whether a connection for a remote user is at a fixed location using routers or branch-office routing capabilities, circuit-switched, dial-up telephone networks, or wireless communications, security is always a concern. Any remote access provided through the client/server internetwork is always at risk. No doubt about it, the network can be penetrable and is always subject to security breaches. It is incumbent upon the client/server internetworking manager to prevent unauthorized access and to prevent breaches to the integrity of the data. The role in providing security is to prevent unauthorized access, alteration, manipulation, or disclosure of information to unauthorized persons. Data moving across an internetwork should be secured while in transit. Several techniques should be used to secure the amount of information and the integrity of the data as it transmits across the network. This book is not intended to be a book on security, but the issue must be addressed. When dealing with this internetworking architecture, several techniques can be used to provide for enhanced security. One should not assume that by taking some simple steps that a fully secure network can emerge, but at least rudimentary procedures and safeguards should be put in place to prevent unauthorized access.

Using firewall communications stoppers prevents remote access to your network in at least a rudimentary form. Figure 11.11 shows a dial-up firewall arrangement. Here, as a dial-up network user uses the facilities of the circuit-switched, dial-up telephone network, he or she connects to the client/server networking architecture through a modem pool or an asynchronous communications gateway. Once there, the user then begins the logon process, which must be processed through a firewall before access to the actual server is allowed. Although this drawing is somewhat simplistic, it conveys the intent and the concept. Specialists can provide highly reliable firewall protection for both hard-wired and dial-up, circuit-switched users. No exceptions should be allowed when dealing with firewall connectivity. Any door that is left open will become a possible entrance point for unauthorized users.

The use of a firewall, also called a *bastion router* or a *choke router*, could be provided either in series or parallel or individually to prevent unauthorized access to your network. If a connection exists to the circuit-switched public telephone network at some point in time, someone will find it. Once someone finds it, it becomes a challenge, and that person may attempt to defeat all of the security and logon procedures, as well as password protections, that are already in place. The firewall just adds one additional step. Firewalls add to the complexity of keeping an unauthorized user from accessing the data. With a remote access, the use of one or more firewalls is an absolute necessity. Too many cases have been seen

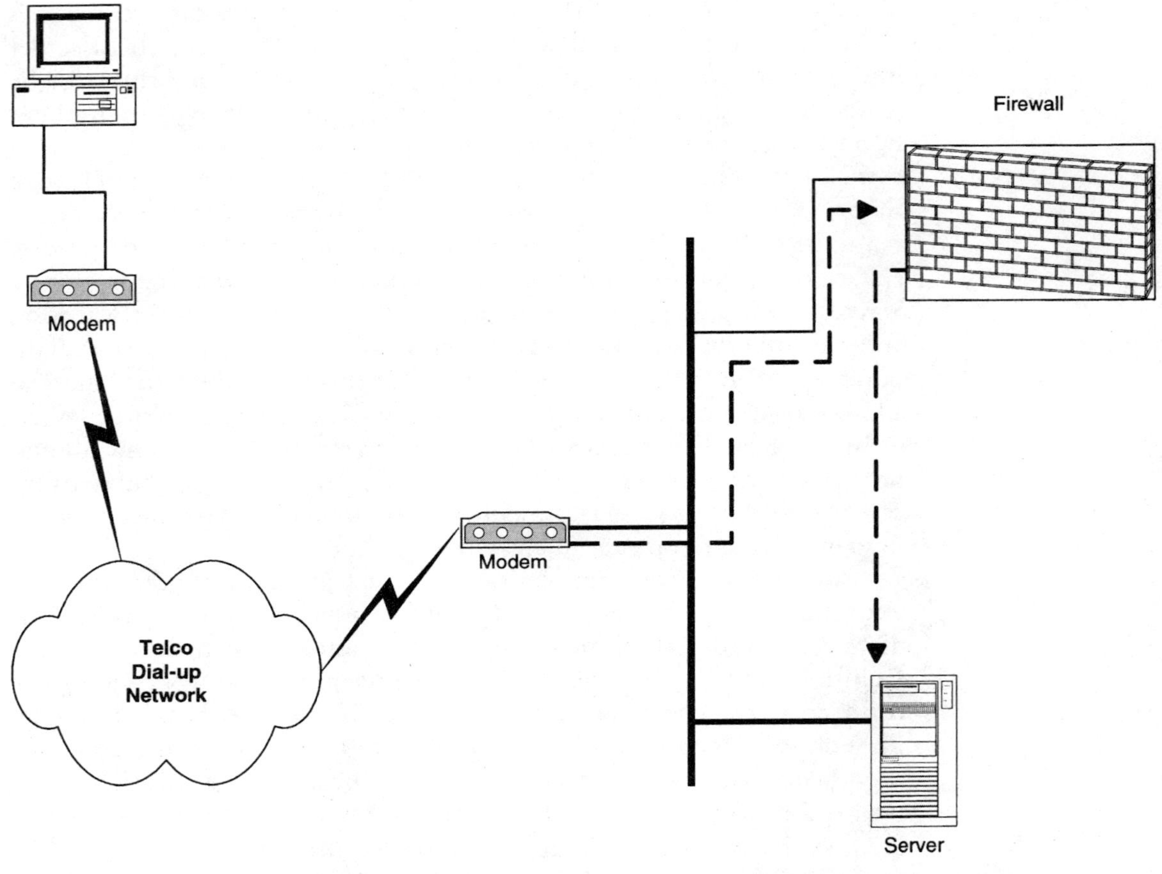

Figure 11.11 *Dial-up firewalls: Build a firewall through a server, router, or hub. Make no exceptions!*

in which client/server internetwork users did not take the time or invest the money to protect the network. The results, of course, were that unauthorized users penetrated the network and caused havoc. Whether it was deletion or manipulation of the data, disclosure of confidential and proprietary information, or the implanting of viruses and Trojan horses into the network, the results were still the same. Management loses confidence if a network is penetrated. Users also lose confidence when network penetration occurs, but penetration can also occur internally as well as externally. If users know that the data is prone to being viewed or breached, they tend to lose confidence in keeping their data on the main server. As a result, demands for larger internal hard drives on their individual PCs immediately begin to escalate. Although it may seem like an alternative solution, it is merely shifting the decisions and access to a different location. Yes, it is more expensive. Moreover, moving more and more data to a user's hard drive provides easier access to the data than if a server was used. The NOS provides for certain rudimentary access rights and privileges and prevents the unauthorized deletion or editing of data, but it is still only a front-end process. One must keep unauthorized users off this network at any cost. Using the firewall on a dial-in service or a leased-line service allows the client/server internetworking manager to provide a more sophisticated security system. No single solution covers all bases. However, putting pieces together, such as these firewalls, as well as the features and functions of the NOS, prolongs and postpones the inevitable breach. Browsers, salami attackers, and disgruntled busybodies on a network will still try to penetrate and read other users' data. The use of the firewall merely slows this process down and in some cases stops novice hackers from gaining access. In many organizations within a client/server architecture, two or three layers of firewall would therefore be used. The firewall can selectively pass or deny database access on certain criteria:

- User ID
- User password
- Calling-number identification, using a technique called ANI (automatic number identification)
- Application-specific access
- Protocol-specific access

If, in fact, filtering can be done and denial can be provided on any one or all of these five criteria, then more sophistication can be provided to the security arena. It is incumbent on the client/server internetworking manager to ensure that the necessary procedures are put in place up front. Any firewall or security protection that is going to be used should be one of the first tools that is rolled out and tested before the actual implementation of the full client/server internetwork. Whether access occurs through a router, a server, or a hub, the use of security stopgaps is absolutely necessary. Note the emphasis on requirements and necessity of providing security. When one thinks about the type of data stored on a network—the entire corporate data sets—it is easy to understand the emphasis on security issues. Dial-up firewalls provide for rudimentary connections and protection against the casual browser. Other measures may still be required.

Figure 11.12 shows another service that may be included along with the firewall capabilities. In this illustration, the use of authentication and challenge/response systems could be added. Several vendors have exceptional packages that add the degree of security necessary from casual and hacking environments. Using an authentication server and an authenticating modem provides some enhancements to the security of the network. Shown in this figure is the capability of using the authentication process for the dial-in remote user. As the remote user dials into the network through the circuit-switched, dial-up telephone network, a packet-switched network, or any other public service, the connection is made to an authenticating modem. This authenticating modem, upon going off-hook, immediately issues a challenge command. The challenge is to the sending modem to identify itself with either a preprogrammed key or a changing-key authentication system. Several vendors have products that will provide the capability of securing the network. As the authentication process takes place, the modems using this authentication procedure go through a handshake and dialogue that is security-aware. If a challenge is issued to a sending modem, and the sending modem is using the same algorithm and changing-key authorization, then the connection into the server will be allowed. However, if an unauthorized user is attempting to access the network and the challenge is issued to the sending modem, the access is easily denied. The sending modem, not being programmed to issue a response, would therefore wind up timing out. Upon time-out, the modem at the receiving end (the challenging modem) recognizing that the sender is a nonauthorized user, breaks the connection. Assuming that the challenge is identified by some adept hacker, and a response can be issued by the sending modem, additional tools are still ready to kick in. Upon the successful authentication with just the modem, a changing-key authentication process then activates. Every 30 seconds, as a default, the authenticating modem issues a new challenge and expects a new response. A hacker may be adept enough to penetrate the modem at the onset, but should not be able to regenerate a new response using the same algorithm that the issuing modem is looking for, which means a hacker may be allowed only 30 seconds on the network.

Once through the authenticating modem, an authentication server is used. This server is a specially equipped server that has a custom database that an authenticating modem will be able to use. After successfully

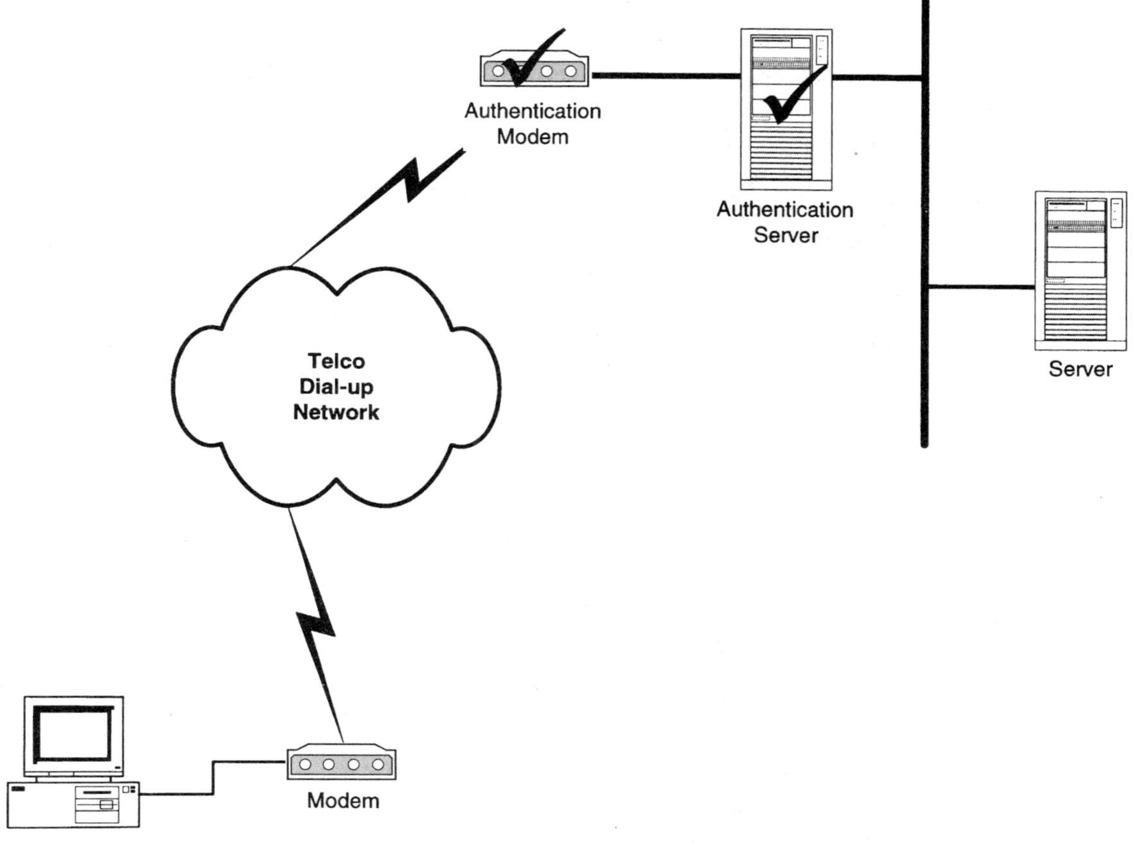

Figure 11.12 Authentication on a per-call basis provides some level of security on the client/server internetwork.

getting through the authenticating modem, the end user must go through a specific logon procedure through the authentication server. The user ID and password, and possibly even an additional challenge response, would be required. Only upon successfully achieving the necessary password generations and authentication challenge/responses between the modem and the server is the user allowed onto the network. This front-end process adds some considerable depth to the security of the network and the security of the server in a client/server internetwork. The additional cost can be significant. These changing-key authentication modems and servers can have up-front costs of tens of thousands of dollars just for the server end. At the remote user end, the keys and the programming capabilities could be as much as $60 to $100 per user, if a hardware solution is used.

Another choice is to use a software-based solution, which costs as little as $35 per user. The difference here, of course, is that the changing key is a physical and hardware-oriented system that can be lost. Conversely, the software-driven system is preprogrammed with a challenge/response functionality, which could add some new complexities to the picture. In dealing with many client/server internetworks, it was noted that many of the end users who had software-driven systems preprogrammed their individual PCs with onboard internal modems with all of the appropriate challenge/response password and user IDs preestablished and saved. Logging onto the server was as simple as powering up and going through the communications software program. The rest was all stored program capabilities; therefore, if a user lost his or her PC (which is an everyday occurrence), then whoever has the PC has the ability to access the server.

It is imperative that if a user experiences a loss, he or she immediately notifies the client/server internetworking manager. Unfortunately, this doesn't always happen. While standing at a train station, an auditor for a large accounting firm set his laptop on the ground next to him, and it disappeared into the crowd. Although this particular auditing firm had taken all the necessary steps and procedures to protect its network, it was still prone to penetration. The auditor was so embarrassed that he chose not to report the loss to management. Instead the auditor procured a duplicate system just like the one he had. From all visible indications, nothing had changed. However, the auditor was not able to dial in and log onto the network because the authentication process and software was not loaded on this new computer. It was only about 10 days later that the client/server network manager noticed this particular auditor had not logged in and began to get suspicious. When day-to-day activities such as normal logon procedures suddenly cease, someone may get concerned. The astute manager quickly queried the auditor. It was only after this challenge that the auditor finally admitted he had lost his PC and replaced it with one of his own. Unfortunately, for 10 days, whomever had the PC had the ability to dial in and log onto this network. Fortunately, there was no indication that this breach actually happened. Whoever stole the computer probably was only looking to move the hardware as a resellable piece of equipment. Let's not forget, though, when someone buys that PC or notebook, that person may discover the access methodology. Immediate action must take place whenever some loss or some difference occurs on the network. The client/server internetworking manager must constantly monitor usage statistics, changes in the amount of usage, or any variations to the normal logon procedures. The manager might consider verifying every user on a periodic basis. If someone is on the network and statistics show that individual's usage is inordinately high, it may be beneficial to kill that particular user's access until validation can be made. Although it is inconvenient and obviously disruptive to the end user, it is one of the methods that could be used. Furthermore, auto-logoff tools can be installed on the server or on each individual client to prevent loss and breaches. If a hacker is trying to breach security systems or just sitting there and monitoring or capturing data, the network could sense a period of inactivity or lack of data transfer and log the device off. One must be aware of the complications as well as the risks when dealing with these client/server networks and security tools that may cause an uproar from end users.

Still another issue that must be addressed is the security of the data itself from prying eyes. Encryption is a suggestion when remote access is being provided. One can never know, or even suspect, when a tap or a bridge exists on a circuit. Essentially, a hacker can tap into the internal wiring in an organization. By tapping incoming telephone lines, for example, a hacker could merely sit on the wire and watch users dial in and log onto the network. By using a data capture, every single password and user ID could be obtained for all dial-in users. The rule and the law of averages state that as long as multiple users are dialing into a network at some point in time, they will come across this link. By the sheer nature of this transport and by being able to gather this type of information, a complete database could be built on user IDs and passwords. From there, a hacker could merely login at different times pretending to be someone else. The real issue here is that it will be somewhat invisible to the client/server internetworking manager because the logons are valid user IDs and passwords; nothing appears to be out of the ordinary. Consequently, encryption of the information as it moves across the network is something that is more important to consider (Fig. 11.13). By encrypting the data at the end-user device (the actual PC) and at the server level, one can prevent the unauthorized capture of this type of information. But this issue goes beyond the capture of passwords and user IDs; it also involves the capture of the actual data moving across the network from the remote user to the server. If user IDs and passwords can be captured, so too can real information. Therefore, encrypting tools can be used to prevent the unauthorized access

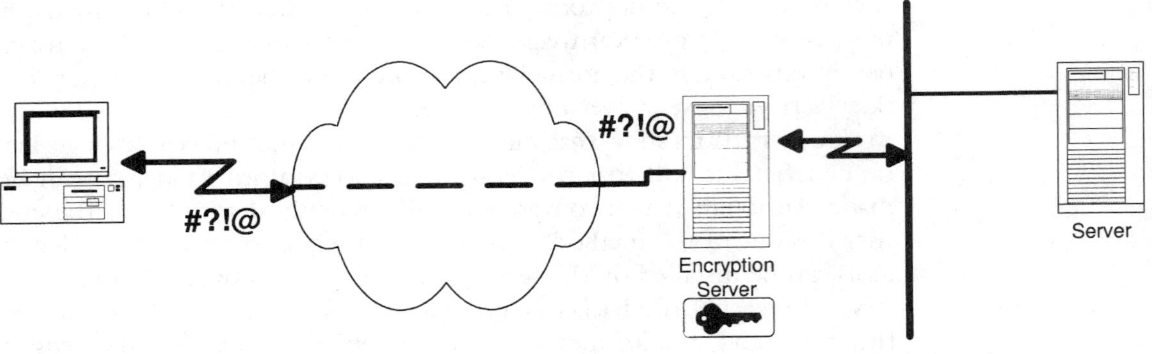

Figure 11.13 Use encryption techniques in the PC and server to protect access and secure the data.

and disclosure of information. By using an encryption technique, whether a private key or a public key encryption tool, the data is encrypted before being placed across the circuits.

Many of you reading this book may think it will be impossible for someone to tap into *your* wires. The chance of someone getting into your building and tapping in, say, at the telephone company's demarcation point is mostly unlikely. It is not the intent of this book to create paranoia among client/server managers, but to provide an awareness that these security breaches happen regularly. If the tapping is not accomplished inside the building, it could be accomplished outside the building. The telephone company brings all of its wiring to pedestals that sit outside buildings. These small green boxes, sitting on sidewalks or curbs or telephone poles anywhere along the line, are accessible. Although the telephone company personnel lock these boxes, they can be broken into. How many client/server managers or internal employees would challenge what appears to be a telephone company employee out on the street line working at a pedestal? What are they doing there? Would we challenge that individual for an identification card? The answers are probably zero and no. In most cases, an employee of a telephone company working on the cable systems outside the building would never be challenged. Again, creating paranoia is not the intent of this particular chapter, but it is important to have an awareness that things can and do happen every day.

Recently, a client/server network manager told me that his company had fiber optics coming into its building, which were highly secure. Although fiber is more secure than a copper-based connection, they are not highly secure connections. Simple fiber taps that take as little as 10 minutes to cut into a cable are available on the market today. In using this connection, one could sit on the data network and capture every bit of data going down the wire. The use of encryption capabilities would be a wise investment. Encryption can take place at the PC, as previously stated, as well as at the server, so that only garbled-looking data moves down the wires. It will only be useful to those who have the decrypt keys. Encryption requires additional overhead, make no mistake about it. When using various encryption techniques, an additional 5 to 20 percent of overhead may be required. Overhead costs time and money. Decisions like this continually draw down on the ability to move information in a fast and efficient manner. Any time overhead is involved, less data is moving down the wires. Combining all the overhead that has been discussed for a remote user, one could experience a 10 to 60 percent overhead demand, depending on the various tools being put into play. Using strictly a 9.6-kbps, dial-up, circuit-switched channel capability, the effective data throughput could be as little as 4800 bps or less. This statement is devastating to someone trying to build out and manage a client/server internetwork. Think of the users who are expecting the same high-speed communications they might achieve on the LAN level at the office being exposed to an approximation of 4800 bps. They will not be totally happy and will begin to complain quickly. One must be prepared to deal with these issues.

Unfortunately, in the past, client/server network mangers have turned off some of the tools that were necessary to provide protection merely to satisfy the complaints and demands of the end users. Exposing a network because of user complaints can be as devastating as having no protection whatsoever. Confidence at management and user levels wanes quickly. The client/server internetwork will be perceived as a bottleneck, therefore driving up the demand for high-speed communications. But any tool and any change in speed or architecture costs money. Budgetary constraints are one of the first things that tend to get in the way of trying to build out and continually fine-tune these networks. The client/server network manger is therefore under constant pressure to match the necessary speed, accessibility, throughput, and security all on a limited budget. At this point, networking mangers will probably ask themselves, "Why bother?" The answer, of course, is the demand for the availability and accessibility of the data regardless of where the user might reside. Therefore, the tools are necessary and cannot be overlooked.

As a final statement on remote access, one must be aware of the dynamics and the constantly changing structures within the actual carrier community to provide higher-speed data communications and better throughput and reliability. In many cases, these network carriers attempt to provide more secure communications through their PVC (permanent virtual circuit) connections. Using a private-line infrastructure may be a better solution than a dial-up solution or access, but it cannot always be achieved for every single site and every user. The client/server internetworking manager must continually balance budget, satisfaction, perception, and confidence from management. If any one of the goals along the way gets out of balance, it could throw the entire scheme off balance. If, in fact, the pivot shifts from one direction to another or to a budgetary constraint only without regard to security or speed or throughput, then the network is not going to function properly. Moreover, if the balance goes the other way, to a more secure environment, the users' acceptance and willingness to use the network will wane. The client/server network manger faces these challenges on a day-to-day basis.

CHAPTER 12

Client/Server Internetworking Applications

In the preceding chapters of this book, several issues concerning hardware/software decisions and other services have all been discussed, but what of the actual applications? What is the purpose of installing a client/server internetwork? Clearly, what one is actually trying to accomplish is the linking together all of the goods and services available to fulfill an organization's data needs and to satisfy the business functionality. The applications become some of the more critical components that must be considered in a client/server architecture. If localized area networks serve all of the business needs in a very small environment or a branch office, then there is no need to provide internetworking. However, as users need to share information or dynamically work together in a virtual-office environment, or if duplication of data and applications is necessary, then the client/server internetwork becomes far more justifiable. A client/server networking manager is responsible for the access, methodology, and connectivity solutions for users to be able to use the organization's data in the performance of its mission. It is through this goal that the infrastructure is built upon. Using the architecture and the needs and demands of the end-user function, the capabilities must be rolled out within a reasonable budgetary limitation.

At this point in the decision-making process, the hardware and protocols have been determined. The protocols must support the applications. It is these protocols and applications to which the client/server networking manager must pay particular attention. The operating system has also likely been chosen. The pieces are starting to come together to create internetworking between multiple sites, multiple subnetworks, multiple division and department environments, or even multiple departments. The necessary devices have been selected. Whether bridging or routing, linking systems together through high-end hubs, building virtual LANs and internetworks, or a combination and hybrid of all of these choices, the decisions have been made in earlier chapters. Hopefully, as you've gone through this book you've been able to select and use a checklist to compare what you're currently using versus some of the decisions you may want to make in the future. The decision about carriers on the internetwork across the wider and metropolitan areas may have been made already. These choices include the differences between circuit-switched, packet-switched, fast frame relay, or cell relay applications. All of these operations and all of these pieces have been carefully considered and the options selected; the pieces continue to come together. The interconnectivity is becoming a reality. It is now time to consider the actual applications for which this network was built.

Typical Candidate Applications

There are many applications that fit the client/server internetworking architecture serving business needs reliably, quickly, and efficiently, but some of the ones that jump to the forefront are those that have been implemented by many others. In looking at more than 100 various client/server internetworking applications used by many organizations spread throughout the world, the more common applications include

1. Database networking
2. Human resources applications
3. Finance and accounting applications
4. Payroll situations and services
5. CAD development
6. Purchasing and order entry/processing
7. Maintenance and facilities within an organization
8. Electronic document interchange (EDI)
9. Distribution management services and functions
10. Publishing systems

As mentioned, hundreds of applications may fit the role of the client/server internetwork model, but these are the primary uses today that have been implemented in a global information system (GIS) to provide interconnectivity within various organizations. These applications, already seen in other organizations, are looked at in the following discussions and figures. The intent is not to steer you in a specific direction or tell you this is the only way it can be done; instead, it is to give additional ideas in terms of how the implementation of a client/server internetwork might take place.

Figure 12.1 shows an example of using order-processing capabilities with a Lotus Notes application running in a server environment. This particular application involves an order-processing function using the Notes system as a means of handling the full order-processing capability, much similar to an EDI environment. In Step 1, a user would access an online catalogue of all of the organization's products and services. This online catalogue allows the customer to select an item that is needed. In this particular application, the catalogue could be internal, for internal users ordering stationery supplies, inventory, or services. The other alternative is to

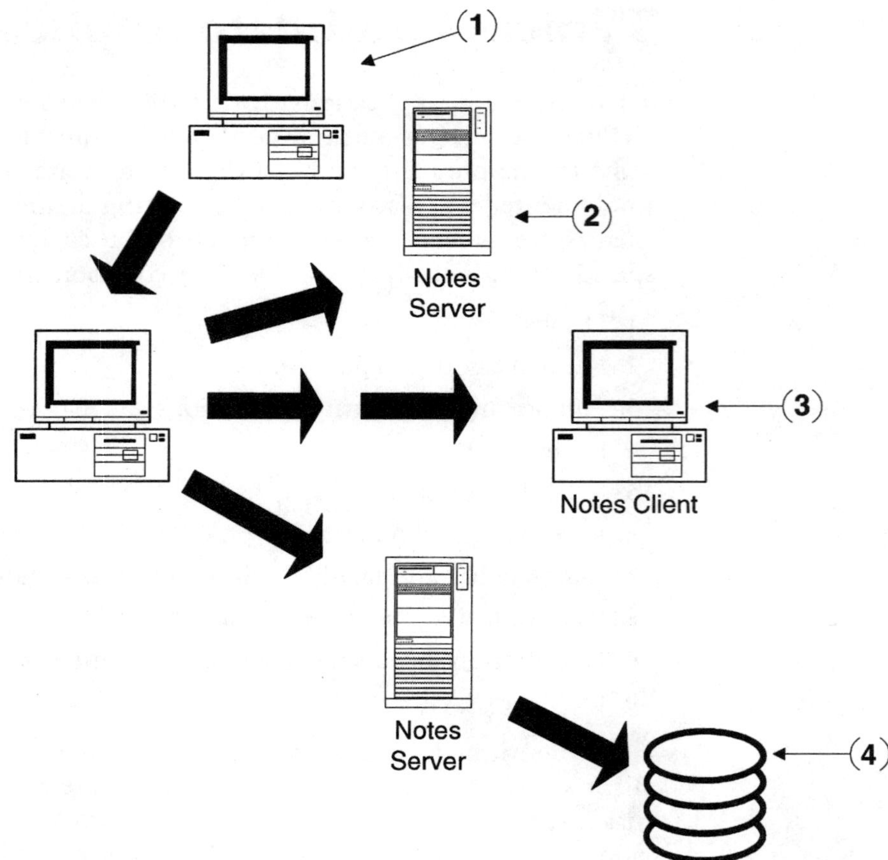

Figure 12.1 Order processing with Lotus Notes is a form of client/server internetworking. (1) User accesses on-line catalog to select item, then forwards order request. (2) Once order approved, is forwarded to project planning, distribution, and engineering. (3) Production builds product and ships to customer. (4) Host asset management system, inventory, and purchase orders automatically updated.

have an outside user, such as a customer, access the online catalogue to select from the goods an organization has to offer. Of course, it goes without saying, this application could also be a hybrid combining both the internal and external cataloguing services. As the customer accesses the catalogue and selects from the goods and services available, he or she fills in an order request interactively. This order request or order form is then submitted to the order-processing function. In the next step, once the order has been submitted to order processing, it must go through the normal order-approval process prior to any form of manufacturing or distribution. This order-approval process may well include a credit check on the customer and a quick inventory check to determine whether the product is in stock or not, or it might be a whole new order process that requires full manufacturing and distribution. Upon completion of the order, a request is forwarded through the Notes server to the various departments that would have interaction for fulfilling this requirement. The departments that may have some interaction include

1. Project planning
2. Distribution
3. Engineering

This system would allow for each of the appropriate departments to schedule and order the raw materials necessary to fill the order for the customer, whether internal or external. The Notes server now becomes the repository, or the server function, of the information that allows various organizations or departments to query or check the status or product flow throughout the entire process.

The production department is then alerted through the Notes server to schedule an event such as manufacturing or building the product that has been ordered and to ship it to the final destination, ultimately the customer. Once again, this whole process can be interactively worked with by various organizations to track the order, check the status of the production process, or determine where in the shipping flow the order actually stands.

Ultimately, the information is then forwarded on through the Notes server to a database such as a host-based assets-management program, inventory control department, and purchasing department so that purchase orders can be automatically updated and shipped out to the customer or to the various user departments. Throughout this whole process, the entire organization can be interworking and internetworked such that at any point in time any query can establish exactly where the flow is. One might assume that there is some proprietary nature built into Lotus Notes. In the past, Notes traditionally has been a proprietary application or front-end process. Rumor has it that IBM/Lotus is continually looking to open the platform into a nonproprietary architecture so that other interfaces and operating systems can work smoothly with Notes. Upon completion of that openness, a Notes environment might well be a suitable arrangement for the average order process and order-taking function. One derivative to this illustration, as shown in the flow, is handling the order-processing function through an automatic call distribution or some form of a call center. The call center agents would be sitting at the terminal device (be it a dumb terminal or a PC-based network), and the call agents would be the ones accessing the catalogue and placing the order. It would only be when custom products are required that are not found in the standard catalogue that this system could become a problem. For the average consumer, however, a Notes-based environment for a customer-oriented function would probably serve sufficiently.

Figure 12.2 shows another application that might be considered in a publishing environment. Note that where a specific application is highlighted, one could substitute some other process or operation within an organization. In this particular case, there would be a midrange server platform, perhaps an AS/400, a RISC device, or a high-end midrange platform from several vendors. Using the midrange server with attachments from various departments within the organization, several different applications can be used here. Let's look at the first environment where a customer might come to a publishing organization in need of some form of advertising or other product that this publishing department would satisfy. First, a group of designers and layout artists would be involved in working with the specific customer. As the customer details exactly what he or she wants, these designers would then start to build a storyboard, either on an individual copyright/designer function or one of those virtual dynamic workgroup applications where several personnel would simultaneously be working on the project. By using this entire function, the designers would go to work and subsequently create copyrighted materials and so on. That information would be stored on a database server that front-ends the midrange server that provides back-office functionality.

Note from the midrange server there is a design department hook that allows the designers to come up with the creative copy. Yet a design/layout group is attached to the LAN. These two groups would work harmoniously together across the client/server internetwork from the LAN as well as from the terminal or even in an Apple (Mac) environment. As the production departments take care of this information, other pieces are still going to be needed. What might happen is that as the design and layout department determines whether they need a specific type of ink or stock of paper or any other custom needs, a specific request would be sent to the purchasing department. Purchasing, in turn, would seek out the suppliers and generate a purchase request. While that takes place, note that the purchasing buyers located on the same LAN would be able to access through the database server to the midrange and pull up any kind of database that exists on the products that are needed and the list of vendors that can supply these

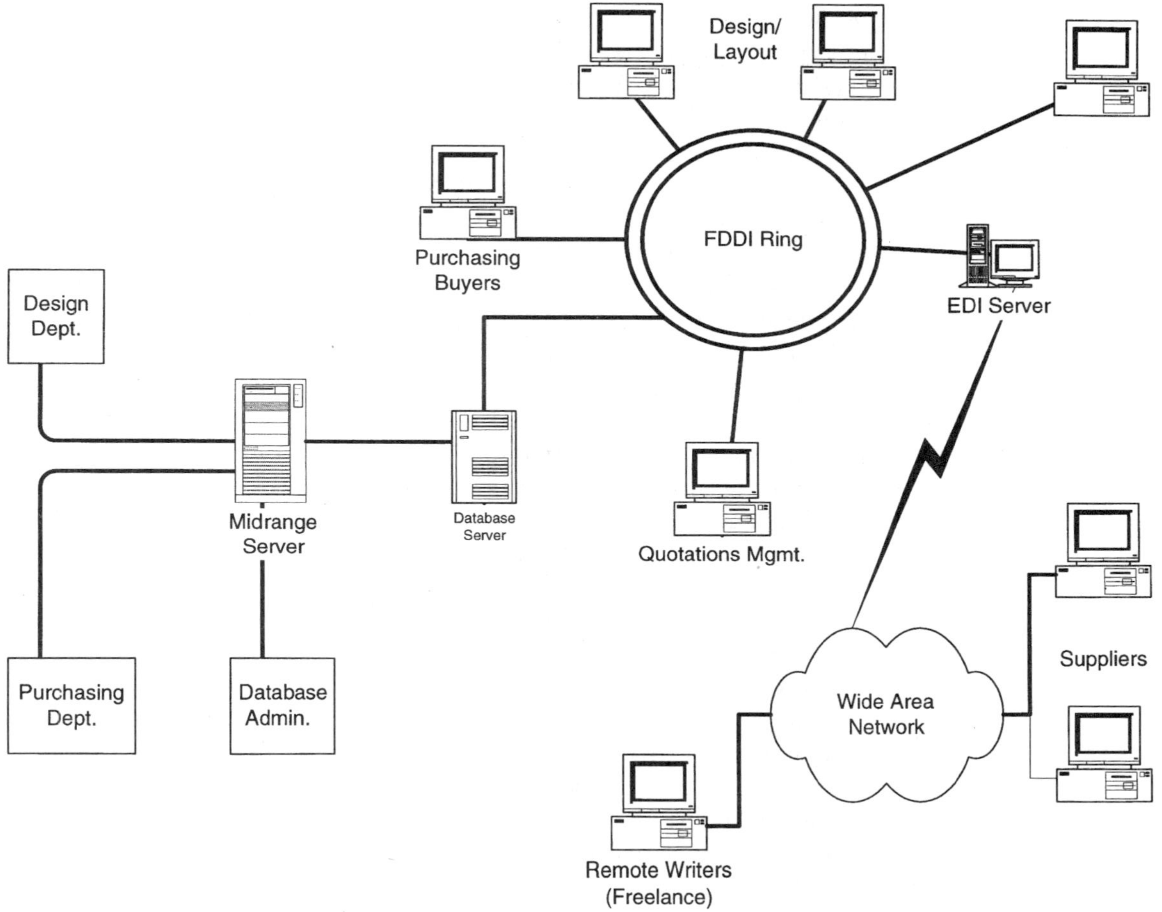

Figure 12.2 Publishing organizations can take advantage of client/server networking.

products. In the event that a particular product or service is not available or not readily available from suppliers, a request could automatically be sent to the quotations management group attached to the same network. Quotations management would then build a database containing descriptions of the products and quantities that are needed and network this information to a group of suppliers for quotes. As the suppliers produce their quotes for a particular product, they then return their information through an EDI server to the quotations management group. This information would then be entered into the database server, where it would be stored by database administration. The production process can continue or the creative copy can still be worked on while all the products that are going to be used in the production process are in the quotation step.

An additional hook is built off the network through the EDI server and across the wide area telecommunications network. It involves remote writers who can be activated if needed. In this particular case, these remote writers include freelancers who produce the ad copy or creative ideas and designs; they could be working remotely on the same project while the design and layout groups are laying out the total production and the purchasing and quotations management groups are getting the necessary quotations from the various suppliers. All of this information would be stored on a centralized server, where each of the departments could always find out the status and the timelines of the project at hand. By moving the information electronically across the wide area network into the client/server networking environment here, it would not be necessary to retype the copy, as is customary, or to re-edit the entire document. Any edits that are required can be done electronically from the server at the client's workstation. Any necessary changes or redlining and markups that are required can be immediately sent back to the freelance writer across the wide area network and delivered for appropriate action. Total control over this production process in a publishing environment can be achieved through a client/server internetwork using the local and the wide area network, the services of the three-computer architecture, and the database hooks for pricing information, scheduling information, design and layout, and all of the creations necessary to provide this total integrated package. By using the suppliers engaged in this EDI function at the same time, the scheduling and the production process for the supplies used or to be consumed can all be integrated tightly within the one server environment.

This example is a classic one of using a true client/server internetwork in a production process. One key point on this wide area network (as shown in the cloud in Fig. 12.2) is that this network can be a wide area, but it can also be a metropolitan area network. Using some of the capabilities of the local telephone companies and SMDS as discussed in Chap. 8, the SMDS network can provide the high-speed 4-, 10-, 16-, 25-, or 34-Mbps throughput capabilities. Linking the SMDS from a telephone company to an interexchange carrier, the SMDS can be hooked to a wider area network. There are several cases documented using SMDS on a wide area and a metropolitan area in a publishing production facility where all of this could take place. One such example involves a publishing house in the Montreal, Canada, area with SMDS links within the greater Montreal area but also with a longer-distance network hook to a production facility located in Philadelphia. This particular publishing house uses this type of a network extensively and has touted significant increases in its ability to produce the product and overall productivity with the decreased costs and decreased lead times necessary to satisfy customer needs and, therefore, increased sales and revenue. It is through the client/server internetwork that these pieces start to fall together.

Figure 12.3 shows several different approaches to a cooperative processing environment. In this particular case, a host-based system exists. The host may be a mainframe platform, a midrange server platform, or could be as simple as a PC-based platform environment. What is different in this illustration is that in cooperative processing, the question now is where does the information reside? You will recall from earlier chapters that there were three pieces to the application in a client/server network that were discussed. In many cases in dealing with the client/server architecture, it was mentioned that we had the application, the data, and, finally, the presentation or the GUI to prepare the information and to present it to the actual user's screen. This illustration tries to depict where those pieces can reside. Looking at the top of the graphic, in the cooperative processing environment, the three functions—data management, application logic, and actual presentation—can all reside right at the front end of the host. These three functions may reside here at the host as a link is used across the wide area in an internetwork through a routing function. A distributed database may reside somewhere else across the country or somewhere within the organization. Through the router, the management of the data, the subsets of information, the access to the individual records and files, as well as all of the logic required to do the queries, the database structure, and the user interface in the form of presentation can all reside at the server function. This figure shows one way in a cooperative processing environment that these choices can be made.

The second choice, directly below the distributed database, is the function of remote data management. Note the illustration has changed a little bit. In this particular case, actual data management is controlled by the remote device across the internetwork. However, the actual logic and presentation are still controlled and delivered by the host in a server environment. Thus, the client may have the ability to manipulate the

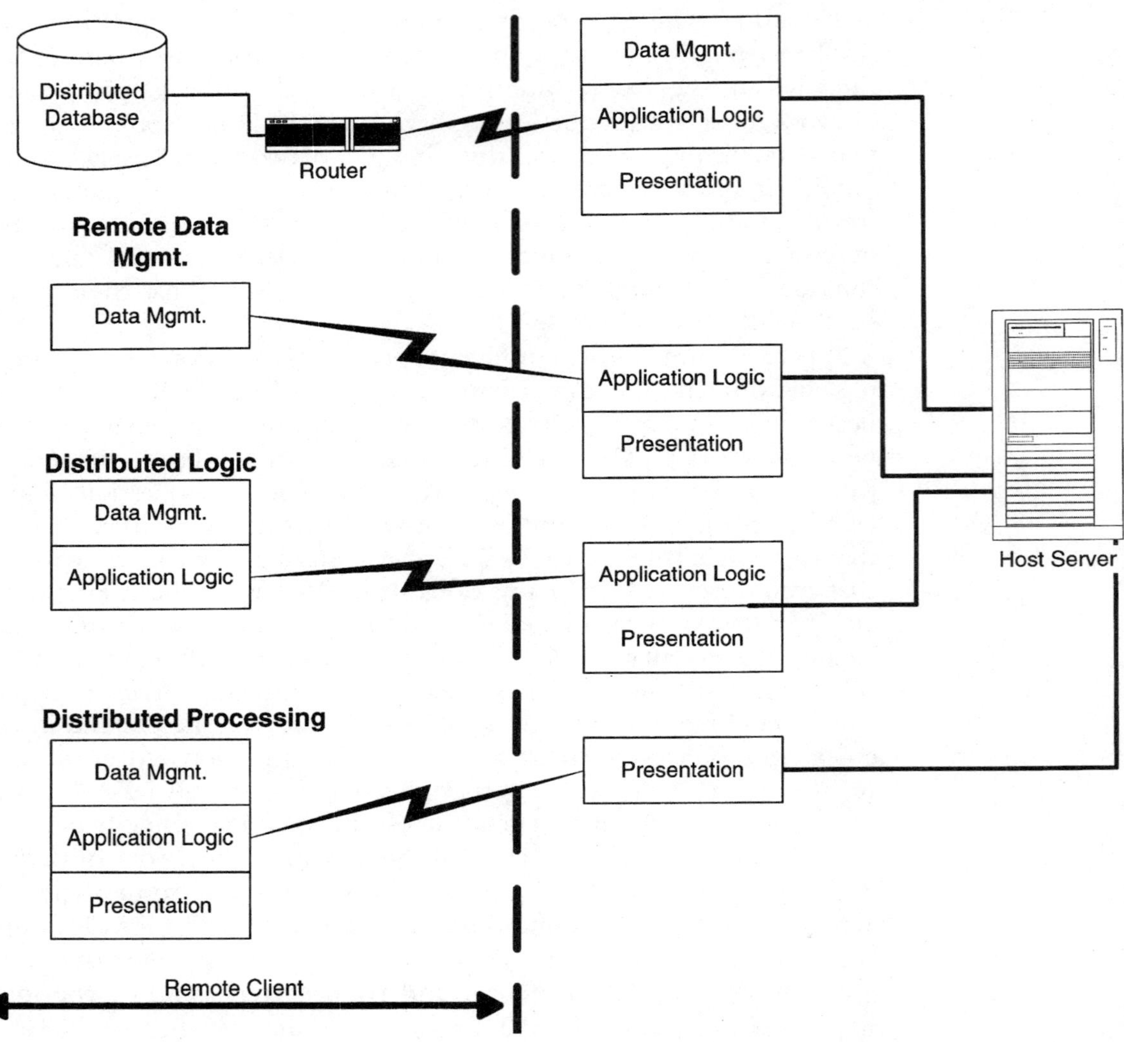

Figure 12.3 Cooperative processing places the various components where they are needed.

data, whereas the server controls the logic and presentation across a GUI via a Windows, X Windows, or some other environment.

Still a third approach is being used directly below the second. It uses a distributed logic function at the client level as opposed to the server. Note here a slight difference has occurred. In the distributed logic, at the remote location or client device, data management capability and a portion of the application logic (possibly a shell) are located at the local workstation itself. This portion internetworks with the host, which also controls a portion of the application logic. Therefore, the logic is actually distributed between the client and the server together. As these two pieces of the logic work together, the presentation and the GUI-type interfaces are still controlled at the server end. This is merely another means of distributing the data-processing capability among multiple computing platforms across the client/server internetwork.

Finally, the last function shown in this graphic is a fully distributed processing environment. In this particular case, the remote client device has the three functions, that being data management, the application, and logic, the structure of the shell and so on, as well as a portion of the presentation to the user device. Note that the presentation is still distributed between the host-based server and the client itself. In this particular case, it is only the presentation of the data that works between the server and the client, whereas the application logic and the data management still reside at the local client itself.

These examples are just several different ways that a cooperative processing environment can emerge in a client/server internetwork using a high-speed communications facility to link this information together. It should be noted that, depending where these functions reside, various amounts of information are required to pass between the client and the server. In the final example of a distributed processing environment, all of the manipulation, presentation, and logic reside at the client, so only some data sets are necessary to achieve access in a distributed processing capability to the server. Conversely, in a distributed database environment, all of the logic and control is controlled at the server. Therefore, it is the data that would be moved back and forth between the server across the internetwork, which means that more information must flow between the database and the server in the second example than in the first. How much data we wish to move across the network is important in the design and structure of the client/server applications. More data moving across the network requires faster, higher-speed communications channels, which in turn could require more cost. Less data moving across the internetwork requires more processing power at the desktop or the client level, meaning higher-cost hardware but lower-cost communications channels. The two examples in between these two extremes are the remote data management and the distributed logic function, but in this particular case, it would just be a variation of one of the two examples already cited. These considerations are part of the design criteria that a client/server networking manager must take into account as a full client/server architecture is built out. No one answer solves every organization's needs. These are but four different choices in a cooperative processing environment that can be selected. Other options are available.

In many cases, if the data is distributed, as in the fourth example, for distributed processing and the data resides at the client location, backing up that data is far more complex than if it were located at a centralized server. The other side of that equation, however, is that if the server is lost, all the data would be lost simultaneously. Using the distributed processing environment, if the server is lost, the client could still work independently without the use of the server for short periods of time without the risk of lost data. The burden of the data backup, protection, and security is placed on multiple devices as opposed to a single device. In the case of the distributed database, all of the information—the data—resides at one location so a single, regulated, scheduled backup function could protect the data much more cleanly.

In Fig. 12.4, another application for the client/server internetwork involves the ability to universally access data for remote computing capabilities. In this particular figure, a group of users connected to a LAN would access the various organizational data sets via an application server. The three-computer environment is now a little more visible. From the LAN, users would request information from a shell that might exist on the application server. This server would then spawn off a process on a mainframe or a midrange server, depending on the data the user is looking to access. By using this application server, remote procedure calls can be extended to the mainframe to access any system files, any virtual system access method (VSAM) files or any relational database, whatever portion of it may reside there. Where a user needs access to other portions of a relational database or hooks to a completely different database, that access can be spawned from the application server to the midrange server housing that data. Very specific, confidential files may also exist at the midrange server accessible to some users based on authorization through the application server. By segmenting or keeping these confidential files separate, the application server sitting between the client and the large servers would be able to determine who and what applications could access these confidential files. This function brings that three-computer architecture to the forefront by using the application server as the front-end process, allowing the client working at the desktop to access whatever data sets are necessary spread across distributed computing platforms. It would be the application server that provides a

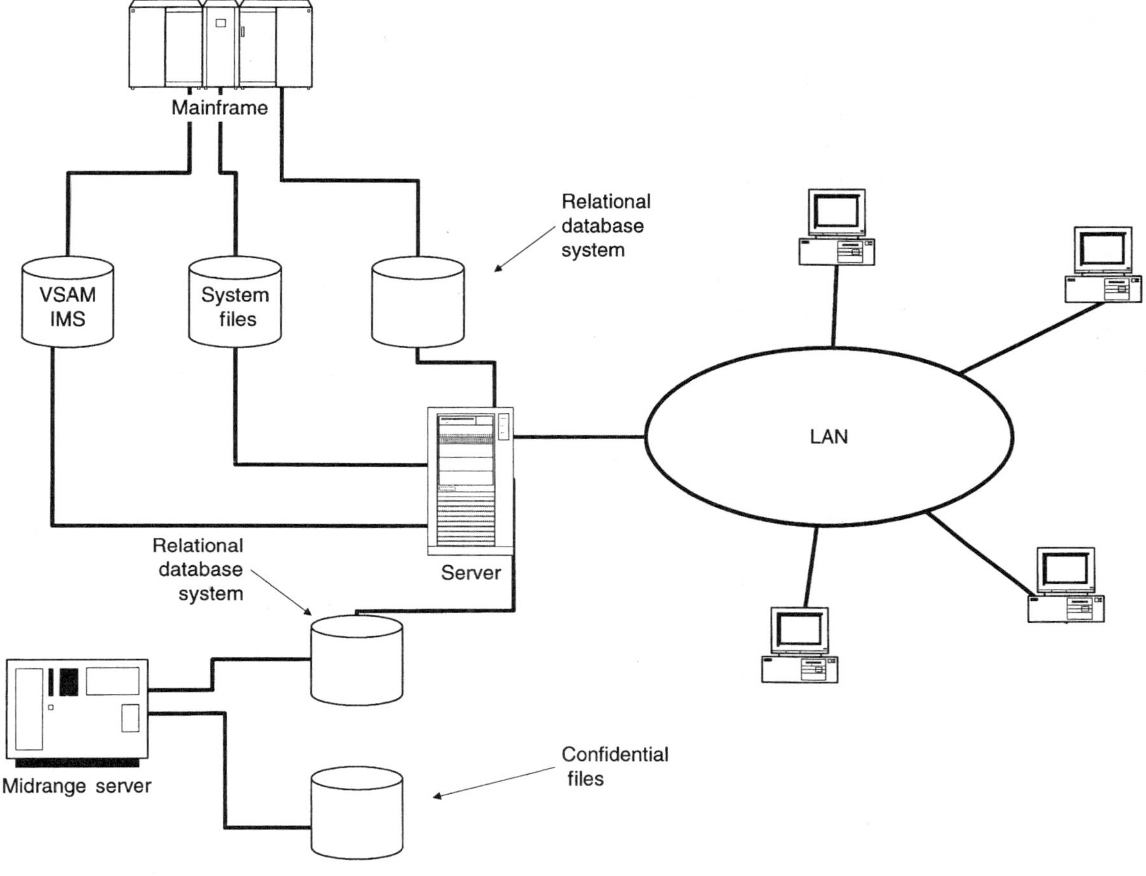

Figure 12.4 Universal data access/remote computing is a natural fit for client/server networking.

good portion of the presentation as well as the data management and the data logic capabilities.

One can begin to see how some of the client/server internetworks function within an organization to allow universal access to data regardless of the platform where it resides. With these particular platforms, the LAN user may be on NetWare, OS/2, or NT, yet by transparent use of a TCP/IP requester, the information would then be sent to perhaps a PC-based application server. The mainframe may be running SNA/SDLC architecture, whereas the midrange could be running a completely separate set of protocols. These are some of the pieces that start to pull it all together and make the transparency and the usability of the data ever so evident. There is no major mystique involved here—strictly the ability to establish the remote procedure calls, spawn off the processes through threads, and bring the information back down to the individual client workstation, regardless of the source. The client workstation, on the other hand, may be running one window or multiple simultaneous windows to view and manipulate the data. It depends on how the client/server networking manager has established the connection and the database in which to access these different data sets of information.

In contrast, Fig. 12.5 represents a different way of accessing the data in a distributed client/server environment. In this figure, several different components are used to link all the different pieces together. For example, a midrange system may be positioned in the middle of the figure. Regardless of the manufacturer or the operating system run here, the server is really the piece that most people are trying to access. Note several different pieces now come into play. From the wide area network, two different architectures can be used to access this information. On the left of the figure a frame relay service may be used. Note that individual locations serving PCs, terminals, or high-end workstations can all use the permanent virtual connection across the frame relay network to access this midrange server. The data is readily available to these devices—for all intents and purposes it appears that they have a dedicated link, even though they don't. Access to the server or midrange platform would be fairly straightforward based on the addressing information that is being handled. Other pieces involved in this architecture, such as a router or bridging capability, would exist at each of the three sites attached to the frame relay network, as well as at the main corporate site where the main server exists.

To the right of the figure, a different scenario plays out. In this case, an entire LAN, such as a branch office or remote field office, can access all its own data on its own localized network. However, when occasional access is needed to the midrange platform again, a router or some other technique is used to access the server on a dial-up, circuit-switched telephone call. This access can also be achieved on an ISDN link using either 64 or 128 kbps. Remote dial-up access from a terminal device at a telecommuter's office or home can also be used across this dial-up telephone network to access this midrange platform. It would be a distributed client in a client/server environment with a centralized server providing all of the access and the data necessary to support the completion of the mission of the organization.

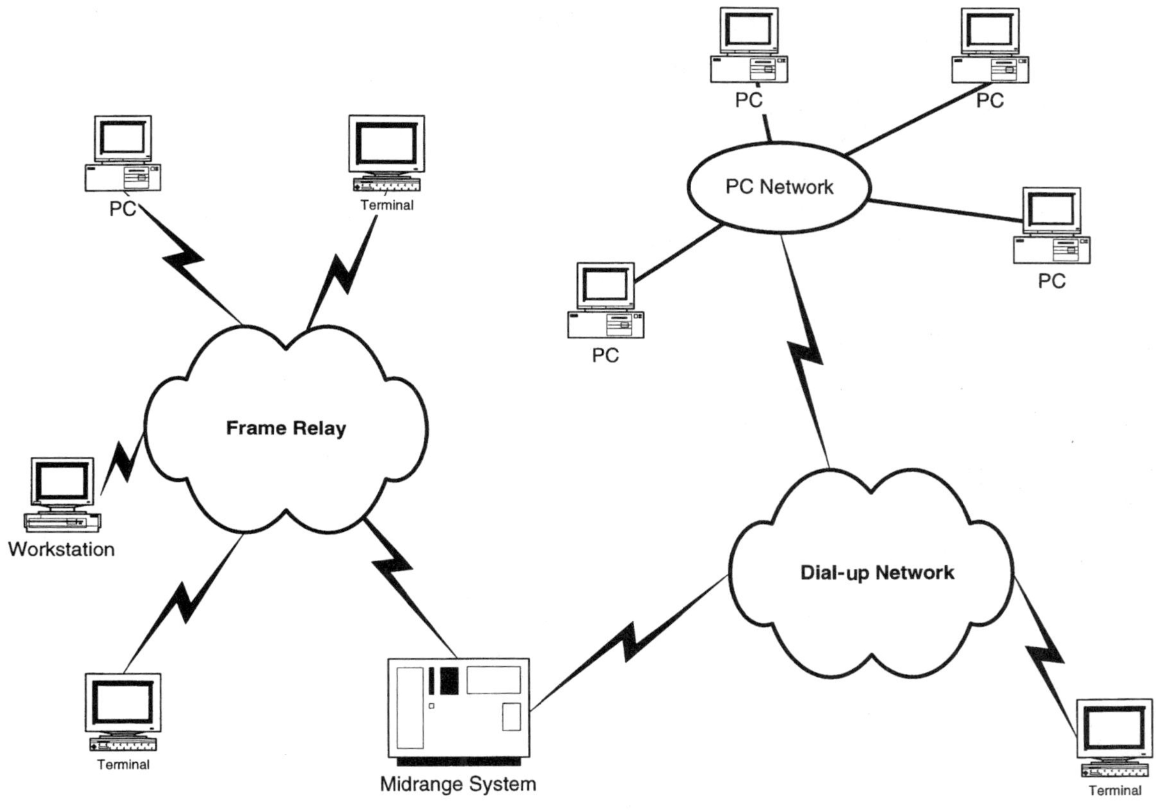

Figure 12.5 Distributed client/server components internetwork across the WAN in many forms.

Still another possible way of using this client/server internetwork is to consider the connectivity shown in Fig. 12.6. Here again, several different alternatives may be available to an end user or to an entire organization. In the core of this client/server information delivery mechanism, a high-end server function is available through each of the users located, for example, in the Boston area. Here in this high-end server, we know that several different pieces or applications are running on the particular server. First, a database system is available to users. Second, all e-mail applications, such as the post office protocols, would be supported on this server. Spreadsheet applications for the PC-based LAN would be available. Human resources information, such as a database of all employees and benefits and a list of applicants, can all be housed on this

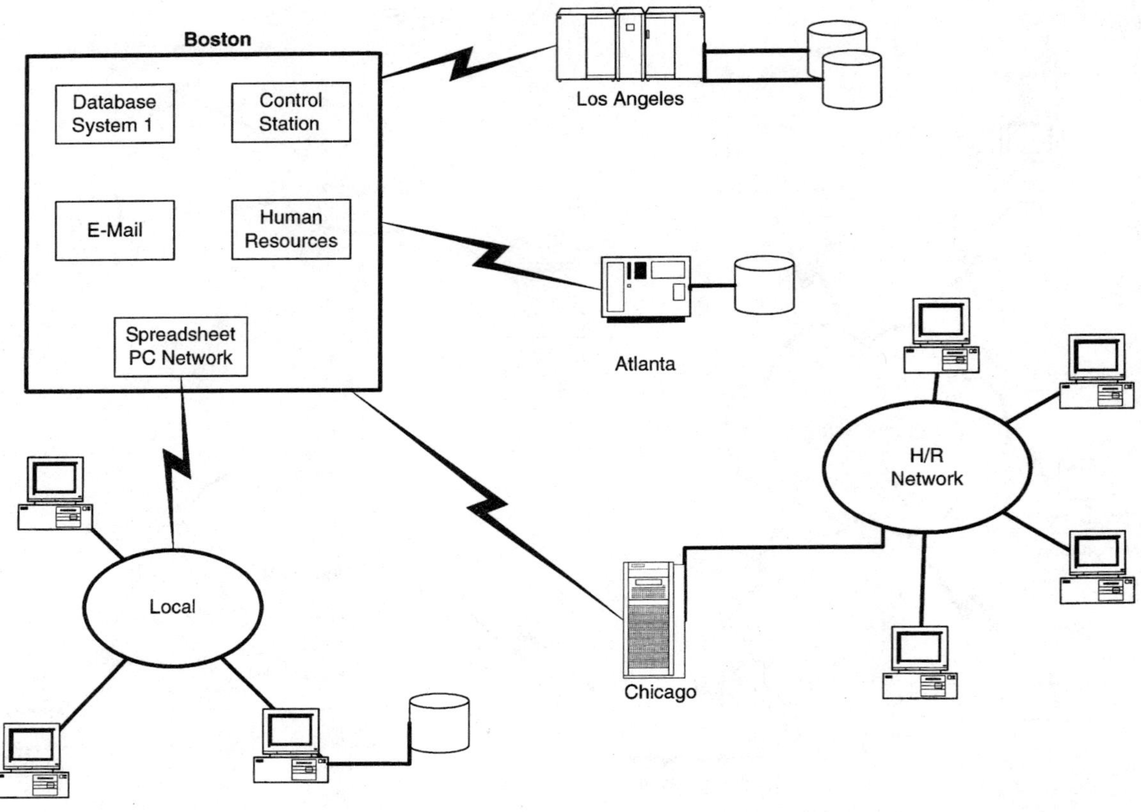

Figure 12.6 Information delivery is a prime application for client/server internetworks.

one high-end server. And lastly, control-station information or control of the entire network could be provided at this Boston location.

Working out from this location in Boston, a point-to-point or a frame relay circuit may be used to a server located in Chicago, providing capabilities for the human resources department in the Chicago office. Here this server acts as the middle-of-the-road server for the human resources LAN located in Chicago to access the human resources database located in Boston. This access can be achieved across a point-to-point or frame relay circuit, as already mentioned. As the users bring up the shell or the application they need to access, they would be doing so on the server located in Chicago. This server, recognizing it does not have the information, spawns a query out to the centralized database sitting in the Boston area and draws down the human resources information requested.

Also away from the Boston area is a midrange server located in Atlanta. Atlanta may have information that resides on that midrange server, such as portions of a database or an entire database, which again can be linked together through some virtual or some physical link between Boston and Atlanta. Users trying to access information from the LANs in either Chicago or Boston would go through the main server that would then spawn a process off to the Atlanta midrange platform to gain access to the data. Lastly, at a site in the Los Angeles area, we see a mainframe environment. This legacy system would probably support multiple databases, containing information that spans decades for this organization. In this particular case, the disk farms may have pieces of the database or may have just access to corporate information that would be used in a database. As any one of the users sitting on the LANs in Boston or Chicago requests information through the Boston server, it in turn would spawn off a process to Los Angeles to retrieve or query the data and bring the results down to the client workstation. Regardless of where the information exists, the data is truly accessible for information delivery purposes. The transparency is what is important. None of these users would recognize that they were connecting to different sites; instead, they would strictly look at it as a desktop operation that they're running from their own desks.

Figure 12.7 shows a slightly different variation to this client/server architecture. A server-based data distribution system is used here. A single, high-end server with all of the data is located between two different LANs. They can either be local or distant across the wide area. Regardless of the distance or the proximity of the device, each of the LANs has equal access to this high-end server. A high-speed Ethernet connection serving one group of users can be used for normal day-to-day activities, but when access to the server is needed, an application server residing on the Ethernet would spawn off the remote procedure call and create a thread to the server. This access may be achieved on a point-to-point leased line, a frame relay, an ATM network, or just a local attachment, depending on the LAN where the server is located. It can also be mirrored with a token ring operating at 4 or 16 Mbps with the same structure and the same access methodology. Note that regardless of whether a bus or ring topology is used in the local area environment, the access to the server is what is important. In each case, both of the application servers residing on each of the LANs provide the connection to the server to access the data. This data, when manipulated, entered, or altered at the high-end server level, would be available to all users regardless of their location or what type of LAN they have. Each of these networks could also be operating on disparate operating systems. The connections are made somewhat transparently. The true intent of the client/server network is to provide the internetworking capability so that the data can move quickly and efficiently from device to device regardless of its location, the topology it resides on, or the operating system that is being used down at the desktop level. The internetwork provides the transport of the information from point A

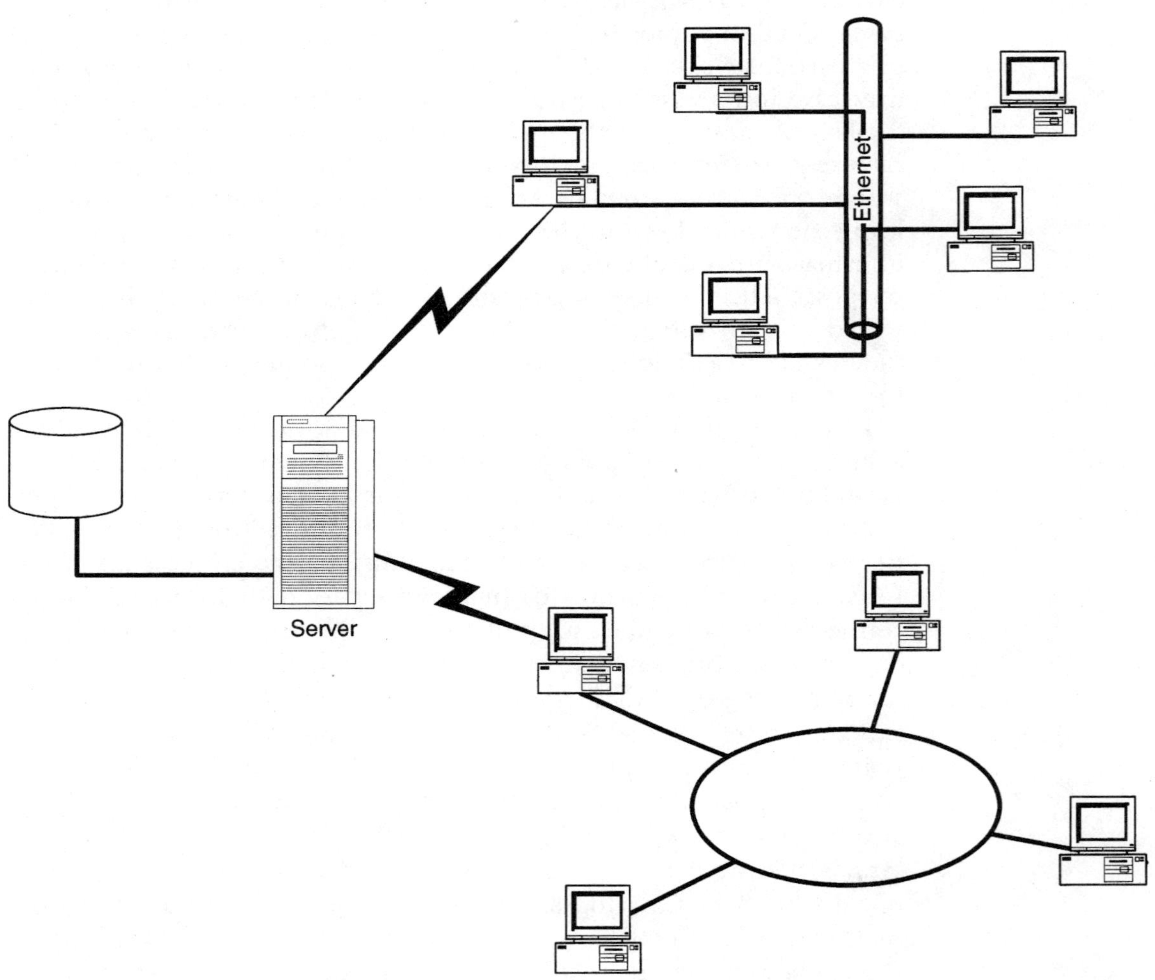

Figure 12.7 Server-based data distribution is another prime application.

to point B, but it allows the sharing of information between disparate devices or disparate LANs, again regardless of where they reside. This is what client/server internetworking is all about.

The intent of these examples is to give the reader some idea of the variations in how such a network can be set up, and still other examples will mirror the same applications or same infrastructure or will be totally different. It all depends on how the client/server internetworking manager chooses to establish and set up the total configuration. One only needs to use imagination to determine which way to set up the configuration. No single solution solves all needs.

Figure 12.8 shows a simplistic approach to the client/server internetwork. The intent here is to draw back a little bit and view what we're trying to accomplish with an internetworking function. Here we look at a client/server internetwork for remote computing functions. The client, located on the right of this figure, may be a stand-alone PC or a device attached to a LAN. At this point, it really doesn't much matter, as long as it is understood that the data resides somewhere else. A user at the individual client device may have a shell for an application and need to access the data for the remote computing architecture. This shell, of course, shows that the information is not available to the client locally. Therefore, as the user tries to open up a particular application or a specific data set within the application, the shell recognizes that this information resides somewhere else. A remote procedure call, in the form of a remote request, is sent across the wide area network to the server. The server houses the data in a database or in a disk farm, as well as all tape backups, catalogues, and libraries of all other data sets that are available. As the remote request is generated across the network, it moves to the server device, where the server will then determine the location of the data or the application and open up that process. Now what happens is as the request is generated to the server and the server executes the appropriate commands, the result of the action or command is then generated back across the wide area network.

This is as simplistic as it can possibly be, but careful thought about where to place the server and where to keep the clients is required. Placing all clients at a remote location with the server at a single location device places the burden on the internetwork to carry more and more data back and forth. If the information is to be generated locally and only a request for a particular file or record is being used, then less data has to move across the network. This tends to drive home the point mentioned earlier about where the effort and budgetary expenses will

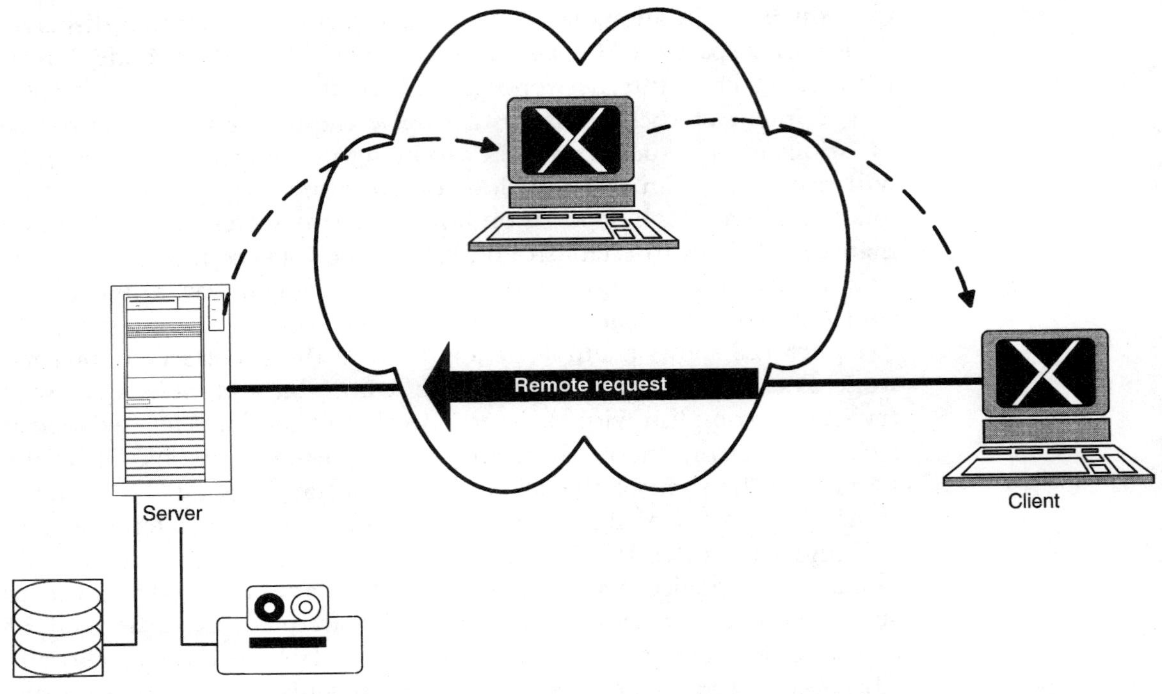

Figure 12.8 Client/server remote computing works across the internetwork by spawning a process.

be spent. Does the client/server architecture require higher-end processing power at every single device, or should it just be a high-speed communications network with low-power devices sitting at the desktop?

Throughout these different applications and different uses of the client/server network one merely has to look at how the data and the organizations happen to coexist. Not all users need a dedicated server, nor does replication of the data make sense. Consequently, it is the internetwork that would be used to provide the access to data that is needed occasionally or even more frequently so that the data is not duplicated in many different locations. This duplication would cost capacity, processing power, and facilities. Using high-speed communications links can minimize such duplication, but it does require additional communications networking support. In the figure, the individual client device may be strictly a stand-alone PC operating at maybe a 586 (Pentium) platform with a standard configuration, graphics, graphics cards, monitors, memory capacity, and disk storage. One would not want to build out high-end processing at the desktop if this capability exists at the server and can easily be achieved through the network.

Another application that has been fairly well deployed throughout many organizations is the use of human resources information. Figure 12.9 shows a human resources server. This server may be attached to a LAN, or it may be strictly a stand-alone device with connectivity spread throughout the country. It may also be accessible through an application server on a LAN or from the remote computing users at individual branch offices or telecommuters working from home. The real intent is to bring all of the pieces together into a single computing environment that allows access to the information based on users or on need. Human resources information would therefore be a large database that serves multiple different subsets of the application. In this particular case, a database of all human resources activities may support the following:

1. *Application tracking.* The ability to track all applicants who have ever submitted an employment application might be useful to determine at which step in the review process an application is currently.

2. *Applicants interviewed.* A list could be generated to determine with which mangers or supervisors the applicant has met. This information may be useful in the event of defending against a suit for discrimination or as a tracking method to determine the historical evaluations from individual supervisors based on the applications that had been sent to them.

3. *Americans with Disabilities Act compliance.* ADA compliance requires that specific actions and concessions be granted to employees who have disabilities. When disabled persons have applied for employment within an organization, the government has certain requirements for reporting the status of applications. A database can be used to track any disabled individuals in the recruitment process.

4. *User-defined personnel actions.* Users might be able to apply for other jobs posted within the organization or update their files with new information, such as completion of degrees, changes in status, or other information.

5. *Skills, training, or educational tracking.* A database can be built listing all the skill sets, additional training, and education an employee may acquire while a member of the organization. Whenever a manager or supervisor needs a specific skill set or

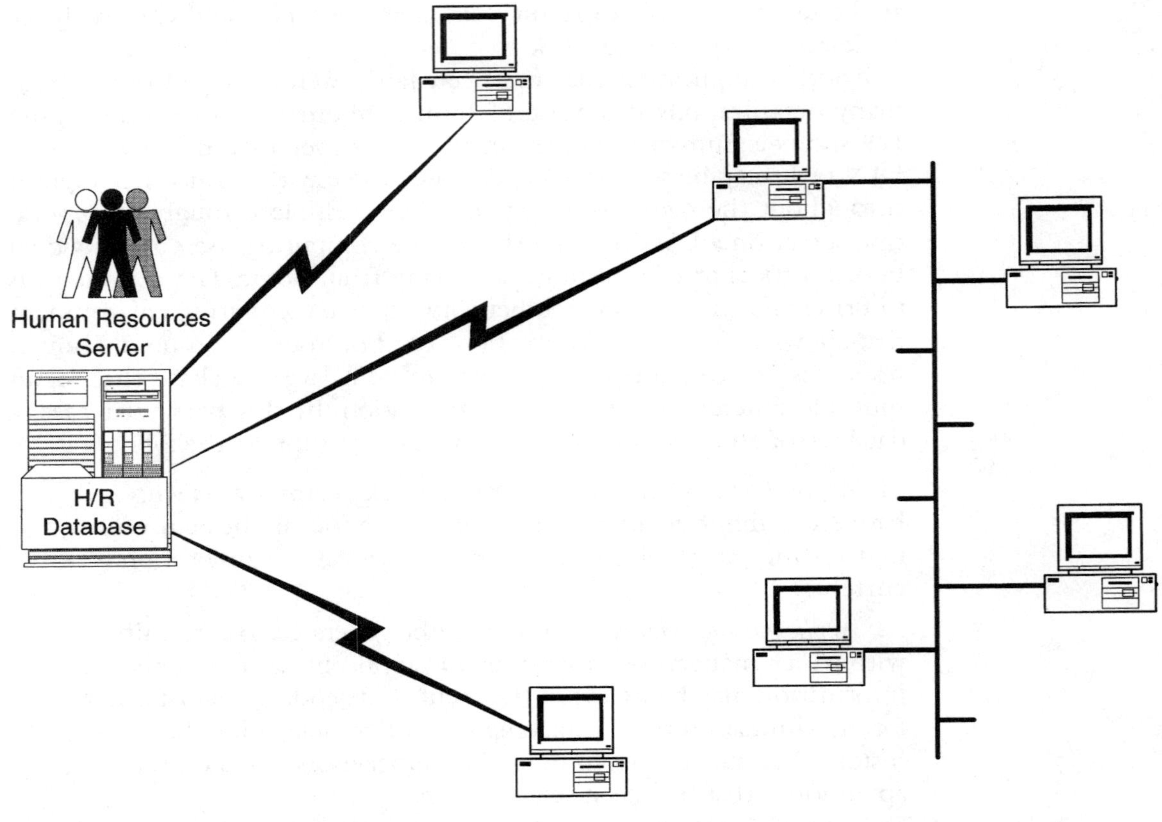

Figure 12.9 Human resources applications work nicely on a client/server internetwork.

specific types of training, this database can be accessed to determine a list of possible candidates to fill that position.

6. *Employee history/review scheduling.* A historical file pertaining to each employee, including date of hire, scheduled dates of review, past performance reviews, and so on, can be compiled and used in this database. It would be a useful tool for managers as well as human resources personnel in determining compliance with legal guidelines or in determining availability of employees for promotion, transfers, or new assignments.

7. *Wage and salary administration.* A database can be used to track conformance as well as incremental increases that are expected or

demanded by employees. A supervisor can scan the database and determine the historical file of an employee in terms of escalation in the salary range. Human resources, on the other hand, may look at the wage and salary portion to ensure that supervisors are giving regular evaluations and increases, based on the organization's policies and procedures.

8. *Planning the workforce.* Human resources personnel, recognizing that managers and supervisors are continually requesting additional skill sets or personnel to meet job demands, can use the database in planning for the workforce. This tool allows a scheduled hiring in advance of actual need, allowing for the orientation and custom training necessary for employees before the actual job demand exists. While planning the workforce, supervisors and managers would have a significant amount of input to the human resources department so that they can determine if any in-house employees already possess some of the skill sets necessary for future job requirements.

9. *Basic inquiry information.* Employees might send inquiries to human resources about possible job opportunities, training opportunities, transfers, or lateral movement capabilities. This type of database would allow various departmental managers and supervisors, as well as the human resources department, to interact with each other more efficiently.

10. *EEO/OSHA reporting.* The legal system requires that human resources departments submit regular reports regarding Equal Employment Opportunity and Occupational Safety and Health Administration compliance. This database can be used to track the degree of EEO compliance, the variations or the incidence of accidents on the job, as well as illnesses that may occur as a direct result of the job. Without such a database, gathering the information is a manual and tedious process that would require various managers and supervisors to submit regular input, which would then be regenerated on the forms required by the government. If all of this information resided in a single database that has input capabilities from the various supervisors and managers, the duplication of effort can be eliminated.

11. *Job searches by employees.* Employees could periodically log on to the human resources database to determine if any new jobs have been

posted for which they meet the skill sets required and what the minimum or maximum skills are for this position. If the employee is qualified, he or she could then use an input form to submit his or her name and skill sets. This information can be hooked to the database to allow human resources personnel to pull up the employee's file for consideration.

This human resources server and the function that is being used throughout many organizations are part of the client/server internetwork. It is particularly valuable with widely dispersed geographical locations housing multiple sites around the country or the world, allowing the various departments to use and access the data as needed. In no way does this whole database become available to all users; therefore, using the internetwork, only the pieces that are allowed to be used based on user ID or password as well as some protocol discrimination could be accessed. The information that resides on this server is still confidential, and the appropriate steps must be applied to protect that information from unnecessary or unauthorized altering, access, manipulation, or disclosure.

Another very popular application in a client/server internetwork environment is the use in a manufacturing environment of a heavy GUI-based menu system, as shown in Fig. 12.10. This menu system is used extensively in manufacturing operations, but it could be modified to meet just about any application as necessary. Note that 12 icon-based menus are available on the screen for the menu application. In this particular case in the client/server architecture, the server can be just about anywhere in a manufacturing environment, such as process control or production control, that would be accessible to the various organizational departments in scheduling or coordinating the manufacturing process. This application can include such things as

1. *Work-order generation and tracking.* An icon-based work order to submit or track a work order by number can be sequentially driven by the server.

2. *Time-keeping events.* Employee hours, time in work in progress, and other timed information can be tracked very effectively throughout the entire production process.

3. *Setup icons.* These icons are available only to certain limited users based on setting up or reconfiguring some of the icons that already exist or to change some of the database applications. This setup menu

Figure 12.10 The client/server internetwork uses GUI-driven menus to provide the interface in a manufacturing environment.

would allow administrators to configure their particular departmental needs or their particular screen needs by user.

4. *Inventory control and status.* Checking availability of inventory in stock, checking raw materials in stock or on order, tracking work in progress, and locating the final product could be supported by this database.

5. *Purchasing icon.* Managers or supervisors could use this icon to generate a purchase request or request for quote. It would bring up a form that would allow the individual user departments or production departments to generate a request for a product or raw materials needed for the manufacturing process.

6. *Preventative maintenance icon.* This icon could be used for scheduling downtime necessary on machinery or on facilities, such as the building HVAC and lighting facilities. This icon, again, is not available to all users for updates and status, but could be available when preventative maintenance is scheduled so that the production-line personnel know when

particular portions of their production space will not be available.

7. *Drafting icon.* This icon would be used for the engineering department to generate new drawings on a separate server and still make the information available to the production process if new forms or new drawings are needed. This icon might access a database for engineering services so that if a particular product needs to be built to specific specifications, the engineering drawings can be pulled down and viewed at the workstation level.

8. *Utilities icon.* This icon could be used for several different processes. Utilities may involve just a reporting or updating of the database functions. Another use may well be in utilities such as electrical, water, sewer, and so on, where tracking can be provided to determine the cost for utilities in the production process. This information could be particularly useful in the event that custom devices and manufacturing are being generated and additional electrical and other facilities are required, which can be billed back as part of the production process.

9. *Notes icons.* These icons are available for ad hoc information such as e-mail or technical notes sent to engineering or purchasing departments in the event of a quality-control problem. In this particular case, the notes could be available to all for reading but not necessarily for editing or deleting.

10. *Labor icon.* A labor icon might be used for the scheduling of labor necessary in the production process, such as shift work, overtime, holiday work, and schedules.

11. *Calendar icon.* This icon is used to schedule the production process out over a longer period of time. It can either be a monthly, quarterly, or annual calendar, based on how the production department wishes to forecast and project the availability of resources, production capacity, or shutdown activities.

12. *Machinery icon.* This icon would be used to schedule specific or particular pieces of machinery necessary in a production process so that back orders or backlogs do not occur or are minimized. Any new machinery that is scheduled to be brought on line can be shown through this database, and it can also show how resources can be enhanced or brought up to speed based on the new availability of machines during a production process. This machinery icon can also be hooked to other facilities, such as preventative maintenance and utilities, to give an overall picture of the manufacturing process.

This type of menu system allows for a lot of flexibility within a manufacturing process so that supervisory and managerial personnel can access the databases or subsets of databases to do scheduling, time keeping, and cost tracking for production purposes. For this type of process, the server can reside just about anywhere, so long as it is available across the internetwork to all the appropriate departments that need access to the information or need input capabilities. In the event some of the data does not reside in this particular database, the server could spawn off the remote procedure call to a remote server elsewhere, such as an engineering server where the drawings can be brought down on an as-needed basis.

One can see how the client/server internetwork mixing and matching of interfaces and applications can add some depth to the organization's ability to meet the demands of its customer base. This ability is what the client/server internetwork is all about—the ability to meet the demands of the organization within a reasonable amount of time without replicating the data in multiple places. One can imagine how big the databases would be and how much additional data would be kept if these devices were independent of each other as opposed to internetworked to each other. Keeping the databases up to date would be the responsibility of the individual departments that have the input capabilities in each one of these icon-driven applications.

Figure 12.11 shows a fully distributed platform in a multiserver environment across the client/server internetwork. Note the numerous servers that would reside on a single LAN environment, such as an Ethernet bus. In this particular case, several different components come into play, making the variations in data and operating systems available to all users across the internetwork. Servers can provide the following types of services:

1. DOS applications, for those that still exist in a operation
2. OS/2 network systems where an OS application or operating system resides for specific uses
3. A NetWare server where specific applications and LAN operating systems are based on Novell's architecture

4. A UNIX server for specific applications that may be running, such as midrange platforms on a UNIX-based system
5. A mainframe legacy system, where legacy data resides on the IBM mainframe front-ended by either a gateway or a bridge function
6. A gateway server, although shown as a gateway PC, provides the access for the dial-in or local attached users who would be dialing into a gateway to access any one of the different operating systems listed, for total ubiquity and transparency for the end user

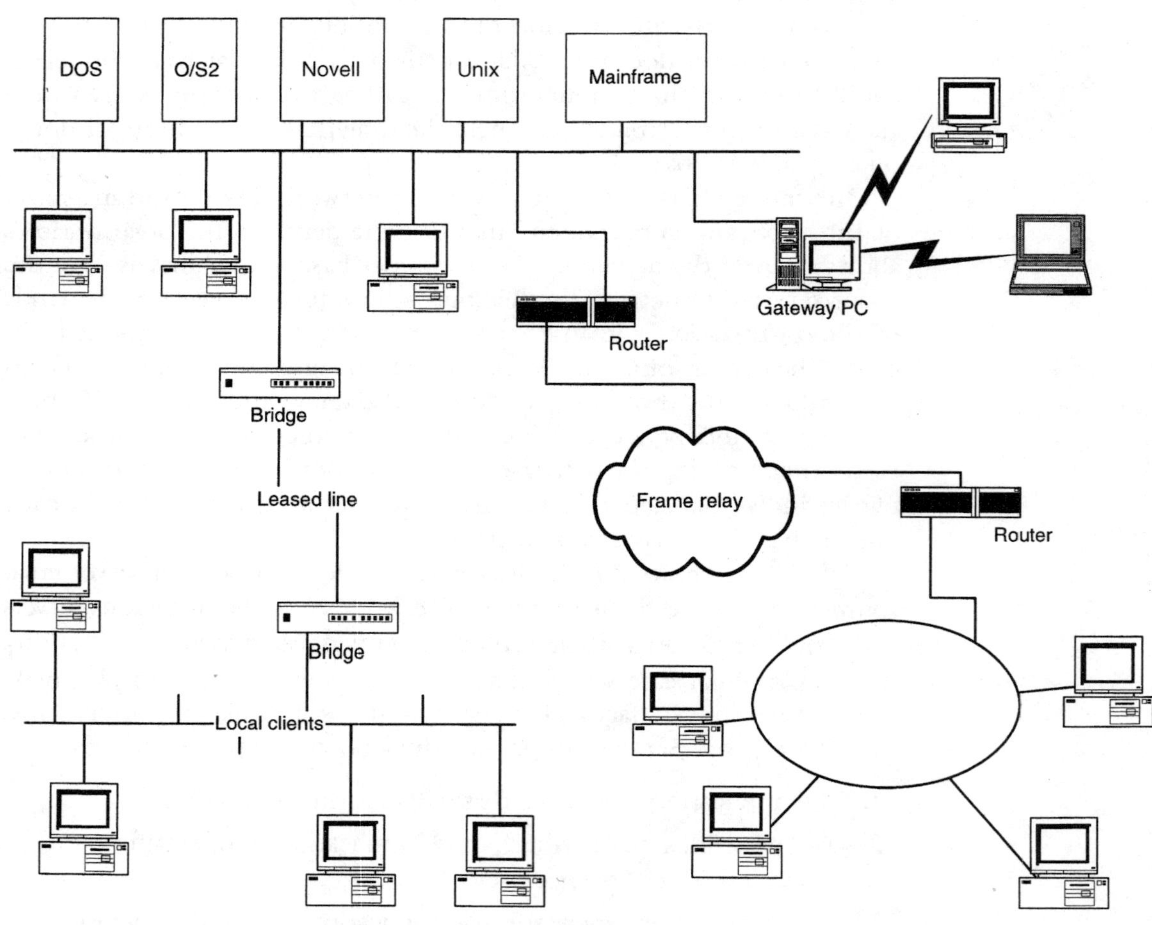

Figure 12.11 The internetwork connects multiple platforms in a distributed network.

This particular figure is useful in showing the multiple server platforms that can be supported on the client/server internetwork. This one high-end Ethernet with multiple servers shows that several different applications or several different operating systems can be accessed from any one of the remote clients, no matter where they reside. One LAN is attached through a leased line and bridging capabilities at a LAN-to-LAN environment using Ethernet, allowing all of the local clients access to any one of the servers necessary, either through a GUI or through a command-line interface (preferably the GUI). Additionally, token ring environments can be connected across the wide area network on an internetworked basis through routers connected to a frame relay network. Any user at one of the token-based PCs at the remote location would be able to spawn a process off to any one of the servers—DOS, NetWare, UNIX, or mainframe—allowing anyone within the organization to access the data regardless of location. This environment does not limit all of the access strictly to the servers that are shown on the drawing; other servers may reside at different LANs across the internetwork that would be available and accessible across the frame relay capability. What this figure really shows is the ability to mix and match the various operating systems and computing platforms, from single PC-based servers to midrange servers to the full mainframe, and still allow total ubiquity and transparency of the data to the end user sitting at a GUI-based workstation device. Regardless of whether it is bridged or routed, the network will find the connection to the appropriate server and open up the application as necessary.

Several of the applications that have already been discussed have addressed the various organizational departments in terms of the use and sharing of information throughout the client/server network. Figure 12.12 shows some of these pieces brought together in a slightly different fashion. Here, a centralized operational control server in the center of the figure is used for a control and access functionality between multiple departments within an organization. Notice that the MIS department, using a Windows-based capability that provides client/server applications and capabilities, could access servers that are running OS/2, NetWare, and UNIX. This access satisfies the needs and demands of the MIS department; however, some of the information may be extracted or deposited onto the central operational control server, which may be running a completely different operating system.

The maintenance department might have the capability of accessing several different applications, such as a CAD system where engineering

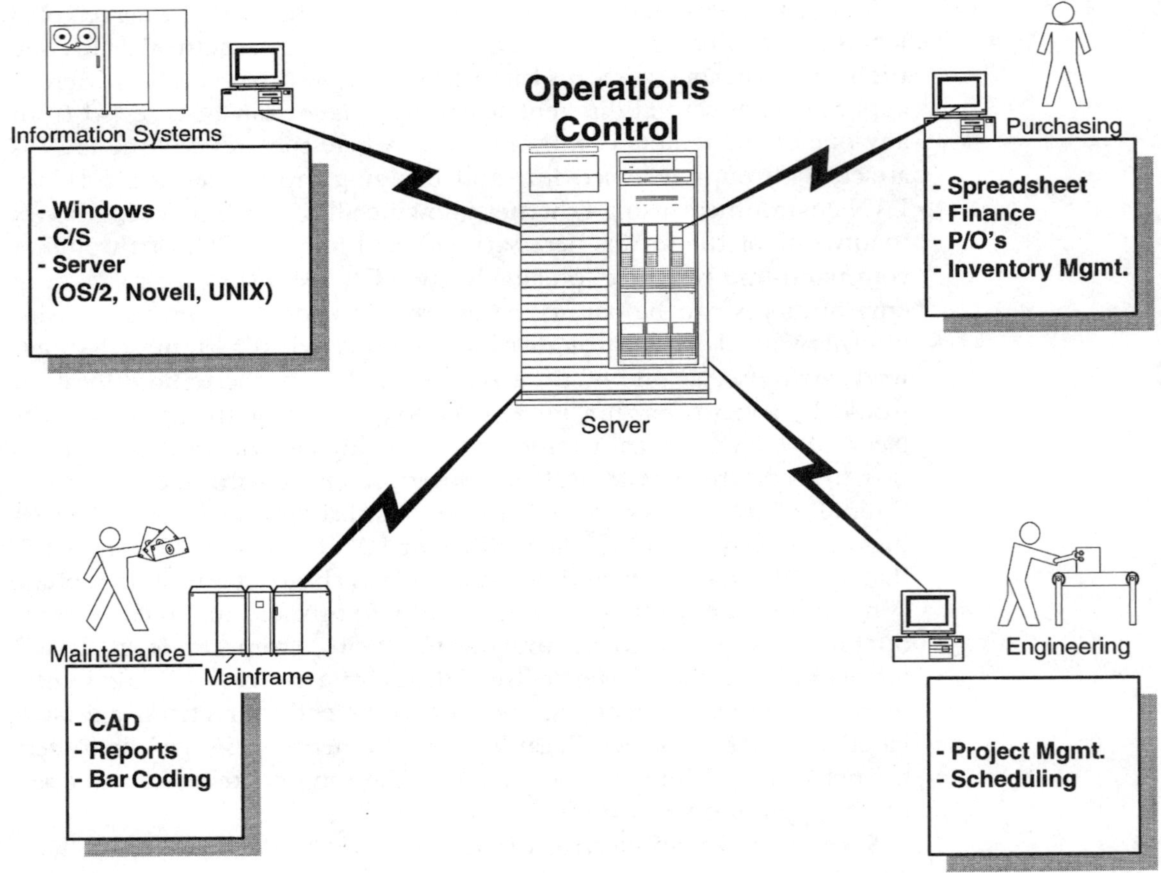

Figure 12.12 Operations control can be spread across the network, providing remote access.

drawings can be created and stored at the operational control server or locally at its own server with the database hooks from the operational control function. Additionally, report generation and bar-coding capabilities might also be available for inventory tracking as well as necessary maintenance reports.

Purchasing, in the upper right-hand corner of the illustration, is served by a server in the department and has access to specific pieces of information not necessarily accessible or available to others. This information would include such items as spreadsheets containing tracking and costing information, access to a financial database, and generation and access to a purchase-order system for order tracking and sequential order numbering and the like. An additional capability in the purchasing department would be inventory management and control information, all of which might reside on the centralized server or on the individual purchasing server, making it available to all.

Engineering, at the bottom right-hand side of the drawing, might use the operational control server for project management and control information, project timelines, and scheduling and maintenance information. All of these pieces come together through this central operational control server that would build the hooks or control the information locally. It is through the internetwork that these pieces are accessible and available to others as needed. The data would then be tightly integrated, or coupled, so that if the purchasing department needed to see something that was based on a schedule for project management in the engineering department, it would be readily available. Again, this is a simplistic approach to the client/server internetwork. The links between these various workstations or servers could be LANs, CANs, WANs, or MANs. The result is the same—total availability and accessibility to the data through a centralized high-end server device that either controls and houses the data or has the ability to spawn off the information request to multiple other servers.

Each of the applications addressed implies that either a centralized server or individual departmental servers may be used to house and control the information. Figure 12.13 shows the open client/server internetworking function. Here, three separate LANs are positioned in different parts of the country. Each of these LANs has its own attached workstations for local informational flow and work production. Each LAN has its own server that provides the necessary services to each of the individual departments using the capabilities of the network. However, when information must be accessed or delivered to another workstation across the remote wide area, the wide area networking capability comes into play.

Any user would be able to access any server on an open basis across this platform. Regardless of whether they are all rings, all bus topologies, or a mix of the two, the situation is that the data is readily available to any user requiring access to the data who has the right to it. In no way do we mean to imply that the data is readily available to anyone. Moreover, the setting up of the client/server internetwork involves control over by whom and when the data can be accessed. Certain users may be able to see all data, whereas others can only see

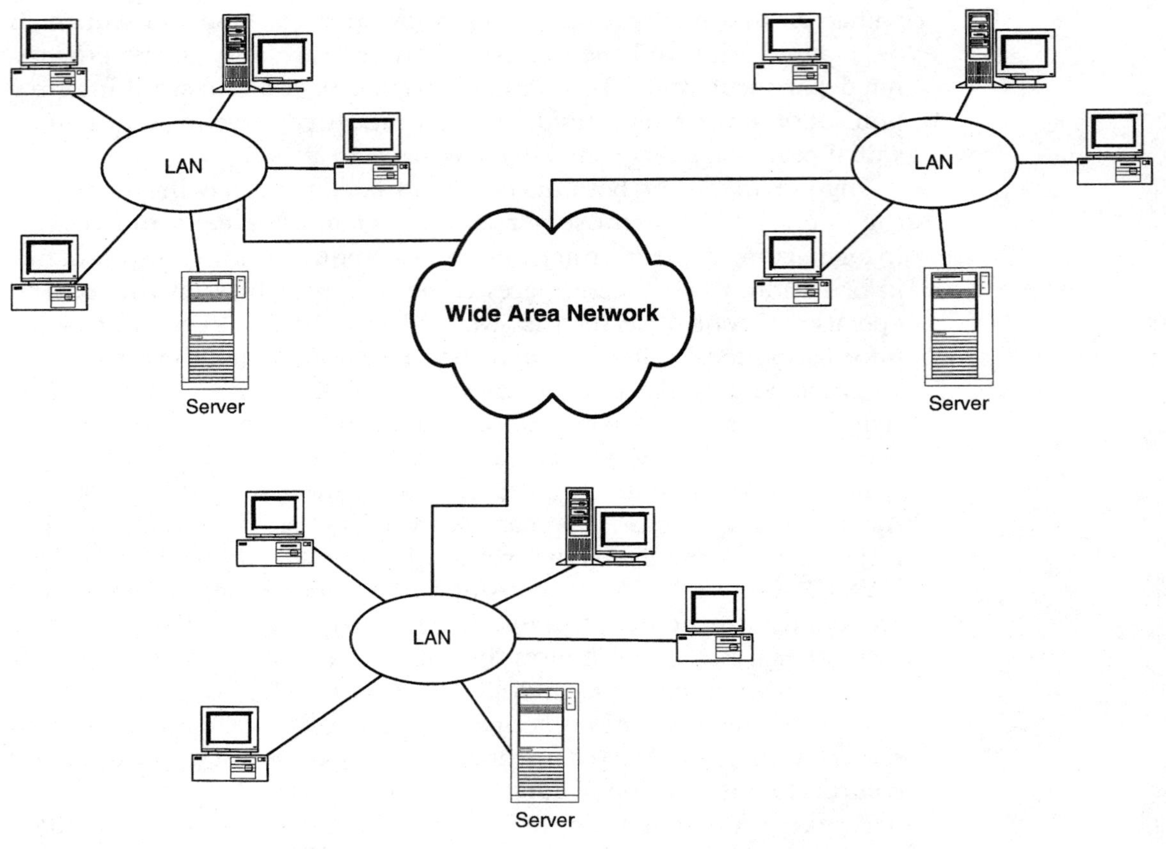

Figure 12.13 Open client/server internetworking becomes a reality.

subsets or just be able to read the data but not edit or delete it. These pieces must be kept in mind as the internetwork is built out so that the same controls can be applied universally across the wide area. Wide area networking becomes a crucial part in the client/server internetworking function. It would be inconceivable to imagine that an organization had to control and manage all the data at one local environment as a direct result of an internetwork. Instead, it is the internetworking functionality—through bridges, routers, or gateways—that makes the data available based on the individual organization's needs.

In the recent past, a lot of hype has been given to the client/server internetwork to support telemedicine and telelearning applications.

Through a client/server internetworking function, in a telemedicine environment, departments may access several different pieces of information from various locations around the country or around the globe. In this particular application, shown in Fig. 12.14, a higher-speed network may surely be needed to support the demands of the data being applied and used. The application may be served across the internetwork with a high-speed ATM or SMDS environment, allowing the end user access at native LAN speeds of 4, 10, or 16 Mbps or at the higher rates of 25.6 or 34 Mbps. Additional speeds are available at much higher cost, if needed.

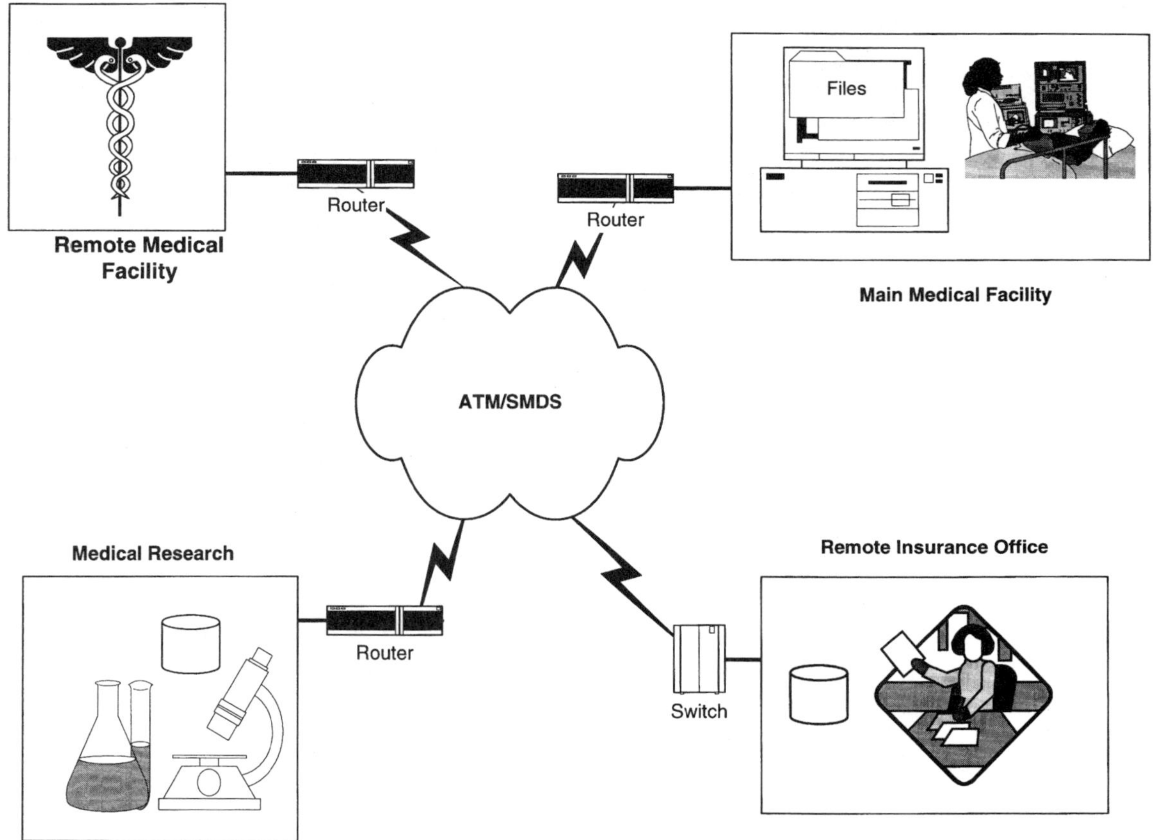

Figure 12.14 Medical applications use the internetwork in a telemedicine platform.

Using the example shown at a major medical facility, a high-end workstation driven by a GUI is being used. The windows can be used to access various pieces of information for a medical staff person to view. Across the high-speed router, a remote medical facility may be accessed where a particular patient file could be brought down to one of the windows in this multiwindowing station. Concurrently, using the high-speed network, a separate process can be opened at a medical research facility, such as a database query for access into the American Medical Association (AMA) on particular symptoms or prognosis of a patient's condition. While all of this is going on, a third window may be opened with a query to a remote insurance office to determine a patient's coverage and for prequalification and approval of procedural billing and services. This single multiwindow workstation located at the medical facility, therefore, has several sessions open concurrently across the wide area network. Using the internetworking capabilities of either routers or switches, the network can provide and deliver the data in a reasonable amount of time into a window environment, allowing the medical personnel located at the major medical facility to see various pieces of information across the internetwork prior to proceeding with a process. Using this telemedicine application, the ability to integrate the various pieces of information and make better decisions becomes a reality. This, of course, will be one of the single largest drivers for the internetwork using high-speed wide area networking facilities in the future. Not shown on this particular drawing is the availability of videoconference through a video server. A video server application exists that could allow two physicians at the remote and the main medical facility to discuss a patient's condition or prognosis.

As glorious and as elaborate as the telemedicine application in an internetwork may sound, there still exist very simplistic applications that need to use the facilities and capabilities of the internetwork, those being distributed databases. As shown in Fig. 12.15, a distributed database would be just an additional application that can be applied using this client/server internetwork. A user on a client device (workstation or PC or Mac) may well have a local database capability at that workstation. This database may reside on the local hard drive of this particular workstation or on a server attached to the same LAN. In the figure it is shown at the local workstation. A local database management system is available with local data attached. All of the structure in terms of the data itself is available to this client. The structure includes data management, logic, and presentation through the GUI-based environment.

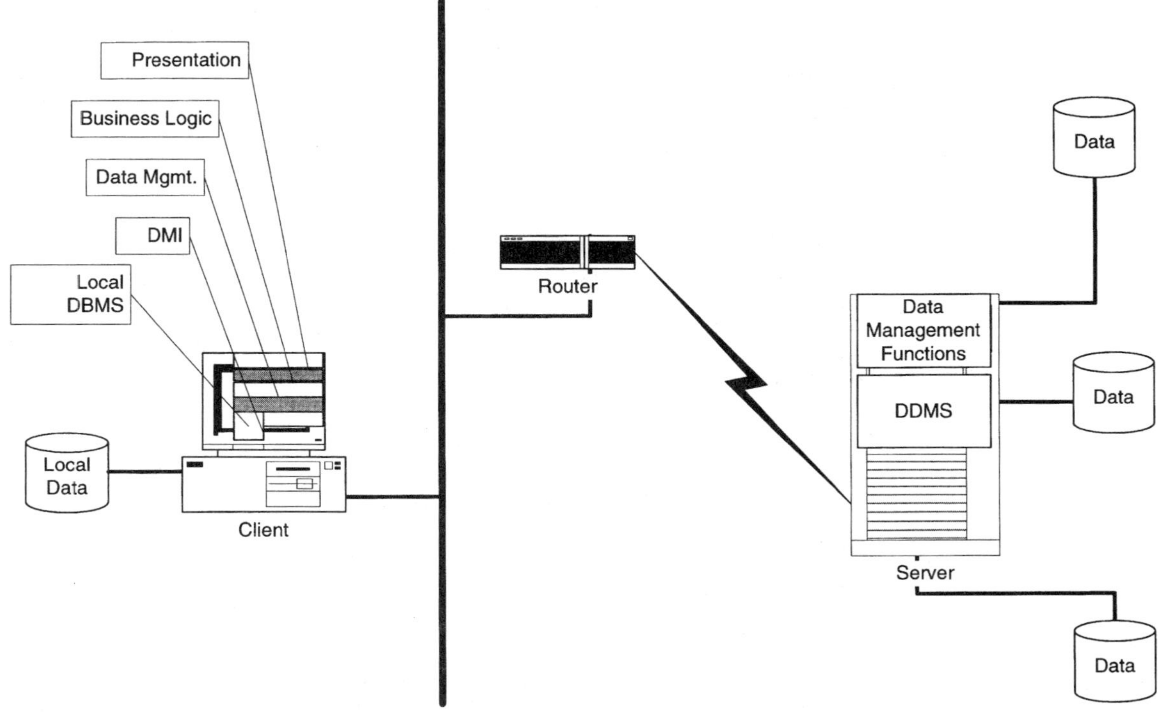

Figure 12.15 Applications for client/server internetworking include distributed databases.

In a distributed database environment, portions of the data may reside at different servers around the organization. From time to time, hooks may have to be built to multiple servers to extract records and files out of a different database to integrate them into a local database. In this particular case, a router would be used across the wide area network to access remote servers, each of which houses specific pieces of the data. Note that the data management functions and the distributed data management system functionality reside at each of the servers, and that the shell would therefore be available from the client to the server to access the data based on this distributed database management functionality. Some of the high-end database providers today clearly point that this is the way their product and market are going. Using this capability, it doesn't matter where the data resides, merely that the devices can internetwork and pass the data back and forth. As the data is updated on each of the individual databases, choices can be made whether to store it locally at the client device or continue to store it at the remote database. The preferred method, of course, is to store it at the remote database where the information already resides. This choice keeps the data in sync with the rest of the organization. It provides for transparency and also for harmony within the data sets that exist at various databases across the country or across the globe. One can just imagine what might happen if each of the database accesses was stored locally, changed, and manipulated, and multiple user departments that needed access to the data, files, and records would see different pictures and different cuts at the same time—total chaos. Therefore, as the user grabs and uses the data, the data would be updated on the database on which it resides, as opposed to just at the local client device. This again is where the internetwork comes into heavy play.

One of the simplest and yet more widely used applications in a client/server internetwork is transaction processing (Fig. 12.16). When looking at the historical content of all of the legacy data and legacy systems that reside across our networks, one must recognize that all of the data stored over 30 years cannot be easily disposed of or converted into some new architecture. Consequently, a good portion of our day-to-day business remains on the legacy transaction-processing systems. A host running an SNA/SDLC platform may still reside on the network. Using a gateway attached to a LAN, for example, the host becomes a main data depository for the legacy data that customers use. Clients attached locally can access the host-based server system and access the data management functions and the transaction-processing functions. The gateway will therefore take the Ethernet data frames that are being generated on this LAN and convert them to SDLC frames so that they are usable and understandable by the host. Moreover, when remote transaction-processing clients, such as a branch office or field office, need access to the host for transaction processing, the user would use the capability of a bridge or a router across a leased line or a virtual network connection. Here the transaction client would run a front-end process such as a shell for the transaction processing to emulate a 32/70-type device. Pulling up a form or a screen that is readily available to the transaction clients, these clients can access and manipulate the data as necessary. Through this architecture, the individual clients are transparent to the network and the host server is transparent to its own operating system. The client merely uses the data, updates the files, produces the transaction, and provides the end result. One can imagine what it would take to change out an

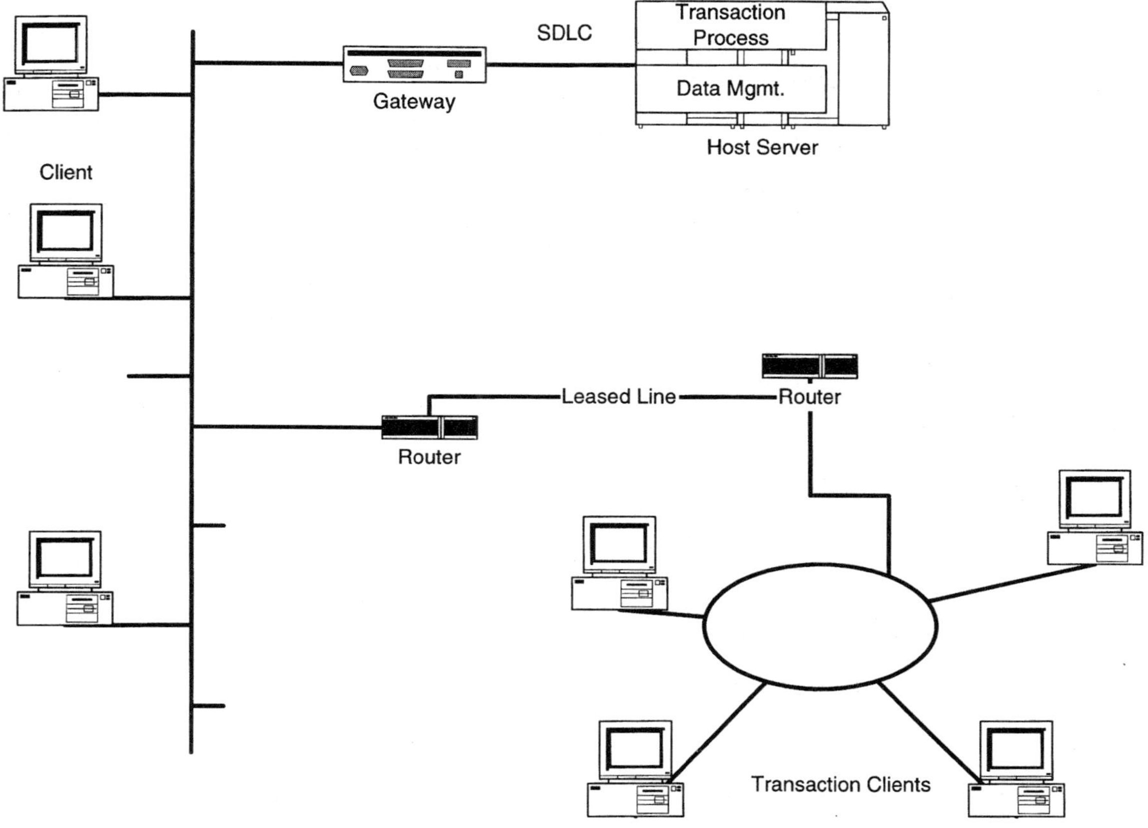

Figure 12.16 Transaction processing is another good fit for the client/server internetwork.

entire architecture like this. There are not enough programmers and not enough time to ever convert all of these processes easily. Therefore, the combined host/LAN/wide area networking capabilities all must coexist in providing a full transaction-processing environment as well as any local data requirements that might be needed. Major insurance and health care organizations are the primary users of these types of integrated access, but other organizations fit this bill as well.

The last, but certainly not the least, application discussed in this chapter is inventory tracking. As shown in Fig. 12.17, an inventory tracking system may employ a high-end host server where the inventory management systems may have resided over the past three decades. Note,

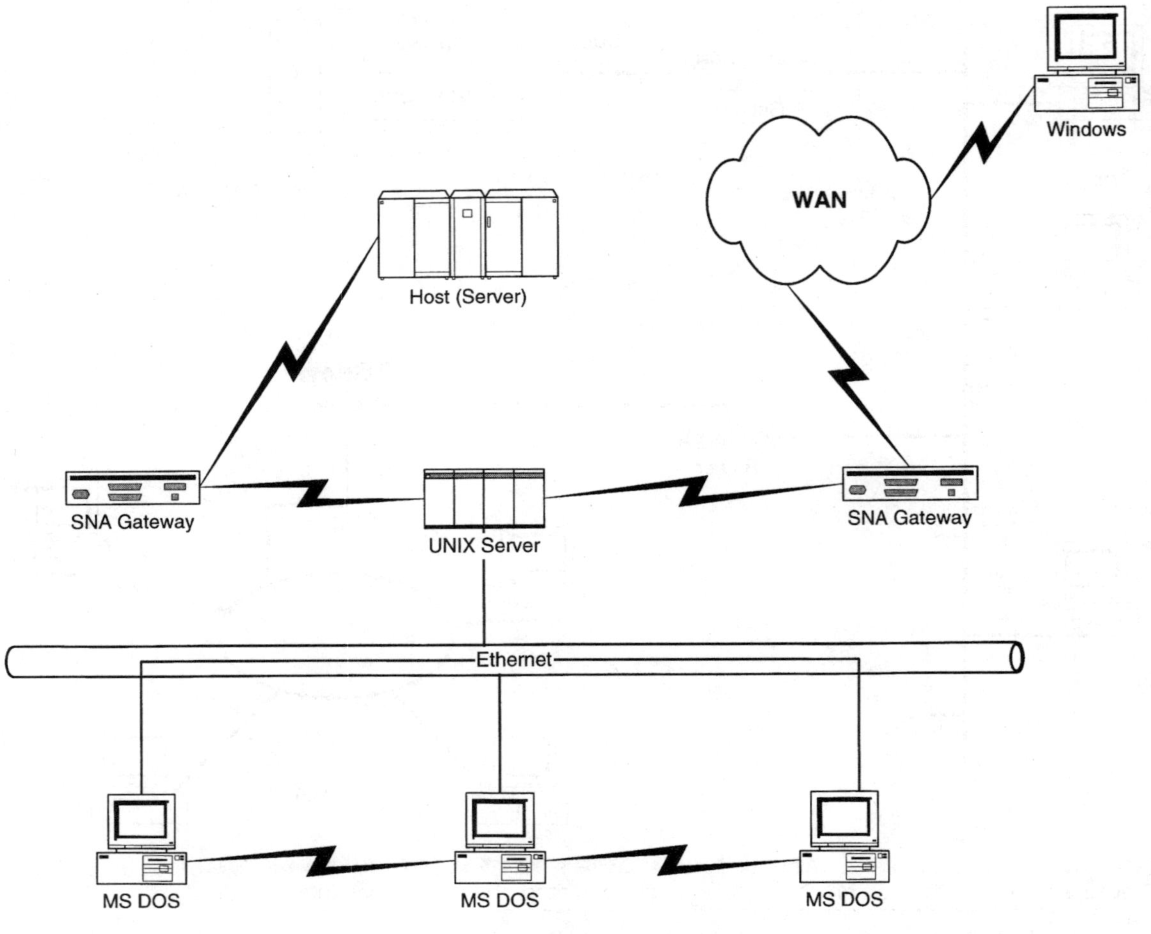

Figure 12.17 Inventory tracking can use the various server platforms of the client/server internetwork.

though, a couple of other pieces may have been implied here. An SNA gateway has been used attached to a UNIX server, going back to our three-computer architecture. The host, the UNIX server, and the client, whatever that client may be, are all implied here. The UNIX server acts as the applications processor that will spawn the process through the SNA gateway into the host-based server. Data mining and data repository capabilities exist at the host but must be accessed through the UNIX server. This UNIX server also acts as the gateway function from an asynchronous dial-up communications gateway into the application server à la the UNIX server. Any one of the MS DOS or Windows-based clients that might exist on the LAN would be able to use the local area network on an internetworking basis to provide access into the mainframe platform. Again, the pieces are merely mixed and matched so that the data is available to those who need it. Inventory tracking then would be readily available to Windows- or DOS-based clients sitting anywhere across the network, who would be able to use the services of the host-based system even though they are not on a 32/70-type terminal device.

One would certainly hope that creativity and imagination would allow readers to see other possible applications that fit the specific needs for their organizations. The pieces can all come together by using bridges and routers, using the carrier-based services to transport the data across a wider area, and using either low- or high-end servers at each of the ends to provide the necessary access to the data and performance of the company's stated mission. One cannot ignore the primary goal of the client/server internetwork—to access the data reasonably, efficiently, and at a competitive price.

CHAPTER 13

Managing the Client/Server Internetwork

Up to now the discussion has centered around designing and building a client/server internetwork as well as the applications that would run on it. This discussion was geared towards letting the reader understand the intricacies and the differences between the various components that constitute a client/server internetwork. Assuming the decision has been made to build and use a client/server network, and that some project planning and some budgetary needs have been met, the next step after the implementation is to recognize how the network will be managed. Network management is one of those needs that tends to be overlooked by most users. Of course, this oversight is not the users' fault; rather it is a culmination of several different fallacies in the industry. Vendors and carriers alike have a tendency of overplaying their particular posture. When asked about managing a network, they typically advise that the tools and procedures necessary to manage any internetwork are readily available and well deployed. In reality, what they are addressing happens to be how they manage their own network within their own environment, not how an individual organization will be able to use tools and techniques in place to provide proper network management.

Network management is a must! Distributed systems require a very aggressive management approach, because the entire organization's data communications and data access reside on this distributed environment. If one cannot support and sustain daily operations, then all is for naught. Remotely distributed systems offer their own unique challenges, due to the distance and the variations in the configuration. One cannot assume that in the event a problem occurs, that vendors and carriers alike will rush to the aid of the customer and solve all problems. What these carriers and vendors will do is to support their own components but not the overall network as an entity in itself. Consequently, client/server internetworks have been built just as many other networks have been built, with the misbelief that the tools and the techniques are relatively inexpensive, automatically built into the systems, and are very effectively used. In many cases, the carriers and vendors alike do not understand the complexities or the uniqueness in using the network management systems to build out their own techniques. They, in turn, use a proprietary network management tool that has been built and geared toward their own components. This tool can involve software, hardware, or a combination of both. In either case, the network management tools are designed to look at one small piece of the overall network and not the global network as a whole, leaving the client/server internetworking manager with a hodgepodge of various tools and techniques that must be used in gathering and maintaining information about the network on a component-by-component basis instead of an overall performance ratio. These disparate tools and pieces of information are not easily brought together when dealing with all of these proprietary systems, in turn creating a nightmare for the networking manager.

Most systems are very specifically limited to performance management techniques or to failed links. Again, it depends on the provider of the service. In many cases, the carriers have taken a slightly different approach by partnering or aligning with the hardware manufacturers. An example of this would be several of the major long-distance providers of communications infrastructure that have teamed up with the major router and bridge manufacturers, including Cisco and Bay Networks, and have begun offering a total package of links and of routers. What they failed to see is the next extension of the router and the link. A network is made up of more than just routers and links; it has a series of other components that all need to be managed and maintained in a uniform fashion. The limitations that these carriers bring to the table, although better than nothing, still perplex and place in jeopardy the overall performance capabilities of these networks. For example, when building out a client/server network, the user may look at

- The desktop device, manufactured by one vendor
- The network operating system with its own set of tools and techniques provided by a second vendor
- The applications, such as databases and human resources packages
- The middleware stack of protocols, such as TCP/IP
- A network interface card, or NIC, which is hardware-oriented and manufactured by another vendor
- The cabling connectors and cables manufactured by still another vendor and installed by a third party
- The interface to the bridges and routers and from there an access method out onto the links into the wide area network
- The wide area network, which would include some digital transmission capability such as a DSU/CSU manufactured by even another party or a modem communications capability manufactured by still a different vendor
- Finally, the local exchange carriers link tied to the interexchange carrier link

Working across this network to the distant end, the interexchange carrier will in turn send information across a set of links connected to possibly a second LEC, which in turn would deliver the information to a DSU/CSU provided by another vendor, and so on and so forth.

Looking at all of the components just discussed, one can see that using perhaps an interexchange carrier integration with the routing manufacturer only addresses two very small facets and pieces of this complex and unique network built around your own needs. By looking at only pieces, when things start to go wrong the analysis and the tools necessary are not available to look at every single step along the way in the data preparation, transmission, and data reception. Systems that are available on the market today from each of these vendors, although proprietary in nature, are also somewhat limited in what they can do. One must be aware that the limited and proprietary solution sets that are being offered may not tightly couple with all of the other components. This situation may leave the user with multiple subsets of network management capabilities, all of which would then pull together small pieces of information that may have to be manually tagged together or may not provide any valid information at all. Standards do exist, but they are somewhat limited. These standards have been based on one or two different protocol stacks that have already been addressed through this book (the OSI model and TCP/IP protocol stack). Proprietary solutions continue to emerge, many of them deploying or taking advantage of some of these de facto or standards-based products. One must pay particular attention to network management when deciding on the purchase, acquisition, or rollout of a client/server internetwork.

Not to unjustly hammer on the vendors and carriers, one must also be aware that when a solution is offered from one of these providers, it must be physically and visibly seen. One cannot assume that just because a provider has indicated that it has network management tools in place that these tools will solve your business needs. In fact, one should look closely at how these tools are used by the particular provider. It is not uncommon when searching and seeking out information to discover that the carriers may have specific tools and procedures in place for managing a network, but the personnel working for that particular carrier do not know how to use the tools. Training was either lacking or changes in personnel have not caught up with the actual implementation tools that are being used. Moreover, policies and procedures are not always adhered to by the providers themselves. One must therefore discern how well the vendor personnel adhere to and abide by the policies and procedures and how that vendor or carrier enforces adherence to its procedures. In many cases, after dealing with client/server managers around the globe, the reality of the situation has been completely different than what was proposed or offered. Many of these carriers and providers, although they manage through a contract arrangement to deliver a specific availability or reliability of data transport or connection updates and upgrades on a regular basis, have fallen down in their delivery. Although customers were paying extra money each month for a managed network service, this is not what was really being delivered. Yes, the carrier would act as the customer's agent in trying to solve problems, but it was no better equipped to recognize and solve the problem than if the customer had done it alone. There was no evidence to indicate that the carrier was able to solve problems faster or better than the client. A significant amount of the funds being expended in a client/server internetwork may well be used for a purpose in which the actual deliverable is not readily available.

One such example of this situation was a Midwestern-based organization that was spending approximately $250,000 per month for a network from a carrier. This network involved frame relay. The carrier approached a customer and offered network management ability. For a 20 percent premium, or roughly $50,000 a month, the carrier offered full network management services from door to door. The customer, realizing that trained staff was not readily available and the dependency on this network would be high, decided to use this service. The carrier had shown the customer a series of reports, management reports, and tools that could be used by the carrier in the performance of its duty. The reports looked fine, highlighting performance, delays, performance throughput, lost frames, average time for delivery, and so on. Once the organization signed up on the network and built the infrastructure, the carrier was supposed to deliver monthly reports to the customer in a format that was readily used. What the carrier actually delivered was a very complicated and convoluted set of reports that were not readily readable, were very difficult to manipulate, showed the overall performance of the carrier's network rather than the specific client's network, and could not be integrated with other management tools.

Moreover, when problems occurred and the customer had specific time frames when actions were to take place, the carrier could not deliver. Unfortunately, after several negotiation steps, discussions, and arguments with the carrier, the customer chose to cease paying for this network management service. Instead, the customer chose to use a third-party outsourcing organization to provide the managed services it needed.

There are very few organizations on the market today that can provide the kinds of services the customer needs or is looking for. By going to a third party, the customer was immediately looking for some resolution and report generation capabilities and so on. This vendor, of course, said it could do just about anything the customer wanted. It was going to charge the customer to customize reports that could be viewed in graphic, as well as in data, orientation. The cost of this custom development was significant. Upon signing of the agreements, this particular third party was to act as the customer's agent in working with the vendors and the carriers to solve problems quickly and reliably. When the network went down, the customer immediately called the third party to determine what was going on, only to be told that it was waiting for information back from the carrier that was running the network. Of course, the customer demanded more information, quicker action, and so on, but was only frustrated in the efforts to gain this information. There was no difference, other than the third party was interjected in between the customer and the actual carrier. This third party could not get the information any quicker—it was depending on the carrier to provide steady feedback. About all it was able to do was to call and constantly badger the carrier for status reporting and updates so that it could relay the information back to the customer. In relaying this information, this third party basically filtered a lot of the information before delivering it to the customer. The customer was no further ahead but was spending a significant amount of money and was locked into a long-term contract for this network management service. After several months of frustration and nondelivery, the customer began to buy some of its own tools to recognize and provide information quicker, which defeats the purpose of having a network-managing third-party outsource group. One must be very careful in selecting how the network will be managed and who the provider of this network management will be. The choices are many:

- The customer itself
- The IECs
- The hardware providers
- Third-party outsource organizations
- Others

Defining Network Management Systems

When addressing the need for network management, the end user must be aware of just what network management entails. As already stated, many of the providers of service have a tendency toward a myopic focus on what network management means. They see it as performance and availability on their network, for example, or if it is a hardware supplier, the up time and the availability of parts. In most cases, they are only looking at one of many facets of network management in their definition. Therefore, it behooves the client/server networking manager to understand just what goes into a full network management system and how those pieces may be provided. One way to define network management is to take the pieces one at a time:

1. *Security management*—the physical, logical access to resources that exist on the network. One must understand how access is provided in a physical and logical arrangement. Further, one must understand how to recognize when that access has been breached. Does the network management system provide alerts and alarms when someone has tapped into the cable or some new device has registered on the network that did not belong there? Is it possible that some other device can receive and capture the data packets as they move across this network? A true security management system in all of its complexities allows the capture of information to determine that all of the devices on the network are appropriate and that the logical connectivity is being physically managed in a robust manner. One must also look at the physical side—the encryption of data. The network management system should provide for autoencryption or at least for the hooks or a third-party encryption package to be able to control and manage this data.

2. *Performance management*—the monitoring and tuning of actual data performance and throughput performance capabilities across the network. Monitoring indicates that statistical information can be gathered and evaluated. Tuning, on the other hand, indicates that bottlenecks and delays and throughput performance degradation can all be highlighted so that some method can be used to work around the problem. Performance management, in most cases, by carrier definition, involves just throughput and performance as opposed to

the ability to gather information and use it as a tuning tool. However, most developed systems offered by these third parties concentrate primarily on performance management and ignore the other pieces.

3. *Operations management*—the planning, distribution, evaluation, and controlling of workloads. Operations management involves the ability to distribute information or workloads across the network so that devices or components are not overloaded while other components sit barely used. Operations management should go hand in hand with performance management, so that as performance degrades, a redistribution of workload or data traffic can be achieved. In the evaluation and control process of workloads across the network, the ability to see where bottlenecks are occurring and the ability to move this bottleneck across that network to a different device are functional parts of operations management.

4. *Change management*—the managing and controlling of changes across the network, i.e., software updates, new releases, new applications, etc. Change management is one of the pieces that falls apart very, very quickly. Change control and management involve the continual knowledge of what devices and software releases exist on the network. Moreover, it goes into the revision levels of the applications or of the hardware solutions that are being attached to the network. All too often users start out with a documented network, but the change management falls apart quickly. Two, three, or six months after the network is installed, additional components change, and new software releases and the like have been added to the network but not documented. When problems begin to occur, there is no harmony in terms of gathering the data and being able to assess what is occurring. A new release in software may change a configuration on an individual device, rendering it unusable on the network. If this new release has not been documented, one can spend a significant amount of time chasing problems and trying to determine what has gone wrong. Moreover, as the network changes, such as with the addition of new links, new speeds on the links, and so forth, when network problems begin to occur it is very difficult to understand where the traffic is rolling and how it might be enhanced or changed. Change management is probably the worst portion of a network in terms of tools and availability because documentation is not readily available.

5. *Configuration management*—the design and internetworking relationships of all of the components on the network. Configuration management involves how each of the components are working, what protocol stacks are being used, and the interrelationships between the hardware, the software, and the network operations systems, as well as many other pieces. In many network management tools provided by third parties or by individual vendors, configuration management is not considered. Again, the primary goal of network management with most of the players is performance management. Therefore, a well-designed network management system should allow the mapping and configuration of how the network components interwork with each other. A good configuration management system also highlights inconsistencies or incompatibilities that exist due to hardware or software resolution problems.

6. *Fault management*—the handling of problem resolution when things don't work properly. This particular portion of a network management system is the proactive result of problems as they occur. Fault management should be one of the tools used to determine where things are degrading or corrupting across the network. Fault management would be another component the carriers and the vendors tend to concentrate on, leaving all the other aspects out of the picture. Handling problems as they occur should also be something that is intuitively built into the system, as opposed to being a new challenge every time a problem arises. A true fault management system is able to determine, based on some thresholds or parameters, how well the links are performing, whether the links are actually there and operating, or if there are other components that have fallen off the network. One should consider fault management an absolute necessity as part of the overall network management function.

7. *Accounting management*—the gathering of usage statistics for accountabilities and for charge-out purposes. In many client/server architectures, usage-based networks emerge. How one will gather the information for charge-out purposes based on application or user traffic loads, and then appropriately apply that charge and usage to the appropriate department budget is always a mystery to most people. The accounting management function within a network management system should be able to capture the data based on specific protocols, applications, or user devices. Using the tools, one can then gather these statistics and apply some algorithm in terms of charging out the network performance and network usage to the individual departments. This method is fair and equitable, but it is nearly always an ignored function. Instead, most client/server internetwork managers apply some flat-rate usage charge (perhaps by percentage points) across the board to each of the user departments. Some users who are low-volume users are being charged to compensate for or contribute to the payment for the higher-lever users. Over time, the lower-end users tend to look at the costs they are being charged and determine that if they went out and built their own network, they could probably do it less expensively. An accounting management function therefore is necessary in the continued justification and support of the users based on their usage.

Figure 13.1 shows an approach to systems management and design. Note the constantly revolving flow as a design and management func-

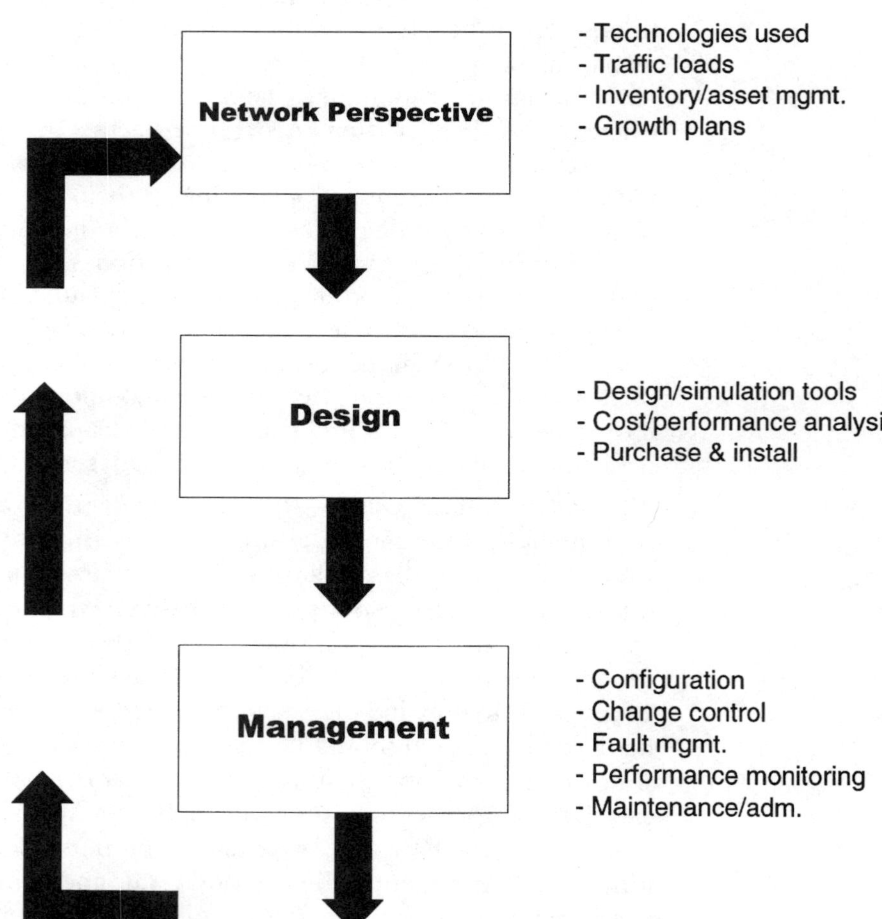

Figure 13.1 *Systems management and design process allows for the design and implementation.*

tion is being used. This illustration looks at the three major building blocks for network management and design systems. Starting at the top is the network perspective:

- The technologies to be used on the network
- The anticipated traffic loads to be carried across the network
- Inventory and asset management capabilities
- Growth plans for future additions or changes to the network

The second component is the design criteria for building out and designing this network. Once an overall perspective of what the network should look like in terms of the technologies and traffic, etc., is reached, the actual design should be applied using the following guidelines:

- The results and analysis through design and simulation tools
- A cost-to-performance benefit ratio analysis
- The purchase of the equipment
- The installation

The third block in this figure shows the management function kicking in. After a networking perspective and design effort has taken place, management issues become most crucial. The design of this network management systems should include

- The configuration management tools available
- Change control functions
- Fault management capabilities
- Performance monitoring and statistics-gathering capabilities to determine that all things are working properly
- Maintenance functions, both scheduled and unscheduled
- Administration, such as charge and accountability information

Note that the three building blocks in a continual flow work from the basic overview of the network right down to the installation, maintenance, and management of this system. Things are dynamic—the static network is a passé environment. Therefore, the figure depicts that as things continue to change or as modifications must be made, the flow line works its way back to an overall perspective. Periodically, the network manager must assess what has changed and what the network has emerged or changed to as the pieces have been reconfigured.

Either on a semiannual or an annual basis, a reevaluation of the overall network in terms of its performance and throughput capabilities, as well as the overall capabilities that users are demanding, should take place.

Systems Management Problems

As already stated, very few standards are available on the marketplace today through a single-vendor environment. Too many proprietary solutions and systems are being delivered on a single-network supplied solution. When dealing with a single vendor, it might be easier because the proprietary standard developed by that vendor can administer its products and services. However, very few networks in the market today are built and based on a sole-vendor solution. Most networks are based on multivendor, multiprotocol, and multiple hardware environments. This fact constitutes a major problem for the client/server networking manager whose primary role is to administer such a network. Different tools exist on a vendor-by-vendor and platform-by-platform basis, which creates several disparate hooks and techniques for gathering and maintaining information about the network. A shell may have to be put on top of these network management tools to draw the information in and remanipulate it so that it becomes a single-entity reporting structure. This process adds to the cost and complexity, and very few exist on the market. The network manager must be aware of this before making the installation and decisions on how to manage the network.

Another problem that exists within the industry is the lack of skilled personnel due to the depth and breadth of client/server internetworking. From a vendor's prospective, turnover and changes in personnel continually occur, causing a lack of the necessary skill sets in the vendor and carrier communities. Moreover, from an end user's perspective, the skill sets and talented personnel are not readily on the market or are priced so that most network managers cannot afford them. A learning curve and training cycle are required to bring up to speed all of the associated personnel involved in managing this network. Finding the right tools is difficult; keeping and attracting talented personnel is an equal challenge; merging the two together becomes even more complex.

Once personnel are trained, their value automatically goes up in the industry. Keeping a maintenance or network management individual in an organization is a high risk due to the demands of the network for such talents. A technician who has been trained in the use of network management tools and performance capabilities can usually double or triple his or her salary in a relatively short period of time, posing a unique dilemma for the client/server internetworking manager. The amount of time and money expended on training the skill sets necessary in people automatically causes them to be more valuable to others. The risk is that they will bail out and go where the money is. Consequently, the pain/reward ratio goes up exponentially. The better trained the individual, the higher the risk of losing the person. Other organizations, vendors, and carriers will be attracted if a highly qualified network technician is available. They will all vie for that person's services. The client/server network manager can write into the contracts with vendors of hardware and the carriers that they will not attempt to hire away any of the network personnel within a specified period of time. This contract covers a small portion of what the worth of this individual would be, but it does provide some limited protection. Unfortunately, many other organizations are also trying to deploy their client/server internetworks, and the skill sets of your technicians will be highly attractive to them. They will be willing to pay the extra money for salary as opposed to losing the time and money necessary to train and bring their staff up to speed. One must be aware of the risks of network and systems management.

Simple Network Management Protocol (SNMP)

One of the more common tools used in the client/server internetwork, due to the disparity of systems and protocols, is the simple network management protocol. SNMP was designed as a superset of the TCP/IP protocol set. In its definition, it is called a simple management protocol designed to reduce the complexities and to standardize, albeit a de facto standard, the network management systems on the market. Two types of SNMP have evolved in the marketplace:

1. SNMP Type 1 provides primarily a network management overview or outlook
2. SNMP Type 2 takes into consideration a desk-to-desk management overview or outlook

The differences here between the Type 1 and Type 2 are primarily in how far the network management system reaches down into the organization. Where Type 1 looks more at the major network components, such as the internetworking devices and the hardware systems at the server level, Type 2 is geared to look right down to the user desktop configuration, applications, and performance issues. Clearly one would assume that Type 2 is the only way to go. It is an ideal solution if we can look to desktop-to-desktop network management capabilities, but it is not yet all it is cracked up to be. SNMP, although not a standard, has become one of the more common interfaces is used by vendors today. It was designed in an overall performance and network management capability to keep overhead low. When dealing with network management systems, one must consider the amount of overhead that is added to the total traffic and throughput across the network. If, for example, a network management system adds 20 to 30 percent overhead, then performance will be degraded by that amount of necessary overhead. SNMP was designed to keep the overhead as low as possible and not degrade overall performance. Otherwise, it would be no better than the tools it is trying to manage.

The Type 1 SNMP services were limited in the approach to the overall network as opposed to further down into the environment to keep the overhead as low as possible. However, a longer-term solution became necessary, and the Type 2 SNMP system emerged as the de facto standard. Because of its ability to look right down to the desktop, it does add some additional overhead but provides a more global perspective in terms of managing the network in general. Therefore, most users look for SNMP Type 2 support in the design of their network management systems and tools.

SNMP was successful in the rollout within the industry because of certain attempts and failures to deliver a network management system. Two strong leaders in the industry that we would expect to be able to deliver high-quality, high-performance network management systems based their network management strategies on proprietary standards. All of the solutions were designed around their proprietary architectures, which were not readily accepted by the industry. The two companies, AT&T and IBM, tried to achieve acceptance as the de facto network management tool. Unfortunately, whenever proprietary solutions exist and they are delivered by two of the higher-end organizations in the industry, the prices are usually prohibitive. This is the case with both AT&T's Network Management and IBM's Netview. Both IBM and

AT&T developed their own proprietary solutions to an open system. As the world was trying to evolve to an open systems architecture with standards-based open systems interfaces, these two big players developed their own proprietary solutions to mimic the open systems arrangement. The prices, of course, were prohibitive, but the complexities of the systems were also disparate. Therefore, new interfaces were needed whenever a new device was being placed on the network. When adding some new component, the client/server manager would have to go to one of the two players and they would have to develop a new interface to support that new device. This process was extremely expensive and time-consuming and therefore discouraged end users from supporting these protocols. Therefore, SNMP emerged as the main system in the client/server internetworking arena. This does not mean that neither the AT&T nor the IBM solution would work—they did, but users were looking for something less proprietary and less expensive.

All of the major players of internetworking hardware today have at least adopted or are deploying SNMP as their network tool. A common interface has now been developed with management information base (MIB) being developed for every component that might exist on an internetwork. The various providers of hardware, such as routers, hubs, and switches, are now on board with the SNMP protocols. Each of these providers has developed a MIB in terms of gathering statistics and thresholds and established counters for use on the WAN links. WAN links, or the network management tools to perform or gather performance on the carrier-community environment, were always ignored in the past. Enhancements to what are called SNMP traps allow for detailed event-log messages that can be accumulated, eliminating or minimizing message flooding. In the past, whenever a device might fail in a very complex internetwork, all of the devices attached or associated with these failed devices would generate network management messages indicating that a failure had occurred. In a very large and complex network, a flood of messages would come into the network management system alerting the network manager that a single device had failed. The enhancements to the SNMP protocols allow for minimization of this flooding.

Further, encryption techniques have been developed in SNMP to prevent unauthorized configurations within a network. In the past, when these things were plain-text open language, a hacker could have reconfigured a network component at will, or a novice could have inadvertently changed a configuration without realizing it. Using set encryption techniques, such a change can be prevented. An additional capacity or enhancement to SNMP is the fact that a direct memory trivial file transfer protocol (TFTP) transfers event logs directly from the memory on a buffer or a card into the management system, eliminating a lot of the older ways in which event messages were continually transmitted from device to device into buffer to buffer along the network.

With all of the benefits that have been provided in the SNMP protocol, it is unfortunate that performance management was never really considered. SNMP, as well as all of the other network management systems that were developed, were designed primarily around fault isolation and resolution. It is only recently that performance management has been introduced into the client/server internetwork, or any network for that matter. Past implementations were designed to resolve and monitor network problems. These past implementations that did not have performance management tools were based on some subjective algorithms that were developed based on other networks of similar types and size. Newer multivendor internetworks also added to the complexity of performance management. Therefore, no real integration plan or integrated tools exist, a major drawback in all of the major network management tools and systems on the market today.

As SNMP techniques were being developed, several vendors jumped on board in terms of its support. However, not all vendors supported the SNMP interface. Consequently, workaround solutions were necessary at the client/server internetwork. When using and linking SNMP-capable and non-SNMP-capable equipment together, one had to come up with some form of a common network management interface. These tools existed on the market, as shown in Fig. 13.2. In this case, a separate integrator was developed to support several different proxy capabilities on non-SNMP systems. The organization could use a product-integration module capability or a product- specific module capability to deal with the different pieces on the network, whether SNMP-compatible or not. Figure 13.2 shows a combination of SNMP and non-SNMP services being used on a single network. Note to the right of the figure are two servers, a Novell and a Banyan server. There is also a workstation using a software subset that would be a MIB browser to determine which MIBs are available on which pieces of equipment and server devices. The Novell server and the router shown in this illustration are SNMP-compatible, so an SNMP product-specific module is used for both the server and the router. The specific modules are written for those products. A separate product-integration module is used for the Banyan server to integrate it into this SNMP network.

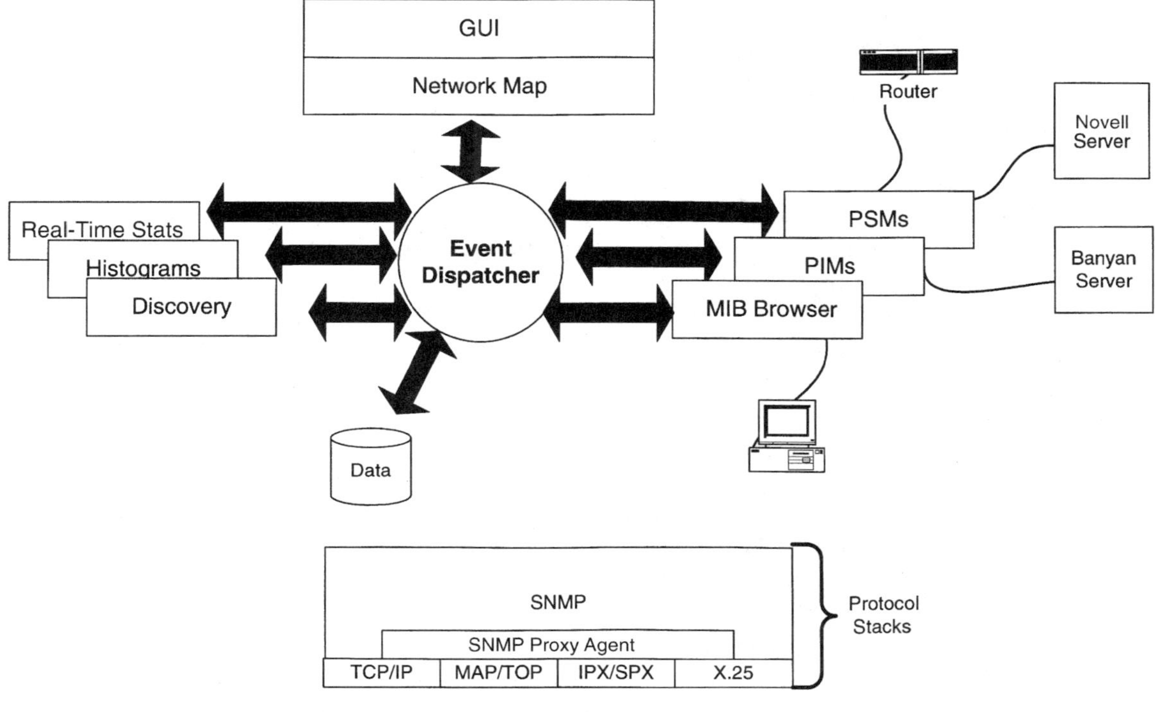

Figure 13.2 Linking SNMP/non-SNMP equipment together can still provide management control. PIM = product integration module. PSM = product-specific module.

Each of these modules and the browser communicate directly with what is known as an *event dispatcher,* the software that controls integration within the various components of the SNMP architecture. The event dispatcher stores the information accumulated from each of these modules in a separate database. The database is shown at the bottom left-hand side of this figure. When specific reports or information is needed, such as traffic statistics or performance management statistics, the event dispatcher is used to gather the information from the database. To the left of the event dispatcher are some of the report characteristics that can be used. They can be used for discovery of all of the devices that exist on the network that are SNMP-compliant. Further, histogram information can be produced in a graphical interface such as line, bar, or pie charts in terms of the availability compared to nonavailability on the network. Additionally, real-time statistics can be accumulated and shown by a separate reporting structure through the event dispatcher. Above the event dispatcher is a separate set of tools that can be used to develop a network map to note where on the network all of the SNMP devices have been discovered. This network map can be used to gather real-time statistics when an event occurs. Any alarm conditions that might arise can be displayed on the map in some form of alerting mechanism (such as a red line). Using this integrated tool for both SNMP and non-SNMP equipment, network management for performance and historical information can be achieved.

Note that at the bottom of the figure, a protocol stack represents the integration between the SNMP and the non-SNMP equipment. At the baseline, the various operating systems protocols are shown. These protocols include the more common ones, such as TCP/IP, manufacturing assisted protocol (MAP) and technical office protocol(TOP), IPX and SPX, or X.25 protocols. Sitting directly above these protocol stacks is the SNMP protocol. However, where this integration tool can link the non-SNMP-compliant systems, an SNMP proxy agent acts between the lower-level protocols and the SNMP higher-level protocols in a common architecture. This solution links the pieces together through a third-party software and hardware package combined. Although not the best of alternatives, it does allow for the linkage on a network to be able to see a graphic and historical trend analysis of the overall network performance.

Open Systems Interconnect (OSI) Model

If this were a perfect world, the open systems interconnect model would be here and in wide use today. Several years ago, the industry attempted to achieve an open systems reference model so that all systems, regardless of manufacturer, could integrate seamlessly. Along with this seamless integration would be the ability to design and manage networks that were consistent across an open platform using multiple vendors and multiple protocols. The open systems reference model that was developed by the International Standards Organization (ISO) and is shown in Fig. 13.3 was based on a seven-layer protocol stack. This protocol stack involves two components. The first component would be the communications component dealing with the bottom three layers of

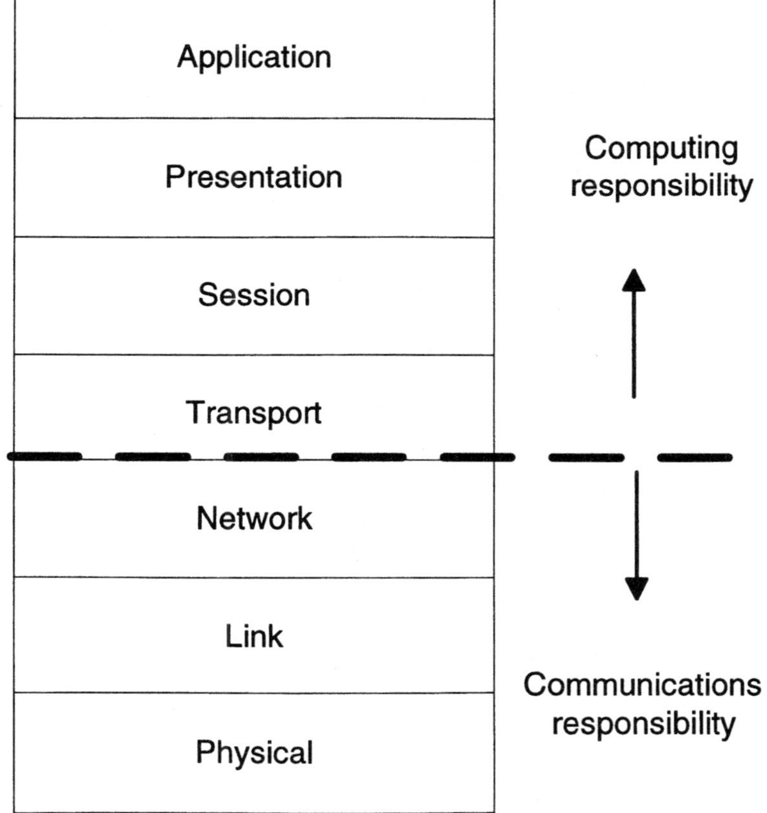

Figure 13.3 The OSI model is split to show the management responsibility on the upper half (the computing responsibility).

the OSI model. From a communications infrastructure, the physical, data link, and network layers would be involved with the communications process. The second component would involve the transparent communications or data transfer between disparate systems and deal with the upper four layers of this protocol stack. These layers are the transport, session, presentation, and application layers.

The goal of the open systems interconnect model was to allow for any-to-any communications and data transfer regardless of manufacturer. It is very complex both in its definition and its implementation. The expense of changing out all architectures already installed throughout the world would be prohibitive. Therefore, subsets of the OSI model have been implemented by various network suppliers to deliver an OSI look-alike capability.

Because of the complexity and the cost in implementing an OSI network, it really has been scrapped in North America. Most organizations have moved away from true implementation of the full seven-layered architecture. Instead, it is a reference model, not a major player in most architectural systems. Each of the vendors producing products and services for network management or any client/server internetworking deployment continues to develop toward this reference model. Unfortunately, they continually add their own proprietary spin to the way that they deploy OSI. The client/server internetworking manager must still be careful in terms of what is fully compatible and compliant versus what is based on a reference model with a proprietary spin. If all things are equal, by 2000 we may see more progress towards an open systems interface. One should be aware that this target date is not necessarily cast in concrete. Too many proprietary investments have already been made in the past. Therefore, until these architectures and hardware components are fully depreciated and changed, there will be no major movement towards an OSI. The client/server internetworking manager must come up with workaround solutions in the interim. In doing so, the choice in the industry today is to continue with the SNMP because of its simplicity and its robustness in meeting the challenges of network management.

Emerging SNMP Tools

Two major SNMP 2 (or II) systems have emerged as the de facto standards in the industry. Although most vendors have deployed some form of SNMP with the communications providers, the hardware providers and now the software providers are endorsing some form of SNMP. The two major players that are making inroads in the SNMP deployment for network management systems are

1. Hewlett Packard (HP), with the Open View product
2. IBM, with the Netview 6000 product

In each case, both vendors have made significant strides in deploying SNMP 2 architectures to support the client/server internetworking management process based on their platforms and developments.

HP Open View

Hewlett Packard is a major supplier in communications as well as computing architectures. It based its Open View network management tools on the SNMP 2 protocols. Open View's primary target today is a client/server internetwork and a Windows-based system. It is also designed around workgroup computing architectures so that the networking manager can see and determine the performance and fault-making capabilities within the internetwork. HP has literally taken the lead in the past in the deployment and the installation of the Open View architecture. It is based on HP's UNIX, or HP UX, protocol and platform. The intent is to discover and map all devices automatically, primarily any devices running specific protocols, such as IPX, IP, and application program interfaces (APIs). The primary goal and service offered with Open View involves the following components of network management:

- Fault management
- Configuration management
- Performance management
- Accounting management where APIs are available

HP's Open View is designed to capture information and discover devices through a common management interface on a console. Several different networks and workgroups can be monitored across the Open View architecture. When alerts and alarms occur, a specific console on each of the LANs may well be used as the data collection device using the TFTP stored in memory. As the memory is ready to transfer the information, it is transferred directly to the Open View console, the management console, and the alarms will then be displayed. This display can be done through a similar GUI environment showing a map of the network, which can then be tunneled right to the actual device that is in trouble. In terms of configuration management, a complete database and asset management program can be used or can be hooked to an asset management program to provide a list of all the products and services that reside on the internetwork. Remote devices, such as PCs attached to a LAN, can also be monitored for fault and performance management capabilities through these applications. In the event a problem exists at the NIC card, the trap can be used to send the alarm condition off to a console, which then will be transferred to a management console. Hubs, routers, bridges, and PC-based NIC cards can all be monitored across this network for performance as well as fault capabilities. Although not inexpensive, the HP Open View system can involve multiple aspects of the network management, but not all. Specific MIBs can be written for devices that are not supported, although HP supports a wide variety of manufacturers and products in the industry. Figure 13.4 is a picture of how the HP Open View running a UNIX platform would work within the data collection and fault management applications.

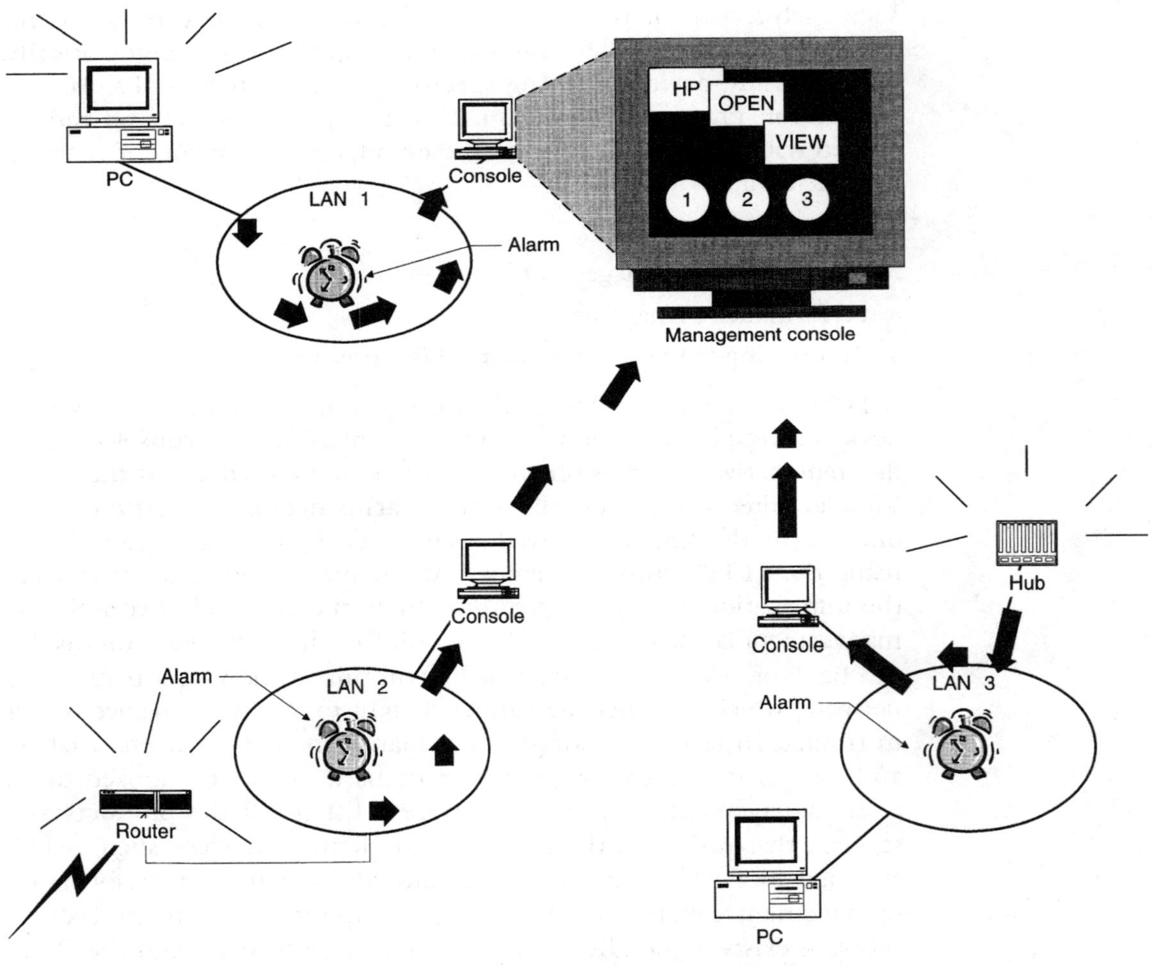

Figure 13.4 Open View for UNIX is one of the two top-end products in use.

IBM's Netview 6000

As a second version of the Netview protocols and products, IBM introduced Netview 6000. It is based on SNMP 2 over a TCP/IP architecture. IBM was looking to provide an open standard capability for the gathering and collection of information from a network management standpoint based on a transition philosophy. In the original days of Netview, IBM's primary architecture was the SNA/SDLC world. It was the single largest deployed networking architecture at the time. Therefore, IBM rolled out its products and services in Netview in support of an SNA/SDLC world. Recognizing that a lot of LAN and internetworking services were based on the mainframe platform, IBM made Netview its network management system of choice in a client/server internetwork. Unfortunately, due to the proprietary nature of this architecture and its prohibitive cost, it didn't go very far in a client/server world. Users could not afford the cost of such a network system. One must also remember this was all in the early stages of the client/server internetwork, which, in all reality, has only been over the past five years. When rolling out a client/server network, most users were viewing network management as an add-on, not necessarily a critical component. When network management systems were priced beyond their expectations, they chose to ignore them or use some proprietary network management tools from each of the vendors. It was only at a later time, when the users discovered that the proprietary pieces did not look at the overall network, but only specific components, that they realized that something had to be done.

IBM, using its transition philosophy from a mainframe platform to a midrange and a PC-based server environment, rolled out its SNMP 2 version over TCP/IP. This version has met with more open acceptance from the end-user perspective. Where IBM did not hold a major portion of the network management systems, it has made significant inroads in capturing a good portion of this market. The Netview 6000 product keeps tabs on inventory within the systems in a client/server network, including the CPU types, the memory configurations, and the applications that are being run on the specific computing systems. Initially, performance data on a Netview 6000 was very, very limited. IBM has since been working together with AT&T[1] (strange partners) in gathering more performance data traffic statistics and is therefore again making new inroads in this marketplace. Also, when Netview 6000 was first

1. AT&T spun off its computing division in 1996, so the names have been changed. Historically, however, it was IBM and AT&T working on the solution.

introduced, it did not capture all of the alarms that would exist across the network. However, as the evolution continues and the products and services supported by IBM expand, so too the capturing of alarms rolls out quickly. IBM's Netview 6000 is becoming one of the de facto standards in terms of network management protocols in an SNMP world. This is good news for the client/server internetworking manager. Not unlike Open View, the same basic infrastructure exists within the Netview 6000. The difference is where HP is designed on a UNIX-based platform, the IBM version is designed around the TCP/IP platform. In Fig. 13.5 is a small table that compares HP's Open View with IBM's Netview 6000. This table was designed around looking at how the protocols are being used between the SNMP agent and the management console. HP uses remote procedure calls based on TCP/IP, whereas IBM's Netview uses SNMP with TCP/IP. As for operating systems that will run Open View versus Net View, the table shows that the systems are pretty much the same. Although variations exist, both were designed to run on a combination of UNIX-type platforms so that the TCP/IP protocol support is fully and robustly available. Note in this figure that both systems support alarm capabilities. From the perspective of the management console and the GUI that is available, IBM's Netview 6000 does support a slightly wider set of applications on several different architectures, whereas the console for the HP Open View primarily is designed around an HP version.

	Agent to Console	Systems	Alarms	Console
HP Open View	RPC/TCP-IP	AIX, HP/UX, SUN OS, SOLARIS	✓	MOTIF, HP/ UNIX
IBM NetView 6000	SNMP/TCP-IP	AIX, HP/UX/ SUN OS, NCR, UNIX	✓	MOTIF ON HP/UX, AIX, NCR, UNIX, SOLARIS

Figure 13.5 Online monitoring changes for both HP and IBM network management tools.

Several different approaches to network management have emerged over the years. Some of these have been very robust, whereas others have been limited. IBM and HP have made significant inroads in providing the services with a base level into network management starting in the tens of thousand of dollars and working up into the hundreds of thousands of dollars. These systems are still somewhat limited to performance and inventory management, not to a full management system as defined earlier in this chapter. Both vendors will continue, as will many other vendors of client/server products, to develop the different interfaces to span the entire range of network management. As each of these new additional pieces are brought on board or APIs are written to support these different services, the price will inherently go up; as the price goes up, the client/server internetworking manager must start to make decisions on what pieces are absolutely necessary compared to what are nice to have. In reality, all are necessary, but certain ones are far more important than others. A true networking management system deals with several other components beyond strictly network, performance, and fault management. Admittedly these management tools are the most important, but the others are still necessities over time. One cannot manage a network, a very dynamic network, without the appropriate tools for configuration and change control, performance planning for future upgrades, and capacity planning capabilities, as well as accounting management for charge-out functions. Management will continue to look at the client/server network and try to determine if the appropriate amount of dollars is being spent in a true business sense. Network management and the tools associated with it will help to justify that process. If one cannot gather data and traffic statistics and determine the average cost per minute or cost per bit transfer in relation to its return to the organizational investment, one has to be constantly on the defense. As a result, without these tools, the client/server manager will constantly be put in a position to try to gather statistics on the fly and manipulate those statistics into some usable and manageable report for management, only to have it be obsolete as soon as it is completed. With the use of network management, the constant gathering of the data, and the reapplication of the management tools, the data is not obsolete immediately but readily available to be used over and over again.

Although the two network management systems discussed here are more of the industry and de facto standards, other systems have emerged. Three major suppliers can provide the network management systems (true network management systems) at a significantly higher price tag.

Several of the network management systems that are available on the market can span into the millions of dollars, which would be far too expensive in a client/server internetworking architecture. Consequently, network management in a real-time, real-mode client/server internetwork is possibly a long way from fruition. Most of the packages that exist on the marketplace are very limited and offer only inventory tracking, but not a lot of real-time performance monitoring and tracking information. The best-case scenario is that within the next three to five years, network management systems will emerge that are reasonably priced. These systems would capture all of the data statistics and traffic statistics, fault and performance management capabilities, and inventory tracking and asset management integration, as well as integrate capacity planning, security management, and accounting information into one major package. Worst case, five years may be more of a reality. This, then, leads the way towards several new introductions if, in fact, the interest and dollars are available.

Newer vendors will be rolling out their products. Hub manufacturers like Cabletron, CISCO, and Bay Networks all are planning on their own integrated network packages that can be used either in lieu of or as a complement to one of the two packages that already exist. One has to look at the pros and cons of using either substitute or complementary products and how it might affect the client/server network that has already been deployed. Whenever a change in architecture is decided upon, it clearly points out that change can cause risk. Risk can come in many forms—the risk of downtime as changes are being made, the risk of incompatibilities that were not foreseen, or the risk of loss of management support and endorsement.

In the event any one of these processes slips into the picture, the client/server manager must evaluate the best alternative available at the time. When a network spans multiple countries and multiple sites, it is very difficult to go through change in an orchestrated fashion without being disruptive. A true client/server internetwork is involved in real-time, round-the-clock data transfer and operations. There is no slack time left to perform management upgrades and techniques that used to exist in a data-processing world. Managing such a network seven days per week, 24 hours per day leaves no time for scheduled performance management and maintenance techniques that were always available in the past.

When any form of change begins, the combination of having to eliminate all existing packages and replace them all in a flash around the world in several countries and in several sites is very complex. Consequently, what might happen is a dual stack of network management, as well as network tools, may have to be run in a short term. This dual stack adds to the complexity of the installation and provides for inconsistencies in data transition and data gathering. Devices may not be seen or visible in a network system while this dual stack is being used. Therefore, as the overall network deploys, one should consider which network management system to use and deploy prior to the installation of the network, not after the fact. Unfortunately, as already stated, most networking managers buy the management tools after the fact. They initially rely on the network services and management capabilities offered by vendors, which are severely limited and proprietary in nature. When they finally discover that management systems are truly needed, it is almost too late. Going around to all of the sites and countries and changing devices is time-consuming, expensive, and risky. Plan the network in advance and plan the tools that will be needed in advance. Take the time up front to determine what the needs and demands are today and what they might look like in three to five years. The decision can then be better made. If, in fact, a low-end solution is all that is ever going to be needed, then the tools available today can be used. If the network is going to be dynamic and grow significantly, or if management is going to demand very specific performance and capacity planning capabilities, then the higher-end tools manufactured by organizations (up in the hundreds of thousands if not millions of dollars) might well be considered and depreciated over the five-year life cycle of the client/server network. When planning it up front, the costs are only made once as opposed to investments removed and new investments being made. It is this reinvestment and changeover of technology that continually places the client/server networking manager in bad light with management. Management expects solid technical as well as managerial business decisions to be made all at once, as opposed to making these decisions after the fact. Network management is a must. One cannot deploy a network the size of these client/server internetworks and expect the vendors and the carriers to provide the necessary management tools and support.

ACRONYMS

AAL	ATM adaptation layer
ABR	Available bit rate
ADPCM	Adaptive differential pulse code modulation
AIM	ATM inverse multiplexer
AIMUX	ATM inverse multiplexing
AIS	Alarm indication signal
AIX	Advanced information exchange
AMI	Alternate mark inversion
ANI	Automatic number identification
ANM	Answer message
ANSI	American National Standards Institute
API	Application program interface
APPC	Advanced peer-to-peer communications
APPN	Advanced peer-to-peer network
ARP	Address Resolution Protocol
ATDM	Asynchronous time division multiplexing
ATM	Asynchronous transfer mode
BCD	Binary coded decimal
BECN	Backward explicit congestion notification
BER	Bit error rate
BHLI	Broadband high-layer information
B-ICI	B-ISDN intercarrier interface
B-ICI SAAL	B-ICI signaling ATM adaptation layer
BIP	Bit interleaved parity
B-ISDN	Broadband ISDN
BN	Bridge number
BPDU	Bridge protocol data unit
BPP	Bridge port pair
BRI	Basic rate interface
BT	Burst tolerance
BTAG	Beginning TAG
B-TE	Broadband terminal equipment
BW	Bandwidth
CAD	Computer-aided drafting (drawing)
CAN	Campus area network
CAP	Competitive access provider
CAS	Channel associated signaling
CBDS	Connectionless broadband data service
CBR	Constant bit rate
CBT	Computer-based training
CCR	Current cell rate
CCS	Common channel signaling
CDPD	Cellular digital packetized data
CD-ROM	Compact disk—read only memory
CIR	Committed information rate
CL	Connectionless service
CNR	Complex node representation
COD	Connection-oriented data
CPE	Customer premises equipment
CRC	Cyclic redundancy check
CRF	Cell relay function
CRS	Cell relay service
CS	Convergence sublayer
CSMA	Carrier sensing multiple access

CSU/DSU	Channel service unit/digital (data) service unit
DCE	Data communication equipment; distributed computing environment
DDE	Dynamic data embedding
DE	Discard eligibility (bit)
DFS	Distributed file services
DHCP	Dynamic Host Control Protocol
DLCI	Data link connection identifier
DLL	Dynamic link libraries
DME	Distributed management environment
DQDB	Distributed queue on a dual-bus architecture
DTR	Delay throughput and reliability
DTSS	Distributed time synchronization services
DXI	Data exchange interface
EDI	Electronic document interchange
EGP	Exterior Gateway Protocol
EIGRP	Enhanced Internetwork Gateway Routing Protocol
EOM	End of message
FDDI	Fiber distributed data interface
FECN	Forward explicit congestion notification (bit)
FEP	Front-end processor
FRAD	Frame relay access device
FTAM	File Transfer Access and Management Protocol
FTP	File Transfer Protocol
GIS	Global information system
GUI	Graphical user interface
HDLC	High-level data link control
HEC	Header error control
ICI	Intercarrier interface
IEC	Interexchange carrier
IGP	Interior Gateway Protocol
IP	Internet Protocol
IPX	Internetwork packet exchange
ISDN	Integrated services digital network
ISO	International Standards Organization
LAN	Local area network
LANE	LAN emulation
LEC	Local exchange carrier
LECID	LAN emulation client identifier
LES	LAN emulation server
LGN	Logical group node
LSAP	Link service access point
MAC	Media access control
MAN	Metropolitan area network
MAU	Multistation access unit
MIB	Management information base
MID	Message identifier
MIR	Maximum information rate
MIS	Management information services
MMF	Multimode fiber-optic cable
MTSO	Mobile telephone switching office
NCP	Network control programs
NIC	Network interface card
NNI	Network-to-network interface
NOS	Network operating systems
OLE	Object linking environment
OSF	Open Systems Foundation
OSI	Open systems interconnect

OSPF	Open shortest path first
POP	Point of presence
POSIX	Portable open systems interexchange
PPP	Point-to-Point Protocol
PRI	Primary rate interface
PTMPT	Point-to-multipoint
PTT	Post telephone and telegraph (local suppliers)
PVC	Permanent virtual circuit
PVCC	Permanent virtual channel connection
RBOC	Regional Bell Operating Company
RIP	Routing Information Protocol
RISC	Reduced instruction set computing
RM	Resource management
RMON	Remote monitor capabilities
RO	Read- only
RPC	Remote procedure call
RS	Remote single-layer (test method)
RSFG	Route server functional group
SAA	Systems Application Architecture
SAP	Service Advertising Protocol
SDLC	Synchronous data link control
SDU	Service data unit
SF	Superframe
SLIP	Serial Line Internet Protocol
SMDS	Switched multimegabit data service
SMF	Single mode fiber
SMP	Symmetrical multiprocessing
SMTP	Simple Mail Transfer Protocol
SN	Sequence number
SNA	Systems network architecture
SNMP	Simple Network Management Protocol
SONET	Synchronous optical network
SPE	Synchronous payload envelope
SPX	Sequenced packet exchange
SR	Source routing
SRB	Source route bridge
SRF	Specifically routed frame
SRT	Source routing transparent; source route transparent
STM	Synchronous transfer module
STP	Shielded twisted pair
SVC	Switched virtual circuit
TB	Transparent bridging
TCP	Transmission Control Protocol
TCP/IP	Transmission Control Protocol with Internet Protocol
TDM	Time division multiplexing
TFTP	Trivial File Transfer Protocol
TLNS	Transparent local network services
VCC	Virtual channel connection
VCI	Virtual channel identifier
VCL	Virtual channel link
VPC	Virtual path connection
VPL	Virtual path link
VT	Virtual terminal
VTE	Virtual terminal emulation
VTP	Virtual Terminal Protocol
WAN	Wide area network

INDEX

A

B

Pages shown in **boldface** have illustrations on them.

D

E

F

G

N

O

P

T

U

V

W

X

Y

About the Author

Bud Bates is President of TC International Consulting, Inc., in Phoenix, Ariz. He frequently consults and lectures worldwide on computer communications topics. Books he has previously authored for McGraw-Hill include *Wireless Networked Communications, Discovery Recovery for LANs, Disaster Recovery Planning (Telecommunications),* and *Voice and Data Communications Handbook.* E-mail address: bud@tcic.com. Internet address: www.tcic.com.

TC International Consulting, Inc., located in Phoenix, Ariz., is a management consulting firm specializing in technological innovations for the present and future. Our expertise ranges from the simplest form of telecommunications (basic voice and data communications) to the future strategies planned in the industry for the year 2000 and beyond.

TCIC is dedicated to helping you and your company control your technology, rather than the other way around. If you are looking for consulting, technical training, seminars (both on-site and public), course development, or the creation of technical presentations, we can deliver.

Some of the seminars we currently offer:

Three-Day Seminar

- Voice *and* Data Communications

Two-Day Seminars

- Disaster Recovery and Restoration for Telecommunications
- Disaster Recovery Planning for LANs
- Understanding Digital Transmission Systems
- Fundamentals of Wireless Communications
- Introduction to Data Communications
- LAN to WAN Internetworking
- PC and LAN Security
- Telecommunications Essentials
- Understanding ATM

One-Day Seminars

- Overview of the SS7/IS-41 (Wireless) Integration
- SS7/CCS7

We specialize in bringing innovations to our clients! At all times our goals are to assist our clients with understanding and selecting the best technical solution that causes the least disruption, to provide excellent service in a timely manner, and to do so at a price that produces the best return on investment.

You can reach TCIC on the Internet (www.tcic.com) by telephone (602/777-7992), or by fax (602/777-7980), or you can write us at TC International Consulting, Inc., P.O. Box 51108, Phoenix AZ 85076-1108 or 1834 East Baseline Road, Suite 202, Tempe, AZ 85283-1508.